Emotion-Focused Therapy

Emotion-Focused Therapy

Coaching Clients to Work Through Their Feelings

Leslie S. Greenberg

American Psychological Association • Washington, DC

First Printing, December 2001
Second Printing, April 2002
Third Printing, July 2003
Fourth Printing, December 2004
Fifth Printing, April 2007

Published by
American Psychological Association
750 First Street, NE
Washington, DC 20002
www.apa.org

To order
APA Order Department
P.O. Box 92984
Washington, DC 20090-2984

Tel: (800) 374-2721, Direct: (202) 336-5510
Fax: (202) 336-5502, TDD/TTY: (202) 336-6123
On-line: www.apa.org/books/
E-mail: order@apa.org

In the U.K., Europe, Africa, and the Middle East, copies may be ordered from
American Psychological Association
3 Henrietta Street
Covent Garden, London
WC2E 8LU England

Typeset in Goudy by EPS Group Inc., Easton, MD

Printer: Edwards Brothers Inc., Ann Arbor, MI
Cover Designer: Naylor Design, Washington, DC
Technical/Production Editor: Jennifer L. Macomber

The opinions and statements published are the responsibility of the author, and such opinions and statements do not necessarily represent the policies of the American Psychological Association.

Library of Congress Cataloging-in-Publication Data

Greenberg, Leslie S.
    Emotion-focused therapy : coaching clients to work through their feelings /
    Leslie S. Greenberg.
        p. cm.
    Includes bibliographical references and index.
    ISBN 1-55798-881-1 (alk. paper)
        1. Focused expressive psychotherapy.   2. Emotions.   I. Title.

    RC489.F62 G739 2001
    616.89'14—dc21

                                                                2001046104

British Library Cataloguing-in-Publication Data
A CIP record is available from the British Library.

Printed in the United States of America

I dedicate this book to my family and my psychotherapy clients and trainees. Here, in these crucibles of development, emotion has been allowed its rightful place. Here, feelings have not been hidden or gone unregulated. Rather they have been validated and expressed. I dedicate this work to all the painful struggles, joy, and compassion you have shared with me. You have given me a much deeper appreciation of what it is to be human.

CONTENTS

Preface . . . .   *ix*

I. Emotional Intelligence: What It Is and How to Promote Its Development

Chapter 1.   Emotions and Emotional Intelligence   3

Chapter 2.   Distinguishing Among Varieties of Emotional Expression   39

Chapter 3.   The Therapist as an Emotion Coach   55

Chapter 4.   The Steps of Emotion Coaching   85

II. The Arriving Phase: Coaching for Emotional Awareness

Chapter 5.   Arriving at a Primary Emotion 109

Chapter 6.   Coaching to Evaluate Whether an Emotion Is Healthy 137

III. The Leaving Phase: Moving on by Accessing Healthy Emotions

Chapter 7.   Identifying Maladaptive Emotions 171

Chapter 8.   The Transforming Power of Affect: Facilitating Access to Alternate Adaptive Emotions and Needs. 193

IV. Applying the Skills of Emotional Intelligence

Chapter 9.   Lessons About Anger and Sadness From
             Psychotherapy 229

Chapter 10. Transforming Fear and Shame in Psychotherapy 241

Chapter 11. Coaching for Emotional Wisdom in Couples 255

Chapter 12. Emotions in Parenting 279

Epilogue 301

Additional Resources 305

References 307

Author Index 317

Subject Index 321

About the Author 337

PREFACE

People have long been unsure of how to handle their emotionality and are given remarkably little explicit tutoring in this complex task. Indeed, some of the lessons about emotion we acquire in life seem contradictory. People are taught to trust their feelings and to follow their heart and yet are also taught to control themselves and to not be so emotional.

Too many people, without explicit tutoring in the emotional arts, flounder along the path of life. Without the skills for dealing with emotional storms and lacking adequate support from caring others, some develop the belief that controlling their emotions is the best solution. Trained in this scientific era to be reasonable and restrained, both in public and at work, people often neglect and lose touch with their internal stream of experience. Others become inveterate problem solvers, thinking everything through and trying to fix things rationally. Still others embrace spontaneity and follow their feelings without deliberation. They extol the virtues of the passionate life, intuition, spirituality, and perhaps mysticism. Some learn that they cannot trust others with their shared emotions and ultimately grow not to trust their own emotional signals, trying not to have emotions at all. Why attend to or experience feelings that others cannot tolerate or soothe and that are too painful to endure alone?

The great complexity of being human is that, in essence, we are two "selves" that do not necessarily get along (Epstein, 1994; Greenberg & Pascual-Leone, 1995). One self drives the rational stream of consciousness, in which people are more thoughtful and often deliberate, pondering the events of the week, plans for the day, and the future. This monitoring aspect of the self becomes an internal critic that represents all the negative beliefs, harsh criticisms, and unassimilated values taken in from others, the "shoulds" and "oughts" that tell people how to be, that manipulate their emotions, and that propel them to conformity, giving rise to feelings of inadequacy and discomfort. This self is also the seat of integrated ideals and values, which reflect the person's healthy assimilated standards and goals.

The other self is more automatic. It derives from an experiential, sensory stream of consciousness that is passionately more impulsive and yet more delicate; sensitive and, in many ways, sensible. Emotions embody our evaluations and goals, and many are prosocial. Human morality has been seen not as deriving from reason but from an immediate sense of feeling, especially a feeling for the suffering of others (Hume, 1739). Feelings such as compassion, sympathy, benevolence, gratitude, and justice come not from reason but from feelings for others.

It is not that one "voice" is conscious and the other unconscious, as Freud (1923/1961) held. Both are available to consciousness, but one communicates in words and the other through the sensorimotor channels of the body. This duality of language and experience is often depicted in dance or drama, in which the actors converse with each other in words while their alter egos dance out the other stream of consciousness, writhing in agony, bounding for joy, or conveying the subtleties of emotion between these extremes.

The resolution to the dilemma of our emotionality lies not in privileging one stream of consciousness over the other but in integrating the two. Allowing emotional experience, attending to it, and reflecting on it does this best. In this way we are processes in ongoing interaction with ourselves, constantly making sense of our experience for ourselves. What we make of our experience makes us who we are.

Through years of study, practice, and reflection, I have come to realize that emotion moves us and reason guides us and that psychotherapy profitably can be viewed as education in dealing with emotion. In all my years of practicing individual, couples, and family therapy, the most striking observation that I have made is that therapists are always coaching people in how to cope with emotion more effectively.

When I began working as a therapist, first with individuals with problems in living, later with couples and families in conflict, and finally with people experiencing affective disorders, I saw that all were struggling with how to deal effectively first with their own emotions and then with the emotions of intimate others. I saw how much emotion influenced people's views of themselves and others and their behaviors. I also began to see, as many had before me, that enduring change often occurs by moving from an intellectual understanding of oneself to an emotional experience of oneself and that therapy works most profoundly to promote change by enlisting deep and often painful emotions. Accessing peoples' core painful emotions —the hidden self-experiences that seemed too painful to bear—often proved to be transforming. I came to see that one had to arrive at a place before one could leave it.

I had begun my training as a psychotherapist in a client-centered approach, and ever since I have been a strong proponent of the importance of empathy, positive regard, and genuineness in promoting change. One guiding concern in this view is that the therapist is a facilitator, not an expert on what the client is experiencing or what is hidden from the clients' consciousness. I thus trained extensively in providing empathic understanding and more fundamentally in following and responding to clients' feelings rather than leading them to a place I thought they should go.

Then I trained in Gestalt therapy. This approach also emphasized the importance of following the clients' process, especially the clients' experiential process, but its form of intervention was more directive. It involved proposing experiments, suggesting "Try this" followed by "What do you experience?" Later I trained in structural/strategic, Milan, and interactional approaches to family therapy and over the years was exposed to myriad other approaches, including psychodynamic and cognitive therapy approaches. All of these, other than the person-centered approach, proposed some degree of leading rather than following. In my entire professional career I have struggled with the dichotomy of nondirectiveness versus directiveness, debating the merits of following versus leading, responding versus initiating, and facilitating versus modifying. Emotion coaching became my answer to this dilemma. Emotion coaching involves both leading and following and above all involves offering attuned process suggestions that help people further process their emotions. Emotion coaching borrows a concept from developmental psychology: Making suggestions in a person's "proximal zone" of development to promote development (Vygotsky, 1986). In this view, if one makes suggestions that are too far ahead of what people can do, those people cannot use the input. However, if one makes suggestions in a zone close to, but just ahead of, people's current state, the suggestion provides the scaffold of a possibility that gives those people a structure to facilitate forward movement.

Another important dichotomy that has governed my professional life has been the one between emotions and cognition. As important as the idea of meaning has been to me, rational approaches in which an expert therapist sees the errors in clients' thinking and helps clients to be more rational appeared to lack depth and an appreciation of the complexity of consciousness. Integrating emotion and reason has always seemed best. Working with emotion in psychotherapy seemed crucial. Expressive and emotive therapies that saw cure as coming about through primal screams, hitting pillows, or acknowledging and experiencing murderous impulses, however, seemed to ignore the importance of idiosyncratic meaning-making and the importance of the human capacity to reflect on experience to create new meaning. Emotion coaching integrates head and heart by promoting both emotional arousal and reflection and by helping people become aware of when to change emotion and when to be changed by it.

Emotion-focused therapy and the concept of emotion coaching are my solutions to the two major polarities with which I have struggled in learning to be a clinician. This resolution involves synthesizing following and leading into (a) being attuned to clients' feelings and offering proposals to help them process their experience more deeply and (b) working to integrate cognition and emotion by using cognition to make sense of emotion.

Emotion coaching is a way of thinking about therapy as training—training people in how to learn which emotions to trust and follow, which to bypass to get to something deeper, and which to regulate or transform and also when to do which of these. An emotion coach helps people identify emotion, differentiate what they feel from what others feel, tolerate emotions, synthesize contradictory emotions, use emotions as information, articulate feelings in words or symbols, use emotion to facilitate thinking, develop emotion knowledge, and reflect on emotions. These all are the tasks of emotional development. They occur throughout childhood and later life and are helped greatly by therapy. Emotion coaching promotes working with both emotion and cognition and with both self and the system. It involves leading and following, being an expert in how to facilitate certain processes, being a coparticipant in an exploratory process, and being a co-constructor of reality.

Valuable lessons about emotion began to emerge in the 1980s from brain and emotion research. The empirical grounding of emotion helped me feel that I might be able to integrate this with the lessons that I had learned from my years of practice, my research and writing on psychotherapy, and my own emotional experience to form a systematic approach for coaching people in the more intelligent use of their emotions. This approach is designed to help people enhance their abilities to use their emotions as a guide to healthy living. I have written several books on emotion in psychotherapy in an attempt to explicate how to work with emotion in psychotherapy. This started with *Emotion in Psychotherapy: Affect, Cognition, and the Process of Change* (Greenberg & Safran, 1987), followed shortly thereafter with *Emotionally Focused Therapy for Couples* (Greenberg & Johnson, 1988). These were the seminal books of an emotion-focused approach to therapy covering work with both individuals and couples. In *Facilitating Emotional Change: The Moment-by-Moment Process* (Greenberg, Rice, & Elliott, 1993), a process-experiential approach was laid out that attempted to provide an overall set of principles for an experiential approach to therapy. This book took emotion as the basis of organismic experience and introduced the idea of synthesizing leading and following into a basic therapeutic style. *Working With Emotion in Psychotherapy* (Greenberg & Paivio, 1997) offered an integrative approach to working with emotion, regardless of orientation. I have only recently crystallized all this into a view of the therapist as an "emotion coach" and have begun to focus my teaching, research, and practice on emotion coaching into what is now generally termed "an emotion-focused approach to therapy." I have found the results most encouraging. The view of the therapist as an emotion coach has helped me to integrate all my previous work on individuals and couples into an integrative emotion-focused approach to treatment. The emotion-focused approach presented here also helps integrate across diverse orientations, combining elements from experiential, psychodynamic, cognitive–behavioral, and systemic perspectives.

I see emotion coaching as an approach to working with emotion that is applicable across orientations. Most approaches to therapy, to some degree or another, involve coaching people in awareness, tolerance, and regulation of emotion. In all approaches, empathic attunement and support help people differentiate and tolerate their emotions. For all clients in all approaches, becoming more aware of their feelings is a first step in problem solving. Seeing their own patterns of emotional responding helps clients gain perspective and control of their emotional reactions. For all clients, changing their cognitions helps them regulate their feelings. Emotion is also regulated by reframing problems in a more positive manner or focusing on solutions. Facing fears in small steps helps people tolerate emotion. All these approaches involve coaching people in dealing with their emotions. In these approaches, emotion coaching occurs in subtle and not so subtle ways. It occurs in direct, psychoeducative ways and in indirect, strategic ways. All train people to deal with their emotionality in a new way. This book offers an explicit framework for thinking about how to coach people on the intelligent use of their emotions and how to help them change emotion with emotion.

PURPOSE AND STRUCTURE OF THE BOOK

This book is intended to serve three audiences. First, for those who are new to counseling and psychotherapy and have not had much experience in working with emotions, this book is designed to introduce the basic attitudes and methods for emotion coaching. It is designed to be useful to educate graduate and undergraduate students on the nature of emotions and on emotion work in therapy. Second, for more experienced therapists, the book provides a set of guidelines to help systematize one's understanding of and work with emotions and a method to help coach clients in using their emotions as a guide. Third, the book provides information and exercises for those seeking emotion self-awareness. In addition to providing skill-building exercises designed for clients to use in sessions or as self-help homework, several exercises are included to increase both professionals' and student practitioners' awareness of their own emotions and the role of emotion in change.

Part I

The chapters in Part I discuss the nature and function of emotion and emotional intelligence, demonstrate (with examples) how to use emotion intelligently, and offer the basic concepts and steps of emotion coaching to help access the wisdom in emotion. Chapter 1 raises the fundamental question of whether or not we are in a position to claim a knowledge base for the ideal way to deal with human emotionality. A brief synopsis of research findings on the nature and function of emotion in psychotherapy suggests that we have progressed sufficiently at the beginning of the new millennium to answer this question in the affirmative. Chapter 1 then suggests that emotion is a fundamentally adaptive source of wisdom and that emotional intelligence involves people being able to access the healthy information and action tendency within emotion, and to use these to make sense of their reactions to situations and to guide adaptive action. Finally, I raise the reality of maladaptive emotion, and emphasize the importance of learning to recognize and deal with both adaptive and maladaptive emotionality.

In Chapter 2, different types of emotion—primary, secondary, and instrumental—are defined. The main characteristics of these emotion types are described as a guide for coaches and clients. Clients need to be coached to make these key distinctions to learn how to use their emotions skillfully.

In Chapter 3, I offer a rationale for viewing the therapist or counselor as an emotion coach and describe the essential elements of the task. An important element of counseling and therapy is to promote emotional intelligence by coaching people in how to integrate emotion into their ongoing self-narratives. Rather than trying to change maladaptive emotion with cognitive therapy, I argue that it is more fruitful to leverage adaptive emotion to facilitate change. In other words, "mood over mood" is more effective than "mind over mood."

Chapter 4 reaches the heart of emotion coaching. I present the eight steps of the process in two phases: arriving and leaving. Coaching clients to arrive at emotion involves promoting their awareness of and receptivity to whatever they are feeling, as well as their ability to describe those feelings in words. Next, it involves coaching clients to evaluate whether the emotion being felt is primary. Finally, it involves coaching clients to make a crucial evaluation of their primary emotion: Is it adaptive, something that can be followed as a guide, or is it maladaptive and in need of transformation? The coaching tasks of the leaving phase hinge on this question.

If an emotion is evaluated as adaptive, one that can be trusted, then emotion-guided, reasoned action is the goal of the leaving phase. If the emotion is deemed to be maladaptive, the client will be coached to access new and healthy emotional resources to transform the less adaptive moods and beliefs. In this step a deeper level of change occurs.

Part II

The chapters in Part II examine in depth the work of the first phase of emotion coaching—arriving at emotion. Chapter 5 describes two processes that are used in coaching people to arrive at their primary emotions. The first process comes into play when the client's feeling is clearly available and intensely felt. This process facilitates the description and appropriate expression of that emotion. The second process, used when the client's initial feeling is vague and unclear, is to promote an experiential search of the bodily felt reactions to help identify and make sense of what is felt. Chapter 6 delves further into how to arrive at and identify four core emotions that are central to therapy: anger, sadness, fear, and shame.

Part III

The chapters in Part III examine more closely the therapist's task of coaching clients to leave behind undesirable states. Chapter 7 details how to help identify whether an emotion is adaptive or maladaptive and how to facilitate the articulation of maladaptive beliefs. Chapter 8 offers various means of coaching clients to identify their adaptive emotional resources, discusses in detail how to change emotion with emotion, and reviews the means of promoting emotion regulation.

Part IV

The chapters in Part IV examine the application of emotional intelligence to problems in living. The skills of emotion coaching are exemplified in the context of individual problems, couples therapy, and parenting. In chapters 9 and 10, lessons learned in therapy about the key emotions of sadness, anger, fear, and shame are discussed. These chapters illustrate the transforming power of emotion, for example, how adaptive anger can be mobilized to empower and overcome fear and shame or how accessing sadness facilitates grieving and promotes letting go and moving on. Chapter 10 offers a view of how access to and communication of attachment and intimacy-related emotion builds emotional bonds between people. I show how this helps transform negative escalation between couples into intimate contact between them. Chapter 11 suggests ways in which parents can coach their children in how best to handle their emotions. Coaching involves parents being aware of and having a positive attitude toward their own emotions and being empathic to and helping children cope adaptively with their emotions, particularly anger, sadness, fear, and shame.

* * *

My hope in writing this book is that it will give therapists the skills to help clients attain emotional wisdom. To develop emotional wisdom, people need to be aware of their emotions, to make sense of their emotions, to regulate their emotions, and to change emotion with emotion. Above all, emotional wisdom involves knowing when to be changed by emotion and when to change emotion. These skills are the key to benefitting from the intuitive sense and passion that emotions bring to our lives.

I

EMOTIONAL INTELLIGENCE: WHAT IT IS AND HOW TO PROMOTE ITS DEVELOPMENT

1

EMOTIONS AND EMOTIONAL INTELLIGENCE

IS THERE A KNOWLEDGE BASE?

Do psychologists and other mental health professionals know enough about emotion to teach people how to live an emotionally satisfying, healthy life? Is there a knowledge base on the best ways to handle our own and other people's feelings? Two major developments in the past two decades form a solid platform for answering these questions and have launched a new era in the understanding of emotion and its role in psychotherapy. The first development comes from the burgeoning investigation and exciting findings on emotion and the brain (Damasio, 1994; Lane & Nadel, 2000; LeDoux, 1996), and the second is an increased understanding of emotion in psychology and in psychotherapy (Ekman & Davidson, 1994; Fosha, 2000; Frijda, 1986; Greenberg, 2000; Lewis & DeHaviland, 2000).

Emotion is a brain phenomenon that is vastly different from thought. It has its own neurochemical and physiological basis and is a unique language in which the brain speaks. The limbic system (the part of the brain possessed by all mammals) is responsible for basic emotional processes, such as fear (LeDoux, 1996). The limbic system governs many of the body's physiological processes and thereby influences physical health, the immune system, and most major body organs. LeDoux (1996) suggests that there are two paths for producing emotion: (a) the "low" road, when the amygdala senses danger and broadcasts an emergency distress signal to the brain and the body, and (b) the slower "high" road, when the same information is carried through the thalamus to the neocortex. Because the shorter amygdala pathway transmits signals more than twice as fast as the neocortex route, the thinking brain often cannot intervene in time to stop emotional responses. Thus, the automatic emotional response occurs before one can stop it, whether one is jumping back from a snake or snapping at an inconsiderate spouse. In some situations it is clearly adaptive to respond quickly, whereas at other times better functioning results from the integration of cognition into emotional response. Thus, human brain anatomy results in two important processes: (a) the ability to have emotion and (b) the ability to regulate it. Effective regulation of emotion, however, is a complex process. Difficulties with over- and underregulation of emotion cause significant problems for clients in therapy.

Stress, a popular topic of discussion in the 1970s, is really an undifferentiated name for the effect of emotion on our bodies. In addition to the visible relationship between emotion and physiology and the immune system, emotion's effects on memory have also been clearly established. Different memory systems have been located in the organized brain: One memory system stores consciously processed information about events, while another stores the actual emotional experience of the event. Sometimes these modules do not communicate, which can cause problems. This may occur, for example, in people who have not recovered emotionally from a traumatic event, such as being trapped in a motor vehicle after an accident and having to be extracted by the "jaws of life." These people can give a factual account of the event without emotion, or they can have the terror of the event come flooding back with little or no detail. The resolution of trauma involves integrating these two memory systems (Van der Kolk, 1993).

Another major emotion-related discovery is that people with brain damage who have lost their capacity to respond emotionally are unable to make decisions and solve problems. They have lost their "gut sense" that guides these processes. Damasio (1994) told the story of a highly rational patient with brain damage who, because he had lost the capacity to feel, had no fear of driving in a snow storm, and one icy day he went to a medical appointment that all other patients had cancelled. When this patient, who showed no intellectual impairment, was asked if he wanted his appointment rescheduled for the following Tuesday or Thursday, he had trouble deciding which day to come. He had no emotionally based preference system to guide his decision making. The emotional brain enhances decision making by rapidly reducing the options that one can consider. The emotional brain highlights certain alternatives with a feeling of rightness and eliminates other alternatives with a feeling of "don't go there."

In psychology, the first major breakthrough in the study of emotion occurred when a reliable way of measuring emotions was developed (Ekman & Friesen, 1975). By the 1970s, at least six basic innate emotions had been clearly established, mainly by showing that facial expression of these emotions was innate. Whether the person is a U.S. college sophomore, a Japanese student, or a Borneo tribesman, he or she will exhibit the same facial expressions in situations that evoke anger, fear, sadness, disgust, surprise, or joy. People might use different words or concepts to describe the emotion, but the expression is the same. What is called "disgust" on a college campus in North America is identified as "the smell of a rotten pig" in the Borneo forest, but both cultures use and recognize the same facial expressions. This universal language of emotion ties human beings together, no matter where they are born. In addition to this universality of expression, other lines of evidence on the innateness of emotion came from the presence of the same facial expressions in people with congenital blindness, from cross-species similarity in expressive language, and from the ability to stimulate these expressions neurochemically and electrically. Thus, even though blind infants may never see the expression of anger or sadness, their ferocious little snarls and sad pouts resemble the faces of sighted infants, as well as those of monkeys. Electrical stimulation of the brains of felines and apes produces facial snarls remarkably like humans'. Darwin first noted this similarity of expressive forms of species in 1872 in his book, *The Expression of Emotions in Man and Animals*. Although it took almost a century to develop this observation into the rigorous study of emotional expression, the ability to finally be able to base emotions on something as concrete as facial expression has allowed for the development of measuring emotion. Reliable measurement, the sine qua non of science, launched the study of emotion in psychology.

Emotions have been shown to provide the very first evaluation of events (Frijda, 1986; Zajonc, 1980) in terms of how they effect humans' well-being. Thus, we automatically feel sad, afraid, or happy without conscious thought. Then we engage in a second-level evaluation (Taylor, 1989) in which we evaluate whether our emotions are adaptive and healthy. Once we have an emotion we need to reflect on it and decide what to do, whether to follow its urging, redirect it, or try to transform it. This integration of head and heart makes humans wiser than our intellects alone (Mayer & Salovey, 1997). In spontaneous living, this integration occurs continuously, preconsciously, in an ongoing process that generates our sense of things and serves as a basis for conscious meaning. Thus, we constantly receive messages from our survival and health-oriented emotional brain that contain a wealth of wisdom that is unavailable to the more conscious cognitive brain, and we are guided by it without thought.

The emotional brain, however, is not capable of analytic thought or reasoning and its rapid evaluations are imprecise; therefore, one needs to attend to and reflect on one's emotion to use its information. When, for example, a person hears a noise in the car engine while driving, he or she needs to integrate the emotional response of surprise and maybe fear with some understanding of how engines work. Then the person needs to decide whether to stop immediately, drive to a repair shop, or leave the car until tomorrow. Integrating the prompts of the emotional brain with the guidance of reason leads to the greatest adaptive flexibility. Relying on a synthesis of the emotional and the reasoning system also enhances the complexity of responses. A crucial next step in personal and cultural evolution involves developing means of teaching people to synthesize reason and emotion in everyday life. Thus, people can become more differentiated in their approach to life and problems.

Wise people have always managed to find this balance between reason and emotion. Aristotle (1941) knew this millennia ago, but this wisdom has often been forgotten through the ages. He noted that anyone can become angry—that is easy. But to be angry with the right person, to the right degree, at the right time, for the right purpose, and in the right way —this is not easy. This represents integrating head and heart. In a clever experiment, Bohart (1977) showed that clients in a treatment that promoted the expression of unresolved angry feelings and reflection on them resolved their feelings more effectively than clients in a condition that promoted either expression or reflection. Synthesis won. In addition, there is growing evidence that integrating bodily sensed feelings into one's awareness and being able to symbolize feelings in words promotes good health. Pennebaker (1990), in a remarkable demonstration of the importance of symbolizing and organizing one's feelings, has shown that writing about one's emotional experience of traumatic or upsetting events as few as four times, for 20 minutes each time, has significant effects on one's health and well-being. Writing in "emotion diaries" helps people make sense of their experience and develop a narrative account or story that makes their experience more coherent. In addition, Stanton and colleagues (2000) have recently shown that women who cope with breast cancer through expressing emotion had fewer medical visits, enhanced physical health and vigor, and decreased distress. The results also suggest that emotional expression is more beneficial than emotional processing alone. The former is characterized by statements such as "I take time to express my emotions" and the latter is characterized by "I take time to figure out what I am really feeling." They also found that emotional expression appeared to drive effective goal pursuit only for those who had a sense of agency and hope.

In the areas of clinical and counseling psychology, time has helped sort out "the wheat from the chaff" of the social revolution of the 1960s. The excesses of the "get in touch with your feelings" revolution have been overcome by the study of how people change and by developments in the practice of psychotherapy. The "touchy feely" era of sensitivity training and encounter groups, of "letting it all hang out," has ended. In the world of work, trying to actualize one's self has moved to surviving and getting a job. In the world of interpersonal relations, terminating an unsatisfying marriage too quickly to try another one is becoming a thing of the past. The value of commitment and the recognition that people need to work on themselves and their relationships has replaced the attitude of instant personal change and the mentality in marriage of shopping for a better version.

In the applied science of psychotherapy research, increasing solid evidence shows that certain emotional processes help promote therapeutic change (Greenberg, Korman, & Paivio, 2001). Having established the fact that psychotherapy leads to change, researchers in the 1980s began to focus on what processes lead to change. With regard to emotion, a complex picture has emerged. The formula stating that getting in touch with feelings will solve problems is too simple. It has become clear that different kinds of feelings need to be managed in different ways (Paivio & Greenberg, 2001). Experiencing emotion is the core of many emotional change processes. In many situations in therapy, arousing emotions seems to be an important precondition to changing emotions. A safe collaborative relationship with a therapist as well as the therapist's empathic attunement to clients' feelings are important preconditions for working with emotion.

In addition, a well-established principle of conditioning is that the only way to get rid of fear is to feel it—changing emotion requires experiencing it. Methods that help arouse feared-emotional states to expose them to new experiences have shown to be important in changing these emotions (Clarke, 1996; Mineka & Thomas, 1999). These methods could involve imagining a painful experience from the past for the purpose of reexperiencing the pain, spinning around in a chair to realize that the dizziness of panic is not a precursor of a heart attack, or realizing that a feeling toward one's therapist is a projection on the therapist from a past relationship. These examples all involve arousing painful feelings to promote therapeutic change.

Mounting evidence that emotional arousal and depth of experience relate to therapy outcome supports the importance of access to emotion in therapy. For example, session emotional intensity was found to be one of the strongest predictors of outcome in a combined sample of varying treatments of depression (Beutler, Clarkin, & Bongar, 2000). In this study Beutler and colleagues also showed that emotional arousal was only predictive of outcome when it occurred in the context of a good working alliance. Underscoring this point, another group of researchers (Iwakabe, Rogan, & Stalikas, 2000) recently have shown that high arousal predicted good session outcome also only in the context of a good working alliance. These findings suggest that processing bodily felt experience and deepening this in therapy in a good therapeutic relationship environment may be a core ingredient of change in psychotherapy, regardless of approach. The ability to experience a full range of emotions also appears important in promoting physical health (Pennebaker & Traue, 1993). The ability to experience, tolerate, symbolize, and express emotion are all aspects of health.

Although research suggests that the expression and arousal of emotion can contribute to change, this is true only for some people with certain types of concerns (Pierce, Nichols, & DuBrin, 1983). The actual relationships among emotion, cognition, and somatic processes still remains unclear. Arousal and expression of emotion alone may be inadequate in promoting change. Venting has not been found to be effective in reducing distress (Bushman, Baumeister, & Stack, 1999; Kennedy-Moore & Watson, 1999). This points to the importance of the further processing of aroused emotion by symbolizing it in awareness and to the clarification of the sources of its arousal. Making sense of emotion in new ways has also been found to help break cycles of maladaptive automatic emotion processes. Mergenthaler (1996) recently demonstrated that in therapy, an emotion cycle of relaxation, followed by an increase in arousal, followed by arousal plus reflection, followed by more abstract reflection alone, and finally back to relaxation is associated with good outcome. Warwar and Greenberg (2000) similarly found that high emotional arousal plus reflection on emotional experience distinguished good and poor outcome cases, indicating the importance of combining arousal and meaning construction. Thus, emotion needs not only be aroused, but needs to be reflected on. This helps regulate emotion.

A progression in depth of experiencing across therapy also has been shown to predict outcome in a variety of types of treatment approaches (Hendricks, 2001; Orlinsky & Howard, 1986). People who do well in therapy move from talking about external events in a detached manner, through focusing on internal feelings in a richly descriptive and associative way, to readily accessing feelings to solve problems. Thus, to change in therapy, clients cannot just talk intellectually about themselves and their feelings; they need to viscerally experience what they talk about and use their feelings to identify and solve problems. The difference between talking about something and experiencing it in therapy is similar to the difference between talking about what its like being knocked over by a wave on the beach and actually experiencing being knocked over by one. In therapy, people who change often need to experience being knocked over by emotional waves before they find their feet.

Emotions are inherently connected to feelings of closeness and trust and are intimately involved in the ability to deal successfully with relationships. Research on couples therapy supports the role of emotional awareness and expression in a satisfying relationships and change in therapy. Emotionally focused couples therapy (Greenberg & Johnson, 1988) that helps partners access and express underlying attachment-oriented emotions has been found to be effective in increasing marital satisfaction.

In addition, couples that showed higher levels of emotional experiencing in therapy accompanying a softening in the blaming partners stance, from blaming to affiliation, were found to interact in a more connected manner and were more satisfied when therapy ended than couples who showed lower experiencing (Greenberg, Ford, Alden, & Johnson, 1993; Johnson & Greenberg, 1985). A similar effect of the expression of underlying emotion was found in resolving family conflict (Diamond & Liddle, 1996).

The above evidence indicates that certain types of therapeutically facilitated emotional arousal and awareness, when expressed in supportive relational contexts, in conjunction with conscious cognitive processing of the aroused emotional experience is important for therapeutic change for certain classes of people and problems. The role of the cognitive processing of emotion is to either help make sense of it or to help regulate it. Creation of new meaning has also been central in therapeutic change (Mahoney, 1991). Thus, not only must people feel their feelings, they also need to make sense of these feelings. Developing a new story of their life is important in change. Therapy needs to help people become the authors of their life scripts and to reauthor their story by organizing it in a new way, making it more coherent and more salutary (Neimeyer & Mahoney, 1995). Feeling one's emotions in therapy thus has been found to lead, not to get rid of them, but to create new stories with new meanings.

Freud originally believed that *catharsis*—the intense expression of repressed emotion—could eliminate symptoms (Freud & Breuer, 1893/1949). He changed this view to one in which repression of emotionally charged memories was as the basis of neurotic symptoms and insight into what was repressed was the cure (Freud, 1923/1961). Out of the Freudian heritage grew a view that certain dangerous or antisocial drives and emotions needed to be repressed or defended against for social adaptation and healthy living. Later, psychologists using ego psychology and modern cognitive therapies saw ideas as crucial in affect and perpetuated the view of emotions as disruptive and often irrational. For example, Beck (1976) proposed that automatic thoughts produced emotion and that rational thinking would produce health. These views emphasized the dysfunctionality of emotion.

Psychologists using humanistic psychology, on the other hand, saw dysfunction as arising from the suppression of the healthy, from lack of awareness of positive or growth promoting experience (e.g., Rogers, 1959). Thus, disowning of emotion and difficulty in tolerating painful but necessary emotions led to disease (Perls, Hefferline, & Goodman, 1951). In line with this more positive view, psychologists with modern psychodynamic views see emotions as playing a healthy role in promoting attachment (e.g., Stein, 1991). In this view the caretaker's response to a child's affect became crucial in how that child experiences self, world, and other. All these views emphasized the functionality of emotion.

From this crucible of competing views and with contemporary emotion theory and research, I came to view human emotional experience as a high level synthesis of affect, motivation, cognition, and behavior (Greenberg & Safran, 1987). The emotion system integrates information across a variety of information-processing domains and is the most complex system of knowing that humans possess (Greenberg & Safran, 1987; Leventhal, 1984). This system can be viewed as involving tacit cognitive–affective structures, internal models, scripts, or emotion schemes (Oatley, 1992). These emotion schemes provide a constant readout of a person's current state and are crucial in determining perception and in helping people mobilize their efforts for goal-directed action.

Developments in emotion research and psychotherapy research have put us in a position to say something about the role of emotion in healthy living. The cathartic dumping or "getting rid" of emotions put forward by Freud and Breuer (1893/1949) as their initial means of a cure is not sufficient. Similarly, total suppression of emotion is unhealthy. In a nutshell, people must pay attention to their emotions and give them equal status to thought and action. It is the integration of emotion and reason that results in a whole that is greater than the sum of its parts. It is not that the experience of emotion alone leads people to wise action. After all, emotion, wise or not, exists in everyone. How people make sense of their emotional experience and how they use it is what makes the difference. Awareness of emotion and the ability to enable emotion to inform reasoned action is what is necessary for emotional intelligence (Mayer & Salovey, 1997).

THE INTELLIGENCE OF EMOTIONS

Robert is sitting at his desk, reading peacefully. A pleasant breeze, coming through the window, cools the warm sun on his face. A loud bang just outside the window startles him. His head jerks up. He finds he has simultaneously almost ducked and drawn back in his chair. His breathing and heart rate have increased. He thinks "Was it a shot? In this day and age, you can't be sure!" He rises rapidly but then peers cautiously through the window. He hears the remains of a speeding car. "It was an exhaust backfiring!" More alert, he sits back and continues reading.

Robert's emotion system sensed danger. His fear rapidly organized him for flight and informed him of possible danger. This happened long before he could consciously assess the situation. He heard the bang; he was startled; and his head automatically oriented toward the sound while his body drew back in fear, readying him for flight. His emotion system automatically told him that his peaceful safety was at risk. Reason then assessed the situation more thoroughly for danger and made sense of what was happen-

EXHIBIT 1.1
How to Use Emotion Intelligently

- Emotion is a signal to oneself.
- Emotion organizes one for action.
- Emotions monitor the state of one's relationships.
- Emotions evaluate whether things are going one's way.
- Emotions signal to others.
- Expression is important but may not always correct what is wrong.
- Deciding on how to act on the signal is important.
- Thought puts emotion in perspective and makes sense of it.
- Emotion enhances learning.

ing. Deciding to get up and investigate the situation for possible danger seemed sensible. Running away from the bang to safety would make him look very foolish. Rabbits are that skittish—thank goodness he isn't. However, some expression or action to handle some of the arousal was good. Carefully checking out the window was a good idea. Analyzing the problem of possible danger posed by fear, Robert rationally determined the source of the sound and established that it posed no threat.

Why do people have emotions, and what should they do with them? They have them because emotions are crucial to survival, communication, and problem solving (see Exhibit 1.1; Frijda, 1986; Izard, 1991; Tomkins, 1963, 1983). Emotions are not a nuisance to be gotten rid of or ignored; rather, emotions are an essential aspect of being human. Emotions are signals, ones worth listening to. They offer messages that one is in danger, that one's boundaries are being invaded, that one is feeling close to someone safe and familiar, or that this person is absent. Emotions also tell people if things are going their way and organize them to respond rapidly to situations to try to make sure things do go one's way. Emotions are most noticeable as changes in a readiness for action; they respond to changing circumstance by changing the person. In fear, people shrink back; in anger, they puff up; in sadness, they close down; and in interest, they open up. People are in a continual process of changing their relationship with the environment by changing themselves.

Like reeds in the wind, people change their inclination and orientation according to what blows in. Emotions particularly tell people about the nature of their relational bonds. They inform people whether their relationships are being enhanced or disrupted or are in need of repair. Emotions, by rapidly communicating a person's current state, needs, goals, and inclinations to others, also regulate other people's behaviors. There is no external signal that tells people that others are thinking, or what others are thinking. Emotions, by contrast, are visible in one's face and voice, and thereby they regulate self and other. Emotions also set up relational themes that become central organizers of relationships. Sadness is about loss, anger is about goal frustration or unfairness, fear is about threat, and jealousy is about perceived displacement or betrayal. Each emotion defines a relationship between a person and other people or between a person and the environment (Oatley, 1992).

Emotions clearly enhance intelligence (Mayer & Salovey, 1997). Fear tells people that they are in danger, sadness that something important has been lost, and joy that a desirable goal has been reached. Emotions give people information related to their well-being; for example, they tell people when their needs or goals are being reached or frustrated. Gut feelings guide decisions by rapidly reducing alternatives to be considered. For example, in deciding what sort of vacation to take, one's emotions might tell a person that he or she prefers going to the beach rather than to the mountains. Emotional preferences narrow the options that people need to consider and keep people from being overwhelmed by too much information.

People definitely are wiser than their intellects alone. By rapidly apprehending patterns in the world much faster than the information can be consciously analyzed, emotions guide reasoning. Emotions are not simply disruptions of ongoing life that need to be controlled; rather, they are organizing processes that need to be attended to. In combination with reason, they help make people more effective in their ever-changing environments by helping them rapidly adapt to the world and by facilitating adaptive problem solving. Emotions involve both cognition, in the form of evaluations, and motivation, in the form of needs, and they are therefore higher level experiences than either cognition or motivation alone. They are richly infused with all that is important to us: our meanings, our needs, and our values. Without emotions, people could not live satisfying lives.

Emotions are among the primary data of existence. Like the senses of touch and smell, emotions course through people's bodies. They comprise intimate, inside information that pervades consciousness, providing people with very subjective information. They tell a person that he or she is feeling proud, humiliated, annoyed, or depleted. Emotions often just happen—they just move people into action in the seamless process of living moment by moment. People constantly act without thought, getting up, moving, hugging, smiling, and scratching without much conscious effort. At the next level of awareness, attending to feelings gives life color, meaning, and value. If a person is unable to attend to this level of experience, he or she will lack orientation in the world and will lose a sense of what is personally significant.

Damasio (1999) suggested that human consciousness came into being in the form of feeling. *Feeling* is one's very first representation that an object has changed one's state of being. Looking at how the brain represents feeling, Damasio concluded that knowing springs to life in the story of the effects of objects on one's body states. The representations of these effects are feelings. The brain maps what happens over time inside the organism, and in relation to it, and in so doing naturally weaves wordless stories about the organism's experience of its environment. Knowing thus first arises as a feeling of what happens to one's body in relation to its processing of an object. Essentially, the brain codes "this happened to me when that object affected my body state in this way." These are the very first stories that help us make sense of our life experiences. People string together the effects objects and events have on themselves, in time-ordered sequences that imply causality.

In addition to consciously experiencing feelings, people also reflect on some of these feelings to make sense of their experience. It is through reflection that people also integrate all their cultural and social knowledge with their emotional sense of being. This ultimately is how personal meaning is created in everyday life. Thus, when people wake in the morning with joy and interest, their organismic feeling signals that all is well. These emotions orient them to begin to tackle projects with enthusiasm and flexibility, and little reflection is needed. If, however, a person wakes with fear or sadness, these emotions signal that something is awry in the way in which the person is conducting his or her life or that something has happened to him or her that requires attention. The person then begins to use all his or her knowledge to consciously reorganize his or her world. This signaling of a problem promotes reflection on what is happening so the person can create culturally derived solutions to the problems that have produced the bad feeling and to act. Emotions thus pose problems that one must use reason to solve. Above all, the information that emotions contain about what is happening to the organism in its environment adds to people's intelligence, just like thought and imagination. Emotional intelligence involves the skillful use of emotions, feelings, and moods to cope with life.

Emotions and the Conduct of Life

Emotional moments occur throughout the day: at home, at work, at play, in parenting, in marriage, with friends and on one's own. The moment people wake up they are feeling. They may feel awake and eagerly anticipate their day, or they may apprehensively dread an upcoming meeting. Each day is a process of ongoing feeling. If all is well people simply feel a background sense of well-being and interest. When all is not well, and when they meet unusual circumstances, they will become aware of specific types of emotional arousal and experience different feelings.

People need to understand what their emotions indicate to them about the way they are conducting their lives. When they experience unpleasant emotions, it means there is something wrong to which they need to attend. Merely expressing the emotion will often not correct the situation, although it sometimes helps. Instead, people need to read the messages of their own reactions and then begin to act sensibly on them to correct the situation.

Emotional Expression

Expression of emotion, in ways appropriate to the context, is a highly complex skill of emotional intelligence, one that involves integrating prompts from both biology and culture. People learn appropriate forms of expression. Even crying at funerals is a learned form of expression. The high-pitched, explosive bursts of crying at a funeral of the Makonde tribe of Tanzania would hardly be recognizable as crying by people from another culture, and vice versa (Kottler, 1996). To the Makonde, crying into a handkerchief is a strange Western cultural form. Expression is thus a socially mediated process, and awareness of emotion is not synonymous with expression. Learning when and how to express an emotion, and when it will not help, is all part of developing emotional intelligence.

People not only are informed and moved by their emotions, but they also need to make sense of them and decide on how best to express them and what best to do in any emotion-evoking situation. Feelings, for example, tell one when something is painful and hurts. Emotions are a very direct way of experiencing what is happening; they send messages and pose problems that need to be solved through reason. Cognition thus often helps people attain affective goals; decisions then need to be made regarding expression and action. Thought also explains the hurt; puts it into perspective; makes sense of it, justifies, or rationalizes it; and helps determine a remedy.

Emotions go coursing through people's bodies whether they like it or not. Early in human history emotions were known as the *passions,* because people were passive receivers of them. It is only in the more recent centuries that the term *emotion*—*e-motion,* to move out, emphasizing the action tendency aspect—began to be used. As our ancestors knew, however, it is folly to try and resist emotions; rather, one has to coordinate one's conscious efforts with emotions' automatic prompting. Human beings exercise agency in how they work with emotions, and in what they do with them, rather than in expending effort in trying not to have them.

Rather than attempting to control, interrupt, change, or avoid the experience of emotions, people need to learn to live in harmony with them. Over-controlled anger or sadness saps energy. Expression of needs and disclosure of hurts often brings better results. To achieve this, people need to learn to integrate their reason with their emotion, being neither compelled by emotion nor cut off from it. To live both passionately and reflectively, people need to integrate their heads and hearts.

EMOTION AND TIME

Present

Emotions by their nature focus on the present. They color the present and guide actions toward immediate goals. Advocates of traditions such as Zen and Gestalt therapy (Perls, 1969; Polster & Polster, 1973) have proposed the importance of living in the present. Some critics have disagreed and do not believe that living in the present is healthy (Cushman, 1995; Lasch, 1979, 1984). They think that it will lead to an impulsive life and argue that using feelings as a guide may lead people to ignore the future consequences of their actions. These critics fail to distinguish between living *in* the present and living *for* the present.

Living in the present is healthy and often involves a heightened awareness. People who live in the present are aware of both the environment and their immediate emotional reactions to the environment. For example, people are aware of joy when a loved one smiles at them. Or, in more meditative moments, they may be aware of a passing breath and say to themselves, "Breathing in, I am calm. Breathing out, I feel joy" (Kabat-Zinn, 1993). People feel at peace dwelling in the present moment. Living *for* the moment however, is tantamount to reckless impulsiveness; people who live for the moment do something if it feels good, without considering the consequences. To critics, living in the present (viewed as living for the present) seems antithetical to the work ethic. This ethic has led many people to view emotion as the enemy of achievement and self-application and has led to the belief that emotion needs to be controlled. Living in the present, however, brings orientation and energy.

Past and Future

Emotions are based in the present, but they are influenced by the past, and they influence the future. The past lives on in the present to the degree that the past influences a person's experience of current events. People's current reactions to circumstances and relationships often are forged from their emotional history (Luborsky & Crits-Christoph, 1990).

Remembering often generates emotions. The lessons people have learned from infancy to adulthood are stored in emotional memory (Singer & Salovey, 1993). Much unpleasant emotion arises as an intrusion from the past. For example, a feeling of sadness may arise when a person sees a picture that is reminiscent of a lost parent. People's current experiences may be pierced by emotional scenes of the past, by memories that rudely intrude into the present. Such intrusions often occur in an uncontrollable way. Present feelings are thus often about past experiences. Emotions about things past differ from vital emotional responses to the present. Emotions of the remembered past are often the source of emotional problems. In coaching people in the use of emotions as a guide, the first important distinction to be made is that unresolved emotions about past events need to be handled differently than emotional responses to present situations.

Anticipation of future events also can produce emotions, especially worry (Borkovec, 1994). Often emotions are difficult to deal with when they concern events that might happen. The past lives on in memories, and emotions experienced in the past at least were caused by responses to actual circumstances. There is something real about emotions felt in response to past events. With regard to the future, however, emotion is secondary to thought, providing people only with reactions to rehearsals of future scenes played out in the internal theater of the mind.

Imagining and thinking of future events, however, are important capacities, because they help one anticipate how to respond to future events. Using this capacity, people can generate "trial run" emotional experiences in the present. If one imagines what life would be like without one's spouse or partner, one might realize how alone one would feel. This might fuel a decision to remain faithful to that person. Only when the mind conjures up anticipated futures that one treats as real are future-related emotions problematic. These emotions can almost be thought of as "virtual" emotions, because they are reactions to virtual realities. Problems thus arise when people confuse their fantasies about the future with reality and react as though the future is occurring now. This is how people get into real knots. They worry, run from paper tigers, fume at insults not yet cast, and weep about the loss of a significant other while that person is still present. To the degree that fantasies about the future motivate planning and action, imagining emotional reactions to future events is healthy. When people stew in events that have not yet happened, as though they are occurring now, they spoil the only-too-brief moments they do have in the present.

There is a second problem with emotion in relation to the future. Although emotions are useful responses to the present, they do not take into account the future consequences of their actions. For instance, fear of surgery doesn't take into account the consequences of having no treatment at all. Emotion tells people there is a current problem or concern and suggests an immediate useful present response. However, emotion cannot peer into the future and tell people about the future consequences of the actions it might be suggesting. Thinking and imagining are required to anticipate future effects.

People's abilities to imagine future scenarios, to evaluate possible courses of action, to think, and to reason add immensely to their capacity to survive and thrive. To act in a healthy manner, people need to not only be prompted by emotion but also to think about the possible future consequences of their actions. For example, every time people decide to use a contraceptive device during sex, reason and emotion are acting together to ensure physically healthy living. If people responded to emotion alone, they might have unprotected sex without thinking of the consequences. The ability to project the future consequences of their actions and to integrate these with present experience will lead to healthier actions. The people will still be concerned about their present satisfaction, but now they can take future consequences into account. People therefore need to distinguish between emotion in response to present circumstance and emotion in response to anticipated scenarios, because each serves a different purpose in life.

Integrating Past, Present, and Future

People need to recognize how profoundly emotion governs the present and orients them in their worlds. Feelings provide them with a constant readout of their current reactions to ongoing events. Their feelings declare who they are in the beginning of any moment. Before people transform their very first self into the more complicated self they always become, feelings tell them the effects of their first contact. These first emotions tell them how they are reacting—not how they should react, or would like to react, but how the self that they actually are is reacting. Emotions, filled with the wisdom of biology, are forged in the crucible of lived experience, into one's current self (Stern, 1985). If one is treated well as one grows up, one perceives the world to a safe place and feels good. If one is treated poorly, one begins to construct a sense of a dangerous world, an unresponsive other, and a fearful sense of self. One's self reacts with this embodied knowledge by feeling things. People thus feel afraid as they interpret looks on another's face as a hint of danger or tension in the air as a signal of impending conflict. Or, they feel pleased that their date's virtually imperceptible lean forward indicates an as-yet-undeclared interest. Without this felt orientation to the world people would stumble through life, clumsily encountering circumstances because of the lack of any intuitive orientation. This wisdom of bodily felt emotions serves as a gyroscope to keep people on an even keel.

If, however, people live only by present emotion, simply surfing on the currents of their next-emerging emotion, they rob themselves of all that humans have learned through language and culture about adaptive living. Language-based knowledge, in addition to biology and experience, has become crucial in transmitting all that humans have learned (Gergen, 1985; Neimeyer & Mahoney, 1995). People thus always need to integrate their emotionally based biological knowledge with their more learned personal and cultural knowledge. Doing something because it feels good, as we know, is not always the best guide to action. People need to take their social context and the future into account before acting. A lot of acceptable and effective behavior in any particular context is learned and needs to be integrated with people's primary biological-based emotional experience. A person who immediately yells at others because they annoyed him or her, or who makes love to another person whom he or she finds appealing, doesn't take enough relevant information into account. On the other hand, ignoring the feeling that one is annoyed or attracted robs a person of a deep source of knowledge, enjoyment, and vitality. However, relying on it alone will not produce wise action. Thus, present feeling must be integrated with awareness of future consequences and informed by past learning. Living only for the present and ignoring consequences is not wise: What one did today will affect what happens tomorrow.

The Embodied Present

People experience the world in the present in their bodies (Damasio, 1999). They gush with feeling and sensation before any words provide containers for their feelings. To exercise emotional intelligence, people need to recognize the present rush of adrenaline in their body when encountering a threat, and, for example, they need to be aware of the hormonal changes that affect their bodies when a sexually attractive person enters their field of vision. People need to recognize the resulting fierce way in which they ache with love, lust, and emotional pain. They need to start this process of recognition by attending to their bodies and then be able to symbolize what they feel, first to themselves and then, when appropriate, to others. People need to be able to say to themselves "I feel." Having acknowledged their emotional experience, people then need to begin to understand these feelings. To do this, people have to "use their heads" to make sense of their experience. The mind needs to symbolize bodily felt experience in words, to synthesize the neurochemical cascades that wash over into conscious experience and symbolize them into personal meanings. Put simply, to live intelligently people need to integrate their heads and hearts. It is to this task—of helping clients make sense of their feelings—that this book is devoted.

EMOTIONALLY SPEAKING, PEOPLE ARE ALL PRETTY MUCH ALIKE

The stimuli that evoke emotions vary greatly from person to person and from culture to culture, and yet there is a commonality that binds people together and makes them human (Scherer, 1984a, 1984b). Little babies who lie in their cribs and go through a parade of emotional expression, their grimaces and smiles only too recognizable, demonstrate this. With these facial displays they begin to communicate irritation, puzzlement, serenity, happiness, and anger. People immediately recognize these expressions, and communication has begun. Human beings could never understand each others' feelings unless they have felt something similar to what they see being expressed (Ekman & Friesen, 1975). Fortunately people, regardless of where they were born—in the Americas, China, Africa, Europe, India, or Australia—understand this language of emotions. All people, regardless of when they are born, come into the world with the same emotional system that serves as the basis of a common humanity. It is true that idiosyncratic experience will put an indelible stamp on people's emotionality, sometimes even twisting and distorting it into something one no longer recognizes. Culture trains people to hide emotions or to express emotions in unique ways. Depending on what different cultures may view as natural or acceptable, people may express themselves, for example, by running amok with emotional fervor or by dancing joyously in the streets during Mardi Gras. Despite varied experience and training, however, people are all pretty much alike. Beneath one culture's self-effacing humility and another's brash assertiveness lies a common core of emotional humanness that serves as a human basis for understanding others.

Emotions automatically evaluate immediate circumstances and consequences of action. With the aid of emotions, people react automatically to their apprehension of patterns of sounds, sights, smells, and to other signs of people's intentions in a way that has served them well as a species for centuries and as individuals for years. Fear-induced flight produces safety and disgust and may expel a noxious intrusion. People respond automatically to patterns of cues in their environments that immediately signal danger, comfort, and loss. This automatic, rapid functioning of the emotion-based, survival-oriented brain was of such advantage that, as the brain developed, the thinking brain emulated the emotion brain's way of being. The thinking cortex added to the emotion brain's wisdom a new form of emotional response. This new emotional response system uses not only inherited emotional responses but also learned signs of things that have evoked emotion in a person's own life (Damasio, 1994; Griffiths, 1997). These emotional memories and organizations have been called *emotion schemes* (Greenberg & Paivio, 1997; Oatley, 1992). By means of these internal organizations or programs, people now react automatically on the basis of their emotion systems—not only to inherited cues, such as looming shadows or comforting touch, but also to cues that they have learned are dangerous or life enhancing. They do this in much the same way as they react to things that heredity has taught them. These reactions occur rapidly and without thought.

ADAPTIVE EMOTIONS AT WORK

Let's look now at an example of how emotions work to make people wiser and enhance their intelligence:

Trevor is away from his wife for the first time, on a 4-month business trip. As he is talking to her on the phone she begins to tell him about how she is doing with him away. She says she is feeling really pleased about being able to be more independent and that she feels good about herself. She goes on to say that she has been able to more easily define her own identity and not feel as reliant on him to help her define herself. Trevor listens with interest and is aware of the excitement in her voice. She continues that she is enjoying being able to do things more freely, on her own schedule, and not have to accommodate him and lose her own rhythm. She reassures Trevor that she misses him and likes his companionship but that she first had to experience her ability to be autonomous before she missed him. Trevor's wife is upbeat and does not sound critical, but something is happening inside of his body. She continues on, saying that it has always been a struggle for her to be separate, to know her own preferences and feel confident in her own identity. The stirring inside him is growing. A feeling begins to course through his chest and stomach. It is like he has swallowed a bad-tasting, oily liquid that he wants to spit out, but he can't because it's already moving through his insides. As he senses this it hinders his concentration. He finds himself less able to attend to what she is talking about. He hears her saying in a joking way, "As you know, it's sometimes quite demanding to take care of your needs, and it's nice, for awhile, to be free of the inevitable compromises a relationship entails."

Trevor now finds himself virtually unable to listen to his wife. He hears her words, even understands them, but he has begun to feel a little lightheaded, and her words seem come to from a great distance. They seem to pass right through him rather than landing in the usual place that gives them their felt meaning. He finds himself steadily withdrawing despite his efforts to stay in contact. His breathing is now shallow, and he is tensing up slightly in his stomach, shoulders, and jaw.

His wife is still speaking, openly and enthusiastically, and Trevor can hear that she is not hostile or critical. In fact, her voice is gentle and warm, but still he feels threatened and rejected. He goes to a place deep inside where he can feel hurt yet protected. He feels sad and alone. This is not a new feeling; he knows it well. But now, sitting with the phone to his ear, he finds it hard to speak out from this withdrawn place. This is different from other times when he has felt rejected—something about being on the phone has made him more able to be aware of his anxiety and the threat. Rather than jumping into his usual coping styles of responding helpfully, asserting his view, getting angry, or analyzing what's going on, Trevor remains quiet, feeling far away. There is a tense silence on the phone. He wants to say something, but he just can't seem to swim up out of his confusion to make contact with his wife.

Finally, somehow, Trevor manages to draw on his internal resources to pull himself out and to get his voice to work, and it strengthens as he musters courage. He says what he feels: "It's hard to hear this, and I feel hurt," or something like that. His wife responds reassuringly, not in her sometimes-defensive manner, but still he feels far removed and still he can hear the echo of his own voice coming back to him hidden in a cavern deep inside of himself. He thinks to himself, "I know she means well, but I just feel so rejected." This helps a bit, but he still has to work hard to draw on some inner resource to help himself struggle out of that walled-off place and say, "I do understand what you are saying, because I have some of the same sense of freedom and less need to accommodate, but you sound so enthusiastic about having me away and so intense about your need to be separate. You always are so involved in your struggle to be you that I feel pushed away. I'd like sometimes to hear more about your need to be connected." He adds, "I know I am emotionally demanding at times, but it's really hard to hear that you find me a burden." She responds in a caring manner, saying that this had always been the struggle in their relationship but that she was feeling clear that she valued him and their relationship, and she wanted him to understand that what she was saying was not a threat. He begins to relax and feels himself coming out of hiding and back into contact. It is his wife's caring tone as much as her words that reach him. He breathes more freely, the spinning sensation in his head begins to leave him, and he notices the bright colors on the bowl he has been staring at on the table. She asks if he is OK, and he feels her concern coming through the phone. They agree to finish this conversation for now and to continue it when he returns home. He talks about a few other details, and they say good-bye. Ten minutes later, she calls to say she felt really sad to hear him without words, so quietly hurt, when he usually is so readily able to talk things through, and that she hopes he is all right. He feels good, especially now that she has called, and says that he appreciates her calling back.

Hard hitting as this conversation may have been, it led Trevor and his wife to a deeper sense of trust based on emotional honesty and concern for each other. Each partner's need for connection and for autonomy was recognized. As a couple, they handled this interaction skillfully and sensitively, and they came through it feeling closer. Others could have gone spiraling out of control. The conversation could have escalated into cycles of attack and withdraw, or attack and counter-attack, and the inevitable efforts to defend. That would have left both feeling battered and diminished, and for a time the connection would have been damaged. Luckily, Trevor was able to come out of his withdrawal, but it wasn't easy. The two them got through it. He spoke from his hurt, and his wife heard and validated his feelings. The following functions (shown in Exhibit 1.1) occurred:

- *Emotion informed him.* Trevor's emotions informed him of feelings of threat and rejection in spite of his rational judgment of safety. These emotions told him that the possibility of something of major concern to him—his need for connection, based on who he was, and his history—was at risk. Like it or not, he felt vulnerable to being abandoned, and he had to pay attention to it and learn how to deal with it. He would have ignored it at the peril of becoming inexplicably withdrawn and disorganized. He didn't always like what he felt, and it was not always adaptive, but it was there, organizing him, and he needed to be aware of it, make sense of it, and find ways of coping constructively with how it was inclining him.

- *Emotion organized him for action.* Trevor's threat organized his complicated withdrawal inside, to a safe place. From there he monitored progress vigilantly, checking for cues of rejection and abandonment and contemplating what he should do next.

- *Emotions monitored the state of his relationship.* His emotions, forever vigilant about the degree of acceptance and rejection and closeness and distance in his intimate bond, reacted to potential rejection, leaving him almost frozen in fear of some form of abandonment.

- *Emotion evaluated whether things were going his way.* Trevor was alerted that his need for security was threatened, long before he consciously determined this.

- *Emotions signaled his state to others.* On the phone, most of the signaling was in the vocal quality. This is a channel rich with signals, second only to the face. Trevor heard his wife's caring and reassurance, and this is what finally saved the day. She understood that his silence, pauses, and hesitation indicated that he was afraid or wary, and she adjusted her behavior accordingly. Without this nonverbal signaling they would constantly have to be talking. As important as verbal communication is, relying on it alone, and expecting one's partner to always read what one is feeling, can cause couples no end of problems.

- *Expressing did not always correct the situation.* Communication helped tremendously, but this was because of Trevor's clarity about his feelings and his ability to take some responsibility for them and his wife's capacity to not get defensive at his concerns. He did not express everything. His expressions were informed by years of interpersonal learning in his culture and by his past psychotherapy, in which he had learned to say what he felt rather than to blame.

- *Deciding what to express and how to act on the signal was important.* Deciding and being able to speak from the withdrawal and about its cause, rather than trying to ignore it, even if he could have, was helpful. Ignoring his feelings or playing at being unaffected would have left Trevor alienated and confused. Deciding to tell his wife what hurt was also important in helping him find his feet again.

- *Thought put emotion in perspective and made sense of it.* Trevor's knowledge of himself and his wife were important in helping him keep things in perspective. Past therapy and work on his feelings of abandonment had helped. He was rapidly able to make sense of what he was feeling, assess that the threat of rejection was not really a danger, and mobilize his view of what was causing him difficulty. He was also able to put this into words and to draw on an inner sense of security that helped him hold onto all the past times of her caring and project these as possibilities in the future. This involved a mind busily at work.

Emotion thus informed Trevor that he felt threatened and rejected, and he signaled this to his wife long before he put it into words. His automatic response at first was disorganizing, and he worked hard to make sense of it so he could communicate it. His wife responded to his feelings, communicating nonverbally and verbally in a confirming, understanding manner. This type of response is highly important in making emotional interactions constructive.

Emotions Also Help People Learn

Another important and slightly different function of emotion, one that has not been covered, is that emotions enhance learning. Emotion increases the rapidity of learning incredibly, because it earmarks certain things with the stamp "not to be forgotten." This promotes one-trial learning. Once a person touches a hot stove, he or she learns to never do it again. People learn things like this because they have such intense emotional reactions that their brains store this experience in emotion memory, never to be forgotten.

Let me now describe a recent two-trial learning experience I had while I was writing this book that was almost as painful as burning oneself on a stove. I was working on a borrowed computer in Spain, where I was on sabbatical. Over the weekend I printed what I had done in the preceding days and put it aside to be read later. When I picked it up late on Sunday I soon realized that I had not saved the last piece I had written—the preceding vignette, about Trevor's phone conversation. I was upset about the loss and tried to make sense of it, because I was sure I had saved it before I printed it out. I never figured out what went wrong, but I quickly sat down and rewrote what I could remember. On speaking to my colleague, to whom the computer belonged, about this loss, I got very good, firm advice: "You really have to save as you go along—every paragraph or two!" Well, Monday came along, and I busily set to work following my old habits. My own computer back home automatically saves every so often, so I don't need to save as I go along. I didn't learn, even though I had received clear instructions.

Tuesday morning I sat down and worked for a couple of hours. The phone rang, and I answered it. I came back to the computer and typed a few more lines. Suddenly the computer froze. The words were on the screen, but nothing moved, and I hadn't saved a thing all morning! I had premonitions of disaster. In a panic, I anxiously started hitting keys. I tried everything I knew to get the computer working and not lose my precious text. Nothing worked. I won't go into a detailed account of my physiology, feelings, action tendencies, or language—I'll just say they weren't pretty. I frantically called a computer assistance service I had carefully preorganized so that if I needed help I would be able to reach someone who could speak English. The truth hurt terribly: There was no way I could save my morning's work. With my consultant on the other end I committed computer hari-kari, by restarting the machine, killing the screen in front of me and losing the morning's work (thank goodness that was all I lost). Well, this time I learned. Thanks to my emotional response this definitely got my attention. I now save my work regularly.

This kind of emotional learning teaches people many things. It helps, for example, to prevent people from losing things. Have you ever lost your wallet, your passport, or your purse? Not only is it a hassle to replace such items, and a possible source of financial loss, but also the immediate emotional experience—the dread, the anxiety, the grief—is so intense you become highly motivated not to be so foolish again. You learn—sometimes!

I am reminded of a joke: What's the difference between rats and humans? Rats learn, and humans don't. If you put rats in a maze and let them explore, they find the quickest way to get to the goal: a food reward. Later, if you shock them for turning left along what they have discovered to be the shortest route, they stop turning left. Same with humans. If you remove the shock, after several trials rats learn that it is no longer dangerous to turn left, and they hurry to the goal along the fastest route. Not humans—they never learn! They don't risk the path again and never learn that the shock is no longer there. People, in fact, learn so well from the fear that they never change.

Intense emotions and the situations that generate them are burned into memory so strongly that they govern behavior for a long time. Once damaged, people often will do all they can to avoid the dangerous situation or ones similar to it. In terms of evolution, this helped people survive. It can, however, be a real problem in complex interpersonal living, causing the unnecessary transfer of much emotional learning from one relationship to another in ways that, unfortunately, can be most harmful.

Thought and regulation are crucial to the intelligent use of emotion. These and the role of learning in the development of maladaptive emotion are discussed next. The chapter concludes with a comment on the importance of empathy in emotional intelligence.

EMOTION AND THOUGHT

Higher level thought or reflection is a pinnacle of human achievement. How, then, is this type of reflective thought used in emotional intelligence? One of the important aspects of human experience, as I pointed out earlier, is that two streams of conscious are constantly being integrated to produce a final sense of who we are. In this process one stream, the more conscious thinking stream, self-reflectively evaluates the first, more experiential stream (Greenberg & Pascual-Leone, 1995; Guidano, 1995; Rennie, 2001; Watson & Greenberg, 1996). Emotions provide first-order evaluations of whether something is good or bad for a person and provide action tendencies that express the associated desires or needs. The distinguishing characteristic of being a human being, however, is the ability to evaluate one's own desires, feelings, and needs (Taylor, 1989). Thus, in determining the self one wishes to be, a person has the ability either to desire or not desire a first-order feeling and desire. In this second, higher order, evaluation the worth of the desire is evaluated against some ideal or aspired-to standard. Being a self thus involves being self-evaluatively reflective and developing higher-order desires. Essentially this means developing feelings and desires about feelings and desires. For the emotion system, the evaluation is simply: "Is it good or bad for me?" whereas in the stronger, self-reflective evaluation there is also a judgment of the value of the emotion and its accompanying desire. People evaluate whether their emotions and desires are good or bad, courageous or cowardly, useful or destructive. People thus form subjective judgments of the worth of their own desired states and courses of action (Rennie, 2001; Taylor, 1989). Thoughtful reflection on emotional prompting is thus a crucial part of emotional intelligence. This is where conscious thought plays its crucial role. Thought must be used to judge whether emotional prompting coheres with what people value as worthwhile for themselves and others.

In addition to the role of higher level thought in reflecting on emotion, emotion itself, as one can verify by attending to one's next emotion, generally is itself not without thought. An emotional experience is a combination of bodily feelings and thoughts. In addition to the bodily sensations, emotion almost always includes mental thought. Whenever people experience an emotion they will find themselves awash with sensations as well as inundated with related thoughts. Anger sometimes involves a burning sensation that erupts up a central shaft through a person's stomach and mushrooms out into the center of the chest. It is accompanied by thoughts of unfair treatment and protest, such as "I won't take this anymore!" or "How dare he (or she)?" At these times images of a cold, heartless other, uncaring and judgmental, may vividly cross the person's mind.

Sadness sometimes comes as a burning behind the eyes that cascades down into the body, especially into the stomach. It makes the person want to curl up into a ball and is accompanied by thinking such thoughts as "I give up" or "I feel so alone." Images of being alone and small in a vast universe sometimes accompany these thoughts. This symphony of bodily feeling, mental thought, and images is emotion. It is this symphony on which people must learn to focus, to understand their inner stirrings and to harness its message.

Greenberg and Paivio (1997), along with others (e.g., Oatley, 1992) have developed the notion of emotion schematic processing as a basic mode more fundamental than thought to account for this type of integrated processing. Basically, emotion, motivation, cognition, and action occur as an integrated response package. There is a type of program or script that is activated automatically and then runs a set of preprogrammed operations. People thus feel, desire, think, and act all in an unfolding synthesized whole. The sequence of thought is generated not simply by association, as once proposed by early associationists (Titchener, 1909; Wundt, 1912), but also by different levels of emotion and desire. Thought rather is motivated by and highly dependent on mood or rapid emotional orientation to what is presented in consciousness. The result is that emotion and thought are highly integrated into conscious experience.

In spite of affect's original independence of conscious thought, most theorists of emotion agree that human emotion involves some form of stimulus appraisal, plus physiological arousal, expressive behaviors, impulses to instrumental behaviors, and some sort of subjective feeling. A debate on the order of these elements has raged for many years. This debate was stimulated by William James's early claim (James, 1890/1950) that a person fears a bear because he or she runs away, which is in opposition to the more conventional view that a person runs away from a bear because he or she is afraid. This whole argument, however, has been based on the assumption that the elements are entities unto themselves that can be linked in linear causal sequences. Interpretations, subjective feeling, and visceral and motor responses, however, are not primary indivisible elements; rather, they are processes that unfold over time. There is no reason to believe that all of one's bodily feedback should reach the brain before any subjective feeling results, or that the interpretation of the situation must be completed before the body can begin to respond, or that a complex emotional experience must occur before interpretation can begin. Instead, interpretation develops over time, as does feeling, in a continuously interactive sequence, often a very rapid one. The process thus is one in which many elements are constantly being synthesized to construct what one feels.

Attention, or very simple perceptual appraisal, often acts as an entry point into the realm of emotions (Ellsworth, 1994; Frijda, 1986; Scherer, 1984b), especially in the context of interactions with the environment. A sense of attention to novelty, of attraction or aversion, or of uncertainty, begins a process. However, rather than evoking complete emotions, each appraisal may correspond to change in the brain, the body, and the subjective feeling. As soon as the organism's attention is aroused by some change in the environment or in the organism's stream of consciousness, neural circuits in the brain are activated (LeDoux, 1993, 1996). The person's heart rate may speed up, the head may turn, or breathing may change. The person now may begin to feel different. Once the organism senses that the stimulus is attractive or aversive, the feeling and the bodily responses change again. As each succeeding appraisal is made, mind, body, and feeling change. When all the requisite appraisals have been made, quickly or slowly, the person may be able to report being in a state corresponding to one of the known discrete emotions, such as anger or sadness. Debates about the primacy of cognition, bodily responses, or affect thus make little sense when experience is considered as a process of construction. What is needed rather is an integrative view in which human beings are viewed as actively constructing their sense of reality, acting as dynamic systems that self-organizationally synthesize many levels of information to create their experience (Greenberg & van Balen, 1998; Guidano, 1991; Mahoney, 1991; Thelen & Smith, 1994).

In addition, emotion–action responses can be activated in a highly automatic manner, without any conscious thought, as when one swerves to avoid another car that suddenly crosses one's path. On the other hand, emotion can be activated by more conscious appraisals, such as when one consciously thinks that a friend has betrayed one. Finally, mood, an emotional state itself, one that endures over a longer period of time than emotional reactions, is an important emotional determinant of both emotion and thought (Forgas, 2000). Mood strongly influences how one sees and feel about things. Thus, there are different degrees of thought in emotion at different junctures and different amounts of emotion in thought.

For simplicity and for use in thinking about this for therapeutic purposes, if one wishes to look at a sequence, Figure 1.1 might help readers envisage the process I am proposing in this book. A more complex form of this can be found in Greenberg and Pascual-Leone (2001).

In Figure 1.1 one sees that attending preconsciously to a stimulus activates an emotion scheme. This in turn gives rise to conscious emotion and need, thought, and an action tendency that all interact to influence

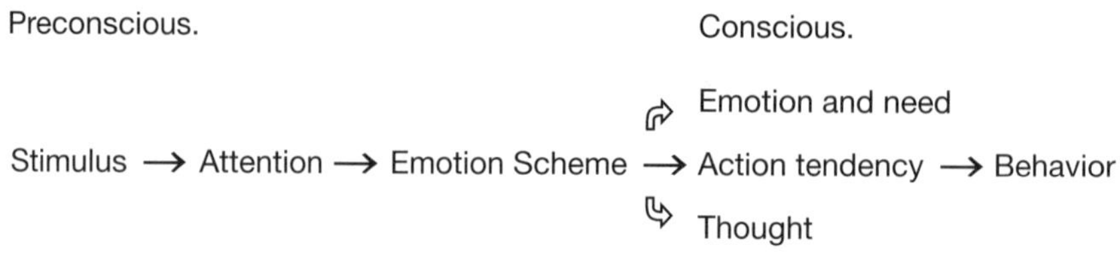

Preconscious.   Conscious.

⤴ Emotion and need

Stimulus → Attention → Emotion Scheme → Action tendency → Behavior

↳ Thought

Figure 1.1. Emotion Process Sequence.

each other and are translated into final behavior. Here the emotion scheme is a fundamental mode of processing information in relation to certain emotion-based scripts that evaluate the significance of the stimulus to a person's well-being. Note that this figure is a tool for thinking: The process is not this linear, and there are far more interactions and syntheses among elements than it is possible to show.

As the 21st century begins, the question of whether emotional reactions precede or follow their phenomenological appraisal should be put to rest. Only if the definition of cognition is arbitrarily restricted to rational conscious thought can it be placed in opposition to emotion—and even then, only weakly. Emotional expression is itself clearly an elaborate cognitive processing task in which data are integrated from many sources in the brain (often in milliseconds), and this occurs, in the main, outside awareness. The conscious narrative flow of evaluations, interpretations, and explanations of experience—the reported story of the emotion—often comes only after the emotion is experienced. The narrative account is significant as a record in memory of experience but often is only peripherally related to the process of generating ongoing emotion.

In psychotherapy, thinking about how the cognitive and affective systems work together and how each is blended with the other appears far more profitable than ascertaining which comes first. What is clear, however, is that the simple linear sequence—cognition leads to emotion, one of the cornerstones of the classical cognitive therapy view of emotion (Beck, 1976)—covers only the most simple means by which emotion is generated. This oversimplification can be misleading in attempting to understand the complex interactions of emotion, cognition, motivation, and behavior, for people often are not witness to the internal processes by which they become emotional (Bargh & Chartrand, 1999).

REFLECTION

After emotion awareness comes the ability to make sense of experience and, in so doing, to receive help from others. Here is where the wonderful human capacity for creating conscious meaning and symbolizing emotion in words and the ability to think rationally, reflect, plan, and imagine the future become so important. Premature application of these talents is harmfully misguided, and a lack of application is potentially disastrous. As people cannot live by bread alone, so too can they not live either by emotion alone or by reason alone. The design of people's emotional brains means they very often have little control over when they will feel what. However, they can be aware of and control the subsequent course of events. They can regulate how long they feel the emotion, what they do with the feeling, and make sense of the ever-important sequence of feelings and thoughts that follows the first rush of emotion. This is demonstrated in the following example.

> Erin sees a man, whom she is eager to get to know, approaching her on the street. She has met him beforehand and, for some unknown reason, she is deeply attracted to him. As she sees the object of her infatuation look her way, her heart skips a beat, and she becomes all jittery. She approaches him, her mind racing as she plans what to say. "How will I start, and what can I do to be interesting?" she asks herself. Then, however, her fantasized perfect partner walks right by her. Does he not recognize her, or is he so lost in thought that he is oblivious to her and anyone else on the street? Erin does not know. She feels devastated. Shame, longing, pain, and loneliness all creep through her body. She continues on her path, almost bent over by the shock of the whole experience. "What happened?" She thinks, "I was just walking along, and suddenly this storm of feeling comes. I must calm down. We have hardly met. I've really no idea how we would get along or if we have anything in common. I don't even know if he saw me or not." Reflection now takes its turn and helps her make sense of this flood of feeling. She begins to think, "These feelings are reactions to a phantom. I guess there's something about this type of man that really sets me aflutter. It's something about his self-containedness, combined with a sensitivity, a kind of sensitive pride, that I like so much. What about me leads me to react like this"? And so a reflection on herself and the situation begins.

In addition to their emotions, people need all their conscious capacities, plus the cultural learnings of their time, to live adaptively. Refusing to let a surgeon cut, so he or she can get to a damaged organ, because of a biologically based fear of incision, would prevent a person from receiving the benefits of modern medicine. However, not being afraid to have one's flesh pierced would make someone a walking disaster. To not be prompted by fear to carefully check out all surgical alternatives, to not pursue with concern whom one lets cut one's body open, and to not find out what will be done to one's body, would be equally reckless. Thus, people need both capacities. They need emotions to tell them, without thought, that something important to their well-being is occurring, and they need their thinking capacities to work on the problems that emotions point out and that reason must solve. There appear to be two types of awareness. One is fully present centered, aware of the here and now. With this type of awareness one knows what one is feeling, but that is all. In the second, higher order, more reflective state of awareness one can consider what one is feeling and can evaluate whether one wants to feel this way or decide what to do with what one is feeling. This state of being aware of one's conscious feeling of emotion allows one ultimately also to be aware of the lived past and the anticipated future and to make decisions about one's emotions in the present. One recognizes what one is feeling and considers whether one accepts one's response as appropriate. Developing and applying this capacity is an important aspect of emotional intelligence.

Thus, symbolization of and reflection on feelings are important. Each inserts mind in between situation and action. Any emotional response ultimately involves excitation and inhibition. What is felt or expressed depends on a shifting balance between letting go and restraint. As is quite common in biologically based systems, emotion involves dual control. Thus, emotion involves a regulatory system, and reason and reflection are important parts of that system. One of the most important characteristics of civilization is that through it people have become more aware of and able to respond to their emotions. This has happened with respect to emotional responses and their reasons. Improved practices of healthy emotion regulation through reflection are a mark of being more civilized. People nowadays all think a lot more about what they feel, and why they feel it, than any previous generation. Herein lies hope for the future: greater integration of head and heart. This integration of reflection and emotional arousal does not necessarily dampen or destroy spontaneity; rather, it can enhance it by recognizing when free expression is appropriate and adaptive and create special times for it and even greater opportunities to develop abilities to be spontaneous.

An additional curious aspect of emotional living is the importance of the time needed to process and reflect on emotional experience. We all know how important it is to take time to reflect on a troubling emotional feeling or how important it is to simply take time out to do other things so that we can later revisit the experience and see it in a new way. Time provides both flexibility and the opportunity to let things reverberate through people's meaning circuits to bring a fuller sense to the meaning and significance of what they are considering. Being aware of a need for pacing when dealing with feelings, taking time to sleep on decisions, and making opportunities to come back and review feelings are therefore all important. This means slowing or delaying impulsive actions that may seem right today but wrong tomorrow. Living in the present, but not for the present, is relevant here. Emotions are spontaneous present reactions. People's lives, however, are textured layers of presentness folded into past and future moments. The past and future, although not present, do exist, in memory and imagination, and they need to be integrated with immediate reactions. Living in the present means being aware of both what one is feeling now and of the implications of past and future.

Writing in an emotion diary has been found to be highly helpful in overcoming painful memories, and it promotes immune system functioning and health (Pennebaker, 1990). It also helps symbolize and reorganize experience and helps people reflect on and make better sense of their experience and thereby assimilate it into existing meaning structures. For example, a girl at age 10 had, without explanation, been prevented from staying with her beloved paternal grandparents during her summer vacation because of a bitter divorce settlement. She had felt confused, rejected, and hurt, because she assumed her grandparents did not love her. As a young adult, writing about her emotional experience in a diary helped her make sense of the experience and realize more clearly that it was not that her grandparents did not care about her but that they all had been victims of the divorce. This helped the young woman forgive them, accept the love she had received from them, and try as an adult to reconnect with them.

MALADAPTIVE EMOTIONALITY

Emotions, as well as being adaptive, also can go wrong (Flack, Laird, & Cavallaro, 1999). Although emotions evolved to enhance adaptation, there are several ways in which this system can become maladaptive. We all know that at times, against our best intentions, we worry ourselves sick, explode at provocation, feel like we hate our children, and rage at those to whom we are close. We sometimes have a paranoid fear of authorities, envy our friends, feel intensely vulnerable with or jealous of our lovers, or feel disgust or anger at only the slightest provocation. We often regret the emotion we experienced, the intensity with which we experienced it, or the way we expressed it. When these undesirable emotional experiences or overreactions are chronic, they stem from complex internal processes based on learning histories in which adaptive emotion expression and regulation have not been fully achieved.

How, then, can one argue that people need to pay attention to their emotions for good information if much of the time they can feel disorganized by bad, vulnerable, insecure, worthless, worried, enraged, resentful, jealous, or hopeless feelings? The ratio of unpleasant to pleasant emotions in the most basic emotion list, based on innate facial expressions, is 2:1, with anger, sadness, fear, and disgust outnumbering surprise and joy (Ekman & Friesen, 1975). The terms people use to describe variations in unpleasant emotions outnumber those used for the pleasant ones by almost 3 to 1 (Shaver, Schwartz, Kirson, & O'Connor, 1987). People often suffer from, and spend much time managing, unpleasant feelings.

If emotions are an organizing force in people's lives, then why can they be so disorganizing and painful? Bad feelings tell a person that something is wrong. They demand attention, set problems for reason to solve, and often even suggest a possible course of action. When people are not feeling strong or well modulated emotionally, they will feel a lot of unwanted emotions, which is difficult; however, avoiding them or trying to control them are not the best answers. A first step in regulating emotions is therefore awareness of them. People need to be guided to become aware of their emotions so they can allow and accept them, be informed by them, and then work with them to solve problems. Ultimately people need to evaluate whether the emotion they are experiencing is adaptive and can be used as a guide or whether it is maladaptive and should not be followed.

Maladaptive emotions develop for a variety of reasons. Most often they are learned in situations that evoke an innate emotional reaction, such as anger at violation, fear at threat, or sadness at loss. The degree to which a maladaptive emotion becomes disorganizing and resistant to change depends on how early they were experienced, how intensely, and how frequently they and the situations activating them occurred. Other temperamental and organic factors also influence people's moods, and these influence activation thresholds of different emotions. When one is tired or irritable, anger is more likely to be activated, and if one has a learning history that leads to maladaptive anger one is more likely to overreact angrily. In addition, the degree to which core schemes or scripts apply to situations with similar themes influences the activation of maladaptive anger. Thus, intense frequent feelings of neglect, rejection, or domination in the past can be activated by current situations with similar themes or storylines. Inattentiveness from a spouse can activate intense feelings of neglect from a loveless childhood. These feelings then become maladaptive responses to the present situation.

Once learned and organized into a scheme or affect program, newly acquired emotional responses become automatic—as automatic as the in-wired biologically adaptive responses with which they integrate. Now people not only flee from predators and get angry at boundary violations, but they also fear their boss's criticism and get angry at obstacles to enhancement of their esteem. The innate emotional responses and the learned ones rapidly become integrated, and they can be activated by learned stimuli (Griffiths, 1997). Emotion responses clearly are open to input and learning; this makes them not only a flexible adaptive system but also open to the possibility of becoming maladaptive. Acquired maladaptive responses then often occur when one doesn't want them to. They are not helpful and are hard to change.

Emotions therefore are neither simple nor infallible guides, and they are not providers of pure bliss. They do produce much of the discomfort and suffering in life as well as joy, love, and interest. They clearly do have to be managed intelligently for people to benefit from their intelligence. The immediacy of emotion, and people's ability to integrate emotions with reason, has made humans more complex and adaptive beings. The sometimes-apparent opposition between rapid, automatic emotional action tendencies and slower, reflective, deliberate action has added to people's effectiveness. An innate, rapid emotion system that just provided fixed action patterns and ready-made courses of action would have had early humans running around like geese, following any stimulus that happened at the right time. That would not do people much good. To simply attack when angry and run when afraid would have made people automatons, highly predictable and manipulable. Instead, humans are complex problem solvers, and emotions tell people what the problem is to keep them motivated to do something about the problem and the situation that is producing the problem. People not only have emotions, but they also have to handle them. The development of skill in emotion regulation is thus an important part of emotional intelligence.

EMOTION REGULATION

To act with emotional intelligence, people need to learn to regulate both their emotional experience and their emotional expression (Frijda, 1986; Gross, 1999). Being able to defer their responses, know what they are, and reflect on them are quintessentially human skills. Affect regulation is a major developmental task. From infancy on, babies learn to suck their thumbs to soothe themselves, and small children learn to whistle in the dark to calm their fears. As an adult, one can learn relaxation techniques and meditation to regulate anxiety. People learn to regulate anger by counting to 10 and even learn to regulate joy and to express it appropriately, depending on the situation. Part of emotional intelligence is the ability to regulate emotionality so that one is guided by it but not compelled by it.

People need to be able to govern what they choose to express and what they suppress. People need to be able to stop runaway anxiety. Ultimately it is the integration of emotion and cognition that leads to health. People need both to be moved by their emotions and to be able to calm them and reflect on them. The first level of emotion regulation involves the capacity to symbolize in awareness bodily felt emotions and action tendencies to produce complex feelings. People need to be able to say they feel sad at leaving home for the first time, rather than just cry. They need to teach their children to be able to say they are angry rather than acting out with anger. If one child tries to take another child's toy, then the second child needs to learn to set verbal limits and verbally protect his or her boundaries rather than hitting the first child.

Emotional intelligence thus involves not only having emotions but also handling them. Emotions are regulated at all levels of the emotional process, from neurochemical to physiological, to psychological and social levels. People can exercise some control by seeking out or avoiding situations and other people depending on how these situations and people make them feel. Once a person's emotions are aroused, he or she regulates them by working feverishly to make sense of them. The person reviews situations and changes the meaning of his or her feelings in order to transform or regulate his or her reactions. If people feel sad because a loved one is going away, they start to cope with this by imagining him or her coming back. They distract themselves by paying attention to other interests. They may say the separation is good, because absence makes the heart grow fonder, and use many other ingenious devices for changing their view of the loss.

People's emotional urges also can be suppressed, so as to disappear from awareness as well as from behavior, or they can be intensified. People can suppress an impulse to act or the action itself. Emotion organizes people to act, but decisions execute the action and its form. Thus people can be angry and rein in their anger, or they can suppress the emotion and not even feel any anger. Once emotions have come alive they can be made to die down. They can be kept within certain bounds by many procedures, some voluntary, some involuntary. People can regulate their emotions by (a) managing the situations to which they expose themselves, (b) transforming their responses by reviewing the situation, or (c) suppressing or intensifying their response. Regulating a response by reviewing the situation generally is far superior to suppressing it.

At the very first level people can regulate *inputs*—the stimuli that activate their emotions. Numbness is one of nature's gifts to human beings; it occurs automatically to deaden pain. It is a protective mechanism to give people time to assimilate loss. In states of emotional numbness people know the facts of the loss or trauma, but they do not feel anything, because their significance is not yet realized. Other, more voluntary processes of handling emotion, as mentioned earlier, include avoiding situations that evoke them. Fear of heights can generally be avoided by controlling where one goes, and jealousy or rejection can be avoided by ending contact with a suspected or rejecting partner. Seeking distractions or concentrating on something else will help take a person's mind off possible dangers or problems about which he or she can do nothing. This can enhance performance: Focusing on the task at hand prevents the intrusion of thoughts of loss or danger.

Emotion, in addition to being activated by external events, is produced by internal, self-generated sequences of prior feelings, memories, images, and thoughts. People can regulate these in ways that can be either to their advantage or disadvantage. People can deny reality, deny their feelings, or they can allow and accept their experience and then construct new meanings to help them manage and transform their feelings. Meaning construction is not a single-level process, and so one can interrupt this process at many points along its path and thereby regulate emotions. Defensive interruption in general is not that helpful. Although denying the horrors of reality, and not focusing on gory details, helps people avoid feeling fear and disgust, the processes of trying to not see what is there, or internally changing the meaning, can be problematic, especially when it is done automatically, without awareness. Thus, denying that one is upset or angered by something is going to deprive that person of certain information relevant to problem solving. Regulating experience by interrupting meaning-construction processes, at different levels of this process, therefore, can be done for better or for worse.

Endeavors to cope by reappraising situations, creating new meanings, and putting things in a broader perspective, once emotion is already aroused and acknowledged, are important aspects of emotional intelligence. These are all important emotion regulation strategies. Although conscious thoughts do not produce the majority of emotions, they certainly help to regulate or maintain them. Thus, trying to change thoughts helps regulate emotions, not because the negative thoughts caused the bad feeling but because they tend to maintain and intensify it. Once people feel an emotion, especially an unpleasant one, they generally have a problem to solve. Rather than concentrating on toning down or suppressing emotions, people need to guide their emotions toward constructive action or transform them into ones that are more favorable and more helpful to problem solving. People can transform emotions by stressing different aspects of what is occurring; they can attribute different reasons to explain what happened, project different consequences, focus on accessing different internal and external resources, and devise different coping strategies. Thus, disappointment can be guided into a renewed attempt, or it can be transformed into acceptance of loss. All of these cognitive strategies will greatly transform emotional experience. Reason is best integrated with emotion, to help guide it once it is aroused. Then people are not working against their emotions, trying not to have them; instead, they are working with their emotions, trying to guide them by integrating their social and cultural knowledge and their personal values and goals with their body-based emotional knowledge.

One of the important issues here is that people can cognitively transform their emotions constructively or reappraise situations defensively. People can try to block certain undesirable things from awareness, or they can permit the undesirable experience and then work furiously to cope with it. People can do something mentally or in action to transform the emotion into something else. The first method generally is far less effective than the second.

One of the paradoxes of defense is this: How it is possible to interrupt or prevent an experience from coming into awareness without first knowing what it is? How can people numb themselves from shattering news without first knowing that the news is shattering? How can they prevent awareness of feeling angry or sad without first knowing they are feeling an unacceptable feeling? The process occurs because people process information at many levels, only some in full consciousness. Thus, at a cocktail party, unattended-to conversations that are going on, some behind one's back, apparently are not consciously heard or understood until an important concern is touched on, such as one's name, or the topic of sex. These unattended-to messages are therefore being processed at some level, but only up to a point. They come into awareness only when they are further processed. This involves attending to them before they decay from very short-term storage and frustratingly leave without a trace of what was somewhat heard but not symbolized consciously.

People's processing of information can thus be interrupted at many levels. It can be interrupted at the stage of processing that determines the meaning of words that are heard, or things that are seen, or they can be interrupted at the stage of linking this to other meanings. Thus, hearing the phrase "she died" may not be linked to her never coming back or what that might mean for one. Numbness is the very early interruption that interferes with taking in anything new; lack of awareness may involve selective attention. Detachment, a higher level interruption, means not processing the personal relevance of something, whereas avoidance might involve strategies of distraction.

Some people can redirect processing at different stages. I suggest that therapists need to help people perceive emotions with as little defensive processing as possible and that emotions need to be made as tolerable as possible. This is the best way to help people cope with the sadness of everyday life as well as with the tragedies. Helping people feel the pain or anger and then see the humor in things, see alternatives, gain a sense of agency in their construction of reality and in their responses to it, gives them a sense of being effective rather than being a victim of circumstance. Choosing how to respond, rather than being a victim of circumstance, provides a sense of self-determination. Seeing things as a challenge mobilizes coping, and seeing things as natural, necessary, or inevitable promotes nonblaming coping. All the means of using people's wonderful capacity to construct meaning is the best way to guide and transform their distressing emotional reactions.

EMPATHY TO OTHERS' EMOTIONS

Finally, emotional intelligence, the ability to integrate head and heart, involves empathy to others' feelings. Empathy is the response of choice to feelings. It is needed not only in response to others' feelings but also in response to one's own feelings. People's empathy makes them, and others, more human. Empathy helps regulate feelings and helps people reflect on them. To recognize feelings in others one first needs to be sensitive to one's own feelings. Once people recognize and confirm others' feelings they also need to help these other people to allow their feelings to inform and guide them. Giving others advice in emotional moments about the merits of more rational or realistic solutions serves only to invalidate their experience. Advice such as "pull yourself together," "calm down," or "take a walk" is not helpful. Even solution-type talk such as "You could give him a call," or do this or that, is not that helpful. People need to validate others' feelings. They need to let them know they understand their feelings and that their feelings make sense to them. Invalidation of a person's most basic feelings is one of the most psychologically damaging things one person can do to another. It is an important cause of emotional dysfunction. Feelings demand recognition; otherwise they escalate or go underground, and everything starts getting very complex. A thirsty child who is told "you're not thirsty, you just had a drink"; a crying child who is told to "stop being a crybaby"; and a crying adult who is told "you have no reason to cry" are all having their experiences invalidated. The best way to validate people's emotional experience is to communicate that their emotional responses are understandable and make sense in the context of their occurrence or their lives in general. Recently, a mother told me how when her adult daughter complained about relationships in her life not working out, rather than giving her advice she for the first time listened and understood her daughter's feelings, and this had a calming effect on her daughter.

Feelings, once they are recognized by others, and by oneself, still need to be guided, but not controlled. Reflection on feelings rather than impulsive action is important in the integration of head and heart. Emotions, as I have discussed, both move and inform. People need to feel their feelings, and name them, not just act on them. One way in which empathizing with others' feelings is helpful is that it promotes this type of reflection. It helps the other person symbolize what he or she is feeling and brings the emotion from the domain of sensation and action into the mental domain. Gaining consciousness of feelings by symbolizing them in words is where the integration of head and heart begins. People need to feel what their bodies are telling them rather than blindly letting impulses determine their actions. As people develop from infancy to adulthood, they have emotional reactions to new situations, ones that are relevant to important needs. The empathic attunement of their nurturers helped them pay attention to and symbolize their own feelings. A caretaker's attunement to and mirroring of an infant's excitement or sadness helps strengthen and confirm the infant's self-experience. People's selves developed out of such interaction in a co-constructive process in which each party added an ingredient and the mixture provided the recipe for the as-yet-unformulated sense of self. In adulthood, new feelings that are not yet fully formed or clear—such as feelings about a recent job change, a recent disappointment, or a meaningful accomplishment—also are greatly confirmed and made clearer and stronger by empathic responses of others who help the adult symbolize his or her experience. People then are able to form a stronger sense of themselves, confirm their experience, and feel more committed to what they feel and who they are. Empathy is a crucial skill of emotional intelligence.

CONCLUSION

Emotional intelligence involves integrating head and heart. This involves awareness of current embodied emotional experience and reflection on and regulation of emotions. Experience and reflection are both important in transforming maladaptive emotions and in creating new meaning. Empathy with others' emotions is a crucial aspect of emotional intelligence.

2

DISTINGUISHING AMONG VARIETIES OF EMOTIONAL EXPRESSION

The word *passion* shares its origin with the word *passive*. This gives the impression that people receive emotions passively rather than creating them. Clients often think that they are victims of their emotions because of their daily experience of feeling good or bad for no apparent reason. Many emotions seem to just happen. Clients need to learn how to intelligently use these emotional happenings as a guide, and they need to learn how to regulate them so they will not be controlled by unwanted emotions. To do this, they need to evaluate what their emotions offer. Just as all thought is not necessarily logical, so too all emotion is not necessarily either intelligent or disruptive, and just as people need to learn how to reason logically, they also need to learn how to tell when their emotions are healthy and adaptive, helping them to live a full life, and when they are maladaptive and damaging.

Because emotions have historically been contrasted with reason, researchers have treated them as a single class of events for the purposes of the contrast. All emotions, however, are not the same. Emotions are not a singular entity; each one has a distinct form and function. For example, in anger the action tendency moves people to expand and thrust forward. The function of anger is to set boundaries, and anger itself varies: It may only last a few minutes, or it can smolder for days. Sadness, in contrast, leads to crying out for a lost object and, after some time, if no one comes, withdrawing to preserve resources. Important distinctions about different types and functions of emotion need to be made in coaching people to use their emotional intelligence. For example, at any one time anger may be an empowering adaptive response to being violated; at another time it may be a destructive overreaction to a current situation, based on a history of prior abuse. Anger may be a person's first immediate reaction, or it may come only at the end of a chain of prior feelings and thought. Men often express the latter type of anger. They might actually be experiencing fear, but because they believe that it is not manly to be afraid, they may respond by becoming angry instead. People may also express emotions intentionally to get a desired result, such as crying to get sympathy. Thus, people need to learn to make distinctions among different types of emotions.

The tradition of believing that reason is the best way to guide life has shortchanged the complexity of human experience. This view has led to an oversimplification of how emotions should be handled: that emotions either should be controlled—the mind-over-mood view—or they should be vented so that one can get rid of feelings—the polarized view. To deal effectively with emotions, people instead need to be able to identify on each occasion what type of emotion is being experienced and to determine the best way of dealing with this emotion in this situation. As Aristotle offered, being angry is easy: It is knowing when, where, how, in what intensity, and with whom to be angry that takes intelligence.

Picture how differently someone might feel in the following situations and what might be the best way to handle these feelings:

- A person has just had a major argument with his or her spouse, and the two of them are not talking to each other.
- A person has just been told that he or she has been awarded a desired promotion.
- A person's parent has just died.
- A person wants to impress a new boss.
- A person's fiancée has just told him that her feelings for him are changing.
- A person is thinking that his or her future prospects are gloomy.
- A person is trying to win someone over to his or her point of view.
- A parent is about to leave for work when the babysitter calls to say she can't come.
- A mother sees that her 3-year-old has just run into the street, and a car is approaching.
- A person wants to get rid of a salesperson at the door who has interrupted an important conversation.

These are vastly different situations and different emotional experiences. Just controlling emotions, simply getting in touch with them, or getting rid of them is not going to be enough. How do people handle this variety of feeling? First, they need to distinguish among different kinds of emotional experiences, and then they need to learn how to deal appropriately with each. An emotion coach will need to help clients to see that their emotions differ in different situations. A coach will need to help clients see that some emotions can be used as adaptive guides to action, others should be faced, others bypassed or explored, and others overcome. Clients need to be helped to learn that some emotions should be expressed out loud, others need to be controlled, others reflected on, and still others are best allowed and used to guide decision and action.

VARIETIES OF EMOTIONAL EXPERIENCE AND EXPRESSION

In working with emotion, the first distinction that an emotion coach needs to make is whether the client is experiencing too much or too little emotion (Paivio & Greenberg, 2001). A person with underregulated emotion who is exploding in rage, overwhelmed by tears, or shrinking to the floor in shame presents quite a different picture from a person whose emotion is highly constricted, avoids feelings, intellectualizes, interrupts any emergent expression, or avoids situations that might evoke feeling. The type of problem and types of interventions required differ vastly. There are two additional important fundamental distinctions that therapists as emotion coaches need to make in accessing emotional experience and expression. The first is distinguishing whether an emotion is a new expression that involves the freeing up of blocked emotion or whether it is an old, stale expression that involves the repetition of emotion too freely expressed. The fresh expression of a previously overinhibited emotion generally is helpful, whereas the venting of too-often-expressed stale emotion that is not blocked is not therapeutic, and does not lead to reduction in expression (Bushman, Baumeister, & Stack, 1999). The second distinction that emotion coaches need to make is whether the emotion being experienced and expressed is a sign of distress or a sign of the process of resolving distress (Kennedy-Moore & Watson, 1999). For example, weeping when feeling overwhelmed and unable to cope is a sign of distress and should be distinguished from weeping as part of a grieving process. Panicky fear or shame at anticipated failure are signs of distress. Fear of risking being assertive, or embarrassment at revealing something new, however, often are signs of facing change. Emotion clearly is not a uniform phenomenon. At the most general level, coaching interventions will depend on (a) whether the emotion is over- or under-controlled, (b) whether it is a newly expressed or stale emotion, and (c) if the emotion is a signal of distress or a process of change.

Criteria for when to facilitate more emotion and when to down-regulate emotion are presented in Table 2.1 and discussed next (Wiser & Arnow, 2001). The first and most important criteria for facilitating more emotion are (a) that there is a relational bond sufficient to contain the emotion that will be facilitated and (b) that there are agreement and collaboration on this task between the client and the emotion coach. Rushing in to facilitate experience and expression with people with whom a secure relational base has not yet been established is unwise, and evoking emotion in an actively unwilling client is potentially harmful. Once a therapeutic alliance has developed, what are the general indications for focusing on emotion? A primary client indicator of the need to facilitate more emotion is, paradoxically, its avoidance. When a person is obviously feeling an emotion and interrupting it, or when he or she avoids the emotion by intellectualizing, deflecting, and distracting, helping the person approach the emotion can be therapeutic. In addition, clients who behave maladaptively because of lack of emotional awareness benefit from being coached toward greater emotional awareness and better access to their own emotion-based action tendencies. For example, clients who do not attend to the information provided by their emotions become passive when abused or depressed when angry, and those who are overly inhibited when they are either happy or sad often lack vigor. Emotion coaches can help people who need to reprocess traumatic experience by facing the feelings stored in emotion memory and putting the emotions into words. Finally, if the problem exists because emotion is preventing the exercise of skills, then exploration of fears and other emotional blocks is helpful.

TABLE 2.1
Facilitate or Regulate?

Factor	Facilitate	Regulate
Alliance	Safety and agreement on task of increasing emotional experience	Relationship cannot yet support emotion
Client	1. Avoids emotion	1. Overwhelmed; emotion does not inform or promote action, or it confuses
	2. Behaves maladaptively; no awareness of action tendency	2. Previous history ■ Aggression ■ Falling apart
	3. Reprocesses trauma ■ Assimilate emotion ■ Create new meaning	3. Destructive coping: drugs, bingeing, self-harm
	4. Emotion inhibits action	4. Skill deficit

There are a variety of counterindications for facilitating emotions. It is unwise to promote emotional experience when the therapeutic relationship cannot yet support it because of lack of safety, when trust has not yet been established, or when the therapist has insufficient knowledge about the client or his or her circumstances. A strong counterindicator for increasing emotional arousal is when a client is feeling overwhelmed by emotion. In such a case, emotion does not inform or promote action; rather, it confuses. This is a clear indicator for emotion regulation. When a person is in a crisis, then crisis management is required rather than facilitation of emotion. A previous history of aggression or of falling apart is a strong counterindicator for promoting anger or feelings of vulnerability. Emotional arousal also is generally counterindicated for people who engage in destructive coping. If a person uses substances to self-medicate, binges, or engages in self-harm to deal with distress, then it is not advisable to activate distress until he or she has learned better coping skills (Linehan, 1993). Finally, if the problem is one of a deficit in emotion regulation, then training in the development of social or problem-solving skills is preferable to emotion facilitation.

To help clients make sense of their emotions and benefit from them, in addition to making the discriminations just discussed, about whether to facilitate or regulate an emotion, an emotion coach has to help clients figure out what type of emotion they are experiencing and when they are experiencing it. This will help clients determine what is useful in what each emotion is telling them. Clients need to be coached to make the key distinctions outlined next to learn to skillfully use their emotions. They need to be coached to become aware of whether an emotional experience at any moment is one of the following feelings:

- a healthy core feeling, an *adaptive primary emotion*;
- a chronic bad feeling, a *maladaptive primary emotion*;
- a reactive or defensive emotion that obscures a primary feeling, a *secondary emotion*;
- an influencing or sometimes manipulative emotion that people use to get something they want, an *instrumental emotion*.

Any particular emotion cannot be put into any one category, because the emotions a person feels at any particular moment could be primary, secondary, or instrumental. Therefore, each time clients feel something, their job is to determine what type of emotion is occurring in that instance. In chapter 6 I focus on how therapists as emotion coaches help clients make these distinctions in regard to anger, sadness, fear, and shame, the emotions I have found most important in coaching. I now describe the main characteristics of primary, secondary, and instrumental emotions as a guide for both coaches and clients.

PRIMARY EMOTIONS

Adaptive Primary Emotions

Adaptive primary emotions are people's core gut responses to situations. They are the person's very first feelings in response to a stimulus situation, such as anger at violation, sadness at loss, and fear at threat. These emotions have a very clear value to survival and well-being. They are quick to arrive and fast to leave. They are reactions to something happening right now, and when the situation that produced them is dealt with or disappears, the emotions fade. These emotions are the main source of emotional intelligence. People have to be helped to recognize these emotions and use them as a guide so they can benefit from them. This is a crucial step in helping people make sense of their emotions. It requires disciplined awareness and practice. The therapist has to help clients get past the clutter of their defensive, secondary emotions and let go of their instrumental feelings to become aware of their core primary emotions. These primary feelings tell people who they really are and what they are most fundamentally feeling in any given moment. These can be basic emotions, such as anger or fear, or they can be complex emotions, such as jealousy or appreciation, as long they are the person's first response.

Maladaptive Primary Emotions

Unhealthy, maladaptive primary emotions arise when people's emotional systems malfunction. These feelings are still people's most fundamental, "true" feelings, but they are no longer healthy. Debilitating fear and anxiety, shame and humiliation, destructive rage, and unresolved grief are the main contenders in this category of emotions. Maladaptive emotions are those that people often regret having or those that they regret having so intensely or expressing in the way they did. This is especially true for maladaptive anger. These emotions can arise through external or internal cueing. They are generally based on past learning. The shame of feeling unlovable, worthless, or no good; the sadness of feeling lonely or deprived; the anxiety of feeling inadequate or insecure; or the rage of feeling wronged or disobeyed arise and take over. People feel stuck in these emotions. They can last long after the situation that caused them. They can stay with people for years as unhealed wounds. When these wounded states emerge, they seem to have a mind of their own. When they are evoked, people sink into them in inexplicable and helpless ways. They might be old, familiar feelings of longing and deprivation, anxious isolation, shameful worthlessness, or inexplicable blame and anger. Every time one sinks into them, they make one feel just as bad as the last time. These are the bad feelings that hold people prisoner and from which people so desperately want to escape. Such emotions are generally disorganizing. They do not suggest a clear sense of direction. Often they reveal more about oneself than about the situation. Maladaptive emotions can be basic ones, such as fear and shame, or more complex ones of empty isolation or alienation.

Each time a person sinks into a maladaptive feeling, he or she hopes that this time it will change, but it never does. Every time the wound is still there. The deep anxiety emerges. Trying to put the feeling into words, the person might say "I feel like I can't survive without you giving me what I need. I'm falling to pieces." A familiar primary sense of shame and worthlessness comes with words such as "I just feel like disappearing. There is just something wrong with me. I'm just no good," "I just don't measure up—I'm not as good as others," or "I'm just a bottomless pit of needs." Negative internal voices and destructive thoughts often accompany these feelings, and the person inexplicably feels shaky and insecure, small and insignificant, defective, or worthless. This awful feeling pervades all—people can't talk themselves out of it; it has them by the throat, and they are helplessly consumed by it.

Certain emotions often become maladaptive through *traumatic learning,* in which an originally adaptive emotion, such as appropriate fear of gunshots in battle, can become so deeply etched into one's psyche that it gets generalized to situations that are no longer dangerous, setting off alarms of danger when no danger is present. For example, a person might duck for cover and relive horrifying scenes of war every time a car backfires. In such a case, emotions from the past are intruding into the present. They are recognizable by their unhealthy effect on the person's daily life. They often disrupt close relationships and destroy, rather than protect, emotional bonds.

SECONDARY EMOTIONS

Secondary emotions are responses to or defenses against a more primary feeling or thought. They are troublesome because they often obscure what people are feeling deep down. For example, a client may feel depressed, but this depression may actually be covering a core feeling of anger. Clients may report feeling resentful but may be feeling hurt at their core and afraid to admit it. Often, men who have grown up being told they have to be strong have difficulty admitting their primary feelings of fear, so instead they get angry. Women who have grown up being told they should be submissive often cry when they are actually angry. If people are not aware of their primary feelings, it is very easy for these feelings to turn into other ones. Thus, anger often obscures original feelings of sadness or primary jealousy, whereas coolness may obscure original fear.

Secondary emotions are the ones clients often find troublesome and want to get rid of. They are symptoms of core feelings that are being obscured. Clients come to therapy wanting to get help so they can stop feeling so upset, depressed, frustrated, and despairing. These troublesome feelings often do not represent people's primary emotional response to situations; they are symptoms of emotions with which the person is not dealing. Secondary emotions often arise from attempts to judge and control primary responses. Thus, anxiety may come from trying to avoid feeling angry or sexually excited, or it may arise from guilt about having felt these emotions. When clients reject what they are truly feeling, they are likely to feel bad about themselves. For example, suppressing anger often leaves clients feeling hopeless or complaining. Disowning sadness leaves them feeling cynical and alienated. Judging their own needs as "bad" makes them feel guilty. Secondary emotions can be basic or complex. It is not the emotion itself that can be categorized as primary, secondary, or instrumental: All emotions, basic or complex, can be primary, secondary, or instrumental.

Clients also often report having feelings about other feelings. They may feel afraid of their anger, ashamed of their fear, and angry at their weakness. These feelings are secondary to more primary, core feelings. A sequence often seen in therapy is one of secondary guilt or anxiety felt about primary anger. In this case the person fears anger or disturbing a relational connection, and this fear prevents acknowledgment of the primary feeling. Feeling or expressing one emotion to mask the primary emotion is a metaemotional process. Feelings about emotions need to be acknowledged and then explored to get at the underlying primary emotion.

Secondary feelings also can arise from thought. These are the feelings primarily dealt with in cognitive therapy. These feelings can take on a life of their own, often reoccurring in never-ending loops, without any overt cause. For example, feelings of anxious worry might go around and around, because every time the person thinks about the distressing situation the bad feeling comes again. In this case, feeling is secondary to thought. In addition, when people think negative thoughts about themselves, such as "I am flawed," they usually feel bad, and when they catastrophize about the future they feel anxious. These are instances in which feeling clearly is produced by conscious thought, and it is helpful to get at the negative thoughts that produce the feeling. The awareness of the role of these automatic thoughts provides an understanding of the immediate source of a lot of bad feeling. It is important to explore all bad feelings to determine what lies behind them. Often there is a complex chain of thought–feeling–thought–feeling that needs to be tracked backward to its origins. This is the meaning of therapeutic exploration: traveling backward along this complex chain. The pay dirt is the source of the secondary feeling. In the emotion-focused view of functioning proposed here, it is the core emotion scheme or program that generates primary experience.

Clients find it difficult to sort out their primary, core feelings from their secondary, negative feelings about themselves. However, they need to learn how to sort out their feelings so that they can identify their primary emotions. Therapists as emotion coaches need to help them do this. This means wading through the chain of all the secondary reactions, which can become quite complicated. As clients tell therapists what they are feeling, or have felt, clients begin to have other feelings in reaction to what they are describing. So, for example, clients often feel frustrated with themselves for feeling weak or angry. This secondary frustration serves to cloud their prior feelings. Helping clients figure out what they feel involves sorting through all these layers. They need time and space to do this, as shown in the following example:

> Joe reported feeling distant from his partner and not knowing why. With the therapist's help, he began to explore this feeling, which arose the day before, during a ride home from a movie. The ride occurred in virtual silence, in which Joe remembered feeling quite confused (secondary feeling). He said that after seeing the movie his wife had said, "I'm too tired to take a walk. I want to go home." He said that he had been looking forward to a walk but figured if his wife was tired then they should go home. On the surface, her response appeared innocuous. Something, however, had not felt right to him. He described how the two of them walked to the car, a few inches too far apart, and as he focused on what he felt he said that he felt vaguely angry (another secondary emotion). At the time, he thought that he was angry because he wasn't getting his way about taking a walk (trying to make sense of his experience). Joe remembered, however, that he decided at the time that his angry reaction was selfish and, wishing to be more considerate, he expressed concern (instrumental emotion) to his wife about her tiredness. Although his concern was genuine, it was restrained because of his mixed feelings. With the therapist's help Joe searched his memory and began to remember that something had happened earlier, at the beginning of the movie, while they were sitting next to each other. He had asked his wife to fill him in on something he had missed during the movie, and she said she couldn't. He had an automatic thought that she didn't care about him. At the time he expressed some irritation at this, mainly in his voice, and had felt annoyed (masking his hurt) at his wife's seemingly offhand response to his request. Things had been fine before the movie, but he remembered now that there had been a few difficult moments between them the day before. His wife had seemed tense and distant in the last couple of days. Joe remembered feeling at that time his old familiar fear and anxiety about being rejected by her (primary maladaptive emotion). This was his core feeling and led him to think she didn't care about

him. He had to sort through a number of reactions with his therapist to get to his primary feelings of sadness and hurt at feeling rejected. Although his secondary bad feeling reactions to his primary feelings were not very pleasant, they still signaled that something was wrong and demanded that he pay attention to what was happening internally.

In another example, early in a therapy session a client said he felt upset about his interactions with his son. The therapist asked him to pay attention to his feeling. At first the client expressed frustration about how irresponsible his son seemed to be, but this soon transformed into his fear that his son would fail and be terribly wounded. The client felt sadness about how he could not protect his son from the pain he had experienced in life. In this case the client's upset feeling was signaling more primary concerns. Vague feelings of sadness or anxiety are often reactions to underlying feelings that need attention to be deciphered. Consider the following example:

> Bill wakes up in the early hours of the morning, in a half-awake state, feeling disturbed. His usual calm is clearly disrupted. Inside, things feel rocky, and he has vague images of a jagged, spiky terrain inside him. This is very different from the calmness he usually feels when he wakes. He normally may not even be aware of the general, calm background feeling when he wakes. It comes to light only on mornings like this, when it is no longer there. These ragged, ruffled, feelings, differing from the smooth plane on which he normally surfs into wakeful awareness, are telling him in a most uncomfortable way that all is not well. He remembers a conversation with his lover the night before that did not end well. Polite friendliness summed it up, which was not the way they usually ended an evening. They had both felt hurt and distant and had not known what to do, except to sleep on it. They had already talked for most of the evening, and things had become worse rather than better. Bill is anxious and disturbed. This feeling tells him, "this relationship is rocky; things are not going well."

Emotional "disorder" of the type described in the preceding example often reflects internal disorganization. Therapists need to help clients pay attention to these states so they can explore them to understand the information they provide. Bill's rocky, jagged feeling of disruption represented a desire for comfort and care. These emotions are constructive and unpleasant, and they tell people something about the way they are conducting their lives.

Feeling upset is a general signal that something is amiss. The term *upset* connotes disorder; disarray; confusion; feeling disturbed, agitated, and stirred up. The state of being upset generally masks a more primary feeling that is not yet recognized. Clients often do not feel their core emotions of anger and hurt; instead, they are aware only of their irritability. However, this irritability is a signpost pointing toward the original feeling. It is an indication that the person needs to search internally for what is troubling him or her by taking time to focus on bodily feelings.

INSTRUMENTAL EMOTIONS

Instrumental emotions are the third category that add to the complexity of sorting out emotions. People express instrumental emotions because they have learned that other people will, they hope, react to these emotions the way they want. Often clients may not be aware that they have learned to use these instrumental feelings for the gains they bring. For example, a client may have learned that when she cried, people were kinder to her. Now she automatically cries to evoke sympathy. Instrumental emotions are expressed either consciously or automatically to achieve a goal. A client may have learned that getting angry is likely to intimidate people or that crying makes them more sympathetic. Instrumental emotions are often more like general emotional styles than momentary reactions. Over time they often become part of the person's personality, such as being dominant, overly dramatic, or shyly demure.

Instrumental emotions that clients express without any awareness of their intention can be quite problematic. The sadness one client expressed with sighs and heavy eyes was quite demanding of attention and support. He was afraid to ask for attention, so instead he hoped that sighing would get the desired response. Another client's uncertainty and anxiety were expressed by hesitating or appearing confused. This attracted helpers who saved her by taking charge. When people use these instrumental expressions too frequently, without being aware of what they are doing, they can often end up driving others away, because the people receiving these signals end up feeling manipulated. Some family therapists refer to people as "showing" emotions rather than feeling them in order to highlight the instrumental use of emotion. For example, a wife may show depression or sadness, whereas a husband may show anger or boredom. This language helps emphasize the communicative aspects of this type of emotion and helps to focus on the interpersonal pull some emotions may be intended to have. A more negative term for instrumental emotions is *manipulative feelings*.

The intentions in instrumental expressions can be more or less conscious. Being consciously coy or seductive may be playful and exciting, but doing this without awareness can be problematic. Consciously expressing anger when feeling offended is quite different from automatically expressing anger to intimidate and control. Coaching here involves helping people become aware of the effects and intentions of their emotional expressions.

Then they need to find more direct ways of expressing themselves and stating their needs.

Instrumental emotions, however, often involve a lot of emotional intelligence. People need to be quite skilled to be able to use emotions to achieve a certain response or to communicate in a social situation. A person may pretend to be embarrassed to indicate that he or she knows the social rules and is aware that he or she is not complying. In such a case the person is skillfully using emotion to influence other people's views of him or her. For example, even though a man may have had no intention of wearing a tie to a meeting, he may pretend to be embarrassed so that others think he made a mistake. Similarly, people may express moral indignation to communicate to others that their values are in the right place and that they are good people. Someone may bow his head and drop his eyes to show deference, or he may stare another person down to show his power. The art of social role playing lies in the instrumental expression of the correct emotion at the appropriate time.

BASIC AND COMPLEX EMOTIONS

Still further distinctions about emotions help in identifying primary emotions. People not only have primary emotions of sadness, anger, fear, shame, and so on, but they also have many more complex emotions, such as love, pride, guilt, embarrassment, compassion, envy, and ecstasy. These too can be the source of great emotional intelligence, depending on whether they are primary, secondary, or instrumental emotions. In early human history, when primitive people sensed danger or violation, the emotional parts of their brains led them to feel a basic emotion, such as anger or fear, and they simply fought or fled. With the development of greater cognitive abilities, more complex feelings, such as guilt, remorse, resentment, and embarrassment emerged as well as subtle feelings of wonder, appreciation, compassion, and love. These complex emotions integrate a lot of information, blend emotions with each other and with cognition, and give people a very high-level sense of themselves and the world, but they do not have as clear an action tendency as the basic feelings do. The complex feelings tell people whether they are feeling on top of the world or down in the dumps. These feelings are more a source of information than of action tendencies. Thus, in coaching people toward primary emotions it is important to not only work with the basic emotions of sadness, anger, fear, and shame but also to recognize that primary feeling is often more complex and that it is idiosyncratic. These complex feelings also need to be acknowledged for the helpful information they can provide.

"ME" AND "IT" EMOTIONS

It is important to make one final distinction to help understand people's emotions. Some emotions are felt in response to an external situation, whereas others arise mainly because of internal reasons related to how people see themselves. Many emotions that people experience in the present are responses to external cues; these emotions give meaning to things in the world, offering information about situations in relation to well-being. For example, fear of the dark alerts people to the possibility that there could be something dangerous lurking in it. People who have a healthy fear of external threats, such as approaching predators, should pay attention and act accordingly. As a rough guide, these healthy reactions to the world are about real threats in the world. They are basic "it" emotions (Dahl, 1991). They need to be experienced in awareness for the information they give about how to act and should be expressed in an appropriate manner. Thus, people need to experience and express their current anger when they have been wronged and act on their fear of being run over by a car. These are healthy experiences and expressions.

Other emotions are more interior. These are "me" emotions, and they often involve people's beliefs about themselves. "Me" emotions affect how people feel about themselves and influence how they handle their emotions. All past- and future-related emotions are by definition internal, because they are not felt in reaction to a current real world situation. They are based on memory of a past event or anticipation of a future event. In addition, specific emotions, such as sadness and shame, tend to be more "me" related, whereas others, such as anger and fear, are often more "it" related. "Me" emotions, such as embarrassment at standing out, or feeling sad and hopeless, often need to be explored for their meaning and the feeling that underlies them rather than expressing them out loud. However, there is no simple formula for this. Clients, with the help of their therapists, always need to figure out whether it would be better to express and act on a feeling or if it would be better to explore and understand the feeling. Clients need to understand what each emotion is telling them about their lives and decide for themselves in each instance what is the best course of action. "Me" and "it" emotions can be primary, secondary, or instrumental.

HOW DOES ONE ASSESS EMOTION?

Assessing emotion involves making a process diagnosis. An emotion coach assesses a client's current emotional expression, not a personality style or trait. This involves determining the type of emotion being expressed in the session. Process diagnosis thus involves the moment-by-moment assessment of the emotional states of mind the person enters, is stuck in, or leaves, and the sequences of these states. The following sources of information are used in assessing emotion states:

1. knowledge of the function of adaptive emotion
2. knowledge of universal emotional responses
3. understanding of the context of the experience
4. observing effects of expression
5. attending to nonverbal expression
6. empathic attunement (putting oneself in the other's shoes)
7. knowledge of one's own emotional responses to circumstances
8. knowledge of the client and his or her issues and ways of responding.

Probably the most crucial information used to assess a person's current state is knowledge of the function of healthy primary adaptive emotion and its adaptive expression. Anger that empowers, sadness that grieves, fear that helps one escape or seek protection from danger, and disgust that expels noxious intrusions are all healthy adaptive expressions. This knowledge of healthy, adaptive expression acts as a baseline against which to assess any current expressions. If a client is feeling anger, one asks whether it is empowering; if the client is feeling sadness, one asks if it promotes the grieving of a loss. It is important to note that, in individual therapy, the healthy function of an emotion is to help reorganize and mobilize the self. It is by organizing and increasing the self's ability to respond (responsibility) that an emotion becomes curative. Emotional experience and expression that are either highly out of control or focused on a desire to change others are unlikely to be primary and adaptive. Anger that destroys or complaining that blames differ from assertive anger that empowers. Sadness that clings desperately, that pulls for a response and demands comfort, differs from the sadness of digesting a loss. Fear that leads to panic and desperately seeks protection differs from a healthy fear that organizes escape or seeks appropriate protection.

In addition to the assessment of whether an emotion is serving a healthy organizing function, therapists as emotion coaches use their knowledge of universal human responses to help assess what type of emotional expression is occurring. They also use their understanding of the context out of which the emotion arises to assess whether the emotion appears to fit the situation and the person's need in that situation. Thus, if someone is only sad at having been violated or only angry at a loss, these probably are secondary emotions, as they do not fit the situation or the person's need, goal, or concern in that situation. Understanding present and past context also is crucial. The immediate context in therapy is important. Knowing what people have just said, and where they are stuck, helps illuminate what is needed. If someone is talking about having been abused as a child and says that he or she feels nothing or that he or she feels resigned or hopeless, an emotion coach understands that fear, anger, shame, and sadness all are possible emotions that are not yet available to this client. Similarly, a woman trapped in a submissive role in a hopeless marriage who only cries helplessly seems to have no access to her anger. Thus, evaluation of prior context helps one see what emotion might be missing or in what emotion the person seems stuck.

The immediate effect of an emotion also helps assess its function. Emotion that informs, opens someone up, promotes deeper exploration, or leads to something new is probably adaptive. Emotion that confuses, overwhelms, or is repetitive and stuck is not adaptive. Therefore, one way of assessing the adaptiveness of an emotion is by observing whether it serves an adaptive function. In addition to the use of emotional knowledge and observation of effects come the attunement skill of reading nonverbal expression and the empathic understanding of the other person's internal experience. The latter is helped by an understanding of one's own internal experience and, on the basis of one's own experience, knowing what it is like to feel different emotions. Finally, as emotion coaches get to know their clients, they learn about a client's particular emotional style and consistent ways of responding, and this helps inform process diagnosis of what is occurring for a client at a particular moment. Here, identifying emotion sequences can be helpful. Learning that a client often obscures anger with sadness but feels guilty when anger is accessed helps client and therapist understand that anger is the primary but feared emotion and that sadness and guilt are secondary emotions that are preventing anger from being acknowledged.

3

THE THERAPIST AS AN
EMOTION COACH

In this book I offer the view of the therapist as an emotion coach who helps people develop emotional wisdom—the wisdom to know when to be changed by emotion and when to change emotion. The view offered in this book is based on a number of propositions drawn from research on working with emotion in therapy (Greenberg, Korman, & Paivio, 2001; Greenberg & Paivio, 1997), on the most recent work on emotional development and emotional intelligence (Salovey & Sluyter, 1997), and on work in parenting (Gottman, 1997).

In what sense am I suggesting that the therapist can be a coach? Among the *Concise Oxford Dictionary's* (Allen, 1990) definitions of a coach one finds that a coach is "someone who gives hints, a private tutor" and that to coach is "to train or teach." These descriptions catch some of the flavor of what I mean by *coach*. An emotion coach helps clients by providing strategies for dealing with emotion. The word *coach* was originally used to mean a carriage for a long journey. A coach is something that moves people from place to place and, as a facilitator, a coach is someone who helps move people from where they are to where they want to be—toward agreed-on goals. In the case of emotion coaching, the goal is emotional fitness. In this age of personal trainers, business coaches, and lifestyle consultants, the concept of an emotion coach as a trainer who helps people to be emotionally fit is highly contemporary.

55

The concept of coaching is based on the premise that individuals have sources of growth and possibility within them and that these sources can be developed by coaching. A coach focuses on strengths, possibilities, and resources and uses language that is valuing and appreciative to help people move forward by accessing positive emotional resources within themselves. Coaches facilitate emotional growth by focusing people's attention on their positive emotional potential and helping them mobilize their inner resources. This is done through moment-by-moment assessments of people's emotional states and by providing guidance that fits people's current states and helps them move toward more desirable states. Guidance also is provided by means of the subtle use of language and through strategies appropriate to the moment that help mobilize resources. Coaching introduces a psycho-educative model of experiential learning in which the coach is seen as a skilled guide. The goal in emotion coaching is to promote higher levels of functioning and to help people learn rather than to treat a deficit or a disease. The client is therefore seen as a trainee wishing to learn and achieve goals. Emotion coaching also offers a concept of *training as treatment*, plus a mentor–mentee style of relating. In my experience, training people in the skills of emotional awareness, regulation, and transformation, and training them how to help others in these areas, are excellent forms of treatment for problems they have.

Some therapists might find the term *coach* or the concept of coaching unpalatable, reacting to the vision of the therapist as a sports coach either yelling at players or inspiring them with locker room speeches. They may see coaches as disrespectful or view coaching as too influencing, involving too authoritative or imposing a role. Perhaps too, coaching might seem superficial, not able to encompass the depth of human experience that working with people's emotions entails. The term *coaching* might imply that change in the emotional domain involves learning a simple set of skills and that emotional difficulties and growth can occur in 10 easy lessons. None of these characterizations is implied by my use of the term *coach*— to the contrary, although the coach is a guide, I view coaching as involving a partnership of co-exploration in a growth-promoting process aimed at helping a trainee achieve goals of emotional awareness, regulation, and transformation. Also, using a developmental and psycho-educative model does not imply purely cognitive or superficial learning. The great leap forward for me in the concept of the therapist as an emotion coach was the realization that it is possible to facilitate change in the most private, tacit, and complex domain of human experience: the domain of emotion. This can be done by carefully following and leading people to become aware of their emotional processes. It is possible to enter into people's inner realms of emotion, places that are beyond reason and often beyond words, and have a positive influence. Emotional learning and teaching are possible. Emotion coaching, as I hope readers will see, is far from being shallow. It requires great sensitivity and subtlety, and it is based on an appreciation of the great complexity of human nature. It is important to note that the concept of coaching is highly respectful and being a trainee often is more acceptable to people than being a patient or a client in therapy. Being in therapy still implies sickness. Training and coaching do not.

Let me exemplify, by means of a recent study my colleague and I completed, how I see an emotion coach as training or moving people from one place to another (Adams & Greenberg, 1996). Readers will see how, rather than carrying clients like a literal coach, from one place to another, an emotion coach uses language in a particular way to help people move. In studying the moment-by-moment effect of therapist responses on clients' subsequent responses, we found the following interesting relation (Adams & Greenberg, 1996): We discovered that the depth of experiential focus with which a therapist responds to a client's previous statement is likely to have a significant effect on the depth with which the client experiences his or her next statement. We found that therapist responses to clients' descriptions of external situations, or of their reactions to these situations, that focus on the client's internal experience promote a deeper level of experience in the client's next statements. Clients tend to follow the therapist's focus and attend to what the therapist attends to in their internal experience of the situation. Clients were found to reliably shift their experience from an external or reactive response, rated on the Depth of Experiencing Scale, (Klein, Mathieu-Coughlan, & Kiesler, 1986) from a Level 3 to a Level 4, at which the client focuses on feeling and internal experience in a descriptive and associative manner. This indicates that therapists are subtly influencing clients' processing by the way in which they respond; that is, they are acting as a coach by providing process hints as to where to focus and how to process that information. We found that clients were 10 times more likely to shift to an internal focus after a therapist's response focused them in this way than when the therapist stayed with the client's focus (Adams & Greenberg, 1996).

For example, a client who recently had been abandoned by her husband, after meeting with him to discuss alimony, made the following statement to her therapist: "When I saw my husband standing there, on the dock, painting his boat, it reminded me how much time he spent doing that during our marriage rather than spending time with us. It made me so mad, I just wanted to throw something at him." In response to this, a therapist's restatement of "just so mad you wanted to hurl something at him," which would focus the client on her reaction, would not be nearly as productive as one that focused her on her internal experience, such as "You just wanted to lash out. It felt like he loved the boat more than you and the kids and this left you, I don't know, sort of exploding inside, so angry and hurt." This latter response, by means of a subtle use of language, helps focus the client's attention inside, on what it was like for her, rather than on the situation or on her behavioral reaction of wanting to throw something. She is then 10 times more likely to explore her feelings of hurt or anger in a more differentiated manner. This suggests that empathically attuned responses, as well as a close following of where clients are, add something in terms of pointing the client to a more internal focus. This provides direction for the exploration not by suggesting on what content clients should focus, or by interpreting the meaning of their experience, but rather by guiding the type of processing in which they engage.

Emotion coaching thus involves both following where clients are in the moment, by reflecting back to them one's understanding of their experience, and leading the client forward by guiding the type of processing in which he or she engages. Sachse (1998), a German researcher, showed that therapist responses focused slightly ahead of the client enhance the creation of new meaning and problem resolution. In his goal-directed view of client-centered therapy, Sachse sees each therapist response as a processing proposal that guides the type of meaning-making process in which the client engages. The type of proposals I suggest in emotion coaching are those that help people symbolize their internal experiences and make sense of them. In further studies of the therapeutic process, Angus, Lewin, and Hardtke (2001) found that successful therapies were distinguished from unsuccessful therapies by the degree to which the therapist shifted the focus from describing events, or discussing the meaning of events, to a discussion of what the client felt internally in response to these events or their meanings. This supported the view that a shift in the manner of processing toward internal experience was an important aspect of good therapy. This subtle process of not only following very closely where people are, but also leading them to another way of processing their experience, is at the essence of emotion coaching.

A further domain of investigation of direct relevance to emotion coaching is that of emotional intelligence. Salovey and Mayer (1990) initially defined *emotional intelligence* as people's ability to monitor their own and others' feelings and emotions, to be able to discriminate among emotions, and to be able to use this information to guide thinking and action. They recently expanded this beyond only perceiving and regulating emotion to include thinking about feelings. Emotional intelligence, according to them (Mayer & Salovey, 1997), thus involves the ability to

- perceive, appraise, and express emotion;
- access or generate feelings when they facilitate thought;
- understand emotion and use emotion knowledge; and
- regulate emotions to promote growth.

Emotional intelligence thus involves the ability to identify emotions in one's own physical states and in others and the ability to accurately express emotions and the needs related to these emotions, as well as being able to discriminate expressions in others. Emotions prioritize thinking, direct attention, influence judgment and memory, and promote flexibility of thought. Emotional intelligence also involves the ability to understand the meaning in feelings; to understand complex feeling; and to recognize likely transitions among emotions, such as from anger to satisfaction. Finally, emotional intelligence involves the ability to regulate one's feelings by staying open to feeling, being able to reflectively engage or detach from emotions when necessary, and managing emotion in oneself and others by moderating unpleasant emotions and enhancing pleasant ones.

Another important domain of study relevant to emotion coaching is that of parenting. Gottman's (1997) research on effective parenting styles has led to the delineation of a number of characteristics of what he called *emotion coaching*. These characteristics are extended in this book to apply to therapy. He found that emotion coaching by parents had a profound impact on children's emotional intelligence. He classified as emotion coaches those parents who had a positive emotion philosophy—who became aware of the child's emotion; recognized emotion as an opportunity for intimacy; and listened empathically, validating the child's feelings and helping the child find words to label emotion. Finally, these parents also acted as guides to their children, by setting limits and exploring strategies to solve the emotional problem at hand. Four- and 5-year-olds whose parents consistently practiced emotion coaching with them, when observed 3 years later, had better physical health and higher emotional intelligence. These children had better general abilities in the area of emotions than children whose parents were not classified as emotion coaches. These abilities included being more effective in regulating their own emotional states. Their heart rates slowed at a faster rate when they were upset, and they were better at focusing their attention and getting along with others. Probably most important of the abilities was that these children were most emotionally resilient to distress. They could soothe themselves and bounce back physiologically more quickly when they got sad, angry, or scared.

The process of emotion coaching as adapted to therapy is as follows:

- Coaches first need to be aware of their own emotions. They need to have a positive view of emotions as resources and see emotions as providing information and action tendencies.
- Coaches need to recognize that when clients are experiencing emotion, these moments offer opportunities for therapeutic intimacy and contact.
- Coaches need to be empathically attuned both to their clients' specific emotions, such as sadness, anger, and fear, and to the tempo, rhythm, intensity, and cadence of their clients' emotional vitality as it changes moment by moment. They need to validate, accept, and respect their clients' emotional

experience and communicate their empathic understanding of clients' feelings.

- Coaches need to help clients symbolize their feelings in words and help them make sense of this experience.
- Coaches, having entered a client's emotional world, need to guide the client in dealing with his or her emotions and offer strategies to help the client process emotion.

GENERAL PRINCIPLES OF EMOTIONAL CHANGE IN EMOTION-FOCUSED THERAPY

Emotion coaching relies on three major principles of emotional change that have been established on the basis of research, theory, and practice: (a) increasing awareness of emotion, (b) enhancing emotion regulation, and (c) changing emotion with emotion. These principles act as a general guide for emotion coaches. They help coaches understand the different goals of emotion coaching at different times.

Emotion Awareness

The first and most general principle of change in emotion coaching is the promotion of increased emotional awareness, which enhances functioning in a variety of ways. Becoming aware of and symbolizing certain types of emotional experience in words provides access both to the information and to the action tendency in the emotion. It also helps people make sense of their experience and promotes the assimilation of this experience into people's ongoing self-narrative. Emotional awareness is not thinking about feeling; it involves experiencing the feeling in awareness. Only once emotion is felt does its articulation in language become an important component of its awareness. Awareness of what one feels has been a long-recognized principle of change and is seen as an important therapeutic goal (Perls, Hefferline, & Goodman, 1951; Rogers, 1959).

Awareness of emotion also involves overcoming avoidance and promoting emotional processing (Foa & Kozak, 1986; Greenberg & Safran, 1987). A long line of evidence on the effectiveness of exposure to previously avoided feelings of fear supports its use in dealing with trauma and anxiety-based disorders. Habituation to a fearful stimulus helps people overcome their avoidance and be able to approach what was fearfully avoided. By facing dreaded feelings and finding that they survive, people become more able to acknowledge painful emotions (Greenberg & Bolger, 2001; Greenberg & Paivio, 1997).

In addition to the informational value of emotion awareness and its role in overcoming avoidance, symbolizing emotion in awareness promotes reflection on experience to create new meaning and helps people develop new narratives to explain their experience (Greenberg & Pascual-Leone, 1997; Pennebaker, 1990; Watson & Greenberg, 1996; Whelton & Greenberg, 2000). Symbolizing traumatic emotion memories in words helps promote their assimilation into a person's ongoing self-narrative (Van der Kolk, 1993). Putting emotion into words thus allows previously unsymbolized experience in emotion memory to be assimilated into one's conscious, conceptual understanding of the self and the world, where it can be organized into a coherent story.

Emotion Regulation

The second principle of change addresses emotional arousal and its regulation. Emotion can be regulated in a variety of different ways. Clients with under-regulated affect have been shown to benefit from validation and the learning of emotion regulation and distress tolerance skills (Linehan, 1993). The provision of a safe, supportive, empathic environment also helps soothe automatically generated under-regulated distress. Emotion regulation skills involve identifying and labeling emotions, establishing a working distance, increasing positive emotions, reducing vulnerability to negative emotions, self-soothing, breathing, and distraction. Regulation can involve putting some distance between oneself and overwhelming emotions or developing self-soothing capacities. Forms of meditative practice and self-acceptance often are most helpful in achieving distance.

Of particular importance in emotion coaching, however, is developing clients' abilities to self-soothe. Soothing involves activation of the parasympathetic nervous system to regulate heart rate, breathing, and other sympathetic functions that speed up under stress. Promoting clients' abilities to receive and be compassionate to their emerging painful emotional experience is the first step toward helping them learn to self-soothe. Amygdala-based emotional arousal needs to be approached, allowed, and accepted rather than avoided or controlled. In this process people need to use their higher level brain centers, not to control emotion but to consciously recognize the alarm messages being sent from the amygdala and then act to calm the activation. Metaphorically speaking, it is as though once the amygdala's message of danger or threat is acknowledged by the higher level brain centers the amygdala, recognizing that its message has been received, can afford to switch off (Atkinson, 1999). It is reassured by the calming effect of recognition and validation of its distress signals and by empathy for it. People thus need to act in terms that will help them turn off their internal affective alarm signals. This is achieved by accepting the emotion; experiencing self-empathy; and by providing cognitive, affective, and physiological soothing. The soothing of emotion can be provided by individuals themselves, in the form of self-soothing techniques, such as diaphragmatic breathing, relaxation, compassion, and in the form of calming self-talk and self-acceptance. People can also soothe and be soothed interpersonally, in the form of empathic attunement to affect and through acceptance and validation by another. Being able to self-soothe develops best by internalization of the functions of the protective other.

This principle of working with emotion thus involves the person acknowledging emotion, creating a working distance, and receiving emotion's message. It is the recognition and soothing of the emergency signal, rather than its control, that helps turn off the alarm signal. Clients in under-regulated states (e.g., rage) are encouraged to access a more soothing, comforting aspect of the self to help regulate internal distress. This process can be facilitated through the use of metaphors or images, such as taking care of the wounded child inside, finding an inner voice of strength or an inner source of wisdom to help calm this distressed child, or finding an imagined safe place to go when one feels overwhelmed. Internalizing the protectiveness of the therapist also is helpful. Having clients imagine taking the therapist back with them into an abusive scene, as a protection against the abuse or threat, combines the client's learning how to self-soothe with his or her internalization of the soothing function of the therapist.

Changing Emotion With Emotion

The third and probably most fundamental change principle involves the *changing of emotion with emotion*. This suggests that a maladaptive emotion state can be transformed best by replacing the maladaptive emotion with another, more adaptive emotion. In time, the more adaptive emotion helps transform the maladaptive emotion. Spinoza (1967) was the first to note that emotion is needed to change emotion. He proposed that "an emotion cannot be restrained nor removed unless by an opposed and stronger emotion" (p. 195). Darwin (1872), on jumping back from the strike of a glassed-in snake, having approached it with determination not to start back, noted that his will and reason were powerless against even the imagination of a danger that he had never even experienced. Reason clearly is seldom sufficient to change automatic emergency-based emotional responses; instead, one needs to replace one emotion with another. As Guidano (1991) noted, "While thinking usually changes thoughts, only feeling can change emotions" (p. 61).

A corollary to the principle that emotion is needed to change emotion is that emotional arousal also is needed to change emotion. Emotional awareness and the use of emotional intelligence also are needed to identify what emotion the person is feeling and to distinguish that the emotion is a maladaptive one that should be transformed rather than a healthy one that should be followed. I discuss how this is done in chapters 4 and 7. Once a person has decided that an emotion is maladaptive and needs to be changed, the maladaptive emotion needs to be aroused, and another, more adaptive feeling that will help undo or replace the maladaptive state needs to be accessed. It is important to note that this principle goes beyond ideas of exposure and habituation, in that the maladaptive feeling is not simply attenuated by the person feeling it. Rather, another feeling is used to transform or undo it. For example, a key means of transforming the felt shame of feeling worthless and the aroused core anxiety of feeling unlovable is by accessing alternate, healthy adaptive emotions, such as pride, anger, joy, or even humor. Instead of attenuating the bad feeling by exposing the client to it, he or she is helped to access another emotion to undo the first, maladaptive one. Such newly accessed feelings are resources that help change maladaptive states. Thus, in therapy maladaptive fear, once aroused, can be replaced by the more boundary-establishing emotions of adaptive anger or disgust or by the softer feelings of compassion or forgiveness. Similarly, maladaptive anger can be undone by adaptive sadness, and maladaptive shame can be replaced by accessing both anger at violation and self-comforting feelings and by accessing pride and self-worth. Thus, the tendency to shrink into the ground in shame is replaced by a thrusting-forward tendency in newly accessed anger at having been violated. Withdrawal emotions from one side of the brain are replaced with approach emotions from another part of the brain, or vice versa (Davidson, 2000). Once the alternate emotion has been accessed, it either transforms, undoes, or replaces the original state. In this view, the new, alternate feelings may have been present in the original situation but were not accessed or expressed, or they may be new, currently available responses to the past situation.

Empirical evidence is mounting to support the importance of a process of changing emotion with emotion. Berkowitz (2000) reported a study on the effect of muscular action on mood. Participants who had talked about an angering incident while making a tightly clenched fist reported having stronger angry feelings, whereas fist clenching led to a reduction in sadness when talking about a saddening incident. This indicates the effects of motor expression both on intensifying congruent emotions and on dampening other emotions. Thus, it appears that even the physical, muscular expressions of one emotion can change another emotion. In addition, in line with the James–Lange theory, Flack, Laird, and Cavallaro (1999) demonstrated that adopting the facial, postural, and vocal expressions of an emotion increases the experience of the emotion regardless of whether the individual is aware of which emotion he or she is expressing. The experience of an emotion can thus be induced or intensified to some degree by using one's body to express it. It is interesting to note that there are individual differences in this capacity, with individuals who are more body sensitive showing this tendency to a greater degree. A more general line of research in social psychology on the effects of role playing on attitude change also supports the idea that performing actions in a role brings people's experience and attitudes in line with the role (Zimbardo, Ebbesen, & Malasch, 1997). Thus, role playing can transform something that at first is not real into something real, just as saying something aloud can lead one to believe it (Myers, 1996). Therefore, a possible way to evoke another emotion is to have people role play its expression. As they express an emotion, it will change their experience toward the expression.

In a further line of investigation on positive emotions, Fredrickson (2001) reported on how positive emotions undo lingering negative emotions. Fredrickson's basic observation was that key components of positive emotions are incompatible with negative emotions. She suggested that by broadening a person's momentary thought-action repertoire, a positive emotion may loosen the hold that a negative emotion has on his or her mind. The experience of joy and contentment were found to produce faster cardiovascular recovery from negative emotions than a neutral experience did. These results suggest that positive emotions fuel psychological resilience. In a further study, Tugade and Frederickson (2000) found that resilient individuals cope by recruiting positive emotions to regulate negative emotional experiences. They found that these individuals manifested a physiological bounce back that helped them to return to cardiovascular baseline more quickly. In a study of dealing with self-criticism, Whelton and Greenberg (2000) found that people who were more vulnerable to depression showed not only more self-contempt but also less resilience in response to self-criticism than people who were less vulnerable to depression. The less vulnerable people were able to recruit positive emotional resources to combat the depressogenic contempt and negative cognitions. In other words, resilient people after a distressing experience appear to generate a positive feeling, often through imagery or memory, to soothe themselves and combat negative feelings and views of the self. Accessing a positive emotional state helps them counteract the effect of a negative emotional state. These studies together indicate that emotion can be used to change emotion, and the last study (Whelton & Greenberg, 2000) specifically demonstrates that positive affect regulates negative feelings. There is also growing evidence that positive affect enhances flexibility, problem-solving skills, and sociability (Isen, 1999). Fredrickson (1998) also demonstrated how positive emotions broaden and build strategies that enhance problem solving. Positive emotions such as joy, interest, pride, and love broaden people's momentary thought–action repertoires, which in turn helps build their enduring resources to cope with life. In addition, research on mood-congruent judgment has shown that moods affect thinking (Mayer & Hanson, 1995). Shifts in mood have clearly been shown to lead to different kinds of reasoning (Palfia & Salovey, 1993). Good moods lead to optimism, and bad moods to pessimism.

In a different line of research interesting patterns of emotions have been observed in studies of small samples of depressed clients from our larger sample (Greenberg & Watson, 1998). In one sample, in all four of the good-outcome cases expression of fear related to the person's view of self was reduced in the late phase of treatment, as compared to the early phase. In this random sample of four good- and four poor-outcome clients drawn from a larger pool of clients the average percentages of number of fear episodes in relation to all emotions expressed were 4.8% in the early phase of treatment, 4.3% in the middle phase, and 0.5% in the late phase. The fear was replaced with other emotions. For example, in one good-outcome case fear present in the first phase increased in the middle phase of treatment but was replaced with sadness in the late phase. The reduction in fear and the increased accessibility of sadness occurred because the client faced her fear of making decisions and took charge of her life. It was when her sadness at all she had lost started to emerge that she was able to transform her fear. In the given context, sadness was a more adaptive emotion than fear.

Similarly, in another good-outcome case, anger in the first phase was replaced with fear in the second phase, and that fear later was replaced with contentment. In the early phase of treatment the client felt angry with herself for allowing herself the "luxury" of expressing her feelings. Then she realized that, rather than being angry with herself, she was more scared that she would say something stupid without thinking. She was able to face and endure that fear, and that led to its replacement with contentment. Different patterns occurred in different clients. For example, in the early phase of treatment, another client expressed anger and resentment toward her mother because of her neglect. However, in the middle phase of treatment feelings of guilt replaced anger. A continuous focus on these feelings in the final phase evoked feelings of compassion and forgiveness and a reduction in anger and guilt.

In other cases, other patterns of replacing emotion with emotion were observed. For example, in another case the three most dominant emotions in the early phase of treatment were fear–anxiety (28%), shame–guilt (28%), and hopelessness–helplessness (17%). Dominant emotions in the middle phase were sadness (43%), pain–hurt (29%), and anger–resentment (10%). In the late phase, fear–anxiety (16%), pain–hurt (13%), joy–excitement (13%), and contentment–calm–relief (13%) were the most dominant emotions. In other cases, fear or sadness in earlier phases was replaced with anger in the later phases while initial shame was replaced with anger or joy–interest. In many of the poor-outcome cases this type of transformation of experienced emotion and the replacement of one emotion by another was not readily traceable. The reason perhaps was a generally low overall level of emotional arousal in these cases. Lack of deep emotional processing seemed to leave client and therapist stuck in the early problematic feeling states, and the shallower processing did not produce any observable shifts in emotional states by the end of treatment.

The results of the above single-case investigations and of larger groups studies that have related emotional arousal to outcome (Warwar & Greenberg, 2000) have provided evidence that supports the principle that emotional arousal and the attendant replacement of one emotion with another occurs significantly more often in good-outcome cases than in poor-outcome cases.

In emotion coaching, adaptive emotions are therefore accessed to replace and transform maladaptive emotions and to help the client organize him- or herself so that he or she can make adaptive responses. Thus, when therapists help clients attend to, access, and symbolize their most fundamental adaptive experience, they are organized by their feelings of adaptive sadness, anger, or joy to act in the world to solve problems and create new meaning. For example, once an aggressive man recognizes the more primary feeling of hurt or loneliness underlying his anger, he begins to be able to approach his situation in a new way. Rather than pushing other people away with his anger, he is able to seek the comfort he really needs. Once clients who have panic attacks recognize that their momentary sadness at being alone is the trigger of their chain of phobic experiences, they begin to acknowledge their attachment needs and their sadness and then, instead of panicking and catastrophizing, they label their sadness and their need for closeness in words and find new ways of dealing with their fears of abandonment.

In addition to organizing adaptive action, emotions are also involved in reorganizing old, static structures to create new, adaptive structures. Thus, traumatic emotional memories can be evoked in therapy, to be reprocessed and restructured. In addition, maladaptive emotions such as core fears of abandonment or shame at inadequacy can be activated in therapy in order to be reorganized. As I have shown, in these instances emotional change occurs when more adaptive experience replaces or transforms old, maladaptive responses with which they are incompatible. When opposing emotions are coactivated, synthesizing compatible elements from the coactivated schemes may form new, higher level schemes. Just as a toddler scheme for standing and falling can be dynamically synthesized by a dialectical process into a higher level scheme for walking (Greenberg & Pascual-Leone, 1995; Pascual-Leone, 1991), so too can schemes of different emotional states be synthesized to form new integrations. For example, fear can be synthesized with anger to form a more assertive sense of self, or shame and self-soothing can be synthesized into a sense of comfort that results in the ability to make more contact with others rather than avoid it.

Change wrought through emotional processing thus involves arousing and becoming aware of emotion. It also involves assimilating nonverbal emotional meaning into conscious narrative structures and regulating sensation as well as replacing or integrating old emotional responses with newly activated aspects of experience to produce more adaptive responses.

Clients' Perceptions of Their Emotional Experience in Counseling

In a qualitative research study of the role of emotional experience in the psychotherapeutic process, Cummings (1997) intensively interviewed 11 former clients on their experience of emotion in therapy. They had undergone 25 therapies in all, some having had more than 3 therapy experiences. All treatments had taken place in public mental health institutions, for problems of depression, anxiety, and substance abuse. All participants described emotional distress as the impetus for entering therapy and change in or control of negative emotions and increased self-understanding as their goals. They described emotion-based interventions as significant therapeutic events. In successful therapy, clients identified the therapy relationship as the source both of their most positive emotions and of the most therapeutic gain. In unsuccessful therapies the relationship with the therapist was the source of clients' most negative emotions and of therapeutic failure.

The distressing emotions about which participants talked most often referred to the self (Cummings, 1997). These included depression (7 participants); anxiety (5 participants); self-hatred (3 participants); and flat affect, boredom, and ambivalence (2 participants each). The next most prevalent presenting problem mentioned involved difficult emotions triggered by important relationships. These were problems such as stress caused by marital failure (4 participants); loneliness (2 participants); and grief at the death of a spouse, dislike of parenting role, help for a partner or child, and rejection by a parent (each mentioned by 1 participant).

The most prevalent therapeutic issues were (a) a need to control or change negative feelings about the self and relationships just mentioned and (b) learning about emotions (Cummings, 1997). The participants also mentioned fear of rejection, a need for parenting skills, a need to deal with guilt about their feelings or behavior in regard to sexual abuse, a need for self-forgiveness, and a need to deal with feelings toward the therapist. The feelings most focused on were anger, sadness, fear, shame, and vulnerability.

Emotion Work

In terms of how emotion worked in therapy, the participants mentioned the following seven categories of emotion work (Cummings, 1997).

Discovering Connections

In response to the question "What were the most important and helpful things that happened to you in therapy?" clients' answers focused on the importance of discovering connections among emotions, thoughts, and behavior. For example, one participant said,

> I didn't know that I hadn't, or I didn't know that there was anything to forgive. I didn't realize that I had been injured, even inadvertently, by him [my father]. I was surprised.

Another commented, "It was a matter of going back over all the things in the marriage that had led to my sense of frustration and irritation and anger that eventually had gone underground and had caused all these troubles." Another reported, "It's anger. . . . The reason I took up alcoholism was because I had to make an identity for myself, because I was alienated from the Indian culture."

Discovery of Negative Emotions

People reported on the discovery, recognition, and understanding of negative emotions, for example, "[I had to] actually deal with the anger that had gone underground and caused the depression" and "[My therapist] brought out the feelings that I had, the anger, the hate, everything. She brought it out and let me see what it was I was facing." Another person commented,

> You've had [the uncomfortable feelings] all boxed up, and haven't really thought about it, . . . it might be weighing you down, and that's where you're feeling depressed and alone . . . but as you break it into individual pieces than you can finally say "Okay, there you are, you ornery little snot that has been causing me pain and anguish. Bye. We can resolve you and get rid of you." And the weight . . . lifts, so you kinda go through the realization of the pain.

Experiencing Necessary Pain

Clients viewed experiencing the pain (fear, anger, disappointment) of self-knowledge and other negative emotions (ambivalence, despair, grieving, and giving up) as important.

One person said, "You have to bleed a little," another reported, "I had to lose everything in order to get where I am today," and yet another said, "when we open this one, it's a nasty Pandora's box. . . . We need to get into our own emotions to be able to understand ourselves and be able to relate."

Normalization of Negative Emotions

Seeing negative emotions as normal was helpful and reassuring. One participant said, "You actually didn't feel like you [were] the only person out in the world that had the problem." Another said, "You're not the only one, and so you can feel that it's okay. You're not all alone or not, you know, weird or bad."

Experiencing Intense Emotions

Experiencing intense emotions was characterized by the participants' use of some form of the word *intensity* or by their use of an intense form of an emotion word, such as *distraught* or *painful*. Some seemed to feel disappointment about the lack of intensity. For example, one person said, "When I was in therapy, I didn't have any emotional changes in there at all. I just went out and spoke and talked about my feelings. I didn't really have any change of emotions at all." Another, referring to the therapist, mentioned a "profound feeling for him." Another reported that "It just brought tears to my eyes. It was so intense. It was such a profound realization for me." Another said, "It was ecstatic. It was very blissful. That's another good word for it." Finally, one participant said that "there's the overwhelming crying of not having let myself go and. . . . Just finally being given the outlet to say, 'Yes, you are permitted, you are allowed, you can do this' [crying]."

Open Expression of Negative Emotions

Open expression of negative emotions was an intervention participants commonly experienced but did not always experience as therapeutic. The difference between therapeutic results and negative results depended on whether the therapist made the expressive episode useful for the client by relating it to therapeutic issues and whether the expression was simply an outpouring of feeling or was controlled and meaningful. One person said,

> It was amazing to me. 'Cause I—all my life it's felt to me like, don't make noise, be quiet, don't feel your emotions, just hide them or they don't exist, period. And, so that it was real hard for me to even scream and talk to him, to my brother [who had committed suicide] . . . and

tell him how I felt. And I couldn't sustain it, I couldn't sustain the rape or the screaming.

Another person said,

It was a really good outlet where I could feel free to let out my negative emotions and my frustrations and my problems and not be burdening my friends . . . [My therapist] could always make me feel less frustrated and a little more in control, just having somebody to talk to, you know.

A different participant reported that

there was a relief to not having realized that it was really penting up, that it was really getting in the way, that [crying] really needed to be done, and going, "Hey, that's over with, and I'm right here,". . . I can feel this pressure out of the way, or giving way, at least. I was very angry.

Another remembered, "I was very angry. That was a good [session] that time because I told her how pissed off I was, and I swore." One person, however, said, "It brings a lot of emotions out, like, you know, it turned into a battleground. Nothing got solved, but it just kind of, the problem is brought out, but the problem was never solved."

Experiential Learning

Participants described the benefits of emotionally vivid therapy in which experiences were felt in vivo or in memory. Often, in a subsequent session the emotional experience was tied to a therapeutic issue and was completed by cognitive understanding of the emotion, verbalization of the feeling, and identification of the lesson learned. One participant reported, "I relived them from an emotional vantage point instead of settling for this intellectualization that I had engaged in up until that time."

Missing Emotion Work

Participants mentioned missing emotion work. They referred to lack of depth (4 participants), which seemed to mean no work had been done on hidden or denied negative emotions or parts of themselves, no change in problem emotions (6 participants), no increase in self-understanding (4 participants), and no feeling of completeness or success (2 participants). Often it was anger or fear (6 participants) that were not dealt with because the participants hid them or because the therapist avoided them. For example, one participant said,

[My third therapist] didn't want to delve for the depth. He just wanted to fix. I don't think I ever had those depths. I don't think I got into it enough. I always felt I never really quite got into it enough.

In another, more recent qualitative analysis of the experience of emotion in therapy (Stuart, 2000), clients reported, at the termination of treatment, on both the difficulties and the benefits of focusing on emotion in treatment. In this study the clients' descriptions of problematic aspects of their emotions in therapy were clustered into a number of major categories, which are summarized next.

1. *They were not aware of their feelings*: "I had tears rolling down my face, but I didn't recognize my feeling as sadness"; "In the midst of something really sad, I'd start laughing. I didn't know I was afraid."
2. *Their feelings were hidden*: "It's like my feelings were locked behind a door"; "My feelings were deadened."
3. *Their feelings overwhelmed them*: "I felt overwhelmed by my feelings."
4. *Their feelings were confusing*: "My feelings were all jumbled up"; "My emotions were all amiss"; "My feelings were like a huge can of worms."
5. *Problems of emotions obscured other emotions*: "I would turn my fear in, and it would come out as anger"; "I wasn't aware that my fear fueled my anger."
6. *They felt vulnerable*: "I felt like I was on the edge of a big black hole"; "I felt very vulnerable"; "There was a feeling of helplessness."
7. *They perceived distressing bodily components of feeling*: "My body felt like lead"; "It was just like I was in cement"; "I was totally numb"; "My breathing was faster"; "I just got really weird feelings in my stomach, like a big knot"; "I felt sick to my stomach."

These categories and statements clearly indicate the types of difficulties and distress people experience in working with their emotions in therapy. These are the problems with which coaches need to work. The following are the categories formed from the previously mentioned clients' reports of what helped them in therapy to deal with their emotions. These provide a guide for coaches as to what they need to do to help people.

1. *Facing their emotions*: "I looked more intensely at my emotions"; "I needed to face my emotions so that I could get on with life."
2. *Trusting their emotions*: "I didn't think it would ever be okay to trust my feelings"; "I didn't know what feelings were okay and what feelings weren't okay."
3. *Reducing the intensity of their emotions*: "As I dealt with my emotions, they became less intense."

4. *Sorting out their emotions*: "I can identify my emotions"; "I now have these little cubbyholes, and my feelings get put into the spaces they're supposed to be put into."

5. *Overcoming avoidance of their emotions*: "I would push away recognizing the physical aspects of my emotions"; "Avoiding dealing with my emotions was causing me real life physical problems"; "My emotions were ruling my life."

6. *Reowning their emotions*: "After I had explored some of my emotions I just felt different"; "It's like I'm part of my life now because I can feel it"; "My emotions seem to have fallen into place."

7. *Emotions promoted change*: "The big, cold chunk that was part of me had been changed"; "When I began to feel, it felt like a new beginning"; "As the numbness began to thaw, I began to feel"; "When I was in touch with my emotions, I became less volatile"; "As I dealt with the feelings, things came out that I never realized there"; "I started to pay attention to what my feelings meant."

In a final qualitative study, post-therapy interviews of 7 clients from a depression study (Greenberg & Watson, 1998) were examined using a grounded theory research approach to determine the role of emotion in psychotherapeutic change (Gamble, 2001). The analysis revealed that client acceptance of their emotional experiences was at the core of their process of emotional change. The core category of acceptance was comprised of three secondary categories that helped define the core category: awareness of emotion, deeply connecting with emotion, and what it is like for clients to feel that emotion.

These studies highlight that there are a variety of ways in which emotion plays a role in therapy. They are blocked, are outside of one's awareness, are overwhelming, and are a source of confusion and distressing bodily experience. In therapy people need to overcome avoidance of emotion, face their emotions, trust them, sort them out, discover connections, discover negative emotions, experience pain and intense emotion, openly express emotion, reduce the intensity of emotion, reown emotion, and learn experientially. Clients also reported missing deeper emotional work. At the core, clients need to be helped to accept their emotions. This is what coaches need to help clients do in therapy to help emotions promote change.

THE COACHING RELATIONSHIP

The clients in the Cummings (1997) study, discussed previously, reported the therapeutic relationship as the most important source of emotions, both positive and negative. People are born into relationships and develop in them. Given the highly relational nature of emotional development, the helping relationship is an important ingredient of effective emotion coaching. As these former clients pointed out, the relationship with the therapist is alive with feeling.

In addition to the three major principles of emotional change just outlined, the relationship between coach and client is crucial in promoting clients' emotional competence. The relationship contributes to a number of emotional processes that help the client develop skills that make up emotional intelligence. There are a number of major affective competencies that can be facilitated by means of a good relationship with a sensitively attuned emotion coach. The first competency involves clients' acquisition of the ability to become aware of and verbalize their emotional experience through the process of coaches' affective attunement to their experience. The second involves clients' development of a balance between their ability to regulate their own emotional experience and their ability to use others to regulate emotional experience. The third competency involves learning to tolerate and accept painful emotional experience via the process of being in a relationship with a coach who accepts and is able to tolerate both the client's painful emotions and any of the coach's own emotions in response to the client's. People don't learn emotional regulation in the same way they learn, say, math or biology; rather, the skill is absorbed implicitly by being in the presence of a person who has this ability. If, for example, clients see that their therapists are calm in response to their expressions of distress or anger and can contain them, they find this reassuring and are calmed. Greenberg and Rhodes (1991) found that clients in general therapies often felt shame or fear after crying in therapy. They either felt embarrassed at being perceived as weak or were afraid of falling apart. It was the therapists' ability to approach these emotion-laden experiences in an empathic manner rather than deflect the clients from them that was highly predictive of clients' subsequent ability to process their own emotion. Another important relational process in emotion coaching involves coaches giving feedback to their clients to help them develop awareness of action dispositions and experiences that they avoid or interrupt. Clients learn that they are not alone in their emotional world. They experience that their isolation can be broken and their painful feelings can be soothed by connection with another person.

The authentic presence of the coach is crucial in facilitating emotion awareness tolerance and regulation and in dealing with difficult client emotions felt toward the therapist. *Presence* involves being fully in the moment and contacting clients' emotional experience congruently and in a non-power-oriented manner. Being able to be fully present to the other in an open manner, rather than being there for the self, is a highly developed skill that requires letting go of preconceptions and giving full attention in the moment (Greenberg & Geller, 2001). Coaches must not bring extraneous personal baggage, personal needs, or even agendas for coaching into the encounter. They need instead to be fully present with and for the client. To do this, a coach needs to have developed a high level of emotional maturity, or at least be able to attain it while in session.

This kind of presence often allows for the creation of special healing moments. Being fully present in the moment allows coaches to spontaneously draw on the fact that one often knows more than one is able to say. People draw on their tacit knowledge to respond in a manner that fits the moment. When emotion coaches know ahead of time what they are going to say, this is not being present, because what is said is not being formed vitally from contact with the other in the moment. These preformed statements often either come from theory or are technically guided; they generally are not attuned to the moment and do not lead to change.

By contrast, moments of true novelty emerge from therapeutic presence. When a coach is suspended in the present, exactly as it is, with no plan of how to proceed, something novel can emerge. The spontaneous, idiosyncratic responses that come in these moments emerge from the coach's tacit knowledge. Special moments of presence such as these can have a profound impact on the therapist–client relationship. These moments can shift the relationship to another level and can create new possibilities for contact. They are moments of authenticity that help transcend the roles, the familiar positions, in the relationship. They help the participants enter a new intersubjective state. A moment of true meeting occurs in which something new is shared. Both participants now realize that they know something not previously understood, or talked about. This sharing of a new space opens up a new field of mutual experience on which the coach and client can now work together. New possibilities emerge in the relationship. Often this new, enriched relationship need not be talked about; it has been experienced, and this has produced a shift between the participants. Talking about or overreflecting on it can spoil the importance of both parties' experience that each one understands the other's point of view. Moments of mutuality such as this create connections and promote the development of new avenues of relating and experiencing. They also further enhance the presence of both therapist and client, and the connection between them is experienced at a heightened level.

The coach's use of his or her own feelings, and an explicit focus on the patient's experience of the coach's feeling and therapeutic presence, are also powerful tools for introducing novelty (Fosha, 2000). There are several strategies of intervention that make use of the coach's emotions and facilitate the patient's experience of them. Among these are explicit empathy ("It pains me to think of how you suffered"), affective resonance (tensing as the patient is describing a tense situation), and anticipatory mirroring (expressing the emotional reaction the patient would most likely feel, were he or she able to do so). In addition, certain emotional self-disclosures introduce novelty. The explicit expression of the therapist's own emotional experience—for example, saying, "I find myself growing tense as we speak," or "As you lay out all the details, I find it hard to stay with you," or "I sense a wall going up in you as we talk about this—can also introduce something new into the relationship. The therapist also may focus on the patient's experience of the here-and-now contact with the therapist: "What do you see when you look at me?" or "I feel touched when I see your shyness. How do you feel when I say this?" Talking to clients about their experience of you, of your understanding of them and of their relationship with you, also is helpful because it helps them build a representation of their feeling of being in relationship and of being understood and validated (Fosha, 2000).

Given that negative feelings toward the therapist often occur in unsuccessful therapies, learning to deal with negative feelings that may arise in the relationship is important. Client anger and feelings of hostility toward the coach, or client withdrawal and feelings of shame and anxiety, are probably the most difficult emotions with which coaches have to deal in the relationship. Major principles of maintaining good alliances in the face of client hostility or withdrawal are to remain calm, understanding, and curious rather than escalate the situation by defending, explaining, or counterattacking. An open stance toward the client's negativity allows his or her negative feelings toward the coach to be accepted and explored with interest rather than be defended against (Safran & Muran, 2000). This is not always easy and depends on the therapist's ability to remain nondefensive and not become frustrated. In fact Henry, Schacht, and Strupp (1990) found that therapists who were most self-accepting reacted least defensively to difficult interactions with clients.

Therapist anger toward the client and therapist boredom with or rejection of the client need to be dealt with congruently, or they will poison the relationship. Coaches need first to deal with any personal issues that may lead to these reactions, but the ability to be present and facilitatively congruent with clients at these moments is helpful. This involves disclosing these inner feelings as information to be explored for their source and meaning rather than as interactional statements about the client. The roles of congruence and disclosure will be further discussed in chapter 4, which deals with coaches' emotions, but I emphasize here that anger expressed as attack, or a bored feeling expressed as withdrawal, are not facilitative, whereas using these as information on which the therapist can reflect, and disclosing them to the client as information to be explored, when appropriate, can be helpful.

Clients' capacity to experience their feelings without needing to rely on protective mechanisms that interrupt their emotional experience is greatly enhanced by their having the opportunity to do this with a supportive, empathic, and emotionally present other, one who is willing both to share experiences and help with their management. Being in an emotionally connected relationship that is based on genuine empathic attunement and support therefore enhances people's capacity to feel. However, individuals are often in life situations in which they are unable to receive empathic attunement to their feelings. Often, instead of eliciting a caregiver's help and support, a person's emotions have elicited the caregiver's discomfort, withdrawal, or even attack. The emotions, intense and overwhelming to begin with, thereby became further aversive as they disrupt the connection with the primary emotional caregiver (Fosha, 2000). The unwanted emotional aloneness that results when overwhelming emotions are not met with empathic attunement is so unbearable that people learn to avoid their emotions at all costs. Because intense emotional experiences are overwhelming and threaten one's bond with the other, people find ways to blunt, postpone, mute, mask, or distort their experiences of emotion. Instead of experiencing feelings, and using them to navigate through life, people therefore develop protections against feeling. They develop processes such as avoidance, numbing, squeezing, and selective focusing on certain emotions at the expense of others. Empathic attunement to emotions by a responsive other provides people with the safety that helps melt these protective barriers. Empathy is thus the bedrock of emotion coaching.

EMPATHY

The importance of empathy in therapy has stood the test of time (Bohart, Elliott, Greenberg, & Watson, in press; Bohart & Greenberg, 1997). Empathy clearly is a helpful element that is necessary but possibly not sufficient for helping (Greenberg, Rice, & Elliott, 1993). Expression of empathy is a highly complex process, not simply a reflection of feeling. It has many components and is effective for a variety of reasons (Bohart & Greenberg, 1997). It provides confirmation, breaks clients' isolation, promotes the exploration of subjective experience, and helps clients create new meaning (Greenberg & Elliott, 1997). One of its important functions in emotion coaching is to help people focus on, symbolize, and differentiate their emotions.

The following example of a moment in therapy demonstrates an empathic style of responding that coaches need to follow:

Client: So it seems like I just can't seem to get along with people. If there is any criticism or anyone says anything about me, I just can't take it. At my job, when anybody says anything critical, it just crumples me.

Therapist: Uh huh, so it feels like it's just so hard to get along with others, mainly because their criticism is so hard to take; it just leaves you feeling crushed.

Client: Well, it doesn't even have to be meant as criticism. It goes 'way back to elementary school. I never felt I belonged. I worked really hard to get good grades, but I sort of shut myself off because I was hurt so much.

Therapist: I see. You shut yourself off because you felt so hurt? Kind of the hurt of not fitting in, just not belonging. I imagine that must have been very lonely. What was it like for you?

The therapist's first response is interchangeable with what the client said. Responses of this type, that capture the central message and are succinct and not too complex, have been found to be helpful to clients (Greenberg, Elliott, & Lietaer, 1994; Sachse, 1993). People benefit most when these interchangeable responses are supplemented by even more exploratory responses of the second type, which encourage further differentiation and elaboration and focus on the leading edge of client's experience, on what is most alive or poignant or what is just on the edge of awareness. The second response follows the leading edge of the client's experience— the feeling of not belonging. It ends with an inquiry into experience. Asking a question, however, is not necessarily what constitutes an exploratory response; instead, an exploratory response is one that draws the client's focus of attention to implicit experience, to that which is just at the edge of his or her awareness. Notice that even the therapist's first response, the one that is not pushing for as much differentiation of experience, still leaves the client's focus of attention on his or her internal experience of feeling crumpled or crushed. This is one of the major purposes of empathic responses: to focus people on particular internal aspects of their experience.

A balance is needed between *understanding* responses, which convey compassion and provide emotional holding, and *exploratory* responses, which promote differentiation, discovery, and the creation of new meaning. This balance provides a secure base from which it is safe to explore. For toddlers and astronauts alike, a secure base promotes exploration. The situation is the same for an emotional explorer. The provision of a secure base provides grounding, a place to return for refueling or safety in case of depletion or danger. In therapy, exploration of new experience is more likely to begin to take place once a secure base of understanding has been established.

Empathic responding between people can be rated on an empathy rating scale constructed to evaluate the degree to which therapists are sensitively attuned to and communicate their understanding of their clients' feelings (Truase & Carkhuff, 1967). The above interchange would be rated as Level 7 empathy on a 9-point scale. Level 7 is defined as

The therapist responds accurately to most of the client's present feelings and shows awareness of the precise intensity of most of the underlying emotions. However, the therapist's responses move only slightly beyond the client's own awareness, so that feelings may be present which neither the client nor therapist recognizes.

The highest level on this scale, Level 9, is defined as

The therapist in this stage unerringly responds to the client's full range of feelings in their exact intensity. Without hesitation, the therapist recognizes each emotional nuance and communicates an understanding of every deepest feeling. The therapist is completely attuned to the client's shifting emotional content, senses each of the client's feelings, and reflects them in words and voice. With sensitive accuracy, the therapist expands the client's hints into a full-scale (though tentative) elaboration of feeling or experience.

Responding at Level 9 promotes emotional exploration and helps people resolve problems. In being empathic, the therapists take the perspective of their clients in an emotionally compassionate and respecting manner. The therapists try to enter clients' shoes, see the world as they see it, understand their experience, and check with them to see if their understanding matches the clients' experience.

Empathy, as I have mentioned, is a multifaceted form of responding. I like to emphasize the role of imagination in teaching empathy. I see empathy as an imaginative entry into the world of the other. Often, speaking as the client, giving voice to the client's experience, embodies this entry into the client's experience. For example, saying "I just felt like sinking into the ground" involves speaking in the client's voice and helps capture his or her feeling of shame.

A colleague and I (Greenberg & Rosenberg, 2000) recently completed a qualitative study of therapists' experience of empathy and confirmed what we had hypothesized: that empathy is a process that involves thinking and feeling, and imagining and sensing, as well as many forms of responding. What stood out, however, was how often therapists had images in which they pictured their client in situations and scenarios that their clients were describing. They then read the feeling from the image or from their reaction to it, much like one reads the feelings from movie scenes or works of art. Thus, one therapist had a picture of his client as a 10-year-old, walking a fair distance behind her parents, alone, her balloon straggling behind her on the cobblestones on a dreary day. From this the therapist reflected "just yearning for them to turn around and take you up in their arms; feeling so alone." Another therapist saw an image of her client holding the phone away from her ear, shock on her face and silently gasping, and said "It was like I died in that moment."

Empathic attunement to affect, as Stern (1985) pointed out, acts in the context of child development to strengthen the self. An infant whose excitement is mirrored in tone and quality by her caretaker will synthesize her internal experience with its matching external confirmation into a strong sense of her self-experience in the moment as excited. An infant with a depressed caretaker whose face and vocal tone are flat in response to the infant's rising excitement becomes a victim of mixed messages: one from within, expressing excitement, and one from without, expressing sadness or nothing. This leaves the infant confused and unable to form a strong representation of her own self-experience. This occurs because the self is formed at the boundary between self and other (Greenberg & van Balen, 1998; Stern, 1985). Similarly, empathic responses in therapy that confirm where the client is, even if he or she is feeling despairing or weak, has a strengthening effect on the sense of self. Self-experience is confirmed, and the person feels clear, excited, and strong. They think "Yes, that's it —that is what I feel!" This provides the energy and impetus for further exploration. Empathic following helps the client to arrive in a definite manner at what he or she is experiencing. This is an important element of the change process, for one cannot leave a place until one first arrives there.

BEYOND EMPATHY: PROCESS DIRECTIONS

Empathic attunement is one important element of coaching. The other element is the introduction of novelty: leading—not by offering a content suggestion on what a person should feel but by offering a process directive on how he or she can process the emotion or by suggesting a strategy for getting at an emotion. One important way of introducing newness is to offer process suggestions as to a possible next step in dealing with a symbolized feeling. A coach may thus help a client acknowledge an unexpressed resentment by asking "what do you most resent about that?" or by directing attention to a bodily felt sensation by suggesting, "Pay attention to what you are feeling inside right now." The coach may help the client identify an unmet need by asking "what do you need now?" or the coach may suggest that the person express a feeling or a need to an imagined significant other in an empty chair. Coaching thus involves not only empathizing with what the client feels but also entering into a conversation with the client about how best to deal with this feeling. This conversation involves the promotion in clients of the following:

- awareness of what their feelings are telling them
- awareness of the direction in which their emotions are steering them
- reflection on this new awareness
- action on reflected-on emotion
- a search for new ways of handling troublesome emotions.

Coaching does not involve being imposingly directive, giving a pep talk, or providing expert knowledge to clients about their experience; rather, there is a gentle pressure to focus internally and a coconstruction of new meaning. This involves helping clients put emotions into words, helping them become aware of both how they interrupt or avoid certain experiences, and identifying to them the costs of their dysfunctional ways of dealing with feelings. Coaching also involves using methods that help bring emotion alive as well as providing psychoeducation about how to access emotion when it is overcontrolled and how to regulate it when it is undercontrolled.

The coach thus enters the person's emotional world and begins a conversation that opens new possibilities for consideration in a space that was previously closed. The coach is not an expert on what the client feels but rather offers expertise on how feelings work, on means of bringing them alive for inspection, and means of helping clients soothe themselves when their emotions are too disorganized. Emotional experience is so private that people seldom have the opportunity to talk in a safe, reflective environment about their feelings. They have little opportunity to receive new, nonjudgmental input on how to manage their emotions. The coach provides sensitive guidance and feedback to clients in regard to how they are handling their feelings. When difficulties arise, the coach provides this guidance and feedback—not in a directive manner but as a collaborative partner in a search for new ways of handling emotions. The coach is like a guide who knows paths through the emotional terrain with which the client is unfamiliar. The coach, for example, knows something about how to face hopelessness, about the healthy role of anger in grief, that anger often obscures hurt, or that shame needs to be exposed and the self validated. The client, however, is the explorer who sets the goal, decides on the pace, and is in control of the expedition. The coach offers guidance on how to achieve a goal rather than setting the goal.

The coach also helps the client tolerate and contain disjunctive states by helping the self emotionally bridge varying and often opposing states. It often is difficult for people to contain conflictual feelings, such as loving and hating the same person or feeling both hurt and angry. The coach can act as a gentle conductor who guides the person from one state to another by helping him or her shift attention. Pizer (2000) described how a parent promotes affect regulation in a child in this manner. It seems that caretakers' ability to tolerate affective disjunctions in their children—say, a child's rapid movement from anger to sadness or from fear to rage—makes these states more acceptable and coherent to the one experiencing them. If these disjunctions were met with horror or disapproval, or concern for their irrationality, it would become difficult for the developing child to integrate these opposing states into a coherent sense of self. The coach can thus facilitate the transformational process of bridging different emotional states much as a mother adroitly conducts her child from one affective state to another by her affective attunement and coaching. Empathy and acceptance of disparate states and their difference communicates that they are okay and their difference is tolerable. The most important aspect of communication with a client who is dealing with difficult, opposing feelings is an attitude that conveys "you can make the transition." This helps the client go where he or she has not been able to go before or to bridge two states never before felt together. One client said, talking about her father, "Yes, as crazy at it sounds, I feel like I hate him and love him at the same time." It is the actual living through of the experience of bridging affect states—from despair to hope, shame to pride, anger to sadness, and love to hate—that is critical in promoting the development of strength and coherence in the self. Sometimes these polar feelings are experienced and felt toward the coach; at other times they are felt toward other people in the client's life.

FOLLOWING AND LEADING

The view of the emotion coach as both follower and leader recognizes the importance of both following closely where clients are and leading them to new possibilities that are within their grasp. This involves both responsive empathic attunement to clients' affect and the active contribution of new input by the therapist in the form of process suggestions on how to further process their own affect. This form of engagement results in a coconstructive process of generating new meaning. A new conversation about the client's emotional experience develops and opens new possibilities in his or her world. The coach thus both understands and validates where the client is, at any moment, and introduces novelty into a previously closed domain by making suggestions on how the client can better process his or her emotion. Suggestions on what operation to engage in next must be in contact with, but can be slightly ahead of, what the client is currently doing.

Thus, if a client is currently sinking into despair, a processing suggestion that focuses too soon on accessing the client's resources or strengths —a response intended to help the person come out of the despair and master the situation—would be too far ahead of the client's current capability. Clients in these states, however, would be responsive to a confirming response that validates how they feel, focuses them on the feeling and captures what is worst about it all, and symbolizes the meaning of the despair. Any coaching response that would lead these clients toward staying with their despair and differentiating it will help them make meaning from their despair rather than remain stuck in it. Only when the client has emotionally processed the despair by labeling it, differentiating it, and creating a sense of its meaning will suggestions that focus on what the client needs and resources for moving out of the despair be helpful. However, even these need to be just at the edge of the clients' possibilities and should focus on coping rather than mastery.

As a function of this combination of acceptance and change, of validating clients' experience and introducing new possibilities, clients will learn to better attend to and synthesize their experience; to tolerate, regulate, and transform their emotions; and to find new ways of processing their emotions. The essence of this type of coaching work is the art of both being in contact with and responsive to where the client is and having a sense of direction that provides a framework for where the client can be. Both acceptance of the present and projection toward the future are important elements. Helping clients to change to be where they are, rather than trying to be where they are not, as well as helping them by offering new emotional problem-solving strategies that focus on new possibilities within their grasp, are crucial elements of being an effective emotion coach.

It is important to note that, in the view of emotion coaching described in this chapter, people are seen as being continually engaged in a complex, emotionally guided process of adaptation in which they attempt to meet their healthy adult needs in intimate relationships and make efforts to master their worlds. People are seen neither as "red in tooth and claw," needing to control a beast within, nor as being infantile and dependent, harboring a needy baby within. Instead of being seen as constantly in internal conflict, needing to repress or control their emotions, people are seen as needing to pay attention to their adaptive emotions to help them be more viable in whatever environments they find themselves. Emotions keep people active, curious, and connected to others rather than being expressions of infantile dependence out of which the people need to grow. This positive view is not a romantic one, in which people are seen as Rousseaulike noble savages who possess within them all the necessary emotional wisdom for a good life; rather, people's emotional intelligence is seen as requiring an integration of many facets. Emotional wisdom involves the capacity to integrate influences from both inside and outside and from head and heart. The coach is there to facilitate attention to, and integration of, as many facets as seem relevant to help people experience themselves in new ways.

Emotion coaching, then, is based on a basic educational idea about how information and experience are best communicated and assimilated. The idea is that novel information will be heard and processed better by the receiver of the information when it is sensitively attuned to his or her state. This is drawn from Vygotsky's (1986) idea of making suggestions that are in the learner's "zone of proximal development." A math teacher who responds sensitively, and offers something just ahead of the student's level of understanding of mathematical concepts, will be more helpful in moving the student forward in mastering a new mathematical principle. Similarly, a good emotion coach's response does not get too far ahead of the client's level of understanding and stays within the client's zone of proximal development. In emotion coaching the coach takes just enough of a step ahead to help but stays within the person's capability to stretch his or her ability to identify, tolerate, and understand what is being felt at present.

Emotion coaching thus involves the sensitive facilitation of learning by offering input when the client is in a teachable moment. The coach offers input at the edge of the client's experience, in the client's zone of proximal development. This involves suggesting a task, or making a suggestion, that is just a small step ahead of the client. This provides a scaffold for the client to take the step and move to a new place. If the coach makes suggestions that are too far ahead—or, for that matter, too far behind the client—no development takes place. Giving the right input, at the right time, is the challenge. Suggestion or promotion of a new step needs always to be balanced with equal amounts of recognition and validation of exactly where clients currently are in their emotional worlds. This combination of providing support and promoting newness, of following and leading, of confirming the clients' experience and opening up new possibilities (Greenberg, Rice, & Elliott, 1993), constitutes the dialectic of acceptance and change that is coaching (cf. Linehan, 1993).

For example, in working with someone who is talking about a situation in which he is dealing with difficulties with a dependent relative at home, the coach might help symbolize the client's feeling by saying "It sounds like you feel almost despairing, at a loss with what to do." The client responds with "I hate this feeling; it's so childish to feel this way." The coach, after acknowledging the client's frustration with the feeling, might guide him by saying, "Rather than scolding it, try and relax into this feeling of despair. Where in your body do you feel it? Breathe into it." As the client tries the experience, the coach will watch and notice his nonverbal expression and ask him what is happening as the experience unfolds. If the client looks scared, the coach will provide soothing sounds and reassurance. "Uh-humm; it's OK. It's safe here." Drawing on knowledge previously shared by a client of an early loss, the coach might say "You are safe here" and then, in response to the client saying he feels so afraid, like a child, the coach might say "you are not your 5-year-old self who was left so alone. I am here, and so is your adult part with you." After awhile the coach might say, "Talk from the pain of the 5-year-old. Let it have a voice." The client then may allow himself to feel the pain. A floodgate of tears may open. Here the coach might say, "Breathe and let it come." After some conversing, the coach, at an appropriate moment, when the feeling has been more fully processed and the arousal reduced, might ask "What do you need now?" Gentle prompts such as these promote progress through the steps of naming, allowing, accepting, and reflecting on feelings and identifying a need.

These suggestions are offered at the leading edge of the client's experience, in his or her zone of proximal development. At the end of this process the coach might further help the client by symbolizing certain implicit meanings. For example, the coach might say,

> It sounds like you are in the process of accepting that you will never be able to regain the love you lost when your mother died. You are beginning to feel it may be possible to find this source of support from others and within you.

Together the coach and client may explore whether the coach's assessment fits and look at how the pain the client felt connects to other things in his life. The coach, as one can see in this example, is a type of conductor who both affirms where the person is and gently conducts him from one emotional state to the next, in a developmental process.

Emotion coaching involves entering into other people's most private experiences—their emotions—and by sensitive following and leading, facilitating a variety of emotional change processes. The most central of these processes are increasing emotional awareness and acceptance, enhancing regulation, and changing emotion with emotion. The therapeutic relationship helps people develop competencies in emotion awareness and emotion tolerance, as does empathy, and more process directive interventions help focus on and stimulate emotion.

4

THE STEPS OF EMOTION COACHING

Emotion coaching requires throughout a safe, empathic, and validating relationship. A facilitative environment of this nature provides people with the experience of emotional soothing and support they need to pay attention to their bodily felt experiences. This type of relational environment helps people tolerate their emotions, sort out their feelings and develop self-empathy, and it supports their ability to find alternate resources within themselves. Within this relational context emotion coaching helps clients use their emotion intelligently to solve problems in living. In this chapter I elaborate the steps by which therapists can coach people to skillfully experience their emotions.

Emotion coaching in therapy is based on eight major steps on how best to help people make emotions work for them in their everyday lives. These steps are embodied in two phases: arriving and leaving. The first phase, arriving at one's emotions, involves the following four steps that help people become aware of their feelings and accept them.

1. It is important to help people become aware of their emotions.
2. People need to be coached to welcome their emotional experience, allow, and accept it (this does not necessarily mean they must express everything they feel to other people but rather acknowledge it themselves). Certain people who are under-regulated need to be coached in skills of regulation.

3. People need to be helped to describe their feelings in words; this will help them develop problem-solving skills.
4. People need to be helped to become aware of whether their emotional reactions are their primary feelings in a situation. If not, they need help in discovering what their primary feelings are.

The second phase, that of leaving the place at which the client arrived, involves moving on and transforming core feelings when necessary.

5. Once the person has been helped to experience a primary emotion, coach and person together need to evaluate if the emotion is a healthy or unhealthy response to the current situation. If it is healthy, it should be used as a guide to action. If it is unhealthy, it needs to be changed.
6. When the person's accessed primary emotions are unhealthy, he or she has to be helped to identify the negative voice or view associated with these emotions.
7. The person needs to be helped to find and rely on alternate, healthy emotional responses and needs.
8. People need to be coached to challenge their destructive beliefs or views, and their unhealthy emotions, with a new inner voice based on their healthy primary emotions and needs.

PHASE 1: ARRIVING

The first phase of emotion coaching involves helping people arrive at and accept their feelings. As painful as some feelings may be, people need to feel their emotions before they can change them. It is important for the coach to help people understand that they cannot leave a place until they have arrived there first.

Step 1: Promote Awareness of Emotions

First, it is important to help people become aware of their emotions. Emotional awareness helps people understand what they are really feeling at their core, and this helps them solve problems. In this first step, gaining awareness involves helping clients pay attention to and make contact with sensations. This is a nonverbal form of knowing what one is feeling. Here the coach needs to direct clients' attention to their bodies to help them become aware of, for example, the excitement in their stomach or the sadness in their eyes and cheeks. This type of awareness of feelings is not an intellectual understanding of feeling. Clients should not feel that they are on the outside looking at themselves; rather the coach should encourage a bodily sensed awareness of what is felt from the inside—like the sensing of the throbbing of a toothache. Clients are directed to pay attention to the actual quality, intensity, and shape of the sensations at specific places in their bodies to help them concentrate on their sensations. For example, they might be able to experience a feeling such as one of "a hot, tight ball in my chest."

In addition to helping clients pay attention to sensations, coaches need to help them be aware of the thoughts accompanying those sensations, because most emotions include thoughts as well as feelings. When people feel emotions, they often have an inner dialogue accompanying the feeling. They sometimes have images and always some judgments. For example, if a client is feeling sad, he or she might be thinking "Why am I sad? I have nothing to complain about," or "I never get what I need from him." Clients need to be guided to pay attention to the thoughts, pictures, and evaluations that accompany sensations. Emotional awareness thus involves awareness of the feelings, thoughts, and images that comprise the emotion.

Step 2: Facilitate a Welcoming and Acceptance of Emotional Experience

Coaches need to encourage clients to allow themselves to feel their emotional experiences. They also need to communicate to clients that clients do not necessarily have to act on all their emotions. Clients should not, however, be encouraged to avoid or deflect their painful emotions, no matter how difficult it may seem to not do so. They need, rather, to welcome their emotions, dwell on them, breathe, and let them come. They need to accept their feelings as information. People need to recognize their feelings as opportunities to gather information about something important to their well-being; their emotions give them a message about what they are truly feeling. Once they have attended to an emotion, they are more able to let it go. Emotions follow a natural course of rising and passing away, swelling and fading. They come and go if people let them and don't try to block the emotions or avoid them. It is helpful to coach people to become aware of how they interfere with, or interrupt, their emotions rather than allow themselves to experience the emotions. Inquiring as to how clients are avoiding their feelings helps accomplish this.

Clients also need to be taught that emotions are not reasoned, final conclusions on which they must act. They therefore can afford to feel emotions without fear of dire consequences. If a person allows him- or herself to experience a feeling of hopelessness, this does not mean that he or she is hopeless. Neither does this mean that the next logical step is to give up. A feeling is not a permanent state in which a person will reside forever; instead, feeling is part of a process. Emotion is not about a concluded truth; it provides information about one's values and judgments about how things are affecting one's well-being. An emotion says more about the person than about reality. Anger tells someone that he or she feels violated rather than offering a truth that the other person is a violator. People need not fear their emotions because of what they imply. Emotions inform rather than determine. If a client is upset with her spouse and feels "I hate him for what he did," this does not necessarily mean that the relationship is destroyed; this emotion is informing the client how isolated and enraged she feels. Acknowledging this leads to the next step in her own process. She then needs to ask herself "What do I need or want? What do I do?"

Emotion is not an action, and it is not a conclusion. People may want to control their actions, but they should not try to control their primary internal experience. Anger is not aggression. People can feel angry at a friend without hitting him or her. They may possibly not even tell their friend that they are angry; however, they still need to acknowledge their anger and feel it. Telling themselves "I have no right to feel angry" often leads to more trouble, because the anger might build inside them instead of being acknowledged and dealt with.

Expressing how one feels out loud, on the other hand, needs to be appropriate to its context and needs to be regulated. People learn to express their feelings and communicate effectively if they are first able to understand, feel, and welcome their primary feelings. Rather than suppressing their feelings until they blow up, or recklessly blowing off steam at any opportunity, people need to contact and develop their emotional experiences. Once people have allowed the feeling to develop and have made sense of it, then they will be able to decide when and when not to tell others how they feel. Only then will they be able to express their feelings in the manner most appropriate to the context in which they find themselves.

For people whose emotions are overwhelming, the task is not so much one of allowing the emotions and welcoming them as it is learning how to regulate them. I discuss this later in the explanation of Step 7.

Step 3: Promote Putting Emotions Into Words

After helping people pay attention to and welcome their emotions, coaches need to help them describe their emotions in words. People do not always need words for their emotions, but this is helpful when their emotions are signaling difficulties that need attention, or when they want to reflect on or communicate their feelings. Describing a feeling in words makes emotional experience more available for future recall. Once people know, for example, that they are feeling sad, they can reflect on what they are sad about, what this sad feeling means to them, and what they should do. A list of simple emotion words, categorized into the basic emotion they express, follows (Shaver, Schwartz, Kirson, & O'Connor, 1987; see also Exercise 2 in chapter 5 of this volume).

- *Sadness*: sorrow, neglected, misery, despairing, homesick
- *Fear*: distress, panic, hysteria, apprehension, anxiety
- *Anger*: bitterness, fury, wrath, scorn, spite
- *Love*: attraction, affection, passion, infatuation, yearning
- *Joy*: zeal, enraptured, triumphant, eager, euphoria, optimistic
- *Surprise*: amazed, surprised, astonished, wonder, awe.

Metaphors are also useful in helping people symbolize their inner experiences. Thus, conventional images, such as feeling stuck in the mud, feeling dirty, or swimming against the stream are all helpful. Novel or idiosyncratic metaphors, such as "a volcano erupting in your chest" or "just all prickly and sharp," are helpful in catching sensations. More complex images help capture what cannot be expressed otherwise; for example, attempting to catch a client's feeling of a diminishment by reflecting back his image of his loss of substance with "Its like your self is all squeezed up against the back wall of your body, leaving you all hollow inside," or responding to another client's sensation of a lack of solidity with "It's like you are just a chalk outline of yourself on the street that could be erased any moment."

Naming emotion is a first step in regulating emotions. With words people can speak their emotions rather than act them. Attaching words to feelings give clients the ability to reprocess their emotions. Being able to describe their emotions allows them to get a handle on what they are feeling and can help them deal with their problems. Thus, if a client can describe a feeling about having difficulty engaging in social conversations with the words "I feel so left out," then he is better able to understand the experience in a new way, which he might express by saying "I try so hard to keep up with the conversation, but actually I'm often not interested. That's why I've nothing to say. I don't really find it interesting." The client is now in a new place: one where he recognizes that he is often not interested in social conversation. A new meaning has emerged, and this new perspective no longer focuses on his feeling of being left out. New possibilities emerge that were not available in the state called "feeling left out." Another client might describe some of the confusion and difficulty she is experiencing in taking over a job as supervisor of a team. She says, "Whenever I meet with my team, I feel like there's a ghost in the room [the old supervisor], and I can never fill her shoes." The client then moves on to acknowledge "I can't do what she did. It's crazy trying to be like her. I'm different and will use my own strengths." In these examples, describing feelings in words promoted the generation of new meaning. New meaning does not always arise, but often it does, and coaches need to promote it by helping capture feelings in words and differentiating central meanings.

Knowing what they feel also gives people a sense of control of their experience and strengthens their belief that they have the power to do something about their feelings. Being able to label feeling in words facilitates a separation from the feeling. By putting emotion into words, people have in effect simultaneously created a new perspective from which to see the feeling, as well as provided a label for the feeling itself, thereby knowing what they feel. It is now "I" who feels "worthless," and "worthless" is not all of what I am; some distance is created. I now feel that "worthless" is something I am "feeling" rather than it "being" me. This act of naming lets clients experience themselves as agents, having a namable feeling, rather than being passive victims of the feeling. Rather than representing reality or truth, the feeling is seen as their current reaction. This establishment of the self as an agent in relation to a feeling helps establish a sense of distance from the feeling, and this distance provides strength and agency.

Putting experience into language also helps overcome trauma. If clients have suffered trauma or endured deeply painful experiences, coaches can help them begin a reconstructive process with the help of language. This allows them to develop accounts of what occurred (Pennebaker, 1994; Van der Kolk, 1993). The capacity to describe emotionally traumatic experience allows clients to make sense of their experiences. Before, they had not coded the experience in language, and the experience remained as sights, sounds, and images in emotion memory. Now, in a safe environment, being able to put the traumatic experience into words enables people to think about and describe their traumatic memories and thereby gain some control over the terrifying experience. They become authors of the experience rather than victims of it. This process of naming emotions helps marry the verbal and nonverbal parts of the brain and creates an integrated experience in which people can both feel and think about their experience simultaneously.

Step 4: Identify the Client's Primary Experience

Both coach and client need constantly to explore whether the client's emotional reactions are his or her core feelings. Thus, when a client talks about feeling angry when a colleague at work disagrees with her, she needs to explore whether at some level under the anger she basically feels threatened. Or, when a client angrily says his spouse accused him of being inattentive, he needs to explore whether behind his anger he feels unappreciated. A coach will need to help a client who is worrying about her child leaving home for college recognize that, under the worry, she feels sad. The ability to identify primary emotions is one of the core skills coaches train their clients to develop. Coaches do this by constantly focusing people's attention on their bodily sensed feelings and empathizing with their feelings. With practice, clients become adept at monitoring their own feelings.

In life, monitoring whether a feeling is a core one does not mean losing spontaneity. It does not mean becoming highly self-conscious or introspective. Rather, emotional awareness involves the development of an automatic skill that operates at the periphery of awareness. This tacit level of apprehension constantly lets people know what they are feeling, and when a feeling is not a primary one, without them explicitly thinking about it. This form of tacit knowing involves a knowledge that is similar to how people know how to turn a corner on a bicycle without falling off, or how to drive a car without thinking (Polanyi, 1966). To do this, people automatically and simultaneously integrate many cues. In emotion awareness this form of knowing is used not to stop one from falling off a bicycle but to sense when one's emotions are veering off track. For example, people's brains monitor their whole bodies, so, for example, if one is aware one knows when the box one is lifting is too heavy for one's back. When something happens that exceeds the normal level of background sensation, the brain registers this. It sends a pain message to make people aware that they need to do something about this distressing state of affairs. It tells them they need to change their actions to bring things back within acceptable limits. This ongoing monitoring also happens with emotion: The brain can signal people with a feeling, without explicit thought, that the emotion they are experiencing is not their primary emotion. This is how people either simply know they are feeling something else deep down, or they just sense that they are not quite at the heart of the matter.

Primary emotions are based on one's automatic first-order evaluation of the world and what is happening to one and one's body . "Know thyself" means to know one's core emotions, to know one's most basic evaluation and response to any situation in which one finds oneself. This may require hard work; however, it is only by becoming aware of one's primary feelings that one can be in a position to choose whether to follow them. With practice and honesty, clients' primary feelings will start to come to them more spontaneously. They will feel sadness at loss, anger at violation, and joy at connection with others or at achieving goals. They will also more easily discern when their anger is covering fear or when their crying is obscuring anger. Coaches will know that their clients have reached the necessary level of awareness when their clients are more easily able to apprehend what emotion their secondary anger is covering, or that the emotion they are feeling at the moment is not really what's at rock bottom. Some people come to coaches with this skill in place; and Phase 2 is more relevant to such clients, but others need considerable amounts of practice to learn this skill, until it becomes automatic.

PHASE 2: LEAVING

Once people have arrived at a particular place, they need to decide whether that place is good for them. If the place seems like it will enhance their well-being, then they can stay there and be guided by what is in the place. If, however, they decide that being in this place will not enhance them or their intimate bonds with others, then this is not the place to stay, and clients have to find the means of leaving. Therefore, Phase 2 involves helping people decide whether they can trust the feeling at which they have arrived as a source of good information or whether the feeling is not helpful and needs to be transformed.

Step 5: Facilitate the Evaluation of Whether the Primary Feeling Is Healthy or Unhealthy

This fifth and very important step occurs once a client has identified a core feeling. Coaches and clients then together need to ask "Is this feeling adaptive, or is it a maladaptive feeling possibly based on a wound of some kind?" If the person's core feelings are healthy, they should be used as guides to action. If they are unhealthy, they need to be processed further to promote change.

Essentially clients, in collaboration with their coaches, have to decide whether their emotions are healthy responses in given situations. This is often done implicitly but is key: The coach cannot determine what is true for the client. Individuals ultimately have to decide for themselves if their emotion in a particular situation is one to be trusted. No one else can or should decide this for another person. The emotion a person feels at a particular moment is an automatic evaluation of the situation in relation to his or her well-being. This is the automatic first level of evaluation provided by emotion. The person then has to consciously consider this primary evaluation and decide what to do with the feeling. This second-level evaluation, done through conscious reflection using conceptual processing, also is a fundamental part of exercising emotional intelligence. Thus, clients need to reflect on and decide whether their feeling provides good information worthy of following. Coaches can train clients to do this and even can help them decide by coexploring with them and providing input, but ultimately clients have to make this decision on their own. Thus, a client might clarify that his anger is a healthy, adaptive anger and say

"Yes, I trust this feeling. I feel wronged and demand reparation," or he confirms that sadness is the core emotion by saying "I've lost something important and need to recuperate." Clients also might decide that a feeling is not helpful, that their anxiety is unrealistic, their shame reflects a damaging history, their anger is not helpful to them, or their sadness is preventing them from living more fully.

People can recognize that a feeling is not helpful to them once it has been accepted fully. The paradox is that if the feeling is judged as not acceptable—as "not me"—it cannot be changed, because it hasn't been accepted. Only when a feeling has been accepted can it be evaluated and changed if necessary. This second-level evaluation of the adaptiveness or maladaptiveness of an emotion is one of the most complex decisions people have to make. To acknowledge that "I feel angry" but that "This is not a healthy anger that is going to help me" requires balance and wisdom. It involves awareness of the situation that is evoking one's emotions and of one's own emotional history. To exercise emotional intelligence people need to be aware not only of their feeling but also of whether their emotion is a maladaptive response from the past that is still with them. They also have to integrate their emotional responses with all their personal and cultural learnings and with their values. When people function with emotional intelligence all this is integrated in a rapid, silent process of deciding whether a response is healthy or unhealthy. When people sense there are difficulties with their responses, they need to stop and reflect. This second-level reflection involves assessing not the rationality of the emotion but its adaptiveness. If an emotion is adaptive, then it should be followed. If an emotion is maladaptive, then its expression needs to be regulated, and it needs to be understood and transformed.

Greenberg and Paivio (1997) studied emotion in the treatment of affective disorders and childhood maltreatment and found that people's core maladaptive feelings mainly related to two major basic emotions: shame and fear–anxiety. They also related to two very basic views of the self: (a) feelings of worthlessness and a view of the self as a failure—a "bad me" sense of self—or (b) feeling fragile and insecure and viewing the self as being unable to hold together without support—a "weak me" sense of self. In these instances maladaptive core feelings of shame were central to the "bad me" sense of self, whereas fear was central to the "weak me." Fear and shame thus often appear to be unhealthy, even though in some cases they may be healthy responses to situations. To change the core vulnerability that leads them to so much fear and shame, people first have to access it. Next, they need to identify their basic negative view of themselves; finally, they need to heal the basic fault and begin to build a stronger sense of self. Rage, too, can be a core maladaptive feeling, especially in people who have experienced violence. Here the core scheme contains negative views of others. Rage is often very closely connected to fear as a trigger but, as well as being secondary to underlying vulnerability, it can be a primary maladaptive response that needs to be transformed.

Step 6: Identify the Destructive Beliefs or Views Attached to the Maladaptive Emotion

Identifying maladaptive feelings helps people get to the destructive beliefs or construals that are so much a part of them. Maladaptive feelings are almost always accompanied by beliefs or views that are hostile to the self or blaming of others. Destructive thought processes and beliefs need to be identified if they are to be overcome. These beliefs, such as "I am worthless" or "I can't survive on my own," often accompany or help artic-ulate a complex maladaptive feeling state. Such beliefs do not always sit in people's heads, in language, and these beliefs do not cause the problem. Instead, articulating the belief is a way of representing the emotional prob-lem in language. When beliefs are conscious and occur as repeated thoughts they help maintain and intensify maladaptive feeling states. Thus believing "I am a failure" or "I can't cope" intensifies the states that produce these thoughts.

People often experience destructive beliefs as a negative voice in their heads, a harsh, internal voice that has been learned, often through previous maltreatment by others, and is destructive to the healthy self. This internal hostility often leads to vicious self-attacks that leave people stuck in their unhealthy feelings. Whelton and Greenberg (2000) found that the degree of contempt with which a negative belief is expressed is predictive of proneness to depression. Even more predictive, of nondepressiveness, was the degree of the self's resilience in response to the contemptuous beliefs. The more pride and assertion a person showed in response to self-criticism, the less likely he or she was to be vulnerable to depression. To change the contempt, the destructive beliefs, and the totality of the experience they represent, a person must first articulate the beliefs in words. This articu-lation in language gives people something to hold onto in dealing with these feelings. Emotion coaching involves changing articulated beliefs not primarily by confronting their rationality or their validity but by accessing alternate emotions and beliefs that challenge both the usefulness to the person of the destructive beliefs and that these beliefs are the only ones accessible to the person.

In addition to articulating beliefs about self, such as "I am unworthy," into language, clients also need to develop insight into their complex con-struals of the world and the emotional learnings about patterns of conse-quences that govern their worldviews. Thus clients may come to realize that their beliefs that "they had to appease a parent for fear of damaging him or her" led them to view themselves as wrong or useless rather than challenge the parent. They may come to see that it is their inability to trust and the expectation that people will "get you if you aren't careful about what you say" that leads them to such interpersonal anxiety. They may see how this originated in a family culture of hostility in which people never expressed how they felt. Coaches need to help people develop insight into these governing beliefs or construals to help them change.

It is not insight alone that leads to change. Rather, once articulated, these views of self, world, and others can be changed by accessing alternate experiences to undo them. Beliefs and construals are language-based representations of core emotion schemes that need to be changed. Putting the belief or construal into words allows it to be discussed, reinspected, and challenged. Accessing maladaptive feelings and identifying destructive beliefs paradoxically facilitates change, first by accessing the state that needs to be exposed to new experience and second by stimulating the mobilization of a healthier side of oneself by a type of opponent process mechanism. We will now look at how to access people's opposing internal emotional resources and how these resources can be used to challenge dysfunctional beliefs.

Step 7: Facilitate Access to Alternate Adaptive Emotions and Needs

This step is at the core of the leaving phase and involves changing emotion with emotion. How does a coach help a person access a more resilient sense of self to challenge a maladaptive state? A key method is by *shifting people's focus of attention to background feelings* that are currently activated but not attended to. Thus, in response to feeling the core emotion of shame or fear of maltreatment that is leading a client to feel worthless, the coach needs to guide the client toward his or her healthy anger at being treated badly that is implicit in his or her more dominant experience of shame. The anger may be in the client's voice or face or in his or her phrasing. Expressions such as "How could he have done that?" or "It was just awful!" said in a slightly angry way, provide access to the person's subdominant anger at being wronged. The client then focuses on and intensifies this subdominant but present emotion while saying how angry he or she is. Or, a client's sadness at loss, apparent in his or her face or tone of voice, might be focused on.

Bad feelings can also be replaced by happy feelings. This can and does occur in therapy—not in a simple manner by, for example, trying to "look on the bright side," but in a meaningfully embodied fashion. For example, in cases of grief, laughter has been found to be a predictor of recovery. Thus, being able to remember happy times, to experience joy, can be an antidote to sadness (Bonanno & Keltner, 1997). Warmth and affection similarly often are antidotes to anxiety. A coach can transform a protest-filled submissive sense of worthlessness by guiding clients to find the desire that drives their protest. The desire to be free of their cages and to access their feelings of joy and excitement for life. It has been hypothesized that at least some of the positive effect of happy feelings depends on the effects of the neurotransmitters involved in the emotion of joy on specific parts of the brain that influence purposive thinking. Mild positive affect has been found to facilitate problem solving (Isen, 1999). Coaches thus need to help people focus on and feel healthy, adaptive emotions. They need to help people express these adaptive emotions to someone—sometimes to the coach, to an imagined other in an empty chair, to another part of the self, or to another person. This helps people consolidate their healthy experience and expression.

A second and more active way in which coaches can help clients access their healthy, more resilient emotions is *by focusing them on their needs, goals, and concerns.* Asking a client the key question "What do you need when you feel this?" is a good way of bringing goals into awareness. Once people are aware of their goals, then coaches can help them assert their needs and use these needs to challenge their negative beliefs. Focusing people on needs, wants, or goals helps them mobilize themselves to change. People's goals also have been shown to influence their interpretations of situations and their behaviors. Once clients become clear on what they want—once a goal is clearly defined—they can activate their internal resources required to attain the goal. Given that an emotion results from the appraisal of whether a need or goal is being met, goal clarification evokes new emotions and associated action tendencies to facilitate goal attainment.

How does clarifying a need or goal produce change? Davidson (2000) studied emotion and the brain in rats and offered an intriguing suggestion. It appears that raising a goal into awareness may activate representations of certain reinforcement contingencies in working memory by anticipating goal attainment. This produces positive affect that maintains reinforcement-related behavior. Raising goals to awareness, then, appears to activate an automatic process that can provide a reinforcing memory of the positive feeling associated with goal attainment. This process is self-mobilizing, and it generates the positive affect associated with anticipating goal attainment. This positive affect acts to inhibit the emergency amygdala output. Raising goals to awareness also can activate memory or connections of behaviors associated with getting to the goal. Thus, saying "I need comfort," especially in the context of a supportive relationship, opens up people's memories of the path to, and the experience of, past instances of receiving comfort. This is the shift in state necessary to mobilize internal resources. This brain process facilitates more approach-related behavior (Davidson, 2000). People thus can use their cerebral cortexes—the thinking, planning centers—to regulate automatic emotions, not by controlling them but by imagining possible positive alternatives. Emotions can be changed not by reason but by activating representations of alternatives associated with more positive emotions.

Thus, coaches need to help people focus on their healthy needs for protection, comfort, and affection in response to being maltreated as well as on their needs for autonomy and competence so as to free them from the oppression of their desperate need for approval. Having helped a client identify what he or she truly needs, which is usually related to his or her primary motivational systems (attachment, affection, and mastery), the coach needs to ask the client what he or she can do to begin trying to get some of what he or she needs. Identifying what people need is one of the best ways to help start a new, healthier feeling process. It helps people find alternate ways of feeling, being, and doing. The identification of alternate, healthy feelings and needs brings other goals into focus and is the primary means of accessing healthy internal resources.

Thus, when a person feels bad, worthless, or rotten, the associated feeling generally is one of fear, shame, guilt, or sadness. The need or goal at this time generally is to feel acceptable and worthwhile. A person's core healthy emotion is often either anger at being maltreated, sadness at what was missed, or both. When people are able to experience and name their core maladaptive feeling of shame (rather than avoid it), they begin immediately to gain some control over it, and then they can be helped to inspect it. They can identify the destructive voice associated with it and recognize that the self-contempt that produces the shame probably is a result of a past experience of maltreatment or was learned. When coaches help people understand that their shame is produced by contemptuous or threatening voices that they have adopted from their past, then they often are able to focus on their healthier core feelings of sadness or anger in response to the original situation. They now may find it much easier to feel acceptable and to feel they are entitled to have their needs met. This healthier sense of self then begins to reassert itself.

In therapy, I have so often seen that people's healthier life-giving emotions are activated in response to their own experienced emotional distress. People are tremendously resilient, especially when they are in a supportive environment. Everyone has the capacity to bounce back. Ultimately, their ability to take care of and support themselves allows them to face distress in a healthy way. People are able to call on this resilience and use it as a life-giving resource. When people are suffering or experiencing pain, they generally know what they need. They know they need comfort when they are hurt. They know they need to master situations in which they feel out of control. They know they need safety when they are afraid. Knowing what they need helps them to get in touch with their resources to cope. Coaching people to stay with their experiences of their distressing feelings thus helps them get what they need, and this motivates change. Further means of accessing alternate emotions are discussed in chapter 8.

Step 8: Facilitate the Transformation of Maladaptive Emotions and Destructive Beliefs

Having accessed adaptive emotions and needs and developed a healthier internal voice, people are in a position to make the final change. The eighth and final step involves helping people use their emotion to change emotion and belief. As I have argued, it is only through the experience of healthy emotion that emotional distress can truly be cured. Coaches cannot rationally argue clients into healthier emotional processes. They can, however, help them overcome their unhealthy feelings by coaching them to identify the destructive voices inside their heads, access their emotional resources, and then combat their negative voices with their healthier voices. A coach's job is to help clients find their alternate, healthy feelings and use these to transform their unhealthy feelings. Thus, clients' feelings of self worth or self-compassion transform their shame and fear into self-acceptance and self-support. The action tendency in empowering anger is to thrust forward, and this is incompatible with the shrinking away involved in fear or shame. The latter will be replaced or transformed by the former.

Coaching thus involves exposing people's unhealthy emotions to new, healthier, internal experiences. Helping people access their feelings of healthy sadness or anger exposes their fear and shame to new input. The feeling and shrinking action tendencies begin to be replaced with thrusting forward, reaching out, or recuperative tendencies while their self-critical views of themselves as bad or worthless are challenged by the sense of worth accessed in healthier emotional states. People are thereby helped to integrate all parts of their experience into a new sense of self and to feel more self-accepting.

It is important to note that people are continually changing in light of emerging goals and opportunities. People are not static. Thus, once they feel their shame at being maltreated, or their fear of rejection, they also can contact their need to be valued. With their attention shifted to the new goal of being valued, they have in essence presented themselves with a new problem to solve: how to feel valued. When people discover that they can do something about their feelings, they can then prepare to solve their problems. Motivated both by their healthy aversion of pain and by their need for mastery and for human contact, comfort, and safety, people will mobilize new resources to cope better. In this process, an alternate, healthier part is helped to surface and is then used to challenge and change some of the person's core unhealthy feelings, beliefs, and hostile thoughts. The newness in this process comes from within, by accessing previously unacknowledged healthy feelings and needs, and from without by the affective attunement and confirmation of an empathic other.

At times people also need to be helped to get some distance from emotions that are overwhelming. For the process of changing emotion with emotion to be successful, people have to have sufficient ability to work with their emotions in the manner described. They have to name them, evaluate them, and identify the negative voice. When people are overwhelmed by their emotions, this cannot occur; a working distance needs to be created. This is when emotion regulation skills need to be taught and facilitated. I discuss these skills further in chapter 8.

Finally, clients need a facilitating environment in which to engage in the eight steps just described. They need a safe and validating relationship in which they can sort out their feelings; this is what coaches must offer. Talking with an emotion coach helps people sort out which feelings are healthy and useful and which are problematic and need change. Clients need coaches to validate and strengthen their emerging new feelings and new senses of themselves. Recognition from others is one of the crucial components of a new sense of self. People need confirmation from at least one other person. It is important to recognize that this need is a core ingredient of personal development. Thus, coaches need to both confirm clients' experience of what they feel and coach them to reflect on their feelings and access new possibilities.

THE COACH'S OWN EMOTIONAL AWARENESS

To facilitate the emotional work of others, coaches must have engaged in their own emotion awareness process. The exercises in this book offer an opportunity for coaches as and clients to practice this process. Probably the best training in the emotion awareness process is to experience it. It is only by working with one's own emotions that one can help others do this. It is only by allowing and accepting one's own emotions that one can see that emotions inform and organize people. It is only by learning to tolerate one's own unpleasant emotions that one can experience that such emotions come and go, and it is only by suffering one's own pain and triumphing over it that one truly knows that this is possible for one's clients. Thus, this is a case of "Physician, heal thyself" rephrased as "Coach, train thyself." Coaches should train themselves, or receive training, in identifying and staying with their own emotions. They need to learn to symbolize their feelings in words and evaluate their nature, identify their maladaptive emotions and, above all, learn how to access their positive emotional resources to transform and soothe the maladaptive emotions in themselves.

Clients benefit from coaches' emotional awareness in the process of learning to master their own. Coaches need to be authentically present and congruent when working with clients' emotions. Emotional awareness and emotional honesty in coaches promote emotional awareness and emotional honesty in clients. Congruence, however is a complex concept, and I offer some pointers on what I mean by coaches being in touch with themselves and how to use this congruence (Greenberg & Geller, 2001).

Authenticity or congruence can, at an initial level of analysis, be broken into two separate components (Lietaer, 1993): (a) the ability to be aware of one's own internal experience and (b) transparency, the willingness to communicate to the other person what is going on within oneself. Congruence thus clearly has two components: an internal component, which involves awareness of one's own flow of experience and transparency, and an outer component that refers to explicit communication.

The claim that being transparent is therapeutic requires specification of the set of preconditions and beliefs, intentions, and attitudes that are needed for this aspect of congruence to be therapeutic. To simply teach young or new coaches that they should be congruently transparent is not always helpful. This is because being transparent presumes a certain level of personal development and certain intellectual and value commitments. Congruence thus does not stand alone as a therapeutic ingredient. Therapeutic congruence, as well as involving awareness and transparency, also requires that the therapists' internal experience arises out of attitudes, beliefs, and intentions related to doing no harm to clients and to facilitate their development. This is the psychotherapeutic equivalent of a Hippocratic oath.

Being aware of one's own flow of internal experience and connecting with the essence of one's feeling are two central components of congruence (Rogers, 1959). The internal-awareness component is the easiest aspect of the concept to endorse as universally therapeutic. It always is helpful for coaches to be aware of their own feelings and reactions, because this awareness orients them and helps them be interpersonally clear and trustworthy. This inner awareness and contact involve being receptively open and sensitive to one's own moment-by-moment, changing experience and being fully immersed in the moment. With this type of presence in the moment and emotional awareness there is less likelihood of a discrepancy between verbal and nonverbal behavior, and clients come to know that what they see is what they get. They learn that the coach has no hidden agendas. This helps the client feel safe and reduces interpersonal anxiety, which in turn allows clients to tolerate more intrapersonal anxiety and thereby to explore more deeply. If coaches are not aware of their feelings in interaction with their clients they are unlikely to be effective helpers, because they will not have access to vital information being generated in their relationships. It would be like operating in the dark. Therapists know that they are most effective in helping others when they are clear and aware of their own flow of internal experience, especially experience that is generated out of their moment-by-moment interactions with clients.

The case of transparency, or the communication component of congruence, is much more complicated than the self-awareness component. Being facilitatively transparent involves many interpersonal skills. It involves the ability to express not only what one is truly feeling but also to express it in a way that is facilitative. Transparency thus is a global concept for a complex set of interpersonal skills embedded within a set of therapeutic attitudes. This skill seems to depend on three factors: (a) the coach's attitudes, (b) on certain processes, and (c) on the coach's interpersonal stance.

First, and probably most important, congruent responses need always to be embedded within Rogerian therapist attitudes and need to be communicated nonjudgmentally. In life one clearly can be congruently destructive. Therapists know that being destructive is not what is meant by the term *congruence* as it relates to therapy, because the term *congruence* is really tacitly qualified by a number of other beliefs and views on *how* to be congruent. I thus find it helpful to use the word *facilitative* to qualify the word *congruent*. The coach's expression of him- or herself needs to be done for the client's benefit.

When coaches express themselves genuinely, they need to do so in a *disciplined* manner. They do not impulsively blurt out whatever they feel in the moment but communicate important core feelings. To do this, they need first to be aware of their deepest level of experience, and this may take time and reflection. Next, they need to be clear on their intention for sharing their experience—that this sharing is for the benefit of the client or the relationship and not for themselves. It is also important for therapists to be sensitive to the *timing* of disclosure, sensing whether clients are open to what one has to offer or too vulnerable to receive it. Discipline thus involves the therapist (a) not simply saying whatever he or she is feeling and (b) making sure that what is expressed is a core or primary feeling rather than a secondary one. Another qualifying concept that I think helps clarify the transparency aspect of congruence is *comprehensiveness*— that congruence needs to mean "saying all of it." The coach expresses not only the central or focal aspect that is being experienced but also the meta-experience, what is felt about what is being experienced and communicated. Thus, saying that one feels irritated or bored does not comprise comprehensive communication. Coaches need also to communicate their concern about such a revelation potentially hurting their clients and express that they are communicating this out of a wish to clarify and improve a connection, not destroy it. This is the meaning of "saying all of it."

Being congruent may involve the therapist saying what he or she is feeling in his or her body at the time. It may involve speaking of a feeling that has been persisting over time and is not actually being felt at the moment in any visceral way. Also, being congruent may involve the therapist saying something that spontaneously captures the sense of the moment. The current or general feelings being congruently expressed may range from compassion to anger, from threat to joy and, depending on which emotion is being felt, it will be expressed in a very specific way, with its own expressive intentions. Anger, for example, may be expressed to set boundaries and to assist in resolving a feeling of being wronged; compassion may be expressed to share it and to comfort. Fear probably is usually expressed to inform the other person of one's reaction to him or her.

In addition to disclosing what one is feeling, being congruent might involve saying what one is thinking, disclosing an image, sharing a past experience of one's own, or commenting on the interaction between therapist and client. The intentions here may be to convey one's understanding or deal with a relational difficulty. A highly integrated or well-trained coach dedicated to helping will produce congruent responses of a different kind and quality than will an undifferentiated or egocentric therapist or a novice. Being therapeutically congruent thus can be seen as involving a complex set of interpersonal skills as well as the intrapersonal skill of awareness.

Finally, it is the coach's interpersonal stance that is important in understanding facilitative transparency. Affirming and disclosing stances are the key that make transparency facilitative. *Affirming responses* are the baseline responses in supportive therapies. What does a therapist do when he or she is feeling not affirming but angry, critical, and rejecting and cannot get past this feeling? For a transparent response to be facilitative, feelings need to be expressed as *disclosures*. It is not the content of the disclosure that is the central issue in being facilitative; rather, it is the *interpersonal stance* of disclosure that is important. Implicit or explicit disclosure involves a willingness to, or an interest in, exploring with the other person what one is disclosing. For example, when attacked or feeling angry, coaches do not attack but rather disclose that they are feeling angry. Coaches do not use blaming, "you" language; instead they take responsibility for their feelings and use "I" language that helps disclose what they are feeling. Above all, they do not go into a one-up, escalatory position in this communication but rather openly disclose feelings of fear, anger, or hurt. When the problem is one of the therapist experiencing nonaffiliative, rejecting feelings or a loss of interest in the client's experience, the required interactional skill involves being able to disclose this in the context of communicating congruently that the therapist does not wish to feel this. Or, the therapist might disclose these feelings as a problem that is getting in the way and explain that he or she is trying to repair the distance so that he or she will be able to feel more understanding and feel closer to the client. The key to communicating what could be perceived as negative feelings in a congruently facilitative way is generally occupying an interactional position of disclosure that is nondominant and affiliative. Thus, in the context of feeling angry, a coach's facilitative, congruent process involves first checking whether anger is his or her most core feeling; if it is, then this needs to be disclosed in a nonblaming, nonescalatory fashion. If the coach is feeling more hurt, diminished, or threatened, rather than angry, then congruence involves being aware of this and disclosing this in an effective manner.

For example, a very fragile and explosive client once told me during an intense encounter that she hated me because I was so phony and that I acted so presumptuously in assuming that I understood what she felt. She said she saw me as a leech trying to suck her emotional life out of her and that although I professed good intentions I was really out to destroy her. Under this mounting, relentless attack I first felt defensively angry. I succeeded, however, in going beneath my anger and told her I felt afraid of her anger. Tears came to my eyes as I told that I felt hurt. This was disclosed without blame or recrimination and without an explicit power- or control-related intention to get her to stop—just a disclosure of what it felt like inside for me in that moment. This disclosure helped the client stop her attack and drew from her some concern for me. The skills of congruent responding in dealing with difficult feelings thus involve identifying one's own internal feeling response—this is the general skill of awareness—and translating this intrapersonal experience into affirmative, disclosing interpersonal responses.

A VIGNETTE FROM THERAPY: PUTTING THIS ALL INTO PRACTICE

A client in a session appeared depressed and talked about feeling lonely. I guided his attention to his feelings of loneliness with an empathic response of how he was "just feeling all alone." My client acknowledged this. In response to the question "Do you feel this now anywhere in your body?" the client pointed to his chest. I asked him to put his hand there and speak from that feeling. He talked about his deep sense of isolation. He said "I feel empty, like I'm not there unless I talk to someone or do something." His loneliness welled up, and he began to cry. He articulated this feeling, expressing how much he yearned to just be touched, to have a hand placed on his shoulder or his chest to know that he exists, and to be reassured and comforted by the touch. He said all this while gently rocking back and forth in his chair. I highlighted his expressive motion and asked him to develop it into an explicit self-comforting activity. He then described how isolated he felt in his previous marriage. He felt this for years before the marriage broke up, and he expressed how he had felt "unseen" and "uncared" for by his ex-wife. I continued to help him to search for, describe, and express his feelings in words by empathically reflecting both his feeling of having been invisible and his need to be seen and valued just for him. My client then began the inevitable process that occurs in so many of us: that of criticizing himself for being so weak and needing others so much. He worked for awhile on this unfortunate process of self-diminishment, putting his criticisms into "you" language and pretending he was another person criticizing himself; however, he overcame these criticisms by focusing on his healthier aspects. He focused on his ability to read the message from his feelings of isolation in an empty marriage and the legitimacy of his needs for contact. These feelings acted as a valuable source of information to him about what he wanted and led him to reflect on the importance to him of being in a caring relationship. He talked about how amazed he was when his new girlfriend actually wanted him and approached him for physical contact.

As my client talked about his girlfriend's active pursuit of him, he held his arms and hands straight out, gesturing that his response to her pursuit was to protectively hold her at bay. Paying attention to his hand movements, I asked him what it was like when he was approached by her. He said that he initially feels anxious when she approaches and that he internally pulls back. On further exploration of this feeling, I encouraged him first to own this possibly unhealthy fear rather than avoid or ignore it. He talked first about how unworthy he felt and then about how he was afraid to let anyone close for fear of being known and rejected again. This led back to his feelings of having been dropped by his ex-wife, not for another man but for her art. I shared with him that I could imagine how unimportant that must have left him feeling. His experience of feeling rejected was further evoked and intensified when I asked him to pretend his ex-wife was sitting in the chair across from him. I asked him to imagine telling her how unlovable this had made him feel. This helped him access his feeling of having been poorly treated by her. A feeling of anger emerged. He felt more empowered, because he was able to feel angry at the offense rather than rejected and sad. The session concluded with the client clearly describing his need to feel loved and to be self-affirming and his intention to continue to seek the closeness he wanted with his girlfriend. He also said how reassured he felt when his girlfriend told him that she felt insecure and needed his reassurance. He said he saw himself reflected in her. To realize that she felt insecure when he felt so positively toward her must mean that she did love him, even though he felt a similar inner insecurity. He thus reflected on and constructed a new view of his past relationship, of his own worth, and of his ability to be in a new relationship. Although this was a new, tentative outlook in need of further validation, it definitely marked a new beginning in his view of himself. This event involved many of the processes we have talked about:

- paying attention to body experience,
- focusing on what is experienced in the present,
- experiencing feelings,
- describing feelings and meanings in words,
- expressing feelings,
- overcoming self-critical interruptions,
- owning unhealthy emotion (fear and unworthiness),
- contacting healthy emotion (anger),
- contacting needs and wants (the need to be treated fairly and the need to be loved),
- creating new meanings, and
- the coach's presence and sharing.

When people are searching for, describing, and expressing their feelings they need to track their moment-by-moment experience, just as my client did in the previous example. Coaches need to work like artists: continually trying to highlight and develop aspects of their experience, focusing on a phrase here, a gesture there, and the particular vocal qualities of the voices inside their heads or their spoken voices. Feelings of poignancy indicate a direction for deepening an experience. A sigh indicates a sense of sadness; the shape of a person's mouth can indicate that tearfulness is near. People need to pay attention to and allow themselves to feel all these emerging experiences until a core meaning emerges, as when my client experienced his isolation and desire for contact and comfort. Emotion coaching is thus primarily a process of directing attention to internal cues so the client can put them into words and to then help clients make sense of what they are saying. In this therapy example, once the emotional experience of loneliness was aroused it was alive and in the room; there was no need to search for it. The task was to pay attention to it rather than avoid, control, or cancel it. The client needed to put it into words, to allow it to exist and to help him make sense of it. This involved identifying what the emotion was urging him to do and informing him of his needs. After this people then have to decide on a course of action, taking into account all the important emotional information as well as all the external factors. They then need to integrate all of these sources of information into a reasoned course of action.

II

THE ARRIVING PHASE: COACHING FOR EMOTIONAL AWARENESS

5

ARRIVING AT A
PRIMARY EMOTION

Coaching involves helping clients make sense of their bodily feelings. Once people become aware of what they are feeling, they need to either (a) follow their feelings and act on them or (b) judge that their feelings are signaling to them that something within is in disarray. The dilemma is when to be changed by emotions and when to change them. Some emotions tell people that their internal world is upset. If this is so, they need to pay attention to what is awry and figure out how to set it right. In well-functioning individuals, as soon as emotion emerges, so too does recognition of what is felt. Emotion and awareness work together to help people discern appropriate courses of action. Integrating emotion and reason in this way is truly the heart of daily living. Coaching involves training people in this skill if they do not have it or helping them develop it if they already possess it.

The first pivotal moment in the steps of the emotion coaching process laid out in the previous chapter is helping people evaluate whether their currently felt emotion is their core feeling. Having arrived at a feeling, coach and client together must ascertain whether they have arrived at their destination or whether this is simply a waystation soon to be left behind. What cues help indicate whether a state is a primary, one with which a person should stay?

EVALUATING WHETHER AN EMOTION IS A PRIMARY EMOTION

People recognize a feeling as core because it is fresh and new. It arises in the moment in response to shifting circumstance, whether this is internal or external circumstance. It is not an old, stagnant feeling that lingers and does not move. It is not the stale resentment followed by resignation at remembering being overlooked for a promotion 2 years ago; neither is it the sense of complaint that comes from unresolved hurt. Instead, it is a vital feeling that often leaves the client feeling very open and perhaps vulnerable. This can be the anger a client feels at being taken advantage of, the sadness at losing a dear friend to disease, or even the embarrassment or shame of a blouse or fly being open in public. In therapy it is often a previously unacknowledged feeling that is the most primary.

Once a client is feeling something, the client and coach, or the unfolding process between them, need first to answer the following question: Is this feeling a secondary feeling that is obscuring a more primary one? For example, is this anger covering hurt? Is this hurt covering anger, is shame or fear behind the outrage, is there pain lurking behind the emptiness, are there even deeper tears in the despair? Is this emotion a response to another, more fundamental feeling? Is this client anxious about her sadness, afraid of her anger, ashamed of her vulnerability, afraid of her fear, or sad about her shame?

To identify primary feelings, the coach has to promote a process of exploration, helping the client push through the underbrush of secondary feelings and thoughts to see if there is something more there. When clients arrive at primary emotions, a type of internal bell often rings and tells them "Yes, this is it. This is what I most truly feel." Without practice, discerning one's true feelings is difficult, so both coach and client really have to concentrate. Having a coach as a co-explorer, who lends another pair of ears and also concentrates, helps the client pay attention in this search for primary feelings. It helps, too, when the coach knows something about the client's emotional terrain in general. It is helpful, for example, when the coach knows that complaint in the client's voice often signals a fusion of unexpressed sadness and anger and that having each emotion expressed separately helps the client differentiate the feeling.

EXERCISE

Ask clients what they feel in response to something important to them or what they feel in the present as they are talking. Ask them to pay attention to the sense in their body of their feeling. Help them name it and then ask themselves "Is this my primary feeling? Is it clearly felt and fluid?" If it is, they are probably experiencing a primary feeling. Or they can ask themselves, "Is this a stuck, bad feeling, knotted and tense?" Ask them if it is a feeling that they want to be rid of, that feels wrong. Is it filled with complaint, blame, or helpless passivity? If so, it is very likely a bad feeling that is obscuring a deeper primary feeling that needs to be unearthed by further exploration.

Recognizing primary feelings is in part an art and in part a skill that can be learned. Primary feelings feel good. They feel right, even if they are painful. Even if they are unhealthy, they help people feel more solid. They clearly are what the person feels. Thus, a client might say, "I feel like I have failed" or "I feel broken or afraid of being alone." This is said without panic. Rather than leaving the person confused or anxious, it provides a footing. The person will be able to admit "Yes; that's it. That's what I feel."

People cannot determine whether a feeling is primary before they have experienced and explored it; it is the feedback from experiencing it and from the exploration process that tells them whether the emotion is primary. To the degree that there is something more to the emotion than at first seems apparent, it is not primary. If people are able to uncover a deeper feeling by being disciplined and focused and concentrating on their emotion, then the original feeling was not a primary emotion. Only the person can really tell. Although a coach can sometimes see if the client is showing signs of anger, sadness, fear, or shame, and can help him or her concentrate on what appears most central, the coach cannot easily evaluate which is the client's most primary reaction.

For example, in therapy, coaches can see if someone is engaged in a productive exploratory process. They can hear if people's vocal quality has a searching and exploring quality and if their eyeballs are turned inward and they are concentrating in a focused way on what is new and fresh at the edge of their conscious awareness. Coaches can see if clients are trying to bring something from the murky background into the clear foreground, and they can hear when clients have a clarity and sureness in their expression, when there is a release of tension, followed by feelings of relief and confidence. Coaches can see when their clients' eyes shine, when they sparkle with clarity, and when there is a sureness in their voice. One of the best ways of assessing whether an emotion is primary is by observing the effect it has on the client's subsequent process. If the emotion helps the client open up and produces further productive steps, it means the client has contacted an emotion that is functionally productive, and it aids problem exploration and problem solving. It therefore is a primary and adaptive emotion. An emotion coach needs to be trained to notice all the cues—both expressive cues and subsequent process ones—that help determine whether an emotion is primary.

When a coach is helping people sort out their primary feelings, it also is useful to notice whether their emotion is felt in response to something internal or external. Emotions that come from external cues are usually more specific and easier to identify. They might be clients' feelings of anger at a driver who cut across their path, fear at someone walking behind them as they are alone on a dark street, or the joy of getting breakfast in bed on Mother's Day or Father's Day. These responses to external cues have a sense of immediacy: The feeling swells in the moment and provides incontrovertible evidence of what a person feels. There is no confusion as to whether this is a primary feeling; it is spontaneous, fresh, and alive. The feeling will melt away as circumstances change, although the flavor may linger awhile.

Primary emotional responses to more internal processes have a slightly different quality. They are more likely to slowly wash over a person than to rapidly move him or her. For example, these responses may include remembering one's child's first birthday, or recalling the time when a child left home, or thinking about seeing a loved one after a long absence. These feelings are still primary, but they are less rapid and less action oriented. Thus, internally generated sadness about news of a loss received earlier that day may spill over when one is standing at the stove cooking dinner, or mowing the lawn, activities which in themselves do not make one sad. These internally generated emotions are poignant and full. They are felt some place inside, or all over. They may feel silky and velvety when they are soft and pleasurable feelings. Poets and writers, who are experts at capturing emotions in words after the turmoil or ecstasy has passed, can describe these feelings with lines such as "Do not go gentle into that good night," or they may describe "raging at the dying of the light" in response to a death, or combine words to describe the "sweet sadness" of a goodbye. Metaphors capture these emotions, and good actors convey them.

Feelings, however, are most likely not primary when the person is easily able to identify the thoughts that generated them. These types of thoughts could include "I sounded like a fool at the meeting. I didn't make any sense at all," or an internal negative voice that says "I'm bad because I didn't send a condolence card to my friend." Here it clearly is a conscious thought that precedes the feeling. This sample of negative self-talk gives merely a whiff of the type of chatter that can permeate people's consciousness and produce the type of secondary bad feelings that may mask a more primary sadness, shame, or anger. A coach's task in this situation is to help people identify what produces these negative thoughts. Clients may have to work hard to try and actually sniff out what lies behind their thoughts. They will have to discover what it is that they are feeling at their core that leads to the self-critical voices in their heads. Coaches may have to help them go back into the original situation and remember with full clarity the moment in the meeting in which they tried to speak up but the words did not come out clearly. They need to access memories of actual events rather than general memories of the meaning of experiences. Clients who think they will be reprimanded or found lacking if they speak need to go back to the maladaptive experience that is the source of these thoughts. They need, for example, to remember lying on the floor in their bedrooms when they were 7 years old, hearing the creak of the stairs as a parent came up. This will help them access their actual feelings. They will then begin to experience how scared they really were at that time. They will have to dig and search for the buried aspect they felt at that time. Their primary feeling may be a fear of abandonment and a basic insecurity, or it may be shame and a shrinking feeling of failure, or it may even be anger. Whatever it is, it will feel very different from the secondary bad feeling they get from their negative self-talk. A primary emotion is much more of a core feeling about the self, and identifying it is like arriving at a destination. People must then give their attention to this crucial primary feeling and the memories associated with it.

What they unearth initially may be a bitter truffle. They may remember feeling unvalued by parents or childhood friends, or having been rudely dumped by a first love. They could remember a feeling of failure related to a work situation many years ago. Whatever this wound is, however, it can yield a most delicate part of the self if the client deals with it with emotional intelligence. With care, this part of a person can transform itself from a bitter experience into a subtle and delicate part of the self, an essence that gives strength. By going into the wounded part of the self, people can find the gem of their adaptive, essential self. This healthy essence is a vital part that strives to be connected to others and to be effective. This part, once awakened, will resiliently exercise itself, given half a chance. The essential self, however, needs safety and encouragement, both from within and without, to help it emerge.

IDENTIFYING SECONDARY AND INSTRUMENTAL FEELINGS

Secondary and instrumental feelings have a different quality compared to primary feelings. Secondary feelings are too strident, too unbalancing, and too tense. They leave a person in pieces, feeling pulled and ruffled. They leave the person feeling disordered inside, not whole and smooth and not clearly in their center. A secondary feeling does not leave people breathing more freely. Secondary feelings are recognizable first because they make the person feel bad. However, they differ from unhealthy core feelings, which also feel bad, in that secondary feelings often are global or nonspecific. People often come to therapy feeling upset, uncomfortable, hopeless, or just vaguely annoyed. These feelings differ from primary maladaptive emotions because they are global and diffuse and more often are felt in response to situations rather than being about the self. Secondary feelings signal that something is wrong, but the person doesn't yet know what. He or she just feels puzzled, inexplicably angry, or despondent and wonders why he or she reacted this way. These puzzling bad feelings need to be explored and understood.

Secondary reactions, as I have discussed, are reactions to more primary experiences. They are not as deep, and they do not define a sense of identity. They often form part of the symptoms of depression, such as feeling blue, down in the dumps, defeated, dejected, or gloomy. They could be part of the symptoms of anxiety, such as feeling agitated, uneasy, tense, apprehensive, or a sense of dread. They can also be part of anger problems, such as feeling constantly hostile, bitter, scornful, spiteful, agitated, or grouchy. These are not the primary maladaptive feelings of shame, fear, anger, or sadness that may be part of a person's core identity. Of course, any bad feeling could be primary or secondary: This is the unfortunate complexity of it all. Each person has to learn to be his or her own judge of what type of feeling is being experienced.

If a person's feeling is a secondary bad feeling, a coach needs to help him or her explore it to get at the primary feeling. First coaches must help people become aware of, and name, the secondary feeling; then they need to slow things down and try and get at what is generating people's reactive or defensive emotions. The generating cause may be negative thoughts or "shoulds" about a specific behavior or event, such as "You should have worked harder on the report; you were boring people and were not very articulate or responsible." Then coaches need to help people get behind this self-talk to contact their most basic feelings. For example, a man may tell himself, "You should have more courage and be more confident." This tends to make him anxious. He may even say to himself, "Don't be such a wallflower—speak up!" This command makes him feel worse, and he feels bad about being so unsure of himself. This anxiety and despair are secondary—they may be painful and real, but they are not primary. Secondary feelings such as this often come from people telling themselves that what they are doing is no good. These are the feelings of inadequacy that result from people giving themselves "pep" talks such as "You should work harder at being confident" or "You shouldn't feel depressed, anxious, or unsure."

People's primary emotions, on the other hand, are the not-yet-discovered ones that lie at the heart of feeling depressed, unsure, or unconfident. Coaches have to help people discover what their primary emotions are. Sometimes a primary emotion is an adaptive feeling of being angry or sad, or it may be an unhealthy primary feeling that contains destructive beliefs about the person's whole self. The primary maladaptive emotion may be a core fear or anxiety about being rejected or of being unlovable; a feeling of basic insecurity, a feeling that one cannot survive without support; or a feeling of shame at being worthless or bad. Awareness of primary feelings is a first step on the path to intelligent living. Identifying primary feelings is not easy without a lot of practice.

Helping clients recognize their instrumental feelings sometimes is even more complicated. These are so much a part of their normal way of communicating that they just feel natural. One person, for example, may feel a repeated sense of anger or generally feel aggrieved. Another may always complain or communicate in a suffering manner that the world is unfair or that things are too much to handle. People use their voices or facial expressions to convey that nobody cares about them, or they give off "poor me" signals. Others may appear perennially cold and distant, out of a sense of mistrust or a feeling that no one really cares about them. These instrumental emotional expressions have somehow proved useful to them in their lives. They either helped them to get sympathy or to excuse or protect themselves. A way for clients and therapists alike to recognize that such emotions are not primary feelings is the recognition that, rather than being reactions to specific situations, these are a part of a person's manner and occur across situations. They represent a style of interacting with others to get what is wanted or needed. Coaches can ask clients to complete the following exercise to help them identify these feelings.

EXERCISE

To become more aware of your instrumental feelings, ask yourself what your most frequently expressed attitudes are in relation to others. Ask "Do I constantly feel wronged and angry and try to get apologies? Do I complain how unfair or difficult things are and try to get help?" Ask yourself "Do I get any gains from expressing this feeling? Does it give me control, get me sympathy, or release me from responsibilities that are mine?" If so, it is likely this is more of a feeling "racket," a style of expression that in the past has given you some gain, even though it may seem like suffering.

Instrumental emotions are so much a part of a person's style that it is difficult for the person to recognize them. Because instrumental emotions are so familiar and regular that they occur without awareness, people often need feedback from others to recognize them. In such cases the coach's job is to give observational feedback in a nonjudgmental way about how he or she experiences the client's expressions. In general, probably the best way for people to learn about their instrumental emotions is to pay attention to how other people perceive them. Clients can be encouraged to ask appropriate others for feedback on what emotion they most often express to them and what type of impact this has on them. Even more difficult is for a client to ask the people to whom he or she is most close if they feel manipulated by any of the client's emotional expressions. Is one's hurt or long face always making other people feel guilty or forcing them to be one's caretaker? Is one's anger or a raised voice silencing others or making them afraid? If so, people need to ask themselves where they learned this form of instrumental expression. They then need to find some more direct way of asking for their needs to be met. Another way of recognizing that an emotion is instrumental is by a person's ability to put the feeling on the back burner at a moment's notice, without much difficulty. Thus, if the aim of one's anger is to dominate, or if the purpose of one's tears is to evoke sympathy, then when the phone rings the person can switch off his or her feelings with no difficulty. This does not happen with primary feelings.

TWO TYPES OF EMOTION: VIVID AND VAGUE

There are two ways in which emotions emerge and two ways in which emotion coaches can help people become aware of what they fundamentally feel. The first type of emotion is one that is vivid, clearly available, and strong. The second type of emotion occurs when people can feel something in their bodies, but the feeling is not yet clear. Coaching with either type of emotion involves helping people receive brain messages through their bodies. In regard to the first type of emotion, coaches help people make sense of what their emotion is telling them; for the second type of emotion, coaches must first help people find the feeling, then help them symbolize and make sense of it.

The first type of emotion is a powerful experience that washes over a person. It rises up in the person and can take over. There is no need for the person to go looking for this emotion: It comes to him or her very clearly. Once people have learned words for emotions, they can easily describe them in words, such as "I feel angry, sad, or afraid." Being able to name the feeling allows them to reflect on it. They may then say, "I feel annoyed at her constant interruptions and want her to stop," or "I am sad about his departure." When emotions are readily available, they can be intensely felt but not yet easily put into words. As coaches help people pay attention to these clearly felt emotions and begin to speak from them and describe them, the meaning of these emotions emerges. People then begin to speak from the strong feeling and say "I feel hurt by what you said," or "I'm feeling anxious about the meeting tomorrow." I call this process *describing and expressing* emotion.

In the second, more complex form of emotional awareness the feeling does not rise up as readily as in the first case; instead, it is implicitly present in the person's body. Promoting awareness of these bodily felt feelings involves engaging people in an internal search for what they are feeling. I call this process an *experiential search* for feeling, and it often involves the use of focusing (Gendlin, 1996; Weiser Cornell, 1996). In such cases the core feeling is often unclear or initially even absent. When it is unclear, there is a felt meaning that people can physically sense. They know there is something there, but they do not yet know what it is. It is similar to having a word on the tip of one's tongue, but it is a feeling that is sensed somewhere in the body. When people are eventually able to put words to it, it is often not a basic emotion, such as anger or sadness; rather, it is a complex, felt meaning, full of implications such as feeling "over the hill"; "all washed out"; "fulfilled"; or feeling hurt, disappointed, small, unsupported or trapped. I now discuss working with each of these emotion awareness processes.

Describing and Expressing Clear Emotions

When people are clearly feeling an emotion—say, feeling sad—they need to have their feelings recognized and have them named. It is important for coaches to both validate and empathically offer words to clients who are unable to name their feelings to help capture those feelings. Some people first need their feelings recognized by another person before they can come to symbolize them. At first they may not have the ability to name them. This is where validation and empathic understanding help. Just as a parent first helps a child to recognize a feeling by validating it and empathizing with it, so too does an emotion coach help the person at first find words for emotions.

Description of emotion can be promoted in conversation, or in writing about the emotion in a diary. Sometimes it helps to use more nonverbal means, for example, asking people to paint what they feel, to sculpt it, or to play it in music, and then trying to help them put it into words. Once people have words to describe their emotions, they can work with their emotions. The goal of describing feelings is to transform aroused emotion into words. Instead of people simply acting on their emotions, coaches want to help them develop the ability to speak them. A parent coaches a child first by giving words to his experience—saying, "Johnny is angry" when Johnny yells and grabs his toy from another child—and continues by saying to Johnny, "Don't hit the child with your car; instead, say 'I'm angry.'" Similarly, therapists coach their clients to put words to their feelings and then make process suggestions about how to handle the feelings.

The Creating Aspect in Feeling

It is important to recognize that what people feel, in part, always depends on how they describe it. Naming an emotion is not simply discovering the right words to fit the feeling, like finding the right key to fit a lock. There is not only one correct word. Feelings are not sitting inside a person, fully formed and articulated, waiting to be named. People are very active in creating what they feel by the way they describe the feeling. Helping a person articulate how he or she feels is more like the process of looking at the clouds and "seeing" a rabbit in the cloud than like the process involved in seeing an actual rabbit hiding behind a tree. Emotional naming involves as much creation as it does discovery.

Even clear emotions do not simply rise up with a clear voice, telling one what is felt and what should be done; rather, the person's reflective self immediately starts interacting with the emerging feelings so that by the time the person articulates the emotion it is as much created as discovered. What people feel always involves how they explain their experience to themselves. For example, clear, consciously felt anger or sadness starts off as a bodily stirring that could involve a facial expression or a change in breathing tempo. The more the person is aware of the beginning elements, the more he or she begins to put these clues together to understand the emotion. The myriad cues or components are an emotion potential that, when blended with related memories, life experience, images, thoughts, and beliefs, become a conscious emotion. The person's brain preconsciously puts together all the elements to form a feeling with a complex personal meaning. Consciously experiencing an emotion involves an automatic process similar to the brain synthesizing a set of letters into a word. People create their final emotional experience by putting their felt sense, itself a synthesis of more basic elements, into words. They add to what is there by the way they uniquely label it. Feelings thus ultimately depend on the meanings created by the way they are described in words and the story created to explain an emotional response (Greenberg & Pascual-Leone, 1995, 1997, 2001; Whelton & Greenberg, 2000). The coach needs to be aware of the constructive process involved in emotional experience and be aware that his or her presence and input influence this process.

First, a safe, facilitating environment influences the level at which the client will attend. Second, the coach's empathic offerings will help shape the client's experience. It is not that there is not something there that the client is feeling. There is a referent that will not let itself be misshaped into something that does not help it develop, but it also is not clearly formed. The empathic coach cannot influence an emotion into something completely different, like changing sadness into happiness. However, a bodily sense can be called tiredness or can be differentiated into a feeling of disappointment or even helplessness. A coach's differentiating use of language often helps people construct a more meaningful experience. A particular feeling could be described as sad, disappointed, discouraged, or even exhausted with a struggle. Happy would not fit this internal experience, but anger might catch a bit of it. Thus, the feeling is not just sitting there, fully formed, with only one correct name. Certain words will not fit at all, but a variety of others will all capture and help articulate some of the complexity of what a person is feeling. Each method of naming has slightly different implications. Thus, people are always combining many elements of sensation, perception, and thought to form a feeling. The feeling can be articulated in a variety of forms, but only a certain set of descriptions help capture what a person is feeling. Feelings, even when they are very clear, also are also complex. There is always more to a feeling than any one description can capture. A person may be angry, but he might also feel sorry that he is angry. The place from which a person's anger comes may involve either a fear of retaliation or a steely resolve with no fear. People generally also never feel only one thing. In describing a feeling it is useful to pay attention to all that is there.

Focusing on Vaguely Felt Emotions

The second basic emotion awareness process involves helping people focus on a vaguely felt emotion. Often a person may feel something only vaguely rather than being overwhelmed by the emotion. At other times he or she may know rationally that something—for example, a recent loss—is important but just not feel anything. At other times a person may be on a merry-go-round of alternatives and may not know what he or she really feels or wants. To help people in any of the above states, coaches need to guide them in an internal search to get a clearer sense of what they do feel. A coach can help people by acting as a surrogate information processor and empathically offer them symbols to try and capture what they feel or by suggesting the process of focusing, first described a number of years ago by Gendlin (1962, 1996). This process is described next.

Imagine a client who is experiencing a vague feeling about something, such as not getting a wished-for promotion, an acceptance to graduate school, a bid for a contract, a wish satisfied in an intimate relationship, or even an acceptance of a request for a date. A coach might suggest to this client that it could be helpful to focus on the feeling and then would give some focusing instructions, outlined in Exercise 5 (Gendlin, 1996; Weiser Cornell, 1996). The coach might simply say, "Close your eyes and go inside to that place inside where you are feeling this feeling. Just stay with it and see what you feel now in your body and let whatever comes come." The client then needs to stay very gently with the feeling, and the coach needs to encourage him or her to welcome it rather than try not to feel it, and to let it come in whatever way it comes. It can be helpful to tell the client to pay attention to any images that may come, even before words. Here is a more specific example. Jonathan is feeling upset about not being awarded a grant for which he applied. He found out this morning and has been very busy since. He has felt tense and upset throughout the day, but this is the first time he is talking about it. He says to his coach that he is shocked, that he was sure he would get it. After talking about it for awhile, and saying how upset he is, Jonathan says he does not really know what he feels. The coach suggests that he focus. The process of arriving at his feeling goes something like this: After focusing his attention on the unpleasant sensation in the center of his chest, Jonathan says "I feel really disappointed." As he continues to focus on the feeling in his chest he imagines the review committee sitting at a table criticizing his proposal. Then what comes for him is "I feel like a failure; I'm also a bit ashamed." His body sense changes. New words come from this sense: "I'm unsure about what this means for the next steps of my life. Maybe I'm on the wrong path." His feeling develops slightly as he stays over time with his body sense of it. What comes next is,

> I feel really disappointed. I'm a bit embarrassed, but most of all I'm tired and discouraged. I don't want to keep trying and repeatedly not have my efforts pay off. I feel powerless. That's it! I feel so powerless. That's what is so disturbing.

The tightness in Jonathan's body now releases a bit. He feels something shift. The coach encourages Jonathan to stay with whatever is new or fresh that comes from the feeling. Then, out of another place in his body what emerges is "I feel angry at the unfairness. A lot of it is politics and image management." His anger feels better than feeling powerless. Then what comes is "Maybe I was shooting too high. I didn't really want to do this; it's not really where my heart is. Maybe I need to reorganize my priorities." Notice how nonlinear this process is: Accessing his anger allows him to let go of, or reorganize around, the goal that has been frustrated. At this point this emerging sense, that not winning the grant is not so important to him, either feels right to him or does not. Jonathan's bodily sense, if he really listens to it, will tell him if this meaning fits. If it does, he will again feel a shift in his body. The bad feeling will continue to open up and lighten. It no longer will be a tight black ball. It will begin to move and become more fluid, spiraling into a different pattern, letting in more air and lightness. Something will have shifted.

This shift is quite different to what occurs when the meaning created is an excuse, a type of self-deception to save face or deceive oneself. In the previous example Jonathan's statement "I didn't really want this" could be an excuse if deep down in his heart he was still set on doing this type of work and he was trying to convince himself that he did not care anymore. Then his inner bodily feeling might change, but in quite a different way. It would become tighter. His shoulders might tense, and his voice might become strained, even if it is only the voice in his head. He will tense some part in his body in his efforts to distance himself from the disappointment, to support the deception and to protect himself from some feeling he feels that he simply cannot bear.

It is important to note that the whole process in which the coach has encouraged Jonathan to engage is not one of thinking about the issue in any effortful sense. Rather than spinning ideas around in his head, Jonathan is paying attention to his body. Words and pictures are coming from the felt sense. This is quite different from a reasoning process; it is more like seeing than doing. It is a process in which he is more a recipient of impressions than actively problem solving. This process has more in common with free association than reasoning, but it is highly body focused. In Jonathan's experience in this example the following now occurs.

He continues articulating the felt shift as "I wanted recognition, acceptance, material gain. This is what I wanted, and I still feel I deserve it even though the review committee doesn't." Now an even clearer core feeling of anger emerges: "I feel angry at my efforts being thwarted." This combination of feeling legitimate and feeling angry puts Jonathan in a new, more empowered state. This major shift occurs by consolidating what his goal, need, and concern are. An alternate resolution could have been one of Jonathan seeing his goal as unreasonable. The following could have emerged: "I feel angry at the wrong," "I feel sad at the loss," or even "I feel relieved at not having to carry through with what I proposed. It would have demanded a lot. I aimed too high." Then he would be able to let go of his prior goal and construct a new one. He would say, "I'm relieved it is over. I will turn my attention to something else." Jonathan would now feel that the way to attack the problem was to do something active. He would be mobilized, because he would no longer feel hopeless. He might set out to get feedback, change his approach, try again, or change directions. Whatever way he resolves it, it was feeling something new that led to the change. Feeling angry and empowered helped him overcome his hopelessness and clarify his goal. Alternately, the sadness of loss would have helped Jonathan grieve, accept the loss, and give up the goal. He would then withdraw his efforts and recuperate. Later he would decide to focus on a new goal. He might begin to clarify that "Really, I don't want to keep working so hard. I've reached my ceiling. Maybe I will retire. I've always wanted to travel and read more. Maybe this is an opportunity in disguise," or he might say, "I'll change my focus. I really wasn't going with my strengths in that proposal. I need to reorient myself." Whichever solution emerges would come about by means of a body-based feeling process that leads to the creation of new meaning.

What Jonathan did can be seen as fitting into the two previously delineated phases: arriving and leaving. I focus here on describing the arriving part of this process and discuss the leaving part in chapter 7.

EMPATHIC COACHING IN THE ARRIVING PHASE IN THE CONTEXT OF VAGUE FEELINGS

Coaches in this process need to be able to dwell in their clients' feelings, to be able to sit with them, just letting clients be wherever they are. This is often difficult for many helpers, especially in Western "fix-it" cultures in which doing something to modify the problem is favored. In the delicate moment when the other person is experiencing difficult emotions, such as feeling like a failure or feeling powerless, a coach can be most helpful by listening empathically. Then the coach can help in creating new meaning—not by giving advice but by helping the client pay attention to internal alternatives that are at the edge of his or her awareness.

When therapists don't follow this empathic focusing approach they move clients away from symbolizing their experience toward a more conceptual form of problem solving and often to secondary feelings of frustration, as seen in the following dialogue:

Client: I feel upset, like there is something there underneath but I don't really know what it is. It's vague.

Therapist: OK. Let's try and identify what brings this about. Let's try and be a bit clearer. If we could really help you identify the cause of this or what brings it about you'd be better able to cope with it. Right now though, you say you don't know what it is.

Client: Yes, and it's so frustrating. Like I can't figure out what it is and then I feel so out of control. It must be my lack of self-esteem that causes all this.

Coaches, rather than promoting premature figuring out, can be most helpful by being highly attuned to their clients' feelings and by helping them to stay focused on their internal tracks. Recall that people's internal emotional signals might be so slight that detecting these signals might be difficult. They may need to be very attentive, and have their coaches, as a type of surrogate experiencers, running the experience through them, trying to find words to describe the experience, helping make more attention available to focus on these subtle signals. Coaches help clients make more attention available first by providing safety. Safety helps clients increase the amount of attention they have available by reducing their anxiety. Second, by lending support and confirming whatever emerges in their clients, coaches help them internally concentrate their beams of attention to capture and solidify any emerging, newly felt alternatives. Any attempted figuring out, reformulations, new views, or solutions, proposed by clients themselves or offered by coaches, always need to be within the clients' immediate zones of proximal development and in their ranges of readiness. Coaches should not try to focus clients on goals they won't be able to achieve right away; this just increases their senses of failure or inadequacy. Thus, when someone is feeling hopeless or helpless, focusing on his or her coping possibilities before acknowledging the helplessness or hopelessness, and before he or she is ready to concentrate on coping, will just make matters worse.

In the previous focusing example, the coach helped Jonathan to stay very gently with the feeling, to welcome it and let the feeling come in whatever way it came. In this case the feeling that emerged was "I feel really disappointed." Then the coach encouraged Jonathan to dwell on the feeling, to be able to sit in it, just letting it be whatever it was. As I have mentioned, this is often the difficult part for many people, especially in fix-it cultures. Instead of trying to fix what he felt, Jonathan articulated it; he described the feeling in words. What emerged most clearly was "I feel like a failure; I'm a bit ashamed. What will I say to others? I'm unsure about what this means for the next steps of my life. Maybe I'm on the wrong path." He fully received the feeling. Once he did this, he was able to tease apart the different messages the feeling was sending him. The feeling developed into "I feel really disappointed. I'm embarrassed, but most of all I'm tired and discouraged. I don't want to keep trying and not succeed. I feel powerless. That's it! I feel so powerless. That's what is so disturbing." If Jonathan tried to change the feeling at this point, before he had truly acknowledged and accepted it, he probably would have driven the feeling underground. Then confusion would have set in. He would have felt "I just feel confused; I don't know what I'm feeling. I feel nothing."

The next step involved transforming the feeling. What is important to notice at this point is that if Jonathan continued feeling powerless, he might have had a clearer understanding of that feeling, but he would not have moved beyond it. The coach facilitated the transformation of Jonathan's powerless feeling by helping him focus on what was new and fresh in what he was feeling. This is where the leaving phase begins.

EMOTION SEQUENCES IN IDENTIFYING PRIMARY ADAPTIVE EMOTIONS

Once emotions begin to be focused on in their own right as important aspects of the therapeutic process, it is important not only to assess each emotion but also to understand the significance of the sequences in which they occur. The latter is crucial. It has become clear from the study of the process of emotional change that particular sequences of certain emotions are important in resolving specific problems. Facilitating productive sequences, and changing unproductive ones, then become important therapeutic goals.

Two-Step Sequences

Implicit in the steps of emotion coaching are a number of important two-step sequences that occur when one is working to access primary emotion. The first sequence is that anger is often a reactive feeling to, or sometimes a defense against, an original or more primary feeling of sadness, hurt, or vulnerability. Another major two-step sequence is the inverse of the above sequence. This is where sadness obscures the original anger. When clients have learned that it is unsafe to experience and share their original sadness–hurt–vulnerability and they cover it with anger, emotion coaches need first to acknowledge the client's secondary anger and then promote the client's experience of the sadness beneath the anger. After acknowledging the anger, the coach must first help locate its source and target and help the client find an appropriate way to express it. If, however, the process stops at this point, clients often remain stuck in their angry blaming, and no lasting change results. This occurs because the original hurt has not been acknowledged and processed or responded to.

One way to reach the original hurt is to invite clients to examine what they are feeling immediately after they have expressed their anger. After the secondary feeling is expressed, a window to the original primary feeling of hurt or sadness often opens. Another way to approach the primary feeling is to empathically inquire about the original experience that led to the client's anger. For example, "Something must have hurt very deeply to leave you feeling so angry. How did you feel when that happened?"

Three-Step Sequences

A more complex process involves three-step sequences. A major three-step sequence, for example, involves first acknowledging secondary despair, hopelessness, or rage as the first step and then, as a second step, accessing the primary maladaptive feelings of shame or fear that lie beneath the first state. The third step in the sequence then involves accessing more adaptive emotions, usually a healthy anger or sadness that is overregulated or not readily accessible. States such as a shame-filled sense of worthlessness, an anxious sense of basic insecurity, or a paralyzing state of traumatic fear often are found beneath despair, hopelessness, or rage that lie closer to the surface. These are avoided states that need to be approached and faced. This two-step sequence, however, is not yet fully therapeutic. The third step is needed so the person can move beyond the maladaptive states to access another set of healthy emotions and motivations. Thus the person often can access anger at violation and sadness at loss and their associated adaptive needs as healthy resources. These adaptive emotions and needs are used to help overcome or replace the maladaptive feelings of fear and shame. These three-step sequences embody the basic change process involved in changing emotion with emotion.

A frequent, unproductive three-step sequence, however, often occurs when there is a conflict around feeling a newly accessed primary adaptive emotion. Thus, clients may present with a sad feeling of hopelessness, and through exploration may access anger at violation, but then they may feel guilt or anxiety about their anger. In such a case the third emotion interrupts and prevents the second emotion, which is the healthy adaptive response.

As described earlier, in the discussion of two-step sequences, when working with secondary anger the coach's task is to help the client experience the sadness–hurt–vulnerability that is underneath the repetitive anger. Sometimes, however, as soon as the original hurt is activated clients interrupt this feeling and return to the safer expression of anger. Then the coach needs to explore the client's interruption of the primary painful affect. Although clients interrupt their primary feelings for different reasons, it is often because the original affect of pain or sadness arouses a third, aversive feeling of shame, anxiety, or guilt.

For example, if the coach inquires about the client's interruption of the original hurt or pain, clients will often say something like "If I let in the pain, it's like admitting he hurt me" or "I'm weak." As soon as clients who express these types of concerns experience the hurt that underlies their anger, they usually have painful feelings of shame or humiliation. Thus, if the therapist draws out the original sadness that underlies the anger a third feeling of shame or humiliation that is associated with being hurt is aroused as well. Clients then interrupt both the original sadness and the shame associated with it by automatically returning to the anger, which helps them feel stronger. Therapists thus often see repetitive cycles of anger–sadness–shame–anger.

Other clients might experience anxiety in response to feeling the original hurt. For example, some clients will say that if they let themselves feel sad or hurt, then "No one will be there, and I will be empty or alone," or "My need will drive others away." These clients feel painful anxieties on experiencing their hurt or pain, and they avoid this anxiety by automatically returning to their anger. Each step of the three-step sequence needs to be recognized for what it is and worked with until the adaptive emotion is allowed and accepted.

INTERRUPTION OF EMOTION

Arriving at primary feelings, be they vivid or vague, often involves overcoming blocks to feeling. Some people habitually constrict their emotional experience and expression and are cut off from their feelings or from specific classes of feelings. Processes of interrupting emotion vary. Helping people become aware that they avoid their experience, and how they avoid or interrupt their experience, helps them become aware that they are agents in this process and can undo what they have done. These steps of becoming aware of the "that" and the "how" of interruption are important precursors to emotion coaching to help people get to "what" they avoid. People can use extreme avoidance strategies or defenses, such as numbing or disassociation; or they might use more moderate avoidant processes, such as ignoring or distraction; or milder ones, such as stifling tears. Helping people to experience how they squeeze down their emotions, suck them in, and tighten themselves into a knot in order to not feel their anger, sadness, shame, fear, and pain is an important task. Overcoming these interruptive processes constitutes an important subgoal of emotion coaching. Facing dreaded feelings can be threatening, so safety and collaboration are necessary to promote awareness of interruptive processes. Collaboration provides safety and minimizes the development of opposition, misalliances, or impasses.

Coaches, then, need first to heighten people's awareness of their interruptive processes. The objective is for clients to come to experience and understand how they stop themselves from experiencing potentially adaptive emotions. Part of the rationale provided by coaches in helping people not be defensive when they are being helped to see these processes is to note that interruptions happen so automatically that the person has no control over them and that the goal is to regain control. It is important to help people understand how they suppress their emotions so that the interruption is no longer so automatic and they can regain some control or choice in the matter of their feelings. After heightening a client's awareness of the interruption, the coach might have the client practice and enact in the session how he or she does this to him- or herself. Or, coaches might have clients identify with the interruptive process and do it to themselves, or ask them to stop their anger, squeeze back their tears, or look away each time they begin to feel sad. This helps return control of the interruption. Coaches should help clients become aware of how clients are doing what they do and, eventually, what is being interrupted begins to be experienced.

In a recent study of interruption of emotion in therapy clients, a review of therapy session tapes revealed a variety of rapid, automatic affective, cognitive, and physiological processes by which clients inhibited their emotional experience (Weston & Greenberg, 2000). The model built from both clients' performance in therapy and their subsequent recall on reviewing tapes of their experience during those moments in the session revealed that they clearly often were aware of engaging in acts of self-protection and self-control. Their reports indicated that interruptions were motivated by a fear of emotion that led to a desire to avoid it. This culminated in acts of avoidance or control that resulted either in relief and feelings of control or, more often, in discomfort, emptiness, bewilderment, disconnectedness, and hopelessness.

Some of the clients' reports after reviewing moments of their own in-therapy process show how active and aware clients are as they talk with their therapists. Clients reported experiencing opposition to emerging feelings, fear of emotions and of losing control, and a desire to avoid emotions. They said such things as, "I was trying to stop myself from feeling sad. Here something is bubbling to the surface . . . the old reaction to old hurts . . . the physical reactions . . . in the chest, occasionally the stomach . . . It's a case of starting to lose control, so my natural reaction is to take a tighter grip."

In relation to fear, one client reported, "I was just afraid, I didn't know what was there or where it would lead . . . I knew it was important, but I was afraid it would be overwhelming." Another client said, "It scares me when he [the therapist] says 'hurt' because it's like I don't want to go there . . . there's a kind of a click of 'keep that away from me. I don't ever want to get involved with that anymore.'"

In terms of the desire to avoid emotion, one client said, "I wanted to get away from that room . . . physically I wished I could have gone away, because I didn't see it getting any better." Another reported, "It's getting tighter and tighter in here (chest) . . . restricting, so it relaxes and I take a breath, releasing the physical tightness I was experiencing . . . it's controlling it . . . the feeling is allowed to dissipate with the sigh and it slips away."

One sees from these reports how vivid a phenomenon interruption of emotion can be. Clients often are well aware that they are doing it. Although they identified these experiences as difficult and reported that they wished to avoid emotions, they all also said that it was helpful when the therapist focused on their interruptions or emotions. A coach needs to help bring clients' awareness of their interruptive and avoidance processes into the conversation by asking them what they are afraid of, what they are doing internally, and how they are doing it. When interruption is not yet in a client's awareness a coach needs to inquire into his or her subjective experience to help the client become more aware that he or she is interrupting his or her experience. People usually can easily become aware of what they are doing, such as looking at the ground, tapping their foot, or sucking in their stomachs. This is the first level of awareness: an awareness that they are doing something. As they pay more attention to this they will slowly become aware that they are avoiding or interrupting some feeling. They will finally become aware of what they are interrupting.

This often leads to allowing the emotion. One client, for example, reported the following about the allowing of a feeling of sadness after undoing her interruption:

- A wave came up from my belly.
- Tears formed.
- I experienced surprise that it was released from being all closeted up.
- I felt a release in my neck.
- I felt internally angry at people who didn't validate me in my childhood.
- Internally I was sad that I couldn't fix the invalidation.
- It was an unusual, very soft, vulnerable feeling.
- I allowed and gave permission to myself to feel my sadness.

PRACTICE EXERCISES

The first step in emotion coaching with people who have very little awareness of their emotion is to ask them to keep lists of their emotions or to keep an emotion diary or log. Below is an introductory exercise that can be given to clients to increase their emotional awareness.

Exercise 1: Getting to Know Your Emotions

The first task to help increase your awareness of your emotions is to keep an emotion log. Three times a day write down the last emotion you experienced, and describe your experience. Address the following points:

1. What is your name for the emotion?
   - If you find yourself using only a few words repeatedly, such as *frustrated* and *happy*, try and find more emotion words.
   - Words are categorized in chapter 4 in terms of which emotion they express.
2. Was it a more sudden onset emotion or a more enduring mood?
   - How long did it last?
3. Did you have body sensations with your emotion?
   - Tensing of body, jaw, fist
   - Trembling
   - Feeling sweaty or hot
   - Feeling cold
   - Heart beating noticeably
   - Other sensations. What were they?
4. Did thoughts come into your mind?
   - What were the thoughts?
   - Were they about the past, the future, or the present?
5. Did you act, or feel like doing something or expressing something?

- Move closer or away from it.
- Make an aggressive move toward it.
- Make a facial expression.
6. What brought on the emotion or mood?
   - Describe the situation.
   - Was it an internal event?
7. What information is your emotion giving you?
   - Is it telling you something about yourself?
   - Is it telling you something about a relationship?
   - Is it telling about your progress toward a goal?

Reflect on your emotional response to your situation and try and make sense of what you are feeling. In addition, identify what it is telling you to decide.

- Should you follow the feeling?
- Should you get to what's behind your feeling?
- Should you try to broaden your view to change your feeling?

Exercise 2: Emotion Log

Keep a log of your emotions (see Exhibit 5.1) at the end of the day or before bed. Check if you felt this feeling that day.

Exercise 3: Experiencing an Adaptive Emotion

Overcoming overcontrol to access your emotion can be accomplished by following the steps of the attending phase, discussed earlier. This is the most basic process in working with your own emotion. It is simple but crucial. Let's take an experience of sadness in the attending phase:

1. Stay very gently with the feeling.
2. Symbolize the feeling in words.
3. Receive the feeling fully.

Below are some pointers to help in this process using sadness as the feeling to be accessed.

- If when you enter the sad state you interrupt the experiences or avoid approaching the sadness, you need to become aware of how you do this. Maybe you think of something else, get scared, or say "I can't handle this." Be aware that you are interrupting and then choose the alternate route of attending to your sadness. You need to focus on your internal experience, the sensations and the bodily felt sense. When your attention moves away from your internal experience, or your

EXHIBIT 5.1
Emotion Log

Type of Emotion	Monday	Tuesday	Wednesday	Thursday	Friday	Saturday	Sunday
Happy							
Interested							
Excited							
Caring							
Affection							
Love							
Loved							
Compassion							
Grateful							
Proud							
Confident							
Hurt							
Sad							
Regret							
Irritated							
Angry							
Resentful							
Disgust							
Contempt							
Ashamed							
Guilty							
Envious							
Jealous							
Anxious							
Afraid							
Other							

concentration lags, you need to refocus your attention, directing it to stay with the sadness, to let it come, and encourage the feeling to emerge. Stay focused on your present experience, asking and describing what it's like inside. Attend to any current nonverbal aspects of your expression of sadness, especially your facial expression, quivering lip, and sagging cheeks, as well as your general posture, and invite the experience to come more fully.

- Notice sighs. A sigh is an expression of core importance that often indicates both the constriction of sadness and a sense of relief at having touched on it. Sigh again to help you regulate your breathing, letting in more air; this allows the feeling to intensify if that is what it is trying to do. Put some words to the sigh in order to help symbolize the feeling behind it. Evocative language and metaphor, such as "It's like wanting to cry out but being afraid that no one will hear me," help evoke the feeling. Memories of situations in which you have felt this sadness can be evoked by using imagery to make them as concrete and vivid as possible. You may imagine doing something, speaking to people. Thus in grief you may speak to a lost person and say what you miss about or what you got from the person. You may imagine being a child, alone again in the house, feeling afraid and abandoned, and calling out for your mother, who left you alone, or you may relive the experience of being spanked by a cold, harsh father. The goal of this is both to facilitate the allowing and expressing of your feelings, to let the tears come, and to help you experience the release and relief of full and complete expression. This will help you to symbolize the unique aspect of the sadness and its idiosyncratic meaning.

- In dealing with adaptive sadness—say, that of seeing a loved one hurt—you first need to recognize your own sad compassion and be moved to reach out and comfort the other. Be sure to breathe and let the sadness wash over you. Comfort and be comforted by the physical contact. Now the feeling lingers, because feelings always color the situation, and clearly it is sad that your loved one feels defeated, wounded, or like a failure. How do you let go of the sadness and move on? In addition to the skills of allowing the emotion there is the skill of not holding onto it. Here is where what you think about and say to yourself also are very important. Sad thoughts and painful memories at this stage will maintain and prolong the sadness, can produce that kind of wallowing, that type of sadness that you find so aversive, when you use that word to describe it.

- An empathically attuned helper might help you symbolize the meaning of the experience and capture your essential needs and goals, but except in the very distressing moments of life you can do it yourself. For example, in loss you may symbolize experience by saying "You meant so much to me. It's hard to feel any purpose without you." Then you need to establish an intention need or goal. Thus, you may say, "I don't want to ever forget you. I plan to carry on, drawing on what you gave to me." In pain you may symbolize your experience by saying, "I feel like my heart is broken, like I'm bleeding inside" and state that need: "I need to just live day by day until I heal."

- Not dwelling on your sadness and re-engaging with other things of importance to you help. The sadness will just come back in waves. It is important to sigh and breathe deeply, because the sigh requires you to remember for a moment what your sadness is about. Don't tighten up and try to not feel it; instead, let it come, but don't hang onto it—let it go, too. Making sense of it, talking to someone else about it, putting it in perspective, receiving support and commiseration on how hard life can be, all help. Moving on and engaging in life again is the crucial step. Going to bed or sleeping for awhile can do wonders provided that that serves as a fueling station for getting back on the road. When it becomes a permanent stop your sadness clearly has begun to reach depressive proportions, and you definitely need social support to help you get back on your feet. And so your sadness comes and goes, and you are richer for it, deeper, more appreciative of good times and more reflective on life in general: sadder but wiser. When you get stuck in it you are probably experiencing maladaptive sadness.

- To enter a state of feeling, so very different from states of thinking or acting, you need to be able to slow down. To feel is a slow process. It often cannot be done when you are talking rapidly, concentrating on content, or trying to communicate with others. You can of course rant and rave when you are angry and feel the heat in your body, or you can weep in despair and hopelessness. However, you cannot at the same time stay in contact with the complexity of what you feel and access what you are really wanting that lies behind your anger or your hopeless feeling. In this process you need to let thoughts and images go by and concentrate on the slower process of feeling until you are affected and able to receive the information involved in your feeling.

Exercise 4: Getting the Message

1. Imagine a difficult experience in your life.
2. Focus on what it felt like in your body. Don't fight it, just accept that this is what you felt. Breathe and welcome the message about how it was as painful or shameful as it may be. Accept it as this is what it felt like.
3. Receive its message. Give yourself permission to acknowledge that this is what you felt and that you do not have to do anything else right now besides register the message.
4. If it feels too overwhelming to even feel it, that is OK. You do not have to feel it or re-enter the scene; just let yourself acknowledge the message being sent to you by your emergency system about what you felt in that situation.
5. After receiving the message, soothe yourself in whatever way you can. Talk to yourself. Imagine a safe place to which you can go. Breathe. Do something good for yourself.

Exercise 5: Focusing

1. Clearing a space. Take a moment, and just be with yourself, get in a comfortable position, close your eyes. Breathe deeply and relax.

2. Focus on a bodily felt sense. Now pay attention inside your body to that place where you feel your feelings, and see what you are feeling there right now, notice the physical sensations that are happening there right now.

   Note: If your client reports that he or she does not feel anything, suggest the following:

   Think about a major issue standing between you and feeling good about yourself. As you reflect on this issue, notice the physical sensation in your body.

   If there is a particular issue on which your client wants to focus, suggest that he or she notice the physical sensation inside body while focusing on this issue.

   The sense occurs bodily, as a physical, somatic sensation. Often it is sensed in the chest or throat, some specific place usually in the middle of the body. It is an internal sensation and it is important to make the distinction between this and an external physical sense like tight muscles or a tickle on the nose.

3. Describe it in words. Now try and describe the feeling or the physical quality of that sensation that is happening. Where is it happening in your body? Put your hand where it is happening in your body and describe what is happening.

Describe the physical sensations, such as tightness, a knot, emptiness or heaviness, or pain. If your client describes something like "I feel fear" or "I feel rage," ask how that fear or rage feels in his or her body: what is the quality of that physical sensation? What is the sensation in one's body that one calls fear? Is it OK to be with this right now?

Helpful questions to ask,

- Does the felt sense have an emotional quality? If there is a tightness in the chest, is it a scared tightness, and excited, or happy tightness?
- What gets the felt sense so . . . (jittery, hot)?
- What is the worst of it?

Note: Often initially, there is a lack of clarity—that's why it is important to talk about physical sensations. The felt sense differs from an emotion.

It is good to get permission from your client to focus on the felt sense. Ask. Encourage your client to be gentle and accepting toward the felt sense. You can help clients accept and feel comfortable with their felt senses by suggesting that they be caring and interested in their senses even though it may be uncomfortable. Suggest that they accept the sensation in their bodies as an important part of themselves and that it is there because it is informing them of something.

4. Check that the words fit. See if the word that describes the felt sense fits. If the person is having a hard time describing it, it is important to help them articulate the felt sense by reflecting empathically what you sense is there.

5. Asking and receiving. Continue focusing inside where the sensation (tightness, aching) is happening now, receive any pictures or words, or images that come from the sensation . . . Whatever comes to you now, let it come, it doesn't have to make sense, just share whatever comes up. Receive any

words or pictures that come to you from the sensation, showing you what it is all about.

Helpful questions to ask,

- What does the felt sense need? What does the felt sense
  want? What would make it feel better?
- How would OK in your body feel?

6. Carrying forward and closing. Is it OK to stop in a minute
   or two or is there something more you want to say right now?

   Note: Help clients continue their experiential work in the
   session and discuss how they would like to carry forward their
   new understandings. Make sure that the client is okay where
   he or she has ended. If you have had to end before something
   is finished you can ask clients to take note of where they are
   and go back there when they can.

6

COACHING TO EVALUATE
WHETHER AN EMOTION
IS HEALTHY

Intensive observation of the emotions that were most prevalent in the York University psychology research clinic tape library of more than 100 therapies led to the development of a list of 15 categories of emotion, shown in Exhibit 6.1, to assist in the rating of emotional arousal (Warwar & Greenberg, 2000). Of these 14, anger, sadness, fear, and shame, in addition to the more complex emotion of pain, are the five fundamental emotions most important in psychotherapeutic change (Bolger, 1999; Greenberg & Bolger, 2001; Greenberg & Paivio, 1997). In this chapter I look at how to evaluate whether these first four emotions, which occur frequently, are healthy and how, as adaptive core emotions, they enhance people's intelligence. Pain is healthy and it warns of injury. A key feature of healthy core emotions is that they inform and organize people for adaptive action. The first task in emotion coaching is helping people evaluate whether their emotion is a core adaptive emotion. The emotion episode awareness training sheet at the end of this chapter acts as a general guide to the task of promoting awareness of primary emotion.

EXHIBIT 6.1
Emotion Categories

The following emotion categories are most relevant to psychotherapy sessions.

1. Sadness
2. Pain/Hurt
3. Hopelessness/Helplessness
4. Loneliness
5. Anger/Resentment
6. Contempt/Disgust
7. Fear/Anxiety
8. Love
9. Joy/Excitement
10. Contentment/Calm/Relief
11. Shame/Guilt
12. Pride/Self-confidence
13. Anger and Sadness (both present simultaneously)
14. Pride (Self-assertion) and Anger (both present simultaneously)
15. Surprise/Shock

EVALUATING WHETHER SADNESS IS HEALTHY PRIMARY SADNESS

People get sad when they leave or lose the ones they love. Sadness tells them that they will miss their loved ones when they are separated. Without this sadness, people would be a lot less connected and more likely to wander. Healthy homesickness draws people back to security and familiarity. People need to be helped to feel healthy primary sadness without shame or anxiety. Healthy sadness organizes a person to reach out for comfort or withdraw when hope is lost.

> David has recently immigrated. He is talking to his counselor about his experience at the airport when he was leaving his homeland to escape the injustice and tyranny that were prevalent there. He is 22 years old and eager to face his future overseas. He mentions how he wept when he said goodbye to his family at the airport, and he again begins to weep. These tears are healthy tears. They suggest that David will return to his land of birth every few years, when he is able and when his need to be reconnected to his family and friends overcomes his hatred of the horrors of his homeland. This is healthy, adaptive sadness. If David suppresses these feelings he is likely to later have difficulty adjusting to his new life. An emotion coach needs to help David allow himself to feel his sadness and to grieve his loss if his tears persist.

Sadness at the failure and loss of a relationship is another great source of sorrow. People get sad at how difficult their struggles are. They are sad because of the pain of life, and they are sad for not loving or feeling loved.

They are sad when they are misunderstood, when they are isolated, when someone they love pulls away, and when they lose a person forever or even for awhile. The sadness of loneliness is deep and wide.

> Dennis and Sharon came for couples therapy. Their issue is whether he will commit to marriage. Dennis is a 40-year-old lawyer who has never been married. Sharon is a 36-year-old schoolteacher who was previously married for a few years in her early 20s. Her biological clock is ticking; she wants a commitment and a child. After a number of sessions they end their relationship in my office with pain. Sharon weeps, and Dennis feels relieved, guilty, and sad. I feel sad.

Healthy primary sadness is a state that often can appear as a brief moment embedded in the complex ongoing process of life. It is characterized by a kind of momentary sense of loss, hurt, or feeling touched by a goodbye or an ending. At times one can feel the passing sadness of surrender, or the sadness of the giving up of a struggle and acceptance of the inevitable. At other times sadness can be deeply and fully felt. People cry at the loss and share their grief or disappointment. This healthy sadness is free of blame. Sadness often is one of the longer lasting emotions.

> Myriam, an advertising executive, has just received news that the proposal she had worked so hard to complete and on which she had pinned her hopes was rejected. She is crestfallen and devastated. Her partner in couples therapy reaches out to comfort her. She cries. The tears flow as she feels the healthy sadness that will help her let go and move on.

Sadness often involves crying. The general biological function of crying is to signal to oneself and others that something is distressing. It motivates the crying person and others to do something about the distressing circumstance. Crying is one of the first things infants do when they come into the world; it is motivated by the will to survive. It tells the self and others that one is suffering. When the crying genuinely stops, it signals that the suffering has ended. Crying within limits is healthy. Being able to cry and express what one is feeling inside helps promote intimacy. The positive effects of healthy crying need to be communicated to clients who struggle against their tears. When they are struggling, coaches need to say to them in a soothing voice, "It's OK. Let the tears come. There is a lot there that needs to come out." Crying is a means of communicating in addition to using words. It adds meaning. Often tears will flow when words fail. The tears may be saying a variety of things, such as "I've had enough," "I care," or " hurt." In addition, crying can express other emotions, such as joy or happiness, fear, or even anger. However, crying excessively, to the point that one is unable to communicate at all, can be unhealthy. Coaches can ask clients to complete the following exercise to help them identify their primary adaptive sadness.

Exercise: Sadness at Loss

Identify a situation in which you experienced a loss. This can be a loss of a person, a relationship, or a disappointment. Identify your feeling. Find a word or words that fit the feeling. Do you feel it in your body? Describe in words how your body feels. If you usually feel like moving your body in a certain way when you are sad, find some way to express it. Let your body speak. Sigh, droop, curl up, or let your face express your sadness.

Sadness and anger often go together. In grief, and in the separation of an infant from his or her mother, there often is anger at the separation, followed by sadness at the loss, or vice versa. People often feel angry toward the person responsible for a loss and feel sadness or pain about the loss itself. Therapeutic work often involves separating out these two emotions from the knots into which they become fused so that people can clearly identify the source of and the need in each and can express each emotion to completion.

EVALUATING WHETHER ANGER IS HEALTHY
PRIMARY ANGER

Anger is one of the most powerful and urgent emotions. It has a profound impact on one's relationships with others as well as on one's own functioning. Anger can be life sustaining, or it can be destructive. Anger should not be confused with aggression, which comprises attacking or assaultive behavior. Feeling angry does not mean behaving aggressively, and people can be aggressive without feeling any anger at all. A research study of people across four continents showed that anger is most often directed at loved ones because people feel the loved ones have done something wrong or frustrated them (Scherer, 1984a). The typical expression of anger seldom involves aggression but rather is directed to correct the situation or prevent its recurrence. Anger tells a person that something needs to change. This empowering type of anger is what clients need to be helped to feel. People need to know the source of their anger if they are to bring about change.

Felicity is sitting in the car talking to her spouse, Jim, for the first time today about something frightening that happened to her this morning. She had been walking past a construction site and almost been hit by a falling beam. Felicity and Jim arrive home while she is still describing her experience. Jim parks the car, opens the door, and gets out while Felicity is in mid-sentence, saying how frightened she was. She feels angry and offended that he doesn't seem to care enough to listen to how afraid she felt. If this anger is not expressed or used to inform her that she feels wronged, it will become a brick of resentment in a wall that will separate the couple. An emotion coach would help Felicity symbolize what she feels, identify the source of the anger, help her recognize her unmet need, and promote reflection on how best to communicate this need.

Aristotle saw anger as stemming from the belief that we, or our friends, have been unfairly slighted, and he claimed that we get angry with people who are insolent and who injure us by their insolence. Anger is provoked most effectively in an infant by holding the infant's arms so that he or she cannot free them. Anger is evoked by interference with something one wants to do. An offense against, or interference with, one's loved ones or oneself provokes adaptive primary anger. In anger one holds the other person responsible for an action that has injured one. This is accompanied by the belief that the other person could have acted differently because he or she had control over the offending action.

More than 200 years ago Immanuel Kant (1953), the great believer in the power of the mind to form categories that shape one's views of the world, recognized the importance of anger in preventing stagnation and thanked the fates for this "cantankerous capacity." He claimed that human beings wish for concord, but nature knows better what is good for the species. When people are clearly offended and clearly angry, their anger helps protect their personal boundaries from violation. Often, especially in Anglo-Saxon cultures, people experience quite a lot of anxiety and disapproval when they hear others being angry. They have been taught well to suppress their anger. For example, an overly pushy car mechanic who exploits Joan's dependence and holds her ransom when fixing her car offends her. Joan knows she is being manipulated and cheated, and she feels angry but, having been socialized to be polite, she says nothing. Afterward she feels depressed and cynical. It would have been far better for Joan to let her anger move her to assertively express herself than to feel deflated. With the energy and power that anger has provided, she can show that she has teeth and can protect herself from being taken advantage of. I do not advocate anger as a first line of defense, and I believe in the importance of conciliatory methods, but ultimately anger is an indispensable part of one's makeup, and people should not be too afraid of receiving its message.

Adaptive primary anger is often activated without one really knowing why. People do not necessarily have any conscious thoughts, such as "You are offending me"; they simply feel offended. Then they start to think angry thoughts. Anger can be activated by conscious thoughts, but more often than not anger is evoked without thought. An infant's first cry of rage does not depend on conscious thought about the environment. People also are quicker to become angry when they are tired, hot, or stressed. Free-floating irritability does not stem from any conscious thought, and anger felt while one is in an irritable mood lasts longer and is harder to manage because of the effect of moods on emotion and thought. Indeed, anger can actually be induced by certain drugs and diseases, and even by electrical stimulation, not linked to any particular thought or encounter. Anger is easily accessible throughout people's lives. Obviously it is an essential resource. The following exercise can help people access this resource.

Exercise: Anger at Violation

> Identify a situation in which you have felt wronged or unfairly treated or your rights have been violated. Identify your feeling. Find a word or words that fit the feeling. What do you feel in your body? Put some words to this feeling. If it makes you want to move your body, then do it. Find some way to express it. Identify the target of your anger. In your imagination or out loud say "I'm angry at . . . ," or "I'm pissed off because . . . ," or "I resent that . . . ." Find a form of expression that suits you. What happens after you express your anger in this way? Do you feel empowered?

ANGER AND GENTLENESS

Coaching people to handle anger and other hostile feelings in daily living requires special attention. The question always arises of whether one can simply express anger. What about attacking, yelling, or being critical of others? Are such activities healthy or wise?

It is important to help people recognize that angry feelings can be wholesome and are part of being human. Feeling angry or annoyed is as human as feeling sad or afraid. It is important, however, to balance anger with gentleness. Being gentle does not mean never being angry. Becoming increasingly gentle does not lead to the suppression of anger; rather, it will help one accept one's angry feelings as undeniably human. Gentleness is hard to maintain when unresolved anger lurks within. Anger that is driven underground eventually bursts out in uncontrollable and destructive ways. Anger should thus be allowed to come into the open from the beginning and be expressed in wise and moderate ways. For example, this might involve being direct with a friend. One may tell a friend how one feels by saying, "I feel angry because you didn't show up for our dinner date." Telling this to a friend is informative and may clear the air between the two. It helps clarify the relationship and may prevent future hurt or misunderstanding. Bottling up anger; becoming cold and sullen; letting anger out by kicking furniture, crushing things, or lashing out; holding onto it; or developing or embellishing how one has been wronged will not promote a growth of gentleness. Outbursts may relieve pent-up anger, but they might also increase a tendency toward venting and becoming more angry and explosive. Rather than engaging in outbursts or rage, the best way to deal with anger is to talk about one's feelings to others. The goal is to communicate feelings for their information value and not to be verbally aggressive. There are only two circumstances in which a display of anger is justified: to protect one's boundaries and to prevent being violated.

EVALUATING WHETHER FEAR AND ANXIETY ARE HEALTHY PRIMARY EMOTIONS

Fear is adaptive. Humans are among the most curious and the most anxious creatures on earth. Cats are probably more afraid than humans are, but fear has served humans well in their struggle for survival by tempering their curiosity. Imagine you are walking down a dark street, alone, late at night, in an unfamiliar part of the city. You hear footsteps behind you. You cross to the other side. The footsteps seem to follow. Your heart beats faster, you are perspiring, and you increase your pace. You want to run. This is healthy, adaptive fear.

Fear is highly unpleasant and provides people with a compelling survival-oriented signal to escape from danger or seek protection. It is generally a transient response to a specific threat that abates after one has escaped the danger. Anxiety, on the other hand, is a response to "threats" sensed in the mind—symbolic, psychological, or social situations rather than an immediately present, physical danger. It is a response to uncertainty that arises when one feels threatened. People's ability to anticipate lets them experience anxiety. It is a gift and a curse at the same time. Thus, people say they are "afraid" of the dark but are "anxious" about a future exam.

It is adaptive for clients to acknowledge both their primary fears and their anxieties. Acknowledging weakness and vulnerability, rather than having to present a façade of strength, helps people to be more human and stronger. Ignoring real fear or insecurity leads to too much risk taking and needless danger. Acknowledging adaptive, primary fear lets one know that something is threatening and helps one maintain secure connections with others as protection. Fear organizes people to flee long before they are consciously aware of what, specifically, the threat is. Adaptive primary anxiety, like anxiety before a big game or butterflies before going onstage, is not so different from excitement. The positive quality of anxiety is captured when, for example, one says one is anxious to see someone. This positive side of anxiety is about being ready for what one is anticipating.

Fear and anxiety operate tacitly and automatically. Often, however, primary fear and anxiety are maladaptive rather than healthy. Certain childhood or relational experiences characterized by unpredictability and lack of interpersonal control can, for example, produce many maladaptive anxieties in one's relationships with others, including fear of intimacy, fear of losing control, and fear of abandonment. It is more common for people in therapy to have maladaptive primary fear and anxiety than to have adaptive fear and anxiety. Coaches can use the following exercise to help people identify adaptive fear.

Exercise: Fear and Anxiety at Threat

> Identify some threat in your life right now that represents uncertainty or danger, real or imagined. Identify your feeling. Find a word or words that fit the feeling. What do you feel in your body? Put some words to this feeling. If this feeling makes you want to shift your body, then do it. Find some way to express it. Let your body reflect the feeling. Check your breathing. Breathe, and say "I'm afraid or anxious." Identify the threat. Now find some way of calming yourself and coping with the threat. What internal or external resources can you draw on for support?

EVALUATING WHETHER SHAME IS HEALTHY PRIMARY SHAME

Adaptive shame helps people not alienate themselves from their group. This is the adaptive shame that, if denied, causes brashness. Shame generally strikes deep in the human heart. It is about a person's sense of worth; it makes people want to hide, as opposed to guilt, which prompts apology or the making of amends. People feel shame when they lose control; when they feel overexposed, like appearing naked in public; or when they feel that other people see them as worthless or undignified. In shame people often want to bow their heads and sink into the ground so as to not be seen. Shame can arise when people reveal their emotions to another person and do not receive support. A person, for example, may be telling a story in a group, suddenly realize that no one is listening and shrink away inside.

> Sue is telling her therapist how she woke up and remembered what had happened last night. She had lost control. She had drunk too much and was acting silly. That is embarrassing enough, but it was the memory of running to the bathroom and getting sick that made her feel ashamed. Someone had to help her clean up. It was awful. How will she ever face these people again? The therapist realizes that helping Sue face this shame probably will help her resolve to not do these things again.

Children feel shame when no one pays attention to their efforts at exhibiting their prowess or to their emotional excitement at their success. When they excitedly yell "Mommy! Daddy! Look at me!" as they stand ready to jump into a pool, and their parents ignore them, they might shrink away in shame. Shame can be an adaptive emotion if it is felt in response to violations of implicit or explicit personal standards and values, such as shame at engaging in deviant behavior, shame at a public loss of control, or shame at being a neglectful or abusive parent. In such cases feelings of shame need to be acknowledged, because they are providing valuable information about socially acceptable behavior that one might choose to use to guide one's conduct.

Shame can be adaptive because it simultaneously protects one's privacy while also keeping one connected to one's community. It does this by preventing one from erring too much in public or breaking the rules that form the social fabric. Adaptive shame informs one that one is too exposed and other people will not support one's actions, that one has broken a very basic social norm, or that one has violated standards or values that one recognizes as deeply important. The following exercise helps people identify shame experiences.

Exercise: Shame at Diminishment

> Identify a recent situation in which you suffered a sudden loss of self-esteem or remember a situation in which you felt embarrassed. Have you ever waved back at someone on the street only to realize that the person was waving at somebody behind you? Was this embarrassing? Why? See if you can recapture the feeling now. Identify your feeling. Find a word or words that fits the feeling. What do you feel in your body? Put some words to this feeling. If this feeling makes you want to move or act in some way, do it. Do you want to drop your eyes or look down? Let the feeling express itself in your body.

HEALTHY PRIMARY EMOTIONAL PAIN

There is one type of adaptive emotion that requires special attention: emotional pain. Pain is not unhealthy but rather is an adaptive response to loss or trauma. At first blush it might look like it is unhealthy because it feels so shattering and people just want to avoid it, but emotional pain is an adaptive emotion. I now discuss how one must distinguish pain that needs to be faced and accepted from unhealthy emotion that needs to be changed.

Pain is the experience of trauma to the self. As such, pain is an adaptive emotion that tells one that damage has occurred. It differs from other primary emotions that organize people to act to prevent damage. Pain is not anticipatory in this way. Fear protects people from impending danger. Anger organizes them for attack. Pain, however, occurs after the fact rather than being anticipatorily adaptive. It tells a person that something terrible has happened and that he or she had better not go through this again if he or she does not want to feel destroyed. It is a unique primary adaptive emotion.

The experience of emotional pain is something one might know by acquaintance. However, little is known about it conceptually. Pain has until recently defied rational analysis. It is not intense sadness, anger, shame, or fear—it is more than these emotions, and it can include all or any of them. Pain is a unique experience of bodily anguish that concern's one's whole self and survival. It occurs most often when one feels powerless to prevent trauma.

Recently some of my graduate students and I have embarked on a study of human pain. In a pathbreaking study of pain, Liz Bolger (1999) asked people about what they felt shortly after expressing pain in therapy. She found that the primary experience of pain is what she called "broken-ness": a feeling of being broken into pieces, shattered. People in pain always referred to the body in an interiorly focused way. They said "I felt torn into pieces"; "My heart was broken"; "It is as if a big chunk of me had been ripped out, and I was left bleeding"; or "I shattered into a thousand pieces." The metaphors of the body being ruptured helped capture the respondents' experience. This is what it feels like to be in pain: One feels broken.

I have seen clients who have had the courage and support to face their pain and not only survive but also grow from the experience. I also have experienced this myself. It is a phenomenon of transformation and emergence, symbolized so long ago by the image of the phoenix rising from the ashes. Research has shown how people in therapy successfully deal with painful experiences (Greenberg & Bolger, 2001). Experiencing the painful feelings is the first step in the process of change. To do this, the previously avoided painful feelings must be *approached*, then *allowed*, and then *accepted* as part of oneself. The original trauma has to be experienced and faced so the person can experientially know that he or she can survive the pain. People must allow themselves to feel the devastation, helplessness, or pow-erlessness. Accepting the pain helps people endure it, and this allows the healthy survival need or goal to be mobilized. Allowing one's self to feel the pain also results in an organismic sense of release and relief and permits one to emerge from the experience a stronger person. When people deal with primary dreaded painful aspects of experience, they learn that they can survive what they previously believed to be unbearable. People meta-phorically face their own existential death and are reborn.

For example, a client who had lost her infant faced her dreaded sense of rupture and brokenness as well as her shame at having left the hospital before her baby's death. After facing her pain in therapy she forgave herself for not being able to endure the pain of his death and saw how her whole life since then had been a protection against the pain. In finally facing her pain, she decided to face life rather than to protect herself behind a wall of fear (Bolger, 1999).

Once people are able to accept feelings of pain, and acknowledge the experience of wanting to survive, they will feel less threatened by any situation that might be a reminder of the previously avoided feeling. They are more flexible and open to new information. The feelings have less power over them. The opportunity for seeing new possibilities and creating new meaning now exists. This process of allowing and accepting pain therefore requires that the pain be evoked and lived through, not simply talked about. By experiencing the pain in its actuality, people are in essence in a novel situation, in which they learn that the pain is endurable and will not destroy them.

A move to more positive coping after facing pain is in part governed by people's tendency to move on and seek more positive, comfortable, healthier states rather than to stay in pain. The paradox is that avoidance of the pain perpetuates it by interfering with one's ability to move away from it. To be able to truly move on with their lives, people need to restructure their experience of the pain so that they can embrace it and face the hopeless, helpless feeling they have been trying to avoid. Helping people face such feelings is often a key part of allowing and accepting pain. Certain forms of hopelessness or helplessness can be secondary feelings that need to be bypassed or explored to get to more primary feelings. This occurs, for example, in resignation or depressive hopelessness that covers anger, or in anxious helpless feelings about not being able to control the future that cover deeper feelings of shame or basic insecurity. People need to accept other forms of hopelessness and helplessness that arise in life, such as those that surround death and trauma, as primary emotions, and these, too, need to be faced as a crucial first step in change. Giving up a useless struggle against feeling hopeless or helpless and allowing oneself to experience and face the inevitable powerlessness is part of being a vulnerable human being. Facing this helpless, hopeless state involves a paradoxical change process. It appears that hopelessness, for example, generally is undesirable and that it is good to feel hopeful. Similarly, competence is viewed as good and helplessness as bad. However, an emotion coach who is able to help people give up struggles against the inevitable and is able to help them accept feeling hopeless or helpless will help them let go of unworkable strategies or unattainable goals. Acknowledging feelings of powerlessness or helplessness thus involves giving up futile efforts and reorganizing.

The acceptance of these feelings also involves beginning to take responsibility for new efforts and new goals. Facing hopelessness is believing not that "I am hopeless" but that a particular effort is not working and that one's efforts are of no avail. Helplessness means recognizing there is nothing one can do to change a particular situation. Contacting and accepting the experience of the futility of the struggle is often a critical step in an emotional change process. This involves facing what has been fearfully avoided, letting go of unworkable solutions, and setting the stage for creative reorganization.

For example, a client who, for the first time, accessed in therapy a painful trauma experience associated with sexual abuse, let herself feel the intense pain of shame plus a deep sadness at her loss of innocence. Supported by the therapist, she felt empathy for herself as a little girl and quickly switched to intense anger at the perpetrator for violating her. The therapist empathically responded to the client's vulnerability and validated her experience of being violated. At the end of the session the client remarked that despite the pain, she felt hopeful "that things will change. I at least feel like these feelings are my own and [that] I have a right to feel them."

EVALUATING WHETHER AN EMOTION IS A PRIMARY MALADAPTIVE EMOTION

I now discuss some examples of the four basic emotions of sadness, anger, fear, and shame when they are maladaptive, part of an unhealthy wound. Maladaptive emotions tend not to organize the self for adaptive action but instead focus outward and make demands on others or focus on the self.

EVALUATING WHETHER SADNESS IS UNHEALTHY PRIMARY SADNESS

Maladaptive sadness does not reach out for comfort or grieve a loss; instead, it turns in on itself and leads to feelings of misery and defeat. A person's storehouse of life's wounds and losses often is the source of a maladaptive sadness that belongs to the past but still colors the present. The painful state of distress can be evoked by a perceived rejection in the present or even by feeling powerless to heal the pain of a loved one. Being unable to heal or take away the pain of a loved one can make a person feel a deep sense of helplessness and despair. Thus, something in the present is creating a depth of despair that seems disproportionate to the situation. This overwhelming feeling is maladaptive sadness, and it does not help a person solve a current problem.

Unhealthy sadness brought on by personal rejection or loss can evoke a deep sense of helplessness and powerlessness. The pain and sadness seem to envelop a person's whole body; it is as though a sadness "madness" takes over. Feeling secure is instantly turned into insecurity, enthusiasm becomes lethargy, and all is suddenly heavy. Colors, textures, and body sense change as the sadness slowly creeps over the person and permeates his or her sense of being. An internal part of the person that holds the pooled memories of this emotional state has now been activated and governs experience.

> John feels worn down by the stresses of the day. His tank is empty. A little refueling from his partner would be welcome. He would just like to melt into his partner's arms and be transported for awhile into sexual ecstasy. His partner shows no interest and seems distant and preoccupied. He starts to feel that familiar unloved, deprived feeling. A wound opens up, and he hears the old refrain "Nobody really cares about me" echoing in his head. He feels sad remembering all the previous times he has felt deprived. He wonders why this always happens to him. His eyes become downcast, his mouth and cheeks droop, and he feels hopelessly defeated. A coach would help John explore this feeling state, identify the negative voices embedded in it and, most important, identify John's unmet need. Rather than avoiding this need, John would be encouraged to experience it. He cannot go underneath the emotion without first entering it. Once John has felt it, differentiated its different facets, and identified what the emotion has been associated with in his past, the coach will work to help John transition into another, more salutary feeling state by focusing John's attention on emerging possibilities.

People are often overcome by these maladaptive sad states and are unable to focus on what is occurring in the present or on other possibilities. A person does not necessarily have a specific thought that produces this change; he or she just feels it take place. A new and uncomfortable, but oddly familiar, sensation creeps over them. This state is not like having an emotional memory of a particular incident that occurs in a flashback, like the memory of feeling grief at a funeral. It is more like experiencing the essence of a lifetime of emotional memories of sadness all rolled up into one feeling. The older a person is, the deeper the well of sadness.

What makes this despairing feeling arrive one day and not another in response to similar situations? This is the true mystery of people's maladaptive emotionality. One never knows exactly what will activate these bleak feelings of sadness and despair. Sometimes people simply are more vulnerable, and other times they are not. People's emotional states are complex. They seem to have minds of their own and are readied for activation by everything preceding them.

The self is a dynamic system (Whelton & Greenberg, 2000). Like any living system, pools of emotional memories are at any moment more or less accessible, more or less active. An emotional state of mind is like a football player not yet on the field: It is either sitting dormant in the background, with no present possibilities of being activated for play, or it is already warmed up for the game by the preceding circumstance. The emotional state is standing on the sideline waiting to be called, ready to go on the field of play at a moment's notice, eager to exert influence. A similar analogy is that, in the parliament of selves that constitute a personality, the emotional possibility may be like a parliamentarian asleep on the back bench. Depending on a combination of to what degree it has been already aroused, and on the intensity of the current debate, an emotional experience may suddenly wake up and enter into the debate. Once it enters the debate it can strongly influence the outcome of the vote.

Thus, at any moment a person might suddenly be swept over by his or her unique experience of maladaptive sadness, and his or her unique way of dealing with it will appear. Some people will cover their emotional canvas with desperately intense red and purple swirls: a sadness of writhing agony. Others will paint with deeper colors and much slower, yearning, curves of deprivation. On another day, at an another time, the same event that cuts one so deeply today will leave a different impression on the canvas. The same incident on another day might even leave the person untouched. People are never really in the same place twice—what affects them one day may not affect them the next. This is the mysterious unpredictability of emotional experience: It simply needs to be accepted as it arises.

Emotional experience is not the same as logical thinking: It does not unfold in a linear way. Rather, it involves a complex, nonlinear process of emergence and completion. Emotions, however, are not chaotic or irrational. There is order in them, and clients can see patterns in their emotionality and make sense of their feelings. They cannot, however, control or predict the activation of their emotions, and so they must learn to live in harmony with them and learn to deal intelligently with the maladaptive, distressing ones.

Helping clients sense whether their primary sadness is adaptive or maladaptive takes time and involves understanding the context and the content of their sadness. If a situation involves loss or injury to self, the first step is to learn how to describe and feel the sadness in the belief that, over time, this will lead to a resolution of the emotion. However, in certain instances the feeling does not seem to shift, and the client just seems to repeat the same feeling again and again without any noticeable change in either quality or intensity. This is a signal that the person is stuck in a feeling that is unhealthy.

On the other hand, a client might recognize right from the start that her sadness is unhealthy. She may immediately react to a situation with a fearful, helpless, dependent feeling. She feels no sense of personal power that helps her cope. Her sadness feels overwhelming, her distress is great, and she feels a primary sense of weakness. The coach and client understand that this sadness is not adaptive and is not going to pass away. It is sending the client a message, but not an adaptive one. The client will need to work hard in therapy to transform this feeling into something that will be more useful to her.

Complicated grief reactions are another form of maladaptive primary sadness. Clients might be unable to cope with an important loss and unable to move on. Often they need to learn to express unresolved anger and guilt to be able to move forward. They may also need to develop a stronger sense of themselves so that they believe that they can cope without the other person. Some people feel inordinately sad at separations and avoid situations involving endings. Unresolved losses may be involved in these experiences. Finally, another clue that clients are experiencing maladaptive sadness is if they feel sad when someone is being kind and tender to them. This may be a sign of unresolved loss that needs to be addressed. It is as if kindness evokes deep longing, deprivation, and unmet feelings of dependency—a need for the kindness that never was. Clients then need to resolve the feeling of deprivation before they can tolerate kindness again, free of the rising hurt.

Exercise: Stuck in Sadness

> Write down three episodes in which you have felt a similar stuck sense of sadness, a wounded feeling that does not go away. Identify the feeling in your body. What is it like? Accept it in a welcoming manner. Is there another voice in your head criticizing you for feeling sad? What is this voice saying about yourself, others, or the future? Say these things out loud to yourself, such as "I feel all alone," "No one cares," or "I can't survive." Is there another, alternate voice available to you? Access a more resilient sense of yourself. Remember a situation in which you felt connected, warm, or loving. Feel this alternative experience.

EVALUATING WHETHER ANGER IS UNHEALTHY PRIMARY ANGER

An adolescent in a home for runaways goes on a weekend pass and visits his aunt, who has no children. She hugs him warmly when he arrives, genuinely pleased to see him, and gives him a gift of a box of tools, which she knows he would really would like. He brushes off her hug. As soon as she asks him if he would like to return home to his parents, he angrily returns the gift, saying he won't be bribed. He has learned that kindness and concern are not to be trusted. He believes they come only with a price. A coach would need to work with this child to first establish trust. Over time the child's anger would become a focus. To begin, a coach would simply acknowledge the child's anger and empathize with his sensed betrayal or violation, and eventually the hurt would come into focus.

Core anger is maladaptive when it no longer functions to protect a person from harm and violation or when it is destructive. Angry reactions to kindness or intimacy can come from prior boundary violations or from a history of believing that nobody does anything for free. It is maladaptive if a person reacts angrily to true, nonexploitative kindness. This type of anger is similar to learned fear responses, the sort that might result if a child had a history of repeated abuse by his or her parents.

Destructive anger and rage often come from a history of witnessing or having suffered violence, and they cause real problems in relationships. Some people report raging at others without control, being volatile in many situations, having hair-trigger tempers, and becoming easily irritated without knowing why. This type of intense arousal is often connected to past events, and people often try to shut down such arousal. When people with maladaptive rage who have suffered from violence in their past become angry, the anger can become a trigger for an explosion. In therapy they need to learn to pay attention to what they experience before they explode. Coaches need to help people first cope with the intense and overwhelming emotion and then, in the safety of therapy, learn to acknowledge all the feelings and beliefs associated with the rage in the safety of therapy and how to contact another feeling, often fear or grief caused by an unsatisfied need to be loved. Often people's maladaptive anger is not about who or what they are angry at; it is about their unmet need. Once people understand this they can begin to process this experience, thereby preventing their rage.

Maladaptive anger also emerges in response to felt diminishment to self-esteem and causes a lot of interpersonal difficulties. This anger often feels justified in the moment. The person feels wronged and loses sight of all the good things received from the other person. The more fragile the person's esteem, the more easily he or she loses contact with the positive parts of the relationship; then all that is felt is the diminishment and all that is seen in the other person is bad. Often clients later feel bad about their anger, but this guilt does not lead to change. They need to learn how to deal with this maladaptive anger in a better way. The problem with anger has to do with the behaviors it involves. Different strategies are needed for different causes and different types of anger. Anger at disappointment or rejection is not the same as anger at attack or anger in response to another person's anger. Attempts to hurt or destroy a loved one are ineffective responses to being hurt or disappointed by that person. Thus, emotional intelligence involves expressing anger in the right way at the right time.

> Jane's partner is involved in other things and is not paying the kind
> of attention to her that she wants. She has already asked for this at-
> tention and hasn't received the desired response. She starts to feel very
> angry. She begins in her mind to analyze and criticize all of her part-

ner's behaviors. Then she begins to attack. "You're so self-absorbed—so insensitive. You just expect things from me and never care about me. I've had it with you!" This is a familiar pattern of which Jane needs to become aware. It begins when she feels neglected. She gets angry and attacks, and generally this doesn't make things better; it just drives her partner away. Emotion coaching, after Jane acknowledges her anger, would help her to see that these actions do not help her get what she needs, and with appropriate timing the coach would begin to focus Jane's attention on her underlying hurt.

An emotion coach would also work with Jane to help her become aware that her core feeling of being unfairly treated not only does not help her get what she wants but also destroys relationships. The following exercise can be used to help people identify destructive anger.

Exercise: Anger That Is a Trap

Identify situations that anger you repeatedly and in which your anger drives loved ones away. Write down the situations and the way they make you feel. Make sure this is a core angry feeling you felt and that it is not masking hurt. Identify the feeling in your body. Identify the thoughts. Now put words to the negative voice in your head related to this feeling. What do you believe about yourself, others, or the future when you are in this state? Write it down. When you are in this state, try saying these negative things out loud to yourself. See if you believe the negative voice. Is there another voice that is less dominant but still there? Can you use it to give you a different perspective? Now reflect on the opposite of anger: qualities of warmth, loving, and kindness. Is there now a way of letting go of your anger? Picture the person at whom you are angry. Can you connect with what you appreciate about this person? Can you feel forgiving or loving? Try saying "I forgive you." Let go of the anger. Let the curtain of resentment fall and be replaced with warmth and caring.

EVALUATING WHETHER FEAR AND ANXIETY ARE UNHEALTHY PRIMARY EMOTIONS

A woman with a severe history of sexual abuse by her father gets very tense and rigid any time her husband touches her. She loves her husband and wants to be intimate, but any suggestion of sex brings back awful images, and she reacts with terror. An emotion coach would work with this woman to rework her trauma, acknowledge the loss of emotions and their avoidance, and would work with her to develop self-soothing.

Clients often experience maladaptive primary feelings of fear even though the triggering event that is occurring is not dangerous. They may also become afraid simply by remembering or thinking about a past event, especially if it was a very traumatic one. The fear a client felt in the past may have been a normal reaction to a frightening situation, but the client may have problems now if he or she continues to get scared even when there is no real danger. When clients have continual memories or nightmares about a past traumatic event, this is a sign that they have hidden primary fears to which they need to pay attention.

> A man who grew up with an explosive father constantly feels like he has to walk on eggshells. At business meetings he is tense and careful. If anyone shows any signs of anger in his or her voice, he begins to feel extremely anxious. An emotion coach would help this man reprocess his fear and access other, more adaptive feeling responses to help him feel stronger.

Unhealthy anxiety comes from a basic feeling that one is ineffective, unprotected, or both. This feeling of basic insecurity, once instilled, will keep coming up in all a person's relationships with friends or loved ones. If clients have primary maladaptive fears, they might often be afraid of being judged, misunderstood, or rejected by others. They might also have trouble telling people how they feel. Past bad experiences may very likely have left them feeling abandoned or rejected. Panic is a prime example of the fear system run amok. It no longer organizes the person for adaptive action but instead is disorganizing. Panicky dependence—the anxious feeling in adults that one cannot survive if one's attachment figure is rejecting or unavailable—leads people to cling to partners for protection in unhealthy ways. Such people must find inner sources of strength and self-soothing.

Exercise: Fear That Disorganizes

> Identify a primary fear, one that occurs in most of your relationships with other people. This fear could also occur in response to a type of situation. Describe the situations that lead to this fear. Identify the feeling in your body. Is this a core feeling? Make sure it is not masking another feeling. Do you hear a negative voice in your head along with the fear? What is this negative voice saying? What do you believe about yourself or others when you are in this state? Write this down. How can you calm yourself?

EVALUATING WHETHER SHAME IS UNHEALTHY PRIMARY SHAME

A man abused by his priest when he was 10 years old talks to his therapist about how dirty he feels. He says he feels contaminated and will never be able to feel acceptable again. His shame will need to be worked through and transformed.

In this form of shame clients may feel humiliated, dirty, and worthless. These feelings often come from a history of being shamed and are part of the primary sense of the self as worthless, inferior, or unlovable. Often clients may not admit that they feel this sense of maladaptive shame; they might cover it up with other behavior. For example, they might get really angry and blow up at the slightest negative comment. If they have a long history of being treated badly and rarely get any support, they may begin to believe that they are worthless. This leads to a primary feeling of shame in which the self is perceived to be defective. The shame of being treated like dirt makes a person feel like he or she *is* dirt. It sticks to the self. Emotion coaching will help the client in the previous example face his shame and overcome it by accessing other, more adaptive feelings.

Exercise: Shame That Sticks

> Think of a situation when you felt worthless or deeply ashamed. What happened that led you to feel this way? Identify the feeling in your body. Now put words to the negative voice in your head related to this feeling. What do you believe about yourself, or what do you believe others feel or think about you? Write this down. Identify what was done to you that made you feel this way. Find a part of yourself to fight back against the shaming. Imagine yourself back in the situation, bringing in someone to stand up for you. Have that person give you what you needed in that situation: support, protection, or comfort.

I now look at some specific examples of different secondary emotions and try to identify the core feeling.

SADNESS AS A SECONDARY EMOTION

A client says "I feel so sad, just despondent and hopeless. He never listens. Nothing will change. Relationships just don't work. I can never be heard or get what I need. It's always 'Yes, but' or 'My needs are greater than yours.' I give up."

This is the kind of depressive, hopeless sadness and resignation that come from a person feeling that his or her anger will not be heard, that it is not valid, or that it will not make an impact. The sadness is felt in response to a feeling of impotent anger. Here the sadness is a reaction to and masks the underlying core feeling of anger. An emotion coach, while acknowledging the client's sense of hopelessness and hurt, would shift the client's attention to any sound of annoyance in the client's voice and to the unmet need or what it is the client wants. This would begin to mobilize the client's assertive anger.

Coaches need to be able to distinguish between tears of core sadness and pain and tears of sadness that are reactions to core frustration or anger. Helpless tears often occur when people chronically collapse into hurt, victimization, and sadness whenever they feel angry but are powerless to have their anger heard. Lingering depression often results when people deny their core feelings of sadness at loss. This secondary sadness often involves a kind of generalized hopelessness rather than genuine acceptance of loss accompanying core sadness. People may feel resigned to the loss and say to themselves "What's the use, there is no point in trying." They may also feel a sense of hopelessness and sadness when they start to criticize themselves or think in terms of "shoulds." One part of the person might berate another part for not measuring up. A person might think "I shouldn't be angry. I have no right to complain" and then start to feel sad and hopeless. This self-criticism often makes the situation worse, and then it becomes harder for the person to express what he or she is really angry about. The following exercise can be used to identify secondary sadness.

Exercise: Sadness That Is Not Your Most Basic Feeling

> This task will help you ascertain if the sadness you are feeling is your most basic feeling. Identify a situation in which you did not suffer a loss but your reaction was sadness of some sort. First identify the feeling of which you are most aware. Maybe you feel just generally blue, or you are feeling sorry for yourself, or hurt. Then ask yourself "Is there something more basic that I am feeling? Is there anger or resentment beneath my sadness?" Find your most basic feeling. Put it into words.

ANGER AS A SECONDARY EMOTION

Julia's boyfriend criticizes her for not being sensitive to his feelings. He claims he is always very attentive, but today when he told her about having been almost assaulted by a disturbed adolescent neighbor, she had quickly changed the subject to talking about her anxiety about her exam. He resentfully demands that Julia take care of him and says he needed a hug rather than to have to talk to her about her anxieties. She apologizes but feels mad at him for being so critical and demanding. She becomes distant. Here an emotion coach would help Julia and her boyfriend each access their underlying feelings of nonblaming hurt and their need for support and help them communicate this in a disclosing, rather than blaming, manner.

Most reactions of anger mask underlying feelings of hurt or powerlessness. Both members of the couple in the example above feel hurt: Julia's boyfriend feels in need of comfort and unimportant to her, and Julia feels frightened and rejected. Yet both express anger that is secondary to the more core feelings of hurt. One of the confusing issues in dealing with anger is that it so often is a defensive emotion instead of a core response. In these cases, other emotions or stresses fuel anger. Once anger is evoked, it in turn produces more angry thoughts. When people are angry they often may think angry thoughts that produce more anger. People who are quick to anger need to learn ways of coping with their anger and, when the anger is not out of control, techniques such as time outs and counting to 10 can help. Another important skill in regulating anger is learning to become aware of and express rising core anger early, before it intensifies. This is an important means of preventing an escalating sequence of anger.

People might also use anger as a way to block the stress and pain that come from other feelings. Feeling angry removes awareness of other feelings, such as fear or hurt, that can be more uncomfortable than anger. Expressing anger can help release muscular tensions and reduce the high arousal levels associated with these other feelings. Thus, a frightened parent may react with anger at a child who runs into the street. This secondary anger is due to a rapid sequence in which the parent notices danger, feels afraid, blames the child, gets angry, and then acts to let go of his or her sense of fear. Similarly, a person who feels hurt when criticized or rejected can decide that the situation is unfair and conclude that what the other person did was wrong. Similarly, anger momentarily erases guilt, depression, and feelings of unworthiness; rather than feel guilty or worthless, one can blame or criticize the other person. This happens frequently in couples' quarrels and in parent–child arguments. Rather than feel sad or disappointed, people get angry at something or someone else to obliterate the painful sensations and thoughts.

Rage often occurs in reference to, and masks, the shame of loss of self-esteem or the fear of a fragile self. People often feel shame when they are rejected or humiliated, because these are extremely painful emotions, and rage covers them. Much marital violence stems from a shame–rage cycle in which the abuser, most often the man, is unable to deal with his powerless dependence. When he feels powerless he feels ashamed and erupts in rage to mask his core feeling of shame. It also is important to understand how an initial healthy reaction of anger can escalate into a secondary rage by an unhealthy sequence of feelings and thoughts that progressively intensify the anger. In this sequence, every successive provocation—either a thought, a perception, or an interaction—becomes a new trigger for further surges of anger, and each builds on the moment before. Rage untempered by reason easily erupts into violence. Thus, in addition to being able to get in touch with and transform helpless dependence or shame that leads to rage, it can also be helpful to unpack the thoughts that contribute to rage. It often is difficult to distinguish between core maladaptive rage and rage that is secondary to shame. The former often is suddenly triggered and is more like a posttraumatic flash and response to past violence, whereas secondary rage follows shame or fear. As long as emotion coaches follow their clients' processes and help them become aware of all they feel, it is not that critical to distinguish between these two types of rage. In both cases the person's rage arousal needs to be regulated, and another, healthier feeling needs to be accessed.

Another common type of secondary anger is when people get angry with themselves for something they did or the way they felt. This form of secondary anger often takes the form of hostile self-criticism. Getting angry with oneself usually leads to further feelings of shame, failure, guilt, or depression. People may get angry with themselves for feeling depressed, needy, or fearful. In these situations they need to bypass this anger and pay attention to their core feeling instead.

> A client in therapy chastised herself for being unassertive. She felt "childish" and like "such a wimp" because she was unable to say no to other people's demands or requests. The therapist sensed that this anger actually masked a core feeling of insecurity. Rather than focus on the client's anger, the therapist responded, "It's as if you feel like a little child, and there's something very scary, very awful about others' disapproval." This helped the client to focus on her insecurity and her healthy need to be liked. It opened up the session to explore her fear of disapproval and her needs to feel connected to other people rather than focusing on her anger.

The following exercise will help people identify secondary anger.

Exercise: Anger That Obscures Another Feeling

> Identify a situation in which you expressed anger because you felt rejected, as opposed to a situation in which you felt unfairly treated. First identify the quality of the angry emotion you felt when rejected. Then ask "Is there something more basic that I am feeling? What is my core feeling?" Are there fear or sadness under your anger?

FEAR AND ANXIETY AS SECONDARY EMOTIONS

Alex is feeling afraid to speak to her colleague. She feels he wasn't honest with the boss about a situation that had occurred in the office and that he made her look bad. She tells the emotion coach how afraid she is of this colleague now and how she greets him in the hall with a phony smile. As she talks it is clear that she is angry with him but is afraid to confront him for fear of losing his support and friendship. The coach helps the client focus on her core feelings of having been unfairly treated and her need to have the situation corrected. With the coach's validation and her realization that her fear of rejection is preventing her from asserting her rights, the client decides to speak to her colleague.

When fear and anxieties are secondary feelings they do not come from an imminent external danger. Neither do they come from a core emotion of feeling like a lost, insecure child in a big world; rather, secondary feelings of fear or anxiety often arise when people are insecure or anxious that their core feelings of anger, sadness, or weakness might damage their relationships with other people. This results in people trying to avoid experiencing their core feelings. Guarding against their anger and sadness often leaves them feeling anxious or vulnerable. In these cases an emotion coach can guide them toward recognizing the primary emotion.

People often try to avoid core feelings of weakness and may fear that they are too dependent on other people. Instead of acknowledging their dependent feelings and admitting that they feel afraid of these feelings, they may become very anxious when they are separated from other people and not understand their anxiety. Another key means of generating secondary anxiety is by having catastrophic expectations about the future. In such cases people's thoughts are the primary generators of the anxiety. People may imagine that tomorrow's meeting will be a disaster, or that they will be rejected on their first dates. They worry and feel anxious today, and this often interferes with preparations for tomorrow.

Exercise: Anxiety About Another Feeling

> Identify an anxiety you feel about another of your emotions, such as "I worry that I am too dependent on my partner" or "I'm afraid to tell my partner I'm angry." Put the core feeling you are avoiding into words, such as "Deep down I am afraid to be alone" or "I'm angry." Let yourself feel what is at your core. Accept it welcomingly. Identify the need, goal, or concern in your primary feeling.

SECONDARY SHAME AND EMBARRASSMENT

> Bill failed to get the promotion he had expected to receive. He has to go to the office tomorrow, and people will ask what happened. He wants to run away rather than face his colleagues. In therapy he will need to work on his shame-inducing process.

Negative views of the self and feelings of self-contempt generate this form of shame. People might say to themselves, "I was so inept," or "I was so stupid," and this results in secondary shame. They then feel that others see them in this way and look down on them. People can feel secondary shame when they see themselves as cowardly for not standing up for their ideas at a meeting. Their negative judgments and their projection of these judgments onto others are the main problems when dealing with secondary shame. If they are able to deal with the self-criticism, then shame disappears. This is not the case with core shame, which sticks to the self much more tenaciously. In core shame people feel like they *are* a mistake rather than that they *made* a mistake. In working with secondary shame an emotion coach helps the person identify the shaming voice within and then works to mobilize feelings of pride, assertive anger, and self-worth to combat the shaming voice.

A large source of secondary shame or embarrassment involves imagining that other people judge one in a negative way. Social experiences in which people feel foolish or exposed generally involve imagining what other people are thinking about them: They treat other people as mirrors, projecting their own views of themselves onto them. People then experience other people as believing these negative thoughts about themselves. People thus often suffer embarrassment because of their own beliefs. It is these negative thoughts that make them feel embarrassed and foolish. For example, Sue may feel embarrassed for having made social error at a fancy dinner party: using the wrong knife for her butter. No one else was really paying attention to what cutlery she was using, but she felt like she stood out.

Shame also can be a reaction to, and a cover for, other core emotional experiences. Shame may mask core emotions of feeling hurt, weak, needy, angry, or afraid. This is shame about internal experiences and desires and shame about exposing and disclosing oneself. When people feel shame about how they are feeling, the shame is often related to an inability to accept weakness and vulnerability. This is an important problematic situation that most people encounter. It differs from a core shame feeling in that in this masking shame people feel ashamed about how they feel rather than are the objects of shame. There usually is a difference in that people tend to have some separation from that which is shameful. They exist independent of the shame, which is about something they feel or did, rather than about their whole selves. Thus, people may be ashamed about their sexual fantasies or about their weakness in response to criticism. Such people need to learn to tolerate their shame, own their fantasies, and face their weakness.

Exercise: Facing Shame

> Identify an embarrassing situation. Stay with your feeling of embarrassment instead of hiding from it. What was the loss of face you suffered? Is there a voice inside you that is criticizing you? Face this voice. Speak back to it from a sense of self-worth.

I now look at identifying instrumental expressions of the different emotions.

INSTRUMENTAL SADNESS

> Sally is not getting her wishes met. She is frustrated and cries helplessly in therapy. The therapist feels a demand in her crying, a demand that he is somehow to fix this, to make her feel better. Rather than responding in terms of this pull, he comments to Sally that he is having this feeling that he needs to rescue her and he wonders if she feels like she is appealing to him to do this.

A good example of a common instrumental expression of sadness is when someone cries as a way of complaining. This is pejoratively referred to as *whining*. It occurs when tears are a form of protest, expressing how poorly treated one feels, with the hope that it will evoke sympathy, support, or understanding. A person may or may not be aware of the instrumental function of the tears and may be feeling genuinely needy. An emotion coach needs to focus the person on the aim of his or her tears by asking "What do you want?" or "What sort of response to your tears do you hope to get?"

> A student goes to her female professor to contest her grade for a class project. The grade was 69%; if she could get a 70 then her overall course grade would be elevated to a B+. The professor says no, because she has no grounds to change the grade. The student pleads demandingly, and her eyes fill with tears. This young woman for a moment transforms into an angry, helpless baby, crying for somebody to provide her with satisfaction. Her professor declines the student's indirect plea to gratify her, on the grounds that this would be unfair to other students.

This sadness results not primarily from an experience of core loss but from feeling thwarted and powerless. This type of cry often does not elicit the desired support, especially not outside of one's family of origin, where it was probably learned. In therapy people need to learn how to face their own disappointments and feelings of inability to take responsibility for themselves. They also need to become aware that often they maintain their powerless sense by getting others to take care of them.

INSTRUMENTAL ANGER

Schoolyard bullies, who are often frightened or maltreated themselves, learn that they can control others with threatening shows of hostile intent. This carries over into their adult lives in offices and home. By raising their voices or their eyebrows, workers intimidate their colleagues, husbands bully their wives, and parents intimidate their children. This is a learned form of control.

> A male client, smiling coyly, talks in therapy about putting his fist through a wall at work. He says he was expressing his displeasure to his female real estate sales partner because she had complained to their manager about him rather than talking to him. He is in therapy because of the loneliness and isolation he felt after his wife left him because he was so dominant and verbally aggressive. He couldn't understand why she felt this way. The emotion coach needs to help him focus on his primary feelings of hurt and his need to be liked. The coach also needs to help this client understand how he uses anger to get compliance and that this results in people disliking him when he deeply wishes to be liked.

Instrumental anger is the learned use of anger as a means of controlling other people for one's own gain. Getting angry is an effective way to control someone, but it usually results in the other person becoming bitter, resentful, and distant. The best way of dealing with this type of anger is to understand the person's underlying motivation and aims and help him or her develop alternate ways of achieving those aims.

Of course, many people are not aware of the instrumental function of their anger, and often their manipulation is not deliberate. For example, a client was hurt and angry at her parents' lack of support and reacted by "punishing" them, "teaching them a lesson," and "treating them the way they treat me." These are examples of instrumental anger mixed with core anger caused by unmet needs. Therapy helped this client acknowledge and validate her anger at her unmet needs for support. She also came to realize that her attempts to force her parents to give her what she wanted were not helping her get what she so desperately wanted and needed. This helped her let go of futile efforts to control her parents and, at the same time, supported her healthy core desire to get her needs met in the world. She then focused on finding healthier behaviors for accomplishing these goals.

INSTRUMENTAL FEAR AND SHAME

Displaying fear and shame to achieve a goal is unusual and does not present itself that often as a problem. Instrumental fear is designed to avoid taking responsibility for oneself and to have others protect one. Playing at being afraid or helpless is done to evoke caretaking. People may also show fear as a means of trying to prevent another person from being angry at them or blaming them, or to indicate subservience. Instrumental shame occurs when, for example, people pretend to be embarrassed to appear socially appropriate. This is image and role management.

Exercise: Identify Your Own Instrumental Emotion

Identify your favorite, most frequent instrumental expression. Do you pout or yell to get your way? Do you act helpless and in need of rescue? What do you think others would say is your way of emotionally manipulating them to get what you want? Try to be brutally honest with yourself. You need to recognize your own instrumental style of emotional expression. What is the cost?

CONCLUSION

Although emotions evolved to enhance healthy living, there are a number of ways in which they can go wrong. Healthy core emotions based on automatic sizing up of situations in relation to needs and goals are the ones that provide people with a healthy guide about how to act, and they inform people of their reactions to situations. They tell people whether something is good or bad for them and help people figure out what is most important to them and how they should respond. They might alert people to whether they feel they are in danger or have lost something important or whether their sense of space is being invaded.

To exercise emotional intelligence clients cannot just blindly follow their feelings. They should follow only healthy primary feelings. Secondary emotions must be explored to identify their origins, and awareness of the aims of one's instrumental emotions helps one to be more direct in expressing what one needs. Finally, unhealthy core emotions need to be uncovered in order to be transformed into healthier responses to situations. This uncovering often is the main work that needs to be done. The first step in emotion coaching always is helping people becoming aware of what they are feeling. Another important step involves evaluating whether what a client is feeling is a healthy primary emotion by which he or she should be guided or a maladaptive one that needs to be changed.

PRACTICE EXERCISES

The following sheet can be used to help people begin to identify different types of emotion. They can follow the instructions on the sheet to identify their primary emotions in regard to recent life events that caused them to feel something.

Emotion Episodes Awareness Training Sheet

Step 1	Step 2	Step 3	Step 4	Step 5
What is your emotion or action tendency? Is it best described by ■ An emotion or feeling word ■ An action tendency	What is the situation to which you are reacting? ■ An event ■ An internal experience ■ Another person	What are the thoughts accompanying the emotion?	What is the need/goal/concern met/not being met in the situation?	Establish your primary emotion ■ Is your emotion in Step 1 primary? If not, is it secondary or instrumental? ■ Establish your primary emotion

Exercise 1: Identifying Your Experience of Different Emotions

Describe the last time you felt each of the following: anger, sadness, fear, shame, and pain. If possible, describe this feeling to a real or imagined other person to help him or her understand the situation, what you reacted to, what happened in your body, how you felt, and what you did.

Now consider each emotion and answer the following questions about how you typically experience this emotion.

- How long does this feeling last?
- How intense is it, on a scale from 1 to 10 on which 10 represents very intense?
- How long does it take for this emotion to occur? Are you quick to feel anger, sadness, fear, and shame?
- How long does it take for the emotion to leave?
- How frequently do you experience this emotion?
- Is this emotion generally helpful to you or a problem for you?

Exercise 2: Dealing With Primary Sadness of Loss

It is important to stay with any emotion until you grasp what the feeling is trying to tell you. This is especially true with sadness about loss. Give yourself permission to consciously enter sadness by practicing this exercise.

1. Slow down, focus in your abdomen, and breathe deeply. Focus on your sadness. Feel the sadness. Identify your loss.

2. Feel the difficulty of the loss associated with your sadness. Feel what it means to you. Articulate for yourself what it is you miss.
3. What is this feeling wanting to tell you? Feel and wait. Don't analyze; just stay in your feeling.
4. Stay with the sadness until you relax or until tears come. Stay with the tears and sadness as information emerges. Allow the tears to relax you.

5a. Tell yourself something that makes you feel better. Be gentle and caring. Give yourself something specific to encourage yourself.

or

5b. Open yourself to be able to let others help you, or let yourself be affected by others.

or

5c. Reach out. Ask for love, a hug, or attention of some kind. Express the difficulty and consciously ask for help from a friend, a professional, or someone able and wanting to give you love and attention.

or

5d. Engage in a routine or a ritual to help deal with the sadness. Shift to what you love to do that doesn't stress you, or engage in a personal ritual to help symbolize and express your loss.

or

5e. Remember a moment of love, competence, strength, or fullness from your internal store of memories. Savor it.
   - In dealing with grief, you can focus on the thought of loss and let it prolong a feeling of sadness, or you can focus on the feeling of love for the lost person or situation until it produces a warm feeling of love.
   - You can focus on the feeling and recognition of your own love for the lost person or the other person's love for you until it produces inspiration toward more life.
   - You can focus on the feeling of wanting what you lost until it produces desire and the urge to struggle into action.

Exercise 3: Explore Healing Grief

1. Scan your life for a situation of great loss.
2. Focus on the loss. Allow yourself to visualize the full situation again. Feel the loss.
3. Visualize the person or any aspect of the situation where there was love. Feel that love.
4. Experience the differences between the loss and love: Go back to the feeling of loss and experience how loss feels. Then feel again the love and experience how love feels.
5. Dwell on any gifts you received from the person. Feel the loving whenever you want to. Keep on loving, and continue to be affected by the loving.
6. Within your feelings of love, remember the positive characteristics of that person, drawing from your personal experience.
7. Find some way to symbolize those admired aspects, and place those symbols in your memory.
8. Whenever you fall into loss, be aware that you can shift to love.

Exercise 4: Expressing Anger

Express your anger on your own. This can be done in a safe place, such as in your room, in your car, or anywhere you are alone. Imagine what you are angry about. Express it. You may want to kick something or hit a pillow. Do whatever is safe and feels right. The purpose of this is to

1. Find what your anger may be hiding or how it is masking what you really want; expressing your anger on your own helps you to search for what you really want.
2. Identify what triggers your anger; learn your own anger patterns and modes of expression.
3. See, hear, feel, or find anything positive that you can do. Know that anger is a struggle between "I can" and "I can't." You need to search carefully to find an "I can" that will help you pull out of the struggle, with a positive action in your favor.
4. Express yourself until you want to be still and go inward or let go of your anger.

When you know what you really want, rather than just what triggered your anger, you might be ready to express your frustration to the other person. When you know something that you can do about your anger, you are no longer a victim; you are no longer dependent on the actions of the other person. Now you are able not only to express your feelings but also to enter a process of negotiation.

Exercise 5: Expressing Anger to the Other Person With the Intent to Negotiate

Be sure you want to express the anger. It may or may not be in your best interest. Just as you don't express all your thoughts, you don't have to express all your feelings. Be sure you wish to negotiate with the other person. If not, you might just as well express your anger to yourself privately. No one wishes to hear your dissatisfaction unless you are at least willing to look for alternatives. Begin your expression with an "I" statement, not a "you" statement. An "I" statement demonstrates that I own the anger and that the other person is not the cause. A "you" statement fuels the fire, makes the other person defensive, keeps that war going, and results in argument and disconnection. Know how you would like to start. Train yourself to begin with "I." Several possibilities are "I am sorry," or "I don't mean to burst out at you," "I'm angry . . . ," "I'm having a hard time . . . ," "I know it's not your fault . . . ," or "I just can't stand it when . . ."

To express your feelings,

- say what you are feeling,
- say what you saw the other doing,
- say what you want,
- say what the other person can do to help.

Express a desire to negotiate. Say "I would like to work this out," "I don't want to feel angry," or "I'm willing to listen to your side." Say something that indicates your openness to listen and negotiate.

Exercise 6: Identify the Power in Your Anger

In general, anger is your emotional reaction to loss of power. It is a signal to alert you that you care about being powerful in a particular situation or with a particular person. Anger shows you exactly where the obstructions to your power are located. It will locate where you felt or believed yourself to be powerful before you were blocked.

1. Ask yourself what activity you were engaged in when you got angry.
2. Although you may feel powerless at the moment, remember that it was the interruption of a goal that left you feeling frustrated and angry. Identify the activity in which you were feeling powerful before you were interrupted. It may help to

complete the following sentences: "What I care about that got interrupted was . . ." "I felt . . . ," or "I wanted to . . ." This is your goal, need, or concern.

3. Identify what you can do now to get closer to the goal of what you care about.

Exercise 7: Facing Pain

Make sure you feel safe. Identify a safe place within or without where you can go if you feel too much pain and need to retreat for awhile. Imagine the painful event or experience. Breathe. Put words to the image and body sensations. Connect your sensation, images, and elements of the event into a coherent narrative. First, name very clearly what you felt with words, for example, "I felt terrified" or "I felt broken." Breathe. Let your emotions rise up; experience them and express them. Go to your internal safe retreat for awhile if you feel you need to. Then go back to your feeling. Notice that in spite of the beliefs you may have had about being unable to face your pain because it would destroy you, you are still there. Feel yourself against your chair. Feel your feet on the ground. Allow your pain and contact your need. Feel the relief that comes with experiencing and expressing your pain. Now make sense of what happened in a new way. What have you learned? What can you let go of? Make up a new account of what happened that is more compassionate to yourself or to others.

III

THE LEAVING PHASE: MOVING ON BY ACCESSING HEALTHY EMOTIONS

7

IDENTIFYING MALADAPTIVE EMOTIONS

In this section I discuss the second phase of emotion coaching: the leaving phase, in which the emotion coach must evoke maladaptive emotions to make them accessible to transformation. This is the phase in which one changes emotion with emotion. Once maladaptive programs are up and running they become open to new input. Having opened a maladaptive program, the coach then needs to expose it to new, healthy input that will eventually integrate with the maladaptive material and transform it. This is not a purely rational process but an experiential one. Exposing existing structures to new experiences enables them to be changed. As Spinoza (1967) stated, only equal opposing emotions change emotions. Emotion coaches thus need to help people access their healthy feelings and the needs, goals, or concerns that their emotion is telling them are relevant in their particular situation.

Once people acknowledge the importance of their primary concerns, they can reorganize themselves and their emotions in light of them. Humans are very purposive beings: Once they become aware of new goals they almost automatically begin to reorganize themselves to attain them. When one becomes aware of a pain in one's back that is caused by an awkward sitting position, one becomes aware of a need for greater comfort and shifts position. Awareness of needs keeps people active and moves them to contact the environment to get their needs met. For example, when people become aware of needs for greater security—whether emotional or even financial—provided they have sufficient internal support for action and are not demoralized, they begin to do something different to try to get what they need. This is the process of healthy living: becoming aware of needs and acting in the environment to get what is available to meet the need. One of course always bumps up against others engaged in the same process and then must collaborate with these others to reach mutual satisfaction.

There are several steps in the leaving phase that set the ground for helping clients access their needs and goals. Once people have recognized what they feel and have determined whether their feeling represents their most primary, heartfelt emotion, uncontaminated by extraneous motives or self-protective covers, what do they do? They cannot simply translate their primary feelings into action or expression. They now need to engage in the conscious, second-order evaluation of whether the emotion is a healthy response that is worthy of guiding action or an unhealthy response that needs to be transformed. People need to determine whether their emotional responses are giving them good information that is relevant to their current situations or whether their responses are based on unfinished business from the past or catastrophic expectations about the future. People need to learn to evaluate whether the difficult feelings are reflections of the present situation or evocations of past experiences that have left them feeling wounded, inferior, not good enough, or deeply insecure. Although adaptive feelings are sometimes painful, they seem to have a positive trajectory, and they impel people toward or away from the memory-evoking situation. Maladaptive feelings do not.

EVALUATING WHETHER THE EMOTION IS ADAPTIVE OR MALADAPTIVE

Having arrived at a primary emotion, how does a person determine if this is a place from which he or she gains energy and direction or whether it is a place that depletes or disorganizes, one that is best to leave? How does an emotion coach help clients discern whether their emotions are maladaptive? As I discussed in previous chapters, emotions can be recognized by means of several cues. In Table 7.1 cues are listed that help identify primary adaptive emotions and distinguish them from maladaptive and secondary emotions. Recognizing these distinctions in clients' expressions goes a long way toward helping clients recognize them in themselves. Emotion coaches and their clients thus need to work toward recognizing which of their core feelings are healthy and which do not leave them better off and do not enhance their well-being.

TABLE 7.1
Criteria for Evaluating Emotions

Type of Emotion	Characteristics
Primary adaptive (organizing)	Fresh and new.
	Felt in the moment in response to shifting circumstances.
	Changes when circumstances change.
	Externally cued ones are rapid and action oriented in response to the environment.
	Internally generated ones are slower.
	Explore until client feels, "Yes, that's it!"
	Feel whole, deep.
	Promote attachment bonds and self-coherence.
Primary maladaptive (disorganizing)	A familiar old feeling.
	Client feels stuck in it. It is overwhelming.
	Each time feels as bad as the last time.
	Don't shift with change in circumstance.
	Difficult, deep, and distressing.
	Often are about the self.
	Part of a person's identity.
	Accompanied by emotion's destructive voice.
	Destroy bonds and self-coherence.
Secondary (signaling)	Feel unsettled, unbalanced, upset.
	Global, nonspecific.
	Include symptoms of depression, agitation.
	Not specifically about the self.
	Obscure a more primary feeling (e.g., anger covering hurt).
	Might be a feeling about a feeling (e.g., fear of sadness).
	Thoughts generate the feeling.

BEING INFORMED BY ADAPTIVE EMOTIONS

When people arrive at a primary emotion and evaluate it as adaptive they then need to translate the emotion into action. Some emotions are clear and can be followed quite naturally; for example, a person feels sad and grieves. However, feeling something does not necessarily imply immediate action or demand expression. There are still decisions that need to be made to translate the feeling into action that fits the context. When second-order evaluation leads a client to trust that his or her current feeling is healthy, that emotion now needs to be used as information. Even though the feeling is adaptive, it still should not be followed without prior reflection. In a complex social environment, context and circumstance always have to be taken into account in translating feeling into action.

Feelings Are Information, Not Conclusions

One of the important things for therapists to emphasize as they coach people to use emotion intelligently is that feelings are information, not conclusions. *Feeling* helpless does not mean that one really *is* helpless, without skills, resources, or competence. A feeling is an emotional experience, not a decision, a truth, or a fully determined course of action. An acknowledgment of fear does not mean the person must run away; neither does it mean that he or she is a coward. Fear simply tells a person that danger is sensed. Once the pertinent information has been gathered, a process ensues in which this information is used to generate a next step. Thus, feeling is information; it is part of a process and, as such, it must be allowed and assimilated, not interrupted, avoided, or suppressed. The feeling will be transformed as the process of coping unfolds and people are able to accept their feelings.

People generally feel helpless and afraid when trauma or loss occur. Trying to stave off these feelings is counterproductive. Experiencing these feelings is important, but it is not the same as acting on them. It is not giving up or running away; rather, experiencing one's emotions allows the emotions to inform one's sense of meaning about the situation. This may involve adjusting to the fact that someone has died, that someone who committed suicide could not be saved, or that one could not have prevented a criminal attack on oneself. Facing feelings helps people process their experience and move on.

Accepting emotion also does not include impulsive acting out. People may make decisions and act on these decisions as a result of emotion, but this is not always advisable. People make many mistakes if they deal with an emotion as if it were the only reality that determines a conclusion or an action. For example, if a person feels sad, he or she can remain quiet, feel deeply involved, or cry. The emotional experience—the expression of quietness or crying—is not the potential cause of any acting out. What could cause a problem is what the person might conclude or do as a result of this feeling. For example, he or she could go through the following thought process: "I'm sad because management didn't give me a promotion. They don't value me. They don't think I'm competent. Therefore, I'm not going to make any further efforts (conclusion). I am going to change my job (action)." The person may mutter on, in an internal dialogue: "My boss thinks I'm no good. But he's an idiot; he's so rigid." Every step moves the person further and further from the sad emotion. Simply reacting to the circumstance by deciding to quit one's job is not using emotional intelligence.

Immediate reactions can be equally disastrous in love. For example, a person may feel bad because a loved one did not call. The person may conclude "He or she really does not love me" or, even worse, "Nobody will ever love me—I'll never be happy again." Judgments are made, and absolute realities created. This is how people use rational or not-so-rational thoughts against themselves. They rush to a conclusion or move into action because they do not take time to experience their emotions. They often do not take the time to feel their emotion deeply enough to get its full message or to understand what it is trying to tell them. People need to learn to focus, stay in their internal emotional worlds, and describe their experience in words. This makes their emotions more amenable to reflection, clarification, differentiation, and elaboration, which are all important in creating new meaning. For example, once people know that they are feeling sad, they can reflect on what they are sad about, what this means to them, and what they should do.

After clients have become aware of their feelings and have put them into words, emotion coaches need to help guide them toward deciding what they intend to do. This introduces a sense of direction and translates feelings into goals to be attained. It is often only after people are aware of their feelings that they are able to figure out what they need and might want to do. The integration of head and heart at this point involves articulating what the person wants, needs, or wants to do. Awareness of need, and what one wants to do about it, also has to be evaluated and integrated with other conscious goals, plans, values, and realistic assessments of the situation. A combination of both streams of consciousness—emotionally based goals and conscious values and reasons—forms a person's final intention.

The establishment of intentions forms the bridge between personal experience and action in the world. Thus when a client becomes aware that she is sad because loved ones soon will be leaving on a trip, she may realize that she wants to spend more time with her loved ones. She therefore might decide that it is possible for her to take some time off from work so that she can do things with them. If a man is aware that he feels a core sense of fear every time his partner angrily tells him how selfish and uncaring he is because he did not call her, he may decide to tell her that he feels afraid when she gets so angry and berates him. He has to feel strong to be able to be genuine in this way. He has to know what he feels, and he has to decide to not react defensively. He also has to be able to communicate genuinely and nonthreateningly and needs to be able to describe what he is feeling by starting off his sentences with "I feel . . .", rather than accusing his partner by saying "You are . . . ." Exercising one's emotional intelligence is not easy.

Expressing Emotions

How should therapists coach people toward expressing what they feel? How, for example, can people express anger without harming, insulting, provoking, or even attacking others? If people express too much joy or happiness, will others be jealous? If people express pride or jealousy, what will others think of them? The first thing to consider is that the appropriate way to express emotions depends on a person's family, social groups, and culture. Expression needs to fit its social context. Thus, an emotion coach must always take people's contexts into account and find out from them what is appropriate. Next, a distinction needs to be made between *experiencing* feelings and *expressing* feelings. To become conscious of feelings, people need to give themselves permission to feel their emotions: to be in them, feel free to explore them, intensify them, ride them, shift from them, or hold onto them until the emotions yield their significance or intelligence. The freedom to feel first requires the freedom to feel without the obligation of immediate expression. People often seem to be trapped between two extremes: suppressing feelings and harming themselves or expressing feelings and hurting others.

People do not, however, need to be either a victim of immediate expression or a victim of suppression and potentially of subsequent illness. They can instead express their feelings whenever they decide it is appropriate. Instant expression, however, is not necessary. The issue thus is not one of expression versus suppression. People have a choice of expressing their emotions when appropriate or of simply being aware of their feelings and choosing not to express them. If people suppress emotions at a certain moment because they do not know how to express them without doing harm, this gives them the time to pay attention to what they are feeling in the situation. They then need to find a way later either to express their feelings appropriately or deal with them internally.

An emphasis on the expression of feelings has inhibited people's freedom to feel. Imagine if people felt obliged to express all their thoughts: What kind of world would that be? In reality, people think continually and express only some of their thoughts. People can begin to use emotional intelligence to access their internal experience by focusing on feeling without adding the burden of conscious expression.

In short, therapists need to coach people to

1. Feel continuously and be conscious of their feeling.
2. Feel without the need to express themselves verbally. They can express feelings in different ways, such as words, art, facial expressions, body movements, or sounds. All of these media express the message.
3. Express feelings when they deem it appropriate.

It is also important to help people recognize that it is never simply a situation or an event that makes them feel a particular way. People need to take into account that what they were experiencing before a particular event occurred had a part in their emotional reactions. They need to realize they are not simply moved from one stationary, emotionless state to another by a particular emotion but instead are always in the process of feeling something, and their current feelings always influence the way they perceive what is occurring. Thus, when people express their feelings they need to learn not to blame the situation or the other person for the way they feel. They need to accept that they, too, are responsible for their own reactions. It is never a simple case of "You make me angry." It is important that people recognize that when they are overwhelmed and angry this is not only because their partners make demands but also because they are in certain states—for example, having had a bad day—and are feeling stressed because of that or, that if people feel sad, it is not only because their partners did not greet them warmly but also because they have been alone all day and are feeling isolated. People need to take into account the initial feelings that led them to react to the current situation the way they did before they give voice to their emotions.

ACCESSING MALADAPTIVE EMOTIONS

An emotion is maladaptive when it is an old, familiar, disorganizing feeling that recurs across time, situations, and relationships. It is like an old friend who is not good for a person. Unhealthy emotions are always difficult, deep, and distressing. There is something so familiar about these difficult emotions and their repetitive, unchanging quality. It is this un-changing quality and the enduring sense of woundedness that lets therapists and their clients know that these feelings are not current, primary emo-tional responses to a situation. Unhealthy emotions do not shift and move with changing circumstance; rather, they simply stick to current circum-stances and change the person to conform to the unhealthy dictates of the emotion. Unhealthy emotions end up determining people's responses to the situation instead of allowing the situation to determine the response. They are enduring and resistant to change. By contrast, secondary bad feelings, although they also might be difficult, can change readily once the situation or the thought changes.

Maladaptive feelings often are about a person's sense of self: He or she feels diminished, unworthy, or unable. These feelings do not organize a person for adaptive action; instead, they are disorganizing. Unhealthy primary emotions are more a part of people's character and identity than they are reactions to situations. They are associated with primary negative views of the self and with unresolved past hurts and fears. Maladaptive feelings seem very core to the self; they feel like part of one's identity, but not a healthy identity.

Another clear indicator that feelings are maladaptive is that they overwhelm people and suck them into their vortex. Any difficult feeling that repeatedly controls someone, a feeling out of which he or she cannot shift, is probably unhealthy. In general, although these feelings often take over and totally color people's views of reality, at some level people usually know that the feelings are not helpful or healthy. People in their reflective modes often know well which of their feelings are maladaptive and can predict what will happen when they feel those emotions. Sometimes people even nourish this feeling and seem to enjoy the pain of feeling so alone, wounded, and different.

Examples of maladaptive primary feelings that clients often feel are a sense of destructive anger; a sad, powerless sense of victimization; or a feeling of being weak and invisible. Other maladaptive primary feelings involve a deep sense of woundedness, a feeling of vulnerability and fear, a basic sense of insecurity, and a core sense of shame or worthlessness or of feeling unloved or unlovable. Often these feelings are masked by other feelings on the surface: secondary ones, such as feeling upset, depressed, irritable, or frustrated. In addition, as I have discussed, maladaptive emotion needs to be constantly distinguished from healthy, adaptive emotion; for example, destructive anger needs to be distinguished from healthy, empowering anger, and hopeless sadness should be distinguished from a healing grief. Maladaptive fear that is panicky or desperately dependent needs to be distinguished from fear that seeks out safety and protection, and debilitating shame needs to be distinguished from shame that informs a person that he or she has made a mistake. For example, unhealthy primary shame that makes a person feel "I am defective to the core" and encompasses the person's total identity differs from healthy guilt regarding an action about which a person feels he or she can do something. When feeling healthy guilt, a person feels "I can atone for my action," whereas an unhealthy primary sense of shame might make the person want to shrink into the ground. Unhealthy fear grips every fiber of people's bodies while they relive something that is no longer present, whereas secondary anxiety about not succeeding dissolves when they stop thinking about tomorrow's exam. Freezing and tensing in response to consciously desired sexual touch from a loved one is another example of maladaptive fear. In this case, a person's brain sends alarm signals of danger that are based on past sexual trauma, even though no danger is currently present. This occurs because fear is too readily activated by harmless cues due to past traumatic learning.

Dreams are often helpful in identifying people's core maladaptive experiences. For example, one of my therapy clients had a dream that she was forced to eat a shit sandwich by her parents. In the dream she decided that she deserved to eat shit rather than take an opportunity to escape. As she entered the feeling state in this dream, she contacted her deep sense of unworthiness. Another woman, who was infertile, dreamed that she was biting into a peach, fine on the outside but rotten at the core. I asked her to describe herself as the peach, and this helped her access her sense of being rotten at the core. Both of these clients first got in touch with their sense of unworthiness and shame and then changed their views of themselves as bad by accessing their healthy feelings of being angry at violation, their grief at loss, and their basic human needs to be valued for who they are. Another client had a dream of being a baby in a basket dropped at my door, needing to be taken care of. He had been emotionally neglected as a child. Another woman dreamed of herself as a small child, lost and alone in a small clearing in a dark forest, unable to move. Both these clients, after acknowledging their fear of abandonment and grieving their losses in a safe, supportive, therapeutic environment, acknowledged their anger at violation. This led them to acknowledge their needs for boundaries and protection. They were then able to internalize my empathy and soothe themselves, and then they felt more able to be alone. All human beings have a need to be valued, and all people need to be validated to have a sense of self-worth and to be connected to another to provide security.

In working to access maladaptive emotions, therapists need to work empathically with clients to access this second-order level of evaluation and bring it into the open. For example, the therapist might say, "As much as this feeling of anger at being diminished captures how wronged you feel, part of you is saying it comes from this terribly vulnerable feeling that you will no longer be special to her." Often unhealthy primary emotional responses seem very intense and even meaningful, but what is so characteristic of them is that they do not seem to change, get better, or go away. Their constancy is their hallmark. Also, they do not improve people's lives but rather damage them and their relationships. At first people might not see how these feelings do damage, but over time and with reflection they generally learn, often the hard way, that their maladaptive emotions do not do them any good. Emotion coaches need to help clients see that these feelings do not work for them. Coaches do this with a combination of leading and following. Coaches validate people's feelings but constantly focus on anything people say about how the feeling does not work for them or about how it damages them or others. It is important to help people see that they are not bad, or even wrong, for feeling this way but that the feeling is not functional, leaves them feeling bad, and does not help them get what they need. For example, a client might need to recognize that this is the same old sense of anger in which he always gets stuck: anger about never getting what he needs. Or the emotion might be the familiar loneliness or the painful sense of deprivation of which a client can never seem to rid herself. A maladaptive emotion might also be a familiar, intense sense of humiliation so out of proportion to a minor slight, or a recurring sense of devastation at criticism, even though the criticism is minor or even constructive. Coaches help clients realize that an emotion is maladaptive first by validating that the feeling is very real and core and then by highlighting how it is not working for them and does not lead to what they need. Over time, with sufficient support and highlighting of the destructive effect of the maladaptive emotion, clients come to recognize that this old "friend" needs to go.

Emotion coaches highlight maladaptive emotions mainly by re-entering the problematic state; exploring it and its meanings (Greenberg, Rice, et al., 1993); and coming to an agreement with clients that, rather than being an incontrovertible truth, this emotional state is a wound that needs to be healed. Often, identifying the source of the wound helps the client recognize that the feeling is maladaptive. Empathic exploration of the maladaptive state often leads to a deeper understanding of its source. At other times exploration reveals that it is the intensity of the reaction that is problematic. A coach may also conjecture about what must be happening in this state and, occasionally, if a person seems truly unable to discover any connections, the coach may interpret sources of the maladaptive state or its negative consequences. Thus, a coach might conjecture, "My hunch is that this deep anxiety comes from feeling out of control"; "I guess your fear of hurting your colleague's feelings after a disagreement relates to how you felt you had to take care of your mother's hurt whenever you disagreed with her"; or "I understand how bruised you feel from all these criticisms and demands in your job, and I guess you are saying it's the degree to which you feel so shattered that is the problem."

Half of the battle of change is won when people see that it is their states that are problematic, that they are in conflict, or that they are in part authors of their own distress rather than viewing themselves as victims of others or of a lack of support or believing that fate is to blame. Helping people acknowledge maladaptive states as problematic lets them take a form of responsibility for their own experience. This is not to say that people are at fault for having an unhealed wound, or for overreacting to something, but helping them recognize that there is something they are doing in these states that leads to their difficulties and that they need to do something to change is an important goal that is sometimes rather difficult to achieve. For example, consider the case of a man who enters a maladaptive state of helplessness whenever he meets criticism, setbacks, or challenges to his competence. At times he feels competent and feels that he has things to offer, but when he enters this maladaptive state he collapses into feelings of utter helplessness. He panics and sees people as highly unsupportive ogres and himself as weak and without substance. In this state he is sucked into a vortex of powerless and helpless feelings, and he catastrophizes. He lacks any solidity and feels like a fragile glass window that will shatter on touch or like a building held together so tenuously that the slightest jolt will lead to collapse. How can an emotion coach help this person get sufficient perspective on this helpless state and help him see that, rather than this helplessness being reality, or a valid response to mistreatment by others, that it is a maladaptive overreaction?

I have not found it that helpful, with this type of enduring maladaptive state, to try to demonstrate to people that their thoughts or beliefs are faulty. Rather, what I have found helpful is helping them get a perspective that this is a temporary, maladaptive, overreactive state they get sucked into and that this is not all they are or all of which they are capable. In other words, I work toward a view of this being a partial self among many possible selves. In addition, rather than viewing clients' beliefs, thoughts, or perceptions as faulty, I understand that it is their *reactions* that are problematic and that these are what need to be regulated. I therefore work to create a sense of other possibilities based on the notion that this is one of a variety of states available to clients and to help them regulate their reactions. I also try to build bridges to other states (recall the idea of a transitional conductor in chapter 3). A lot of this work depends on being able to maintain the therapist–client alliance and appropriate interactional positioning. The person has to feel throughout that the therapist is on his or her side, validating the person and working with him or her against this problem state. Therefore, what I do first is empathize with the person and validate how awful it is to feel so helpless, and I convey an understanding of what he or she is feeling. For me to truly validate the person's feeling of helplessness, this empathy has to come from a place in me of real acceptance and understanding of what it is like for the person to feel so unable.

At the same time that I validate how the client feels, I hold onto the knowledge of his or her other possibilities, and I wonder aloud about them. I might say, "The issue is how to find a way out when you are feeling so caught," or "The dilemma is how, when you are in these states, you can find your feet, and how I can help you do that." Often clients insist that this is the way they are and that no other reality is true or conceivable. In such cases I might say, "I know this is a part of your identity and that when you are in this state it really feels like this is true and all else is a sham." I might also comment on how important it seems for them right now to convince me that this is the case. I add that this painful place is where they get stuck and lose all their resources, that I have seen them at other times feel differently about themselves, and that I know they sometimes handle things differently. I recognize these as real existential moments in which I help clients face their impasses—the places where they get stuck in their emotional lives. I tell them that if I could help them solve the problem, I would, but that I know that ultimately when they are feeling this way it is they who have to figure out how to find their feet. I can only offer support or guidance; it is the clients who have to find the will to change. If my clients get angry and say I am not helping, I empathize with how frustrating it is and reassure them that I am trying to help. I reemphasize, however, that I know that in this stuck place I can't bring about change, that whatever I do would be a temporary fix, and that the real dilemma is how the clients can find their way to connect with the strengths and resources with which they have lost contact. The whole encounter is aimed at helping people find the sense of the possibility of change and the will to change. It is all predicated on my knowing the person well enough, having seen that he or she has other possibilities and that he or she is able to enter other states, which I refer to at times throughout this encounter. If a client is truly without skills, then more training in emotion regulation is needed (cf. Linehan, 1993).

In situations such as the one described in the previous section, I confront maladaptive emotions while still supporting the healthy ones. It is here that my prizing of the growth-related core of the person, of his or her possibilities, comes in to play. Buber's (1958) view that it is the seeing of the possibility in others in an I–thou relationship that helps possibilities come into being is uppermost in my mind. I also try to position myself at this point in such a way that I can present problems to clients of how to access their resources. I allude to and express faith that there are other possibilities but try to engage clients in the task of how they can find them. We work together on trying to figure out how they can find their strengths and resources when they are feeling so overwhelmed by their maladaptive feeling states. Throughout such interactions it is my valuing of the inner cores of possibility in the clients that is important. I take it for granted that there is strength. The problem is not is there strength but how to access it. I do not try to prove to clients, or have them prove to themselves, that there is another reality. The pertinent issue is how to access another, healthier reality rather than evaluating the truth or falsity of clients' beliefs. I take it somewhat for granted that a particular belief is not true because it is based on a maladaptive emotional state, so it is a case of "You believe this now because you are feeling this way." This therapeutic work is done while the person is feeling the maladaptive feeling, so it is more of an existential confrontation than a conceptual discussion. At these points, using imagery to contact a more powerful sense of self, and actually evoking a feeling of competence in the person's bodily experience, can be helpful. If clients can access a sense of themselves as walking tall and having a backbone, then they can begin to get a taste of alternate self-organizations that can then be developed as a resource.

If people are to live happier, more fulfilling lives, their primary maladaptive emotions need to change. These emotions often, however, have to first be experienced and acknowledged to make them more amenable to transformation. Acknowledging maladaptive emotions is the first step in defining the true nature of the problem. Clients come then to see that the problem is "I feel rotten, powerless, or unlovable" or that "My heart is broken; I don't wish to carry on." People cannot leave a place until they have arrived at that place, and so it is with these dreaded feelings. It is the experiencing of the feeling that makes it unequivocally clear what the problem is: This is a key ingredient in motivating new ways of coping with the feeling. A person's old, unsuccessful coping style might have been to either avoid the bad feelings or to feel overwhelmed and out of control and sink into despair, numbness, depression, and anxiety. Coaches need to help people make sense of their experience and begin to process more information by identifying their maladaptive emotions, and the associated destructive thoughts, in words. Then the coach helps them bring previously unused internal resources to bear on coping with this distress-producing condition. Change comes about by having new, corrective experiences that challenge the unhealthy feelings and beliefs with a newfound sense of worth and strength. Unhealthy emotions cannot be changed through reason alone, or by avoidance. This means that emotion coaches have to help people feel their unhealthy feelings so they can change them.

IDENTIFYING DESTRUCTIVE BELIEFS AND CONSTRUALS

Once an experience is clearly accepted and recognized as maladaptive, the coach needs to help clients identify the destructive beliefs and patterns of thoughts that accompany their unhealthy feelings and access the core negative belief or construal embedded in these feelings. The negative belief is much more easily accessible and put into words when the person is experiencing the maladaptive feeling. The coach thus needs to work with cognition when it is hot. When a belief is just cold, it is not really accessible to change. People can talk about all kinds of negative views of themselves in an abstract and intellectual way, and they will not change. They have to be feeling what they are saying to make the whole maladaptive scheme amenable to change.

As I have discussed, people often experience their negative beliefs as thoughts or critical voices in their heads. A criticizing, internal voice often has been internalized from previous interactions or abstracted from general life experience. After isolating the content of the self-critical thoughts it is helpful to externalize the negative thoughts, as though they are coming from outside the person. This helps separate these antagonistic attitudes from more realistic ones and identify them as the source of the person's distress. Often people's self-attacks at first may be displayed in a rational or descriptive manner. As people verbalize the contents of the criticisms, however, they will spontaneously begin to express emotion. If they do not, then the coach's job is to get at the feeling tone in the criticism. Most evident is contempt. It is this contempt for the self that perpetuates people's maladaptive feelings (Whelton & Greenberg, 2001). Most often contempt is seen in the curve of the person's lip and the raising of the nose or heard in the person's tone of voice as he or she speaks. An emotion coach might facilitate the client's recognition of the maladaptiveness in his or her voice by commenting, for example, "So this is the voice that makes you feel so bad. What do you feel as you hear yourself say these things?" A coach might also say, "Good—we are getting to how you attack yourself and put yourself down. Are you aware of your mouth or your voice as you say these things?" It is also helpful to set the stage for collaborating on the task of combating these negative thoughts by opposing them. Thus, a coach might say "Then we will need to find out how you can stand up to this harsh voice."

Often people find it quite natural to articulate their self-accusations in a statement spoken from the third-person point of view, for example, saying such things as "You're too stupid, ugly, fat, or lazy." It is therefore helpful when dealing with this self-attacking voice to promote a two-chair dialogue in which the voice is truly externalized by being enacted. Here the critic voices its criticism to the imagined self in an empty chair (Greenberg, Rice, & Elliott, 1993). Thus the client might say to himself or herself in a harsh voice, "You're such a coward. You're despicable, worthless, untouchable." After identifying these hostile voices it is much easier to help the client separate out a healthier, self-supportive view. Once the vicious, contemptuous quality of the internal voice is identified, people often recognize that the voice is acting way out of proportion to what has occurred. This helps them overcome it.

Sometimes this internal voice might be overprotectively stifling of spontaneity. It could be saying such things as "Be careful, you might get hurt," or it might even seem like a helpful teacher, saying "You should try harder." Unfortunately, as this voice develops it often becomes highly attacking, malicious, and self-denigrating. The coach's job is to help clients become aware of this voice and to understand the distress these destructive thoughts are causing them. Often these hostile attitudes toward the self sound very similar to what the person's caretakers might have said to him or her, and the person has adopted all the criticisms and now repeats them to himself or herself. It is as though a negative parent or significant other now lives inside the person's head. If these destructive thoughts are to be overcome, then the core criticisms need to be articulated and recognized as attacks that originally came from someone else. Then people will more easily be able to combat them with another voice inside themselves. The coach's task here is to help articulate the negative core belief in words to provide a handle with which clients can hold onto this unwanted baggage so they can change it. Once the content of the belief has been articulated, it can be inspected, and the role it has played in hampering people's lives can be understood.

As noted earlier, the schemes that carry the negative beliefs can be broken into two major categories: bad self and weak self. The bad self-scheme is based on shame and the belief that one is not good enough. The following beliefs about the self operate in this state: The self might be seen as *unlovable*, *flawed*, or *undesirable*, or people can feel *inferior* and be ashamed of perceived *inadequacy* (cf. Young, 1990). People can also feel *guilty* and believe they are *bad* and deserve to be punished. In addition, people might believe they are *incompetent* for *not being the best* or for *not being as good as others*.

The weak self-scheme, in contrast, is based on fear and anxiety and the belief that one is not able to cope and survive on one's own. Here the following beliefs about the self operate. The self can be seen as *dependent*, believing *that the self needs others to survive* or that *the person is unable to support himself or herself*. Submissive beliefs, such as *I must put others' needs before mine*, or *expressing my needs or anger will lead to something bad*, might predominate. Beliefs that the *self is vulnerable* and that something bad will happen or that one *will lose control* also are associated with a weak sense of self. Beliefs about *connection*, *deprivation*, *abandonment*, *lack of trust*, and *isolation* are all associated with this weak sense of self. Being able to articulate these feelings in words, such as "I'll never get the love I need," "I'll be alone forever," or "No one will accept me" help both client and coach refer back to these complex states.

Another set of negative beliefs can be related to maladaptive anger, rage, and a bad-other scheme. Beliefs such as "I don't care," "They don't care," "They are bad," or "They deserve to be taught a lesson" can be used to support and justify maladaptive anger. In addition to these classes of beliefs, people's idiosyncratic construals of how they ought to be, their expectations of how others will react to their wishes, and how they will feel in response are also articulated. Becoming aware of core conflictual themes (Luborsky & Crits-Christoph, 1990) in an experiential manner also provides emotional insight.

My approach to working with negative beliefs and construals is neither didactic nor disputational. I do not try to debate, persuade, or reason with people to see that their beliefs or views are irrational. Neither do I help them inspect their reasoning or the rational basis of their beliefs. I also do not try to get them to collect evidence for or against their beliefs. The issue is not one of the truth or validity of their beliefs but of their usefulness. I take the stance from the outset that these beliefs are probably neither useful nor helpful; rather, they are generally self-evidently destructive. I thus take it for granted that the beliefs are maladaptive if they make people feel bad, and I work to demonstrate this by helping people experience how the beliefs make them feel. There is no evidence as compelling as feeling something. I thus work to help my clients discover what they are telling themselves and how this makes them feel, and I try to assist them in moving away from the negative beliefs and injunctions that are hurting them.

The process of working with negative beliefs often involves first identifying the content of the negative belief and saying this in the second person to the self. Experiencing how the belief makes the person feel is the second step. Reflecting on the sources and destructive effects of the beliefs, and understanding how these beliefs influence the person's life, constitute a third step. Finally, the person needs to formulate a resilient response to the belief so that he or she can separate the self from the dictates of these beliefs and identify with his or her strengths and resources. In the next chapter I discuss how to access the healthy voice in one's personality, but first I outline a general set of strategies for working with emotion up to this point, to help people arrive at their primary emotions and establish their adaptive utility.

Overcoming Hopelessness

People often express hopelessness in working with their emotions. They might say that they feel like giving up and may collapse into despair. In this state the client feels a sense of futility or doom regarding the future, or some aspects of it, and defeat or resignation dominate. Coupled with the hopelessness often is a sense of helplessness and a lack of confidence in the self to cope with the situation. Statements of hopelessness include expressions of futility, defeat, feeling beaten, giving up, inability to fight, doom, feeling that one cannot have or achieve what one wants, resignation, submission, and suicidal ideation. Statements reflecting helplessness and powerlessness refer to a person's feelings of lacking internal coping resources, self-confidence or ability, strength or power, to control or to change one's situation. In addition, there may be statements about feeling small, suffocated, numb, immobilized or trapped, feeling defenseless, tired, weary, destroyed, crushed, weighed down or squashed, or feelings of inadequacy or worthlessness. There also is an adaptive state of hopelessness that informs one when effort is no longer useful and that one should give up. As with other adaptive feelings, this informs adaptive action and once the action is completed the person moves on. In contrast, secondary and maladaptive hopeless states leave one stuck and needing to be changed so that he or she can move on.

Helping people deal with this sense of hopelessness or discouragement is an important therapeutic task. Although it seems very core, hopelessness often is a secondary state masking other more core experiences such as fear, shame or anger, and sadness. Coaches need to help people get to the underlying feelings. Coaching in this area is particularly important because people are often quite discouraged and stuck and need a scaffold to help them come out of this state. In a study of how people resolve hopelessness in emotion-focused treatment, we found that people go through steps with the help of their therapists (Sicoli & Greenberg, 2000).

The first step involves working with the person to identify negative, hopelessness inducing thoughts and beliefs, and to help the person experience his or her sense of agency in the production of the experience of hopelessness. A two-chair dialogue between two parts of the self is often helpful. In one chair the person enacts the hopeless producing agent by saying, for example, "What's the use?," "You will never succeed," or "You're doomed to emptiness." The person might also say "You're useless," "You're such a wimp," "No one will ever want you," or "You always mess up." The initial step thus involves helping clients recognize and explore their own internal hopelessness generating processes. Clients then begin to understand that they contribute to maintaining their hopeless state by their attributions and the way they think and that their hopelessness is not merely a result of an external situation. Initially, clients often are unsure about how they generate their hopelessness and they may experience periods of confusion. With a good alliance, however, there generally is a willingness to sift through the confusion and attempt to understand the process. Ultimately clients learn that they are engaged in internal processes that contribute to "making" themselves feel hopeless and that they maintain this state by the things they say to themselves. The content of the negative cognition is often centered around themes of helplessness, lack of belief in one's ability to cope, self-deprecating statements, negative beliefs about the future, values and standards, and self-blame. The exploration of self as an agent may also involve seeing how inactivity and avoidance such as not talking to a spouse, withdrawal, or procrastination contribute to a hopeless feeling.

After activating the hopeless state, the next step in achieving change is to access new, more core emotional experiences (sadness, pain, anger). The coach helps the client search for a more primary feeling. Clients often identify new feelings in response to identifying the agency and negative cognition involved in producing the hopelessness. Thus, clients may feel pain or sadness in response to being told that they are no good, or doomed to fail. The coach's job is to steer them past agreements with the negative thoughts and hopelessness toward how they actually feel in response to the doom-casting statements from the hopelessness-inducing voice within. The client experiences the emotion but at first may not experience it fully. The feeling is undifferentiated and the client may express some confusion by saying "I don't know what I feel."

The coach works with the client to feel the underlying pain, sadness or anger more fully. It is important for the coach to help the client to shift from a detached description of experience to a more focused bodily felt experience. With people who have some resilience, helping them stay with the hopelessness rather than avoid it is sometimes the best way to get them to bounce back. Hitting rock bottom coupled with the validation and empathy of the coach leads to a rebound. In other cases with people in more desperate states, this method of "staying with" does not lead to resilience. It is better to access alternate emotions by shifting attention to other feelings or accessing needs. The needs that are accessed at this early stage will most likely be global, vague needs, but the coach's mere mention of needs often helps the client shift his or her state to a more forward moving one.

Once the client begins to truly feel and accept any emerging adaptive emotions and is able to express these emotions both verbally and nonverbally, the global hopelessness begins to be destructured. Through this more focused contact with the current emotional experience, the client begins to explore its meaning in more depth and with more specificity. Acceptance of the feeling as well as feeling it is important.

In some cases clients contact a primary fear that underlies the hopelessness—a fear that they are unable to survive in: "I'm just really scared; I feel I don't have the strength" or "I'm afraid it is going to go on and on and I won't be able to cope with it." The maladaptive fear can be manifested in two ways, intrapersonally and interpersonally: fears relating to not being able to cope, fear of collapsing, fear of failure, or a doomed future (intrapersonal fears); and fear of being hurt or tread upon by others (interpersonal fears). Both forms of fear prevent the person from accessing an inner strength to overcome the hopelessness. At core, even in the interpersonal fear is the fear that the self will not be able to cope as in "They'll hurt me and I will not be able to cope with it." This needs to be experienced and then countered with the more adaptive emotion.

The underlying feelings of adaptive anger, pain, and sadness are often intermingled with expressions of unmet needs (i.e., feeling sad about lack of spousal support and stating, "I deserve to be supported and cared for"). Once the client is able to fully "sink into" the newly emerged adaptive emotion, it is time to clarify its meaning and access the need associated with it. This is done by maintaining contact with the feeling and speaking from it. This is the time to focus the client on the wants and needs that have begun to emerge with the expression of deeper, more clearly articulated and more forcefully stated painful feelings. Needs that were once dismissed or tentatively stated are now expressed as valid and legitimate in a convincing manner. New emotional experience helps to strengthen and consolidate the sense of self and the self's needs are asserted in a clear and sustained manner. The self begins to move from feeling helpless to feeling empowered, and a resilient self emerges. The client shifts from a hopeless and helpless stance to one of hope and strength.

The process thus involves helping people identify how they "make" themselves feel hopeless, and having them do this in the session, thereby activating the hopelessness. Then it is amenable to change and the underlying primary feelings are accessed, and the needs within them are mobilized as an antidote to the hopelessness. The person moves from feeling discouraged and hopeless to feeling the courage and hope from acknowledging the motivation to survive and thrive in primary adaptive emotions. People come to realize that expectations are disappointments under constrictions and that hopelessness is often produced by their inability to let go of wishes that will not be met.

GENERAL STRATEGIES OF INTERVENTION

There are three general levels of intervention for accessing emotion. The first level is *conversational*. At this level, reflections of feeling, experientially focused questions, and interpretations are used to try to help identify and symbolize feelings. A second, more process-directive level involves *guiding* a client's attention to a particular aspect of experience or behavior. The aim is to increase awareness of emotional experience. The third level of intervention involves *stimulating* new experience. The goal is intensification of experience.

In addition to these three classes of intervention, I briefly elaborate on a list of strategies for working with emotion, which are summarized in Exhibit 7.1 (cf. Plutchik, 2000). Most of these are conversational strategies, although a few are more process directive or stimulating. Probably the first strategy in emotion coaching is to identify the stimuli that trigger the emotion. Often people experience a puzzling or problematic feeling, without understanding its source. *Identifying the trigger* is important. To do this, ask what about the stimulus (or its meaning to the person) triggered the emotion, and when it occurred. The second useful strategy involves *focusing the person's attention on any of the missing components* in the feeling and fleshing out all the components. Emotion, as I have discussed, is a relational action tendency often produced by the appraisal of a situation in relation to a need. This provides five elements on which to focus in responding to people's emotions: (a) the stimulus situation, (b) the feeling, (c) the meaning of the situation, (d) the action tendency, and (e) the need or goal involved. Often the component that is missing will help identify

EXHIBIT 7.1
Intervention Strategies

1. Identify the stimuli that trigger the emotion.
2. Identify any missing components in the emotion.
3. Verbally label emotions.
4. Identify the directional tendency in the emotion.
5. Identify conflicts.
6. Identify stuck points.
7. Explore idiosyncratic meanings clients give to feelings.
8. Develop capacities to experience and express a range of emotions.
9. Be specific and focus on concrete experience.
10. Use evocative language and metaphors.
11. Use respectful, appreciative language.
12. Share your feelings with the client.
13. Identify the emotions in conflicts.
14. Approach feared feelings.
15. Use past feelings to identify current feelings.
16. Explore origins of current feelings.

more clearly what is occurring. Thus, if the feeling is missing, explore what it is. If the action tendency, the need, or the meaning is missing, explore what they are. Filling in what is not there often helps the person move forward. The next strategy is to help people *find words to verbally label emotions* and to explore physiological and sensory motor experiences. This is followed by *identifying the directional tendency in the emotion*. An emotion is not simply an emotion—it always implies something, a need and an action. It is important to identify what the emotion impels people toward. This is often the impetus for change.

It also is helpful to *look for conflicts* and to focus on the emotions in each part of the conflict. Look for splits between different tendencies, particularly between "I want to, but I'm afraid (or I can't)" and "I should, but I can't (or won't)." Next, *look for where clients are stuck;* identify blocks and interruptions and the shame and fear that may lie behind them. *Exploring the idiosyncratic meanings of clients' feelings* is an essential strategy. This is particularly important in helping people understand their feelings and in creating new meaning. The unique ways in which people construe situations result in certain feelings, and it is these methods of construal that need to be identified so they can be inspected and understood. Identifying people's construals and helping them realize that it is their way of seeing things that led to their puzzling emotional reactions is often very liberating for clients. Next, explore and *promote clients' abilities to express a range of emotions*; help them access emotions that are absent and leave them disempowered. Ask yourself whether the person can express anger, sadness, fear, love or joy. If the client cannot, the coach should help explore what is blocking this.

In addition, always *promote exploration of concrete situations* in all their particularity. Recognize that emotions occur in specific situations, in the details. Therefore, be as specific as possible and explore the details of events, perceptions, thoughts, and especially internal reactions. Next, *use evocative language and metaphors to help elicit emotions*. Also, *use respectful, appreciative language* (Wachtel, 1997). Do not say "You avoid your sadness" but instead "It is really difficult to feel so sad." Disclose your own feelings with clients when appropriate, especially feelings you believe will be facilitative and are occurring here and now, in response to the client. Full presence and disciplined genuineness governed by a principle of "do no harm" are called for in working with people's emotions. The next strategy involves *identifying and exploring the emotions in a conflict*. Often there is a conflict between wishes and fears. It is helpful to identify these and other, related feelings, such as anger at frustration of a wish or guilt at the idea of fulfilling the wish. Help people *approach dreaded states and feelings* they fear to expose and desensitize them. *Use past feelings to identify current feelings*, and explore the origins of current feelings in past experiences.

EXERCISE: RECOGNIZING AND DEALING WITH DIFFICULT EMOTIONAL STATES

First, focus on yourself and what you are feeling rather than on what you are thinking or on what others have done to you.

1. Identify and give direct attention to a troublesome state in which you spend a lot of time, often without recognizing that you do so (e.g., angry, hurt).
2. Allow the emotion and be interested in it. Allow yourself to feel it in your body.
3. Identify how you feel toward the emotion. Do you feel accepting or rejecting?
4. Accept the emotion welcomingly.
5. Explore how this state feels.
6. Identify the voice and the thoughts that accompany this state.
7. Identify what, specifically, triggers this state.
8. Explore the relation of this state to anything in the past.
9. Identify what this state is saying now.
10. Interact with this state. Say something to it—react and notice changes in state. Cooperate with it instead of trying to control it.

8

THE TRANSFORMING POWER OF AFFECT: FACILITATING ACCESS TO ALTERNATE ADAPTIVE EMOTIONS AND NEEDS

Now that a client has identified his or her maladaptive emotions, how does a therapist help the person access healthy emotions, the ones that will help him or her transform the maladaptive feelings and beliefs? How does an emotion coach help move people from feeling hopeless to feeling hopeful, from feeling helpless to feeling strong? First, therapists must help people to breathe deeply while they are feeling the bad feelings of shame, fear, anger, or sadness and must empathize with the feeling. This helps during emotion regulation and is especially important when the distressing feelings are intense and overwhelming. Once the therapist is able to help people regulate the intensity of their distress, then he or she needs to help them identify what else they are feeling in addition to, or in response to, their maladaptive emotions. This is where the therapist will help people find the potential for change. A number of different methods in addition to the power of the empathetic relational connection for accessing alternate emotions with which to change maladaptive emotion are summarized in the following list and are discussed in the following sections.

1. Shifting attention
2. Access needs and goals
3. Positive imagery
4. Expressive enactment of the emotion
5. Remembering another emotion
6. Talking about an emotion
7. Expressing an emotion on the client's behalf
8. Other methods for expressing emotion

SHIFTING ATTENTION

As discussed in chapter 3, shifting people's focus of attention to a background feeling is a key method of helping them change their emotional states. On the edge of awareness, or in the background, behind their current dominant emotion, often lies another, subdominant emotion that can be found if one attends to or searches for it. The feeling is there but is not yet in focal awareness. Behind the anger might be sadness, love, or forgiveness; at the edge of sadness is anger, within the hurt or the fear is the anger; behind the shame are the pride and self-esteem. The therapist's crucial role is to shift clients' attention to this subdominant feeling, to focus on it and elaborate on it, and then to teach them how to do this on their own. For example, one woman talked about how "defective" and "soiled" she felt by the abuse she had suffered, and with the help of her coach she was able to focus her attention on the expression of disgust on her face and become more empowered. She found that her disgust and anger at being violated lay behind her more dominant fear and shame. An emotion coach helped a man with fragile self-esteem find the hurt at feeling slighted that lay beneath his anger by guiding his attention to his bodily felt experience at the time of the slight.

ACCESS NEEDS AND GOALS

A second and more directive way in which therapists can help clients access their healthy, healing emotions and internal resources is by asking them, when they are in their maladaptive states, what they need. People, when they are suffering and in pain, usually know what they need. Once they know what they need in a situation they often begin to feel like they have some control over it. The coach's validation of the need is an important element in strengthening it. A sense of "I can do something about my situation or how I feel" then emerges; they begin to feel that "I can survive. I do have resources, talents, and skills. I am worthwhile." This is the healthy, internal voice. Coaches then need to ask them, "Which of the things that you need can you get from others or give to yourself? How can you affirm yourself, soothe yourself, or care for yourself or get these things from others?" Self-empathy and compassion for oneself are important. Helping people do something in the world for themselves is also important. Asking the question, "What do you have to do to get what you need?" is a helpful question. Reaching out to someone who cares is doing something for oneself, as is doing something that one enjoys. These are all ways that people can help themselves shift out of their negative states.

If people have difficulty accessing their needs, this is an indicator that they need more empathic support. At this time the coach might need to voice the need for them. Thus, the coach might conjecture "I guess you just need some comfort when you are in this place" or "My sense is that your disgust is saying 'get away from me, just get out of my space.' Is that correct?" Alternatively, the coach might validate how difficult it is for the person to form a need, clarify a need, or feel entitled to a need and then proceed to explore this difficulty.

POSITIVE IMAGERY

A third way to activate alternate feelings is to use imagery. Imagination is a means of bringing about an emotional response. Imagery involves using people's more conscious capacities to change their experiences. People can use their imaginations to create scenes that they know will help them feel an emotion, and they can use this as an antidote to a maladaptive feeling they want to change. They can thus change what they feel, not by changing feelings with reason but by using imagination to evoke new emotions. People differ in their capacity to use self-generated imagery to replace unwanted emotions with more desirable ones. This capacity, however, can be developed. For example, when feeling maladaptive anger or dejected isolation, people can be encouraged at an appropriate time to imagine themselves in situations that generate positive feelings. When the maladaptive feeling has been fully acknowledged and validated therapists can ask such clients if they can imagine themselves in strong or capable states, in the arms of loved ones, or as having a police officer or their therapist along to protect them. Imagining loved ones also can be very effective as an antidote to feelings of painful isolation or anxiety. With practice, people can learn how to generate opposing emotions through imagery and to use these to counteract negative emotions. This takes time, relaxation, and attention to breathing to help them relax. To change anger at loved ones therapists also can ask people to imagine more positive attributes of the person with whom they are angry or to imagine a time they felt more positively toward that person. Therapists can invite people to balance their resentment toward another with appreciation to maintain their connection. Asking a person to imagine a time in his or her life when he or she felt happiest, contrasting this with the person's current bad feeling, and shuttling between these states sometimes help people see that states other than the ones they are in are possible. Therapists can ask people to recall an awful memory and then ask them to bring supportive people or feelings from a positive memory into that bad memory. This can help alleviate the bad feeling. Images based on memories of past experience thus can be evoked to generate alternate experience and provide access to alternate self-organizations. These alternate image-generated states are then used to combat negative self-states.

The generation of compassion for the self and others through imagery can be particularly helpful. Thus, a therapist might ask a client to imagine himself as an adult comforting his 5-year-old self, alone and hurt in his bedroom, or a therapist might ask the client to imagine someone—the coach or another protective figure—going into the child's room and giving the child what was needed at the time, be it comfort, support, or protection (see Exercise 6). The goal is to evoke new emotional states that provide alternatives to the maladaptive states in which the person is stuck and then to use these new, more adaptive states as launching pads to help transform the old, maladaptive ones. To do this people need to have internalized enough self-support from others and to have a strong enough sense of self to muster self-support. If they cannot do this, then the therapist's empathic attunement to their possibilities is their only available resource.

EXPRESSIVE ENACTMENT OF THE EMOTION

A fourth way to access alternate emotions is to have people enact a feeling that is not currently being experienced. As pointed out in chapter 3, this goes back to William James's (1890/1950) idea that people feel afraid because they run away from something. A therapist might ask people to adopt certain emotional stances and help them deliberately assume the expressive posture of that feeling and then intensify it. Thus the emotion coach might use psychodramatic enactments and instruct the client to "Try telling him 'I'm angry.' Say it again; yes, louder. Can you put your feet on the floor and sit up straight? Yes, do it some more." Here the person is being coached to express an emotion until the emotion begins to be experienced. This is not the encouragement of phony expression but rather an attempt to facilitate access to a suppressed, disallowed experience. Similarly, taking on a sad posture and deliberately expressing sad things can help access sadness. A therapist might suggest that a client speak to an imagined other person: "Tell her what you missed. Tell her how sad you were." Instructing people to organize their facial expressions into representations of emotions, although difficult to do, is effective, because facial expression appears to have a strong feedback component. An angry facial expression seems to produce angry experience, and a sad expression seems to produce sadness (Flack, Laird, & Cavallaro, 1999). It also is helpful to follow very closely any emerging expression. For example, if a person's eyes begin to drop the coach follows this and instructs the person to develop this movement. "Yes, look down and say this again. I missed you." Asking a client to curl up into a ball can facilitate the withdrawal tendencies of sadness. Having people hold out their hands in a pleading fashion can facilitate the experience of pleading or begging. Instructions to take on expressive postures must always be followed by asking people what they experienced after making a particular expression. Too much deliberate expression without attention to the experience it evokes can become an artificial performance rather than the evocation of experience.

REMEMBERING ANOTHER EMOTION

The fifth way to access another emotion is to remember a situation in which the emotion occurred and then to bring the memory alive in the present. This is related to the imaging processes described earlier. Remembering past emotional scenes clearly produces emotion. The physiological and expressive changes that occur in emotional responses to memories have been shown to closely resemble the changes that occur when emotions are activated in response to present stimuli (Ekman & Davidson, 1994). Memories of emotional events therefore are an important means of accessing another emotion that can then be used to help change a more maladaptive state. Emotion and memory are highly linked. Emotion is both evoked by memory and is important in restructuring emotion memories and the narratives that are built on them.

Emotions revive memories of prior occurrences. Things are stored in memory at their emotion addresses. Thus, a current disappointment links to other disappointments, and a feeling of shame is linked to other losses. Present emotional experiences thus are always multilayered, evoking with them prior instances of the same or similar emotional experiences. If coaches are to help people change what they feel, they have to help people access and restructure their emotion memories. One important form of changing emotion memories involves accessing the emotion memory to be changed and then replacing it with another one. Once another emotion memory is evoked either the new memory dominates, and the old one recedes into the background and becomes less accessible, or the new one eventually transforms the old memory. Emotions are often embedded in relational contexts. They connect self to other in the memory. Thus, people have memories of feeling shame in the face of a contemptuous parent, anger at an intrusive other, or fear of an abusive other. Therefore, accessing views of others helps one evoke emotion, and accessing different views of others helps change the emotions one felt.

One client had discovered the body of her mother (who had committed suicide), and whenever she thought of her mother, it was that horrifying image that came to mind. That image left her feeling cold and clammy, with awful feelings of fear and empty abandonment. After working through her anger, shame, and sadness, and after finally empathizing with and forgiving her mother, she talked about being able to replace this awful memory with previous, happy memories of her mother. These memories, in contrast to the others, left her feeling warm and cozy. She reported later that when she thought of her mother it was this warm, loving memory that she now accessed. Ultimately a full restructuring of emotion memory occurred; the client thought of her mother as loving; and she had good, warm feelings whenever she thought of her.

Another way to work with emotion memory to change emotional states is to access a memory of a person in one's life who supported, or would support, a different, more adaptive emotion and experience of the self. Thus therapists can ask clients if there was someone in their lives who would have seen them, or who would currently see them, as having the qualities that would support a more adaptive emotion and experience of the self. Thus, an emotion coach might say, "Is there someone in your life who believed in you or felt proud of you?" or "Who loved or protected you?" This helps the person evoke feelings of being proud or lovable and the comfort or security that accompany these feelings. One client, who could not permit himself to experience his anger and sadness, said he had no feelings toward or in reaction to his wife. He claimed that he could not feel anything and that he had no feelings, having closed them off as a child to protect himself against a perfectionistic, critical father and a cold, ignoring mother. However, after accessing memories of how his grandmother had cared about him, he wept tears of joy and sadness.

New emotion memories, however they are accessed, help change narratives. No important story is significant without emotion, and no emotions take place outside of the context of a story that give the emotion its significance. The stories people tell to make sense of their experiences and to construct their identities are, to a significant degree, dependent on the variety of emotion memories that are available to them. By changing their memories, or the accessibility of different memories, people change the stories of their lives and their identities. Thus, the previously discussed client's access to positive memories of her mother now supported a view in which she saw her mother as loving and caring rather than as recklessly abandoning, as she had previously seen her.

TALKING ABOUT AN EMOTION

Therapists can help people access new emotions by talking with them about the more desirable emotions. Talking about an emotional episode helps people re-experience the feelings they had in that emotional episode. Opening a conversation about a particular topic often helps generate an emotion relevant to that topic. Psychotherapy is a talking cure, and talk can evoke new emotions. Thus, when someone feels like a failure, talking about success experiences helps him or her contact feelings or possibilities of effectiveness. People can benefit from re-experiencing the feelings they had in past emotional episodes, and conversation can bring forth a sense of how they achieved that feeling. The therapist's response to the person is also helpful in installing the new feeling; his or her support, encouragement, and ability to see this emotional possibility in the person strengthens the possibility that he or she can recall a positive emotion.

EXPRESSING AN EMOTION ON THE CLIENT'S BEHALF

In certain situations therapists can express a particular feeling that the client is unable to express. In these instances the therapist is giving voice to the client's alternate emotion. For example, a therapist, on the client's behalf, can express outrage at a violation by saying such things as "How could they do that to you?" or "I feel furious and outraged on your behalf" or "I want to kick him in the shins." This does not prompt violence, but rather gives the client the potential to express him- or herself on a deeper level than he or she feels entitled to express. The therapist's expression of the emotion helps the client feel supported and validated and gives the client access to this emotion to help promote emotional change. Sadness for the client's loss also can be expressed by saying, "I feel really sad when I hear how alone you felt as a child" or "I feel tears come to my eyes when you tell me about this." These are all times when the therapist deems it appropriate to share these as genuine, helpful responses. The therapist must be clear that these expressions are helpful to the client and are not being expressed for the therapist's well-being or are not coming from unresolved therapist issues. The therapist must also ensure that these are genuinely felt feelings and are not being offered as a technique to get the client to access the emotion.

OTHER METHODS FOR EXPRESSING EMOTION

Humor is another method of changing emotion with emotion. Laughing can change a person's emotional state and the perspective given by humor can reframe the situation. A joke that reframes the client's situation lightens depressed feelings, often placing things in more universal light, and seeing oneself sharing Woody Allen's neuroses is somehow comforting. Many expressive arts methods also help change emotion, and although they are not always easy to use in individual therapy, they are very useful in groups. Music also is a powerful medium for changing emotion. Playing music alters people's moods, as does making music. Painting, working with clay, and dancing all change people's emotional states and can be used to access previously inaccessible emotions. After one has the idea that emotion needs to be changed with emotion, a variety of methods will suggest themselves.

SHIFTING OUT OF EMOTIONAL STATES

In addition to helping people access new emotions, a therapist sometimes needs to help people also be able to shift out of certain emotions and emotional states of mind so they can make transitions from one state to another. If people know that they are able to shift out of emotional states and that they can have some control over these states, they might not be so afraid of feeling their emotions. Getting out of an emotion is often a stumbling block. People cannot become emotionally intelligent unless they have the ability both to focus on an emotion and the equally important ability to shift away from it. People can easily become entrapped within emotions. Anger, sadness, or joy can suffuse a person until it feels like the person and the emotion are one. It is then often difficult to shift out of the emotional state and into another one. The person is so involved with his or her emotion that it feels as if the emotion determines the only reality. It is much easier to shift from one thing to another when one is thinking or imagining, because these do not fill as much of a person as do the person's emotions. As I have discussed, maladaptive emotion has a momentum of its own.

There is no need for people to be passive victims of their emotions. Emotion coaches can help people learn to focus on their emotions and to shift away from them whenever this seems appropriate or necessary. Coaches can help people learn to shift from anger to compassion, from sadness to appreciation, from envy to acceptance, and from inner dread to contact with the calming present. With practice, people can learn to consciously govern their automatic emotional brains. One of the better ways of coaching people in how to do this is by making sure that first they can describe what they feel at the moment when they recognize a need to shift out of an emotion. This helps them center themselves and gives them a handle that they can pick up later when they are able to deal with the feeling. They need to practice being able to put certain experiences on hold with the knowledge that they can come back to them later and process them further. The coach then needs to invite them to shift their attention to the present, outer reality and to focus on what is happening outside of the self. This is also helpful for ending sessions when a person has not fully completed an emotional experience. Coaches can ask clients to complete the following exercise to help them learn this skill.

Exercise: Shifting Out of Emotional States

When you are in an emotional state—feeling angry, sad, afraid, or even ashamed—experience the feeling, and name it. Feel it in your body. Identify the thoughts. Now it is time to shift. Get a clear sense of what you feel before you shift. Put this into words. This will provide a handle you can pick up again later. Tell yourself "I'll come back to this." Breathe. Shift your focus of attention to the external world. Make contact with external reality. Name what you see. Breathe again. Now pick something else that you need to pay attention to in your day, and focus on this new task.

To help people shift out of an emotion, therapists can also help them develop an ability to consider other points of view. People need to be able to recognize that meanings other than their own exist. The practice of shifting away from emotions and focusing on another state becomes easier and more real when people believe that other views exist and that their view is not always the only one, correct view. Other, less conceptual means of shifting states involves use of music to change a mood or engaging in pleasurable or mobilizing activities (see Exercise 2).

TRANSFORMATION IN FOCUSING ON VAGUE FEELINGS

Changing emotion by accessing alternate emotions and needs, as described earlier, applies to experiences in which the initial emotion to be changed is vivid, present, and expressed aloud. The principle of changing emotion with emotion also applies to experiences in which the emotion is originally vague and the process is more internal. Consider the example in chapter 5 of Jonathan, who was focusing on his vague feelings of discomfort. This led him to symbolize that he felt like a failure. He completed the first phase of the emotion coaching process when he *arrived* at a feeling of powerlessness. This acknowledgement was helpful and produced a bodily shift. It was experienced internally and was not necessarily even expressed aloud. As helpful as this step was, complete change requires more than this. Sometimes just recognizing what the problem is, like acknowledging a feeling that one feels powerless or has overextended one's reach, feels like a solution, because then the person knows what has to be dealt with and can begin to mobilize himself or herself to do so. Often, however, the person still needs to shift out of the problem feeling to achieve a full solution to the problem. How does the change to something new come in this internal focusing process?

Gendlin (1996) clearly described how the steps of focusing lead to a bodily felt shift that opens up new possibilities. How the new possibility opens up, however, remains a mystery. In studying very closely the internal process in clients, I have observed that often this process happens by a means similar to the one that occurs in changing vivid emotions: through the emergence of a new, adaptive emotion, one that transforms the person's state. In the example of Jonathan in chapter 5, the newness came from Jonathan paying attention to his newly emerging anger, which came once he had arrived at his sense of failure. It was this new emotion that helped him generate internal alternatives. He contacted an alternate internal voice that was on the edge of his awareness that said, "I feel angry at the unfairness of the grant review process. A lot of it is politics and image management." This is another emotionally based part of himself, a part that is based on his healthy core emotions and has its own voice. This was the newly emerging resource available in Jonathan's background experience. Paying attention to his newly emerging anger at feeling unfairly treated, he organized himself to defend his point of view with a new voice that said, "I'm not going to take this anymore." Contacting new resources to help fight against his internally represented oppressor, Jonathan began to assert his rights, much as he would mobilize against a live oppressor who was trying to render him powerless.

Jonathan's currently felt, emerging feelings either could have been subdominant, background emotions that were there all the time, or they could have been newly emerging ones. When people reinterpret their experiences they often create new experiences for themselves. They always are capable of creating new experiences. People can do this because they are emotionally reactive beings, always in the process of evaluating the emotional significance of what is occurring and what they are feeling. Thus, Jonathan came to feel more than just angry: He also felt relieved that he would not have to carry through with a demanding goal. These newly labeled emotions also helped him reorganize and focus on a new goal.

Awareness of needs, goals, and concerns points a person in the direction of change and development. Thus Jonathan, after he identified his feeling of disappointment, and his sense of failure and powerlessness, contacted his need for recognition, acceptance, or even material gain by accessing his anger. This is what he wanted, needed, or desired, what he had to work toward satisfying. Knowing what he needed, even though this knowledge does not actually satisfy the need, is the first step. Being aware of what one needs is crucial to one's orientation to the current environment and is important in the problem-solving process required to satisfy the need. In this internal process of focusing, therapists must focus clients on the need, goal, or concern embedded in their emotions. This will help them become aware of their needs for closeness, separation, protection, recognition, or freedom. They then can take the process of change into their own hands by learning to pay attention to their feeling in a disciplined way so as to discover their main concern. Explicit focusing on the need, goal, or concern takes people a step beyond simply focusing on the sensation they feel and passively waiting for a shift to come. This more self-directed step is especially helpful in focusing when a shift does not occur spontaneously. Thus, people need to be coached repeatedly to ask of their feelings "What is it I need or really want here?" or "What is my goal in all of this; what is of concern to me?"

AWARENESS OF NEEDS

Once Jonathan knows what he needs or wants, however, he cannot just simply decide to act; instead he again needs to integrate his head and his heart and evaluate the value to him of satisfying his needs. Is it worth it to him to do what he wants? He also must know how to get his needs satisfied. This requires the ability to assess the feasibility of getting needs met in different situations. One's needs set an important end goal. The means whereby one gets one's needs met depends on a lot of factors, such as learning, culture, opportunity, and often chance.

Needs come from deep within a person; they are influenced by biology, experience, and culture. People have many needs, and these needs continually emerge as responses to what is going on around people. They emerge somewhat automatically, just like feelings. Identifying the basic human needs is probably impossible, because they are not fully predetermined. From my work with people in therapy I have learned that needs related to attachment and identity usually appear to be of the greatest psychological concern to most people. Needs to be connected, protected, and effective are related to people's basic interpersonal nature. Love and power and connection and status are important in understanding human experience (Gilbert, 1992). Needs for security and interest, curiosity, and mastery also appear to be basic to human nature. Thus a need to be securely attached, a need for affection to belong and to be valued by others, and a need for novelty and mastery seem of critical importance (Bowlby, 1969; White, 1959). Our ancestors probably survived if they belonged to a group and if they were curious, because they learned about things ahead of time, before the necessities of survival demanded it, and this helped them master their situations. Curiosity in humans, in conjunction with reason, promoted by a group that can support its inventors, has been the most powerful source of progress in civilization. Without attachment, interest, and curiosity we would still be in the Stone Age or perhaps not here at all.

People thus become more empowered when they connect with their need for attachment or mastery and regain their interest and curiosity. They feel more like active agents than passive victims. A person can begin to act on his or her own behalf once he or she can contact his or her idiosyncratic current concerns, such as a desire to relax or even to soothe oneself. The person might listen to a favorite piece of music, take a walk, or go for a swim and thereby begin to mobilize his or her resources to meet the need to relax. Feeling that one has a right to a need is greatly aided by having the validity of that need confirmed by another person. Mobilizing oneself and acknowledging a need also lead people to begin to feel some new, core emotion in response to their prior feelings. Thus, after feeling sad at a loss, people begin to feel joy at what they had. After feeling anger at being neglected, they feel sad at what they missed. This new joy or sadness is highly motivating and, when integrated with reason, often leads to corrective action or coping. Joy leads to the desire to live, whereas sadness leads to assimilation of the loss and to letting go.

At this point one might ask the following important questions: "Is the concern or need at the heart of a core primary feeling always going to be a good guide? Can I trust that it always will point people in the direction of growth and positive reorganization? Could it be a bad, selfish, destructive, disorganizing need?" It may not be reasonable to assume that all people's needs are good and that nothing in people is ever inherently destructive. Buber (1958), for example, suggested that good or evil are simply possible directions people might take, not entities. They are thus choices. If a person has a penchant for both good and bad, can a coach still recommend awareness and evaluation of the person's needs and goals as the best guide to living?

First, it is important for a therapist to recognize that if he or she believes that people are not essentially good, this does not necessarily mean the therapist should assume that people cannot trust their needs. Human beings rely for their well-being on a highly evolved, genetically based biological system as well as on socially developed strategies of survival conveyed by culture. These require conscious reasoning and deliberation to produce behavior. People are neither noble savages, complete with natural wisdom, nor savage beasts without an ounce of prosociality in their nature. Although human atrocities do occur, people are more often motivated by their heads than by their hearts. Political and religious idealism has caused more havoc than individual atrocities. In addition, acts of individual violence and greed are often committed by people who are under the influence of addictive substances or immersed in very violent subcultures. Human hunger, desire, and rage generally do not proceed unchecked toward gluttony, rape, and murder. This is especially true if the person has grown up in a society in which prosocial survival strategies have been actively conveyed and valued. Rather than focus on the potential for dysfunction, coaches need to work toward helping people choose healthy directions and toward engendering healthier steps. People should take steps that help them grow and learn how to facilitate this growth process in others. People not only need to use their judgment in this process, but they also need to be very attentive to what their feelings and needs are and then find a creative integration of these. There may be fundamentally destructive processes in human nature that can be developed. Coaches, however, need to focus instead on the healthy, growth-producing processes and encourage development of these.

How, then, do people know which direction can help them grow? Sometimes directions that will help people grow are clear and emerge with no doubts. Other times, when people are less integrated, a part of the self —sometimes just a small voice—doubts the merit of a certain direction even though the rest of the person passionately desires it. Coaches need to help people incorporate this voice before they act. People need to make a decision about which of their needs they should follow and how to do this. They need to evaluate what part of their core experience is healthy and what part is unhealthy. The art in making this evaluation is always listening to all parts of the self and integrating all aspects into unified action. This results in internal harmony and in taking steps that help people grow.

REGULATION AND SELF-SOOTHING

In addition to transforming emotions with emotions, people also sometimes need to learn the skills of regulating emotion. When emotions such as shame, fear, powerlessness, and rage are overwhelming, helping people regulate their emotions and get some distance from them is an important task. People often try to regulate their emotions by trying not to feel whatever it is they feel. This is not that helpful in the long run. Some people prevent themselves from feeling disturbing emotions by withdrawing from or avoiding situations that evoke such emotions. Others use distraction strategies, such as humming or busyness, or they transform their feelings into psychosomatic complaints, such as stomachaches. Others avoid disturbing emotions by not remembering the painful emotions associated with major life events, even though they remember the events themselves and realize the full impact of what occurred. People also engage in stimulus-seeking or impulsive behavior to blot out their disturbing feelings. They can engage in extreme numbing behaviors, such as self-mutilation, binge eating, drug and alcohol abuse, and excessive masturbation and promiscuity, to block or to soothe painful or overwhelming feelings.

Therapists need to help people learn better emotion regulation skills.

Important means of regulating emotion include regulating breathing and mindfulness—the nonjudgmental observation and description of one's emotional states. Basic emotion regulation skills also involve naming the emotion, describing the experience in one's body, clarifying the event that evoked the emotion, and understanding one's interpretation of the situation and the actions prompted by the emotion.

When people are swept away by the impetuous torrents of their souls, they need to be able to calm themselves so that they can function. Disturbing emotions, especially anger, sadness, fear, or shame, can overwhelm a person. Getting some distance from these painful emotions often helps. Coaches need to teach their clients how to put some distance between themselves and their experiences of being lost in overwhelming emotions and thoughts that swamp their consciousness. Helping clients be mindful of their experiences can facilitate this. Coaches can offer people meditative methods of focusing on their breath as it enters their nostrils and of observing the contents of the mind as engaged in a process of arising and passing away. This helps people regulate their emotions when they know the emotions are unhealthy but still cannot control them (Kabat-Zinn, 1993; Levine, 1989). A meditative approach is an alternative to avoidance; it involves paying attention to emotions in a particular way. A meditative process involves teaching clients the skills of describing their experiences to themselves in an objective manner, as if they were an outside observer talking to another person. This helps people to detach themselves from the meaning of their experiences and to pay attention to the experience's qualities and form. People need to attend to whether the emotional experience is felt in their bodies as hot or cold, a big ball or a small knot. The following exercise is helpful in developing this skill.

Exercise: Getting an Observer's Distance

Begin by paying attention to the swelling and fading of sensation and thought in your disturbing feeling. Attend to the rising and passing away of your feelings rather than to their meaning. This interrupts the runaway process by which your thoughts and feelings interact. Thus, if you begin to notice and label the quality and location of your feeling as "a hot sensation in my chest," to notice its intensity as "moderate" and its shape as "a round ball," then the torrents of emotion will begin to subside. Notice whether the sensation is global or specific, whether it is expanding or contracting, whether it is coming or leaving. Do this for anywhere from 5 to 40 minutes and the intensity of the feeling will subside. After having paid attention to your sensations you then need to pay attention to your thoughts. Do not get immersed in their meaning and content. You need to be able to describe your own thinking process. Say to yourself "Now I'm thinking, remembering, imagining or anticipating . . ." or "Now I'm criticizing, defending or berating

. . . ." Describe the mental process in which you are engaged. You are now in direct contact with the process of your own sensing and thinking and have created a new internal experience, one that provides a better distance from your feelings.

Once people are able to distance themselves from the actual emotion, they will no longer feel overwhelmed by their anger, sadness, fear, or shame. The meanings of their thoughts that keep adding fuel to their emotional fires will no longer absorb them. They have changed their focus from being a victim of the feeling to being an observer of the feeling. They will have focused on describing the emotion rather than trying to avoid it. This will help them master the emotion by using a simple reframing process, shifting from paying attention to the content to describing the process. Now they are concentrating on what and how they are being in the moment rather than being caught in the meaning of their ideas or the influences of their sensations. They have become fascinated with the ebb and flow of their experiences. They breathe more deeply, and their muscles are more relaxed. They have shifted their perspective. Now it is possible for something new to emerge, and people can be helped to focus on something they want, or can do, to help themselves in this situation. They can access alternate resources. They can become agents and begin again to be the authors of their lives, because they are no longer victims of their difficult emotions.

Marsha Linehan (1993), who has worked with people with a lot of dysregulated emotion, offered a variety of behaviorally oriented emotion regulation and distress tolerance techniques that can be taught to clients who do not yet have these skills. These techniques include changing one's emotions by acting in an opposite manner to the current emotion; that is, Linehan suggested reversing the expressive and action components of emotional responses as a means of trying to regulate overwhelming emotions. She also suggested that people, when in a state of fear, should approach the emotion rather than avoid it. Similarly, in states of guilt and shame, people should face the feeling rather than pull away from it. In depression and sadness, the skill is to be active rather than passive and, in anger, be sympathetic or do something nice rather than attack. Other regulation skills involve helping people build more positive experiences in their lives by focusing on positive events and behaviorally increasing positive events. Linehan distinguished distress tolerance skills from regulation skills by indicating that the former are designed to help one survive a situation when changes cannot be made and the latter attempt to cure one's problems. Distress tolerance skills help a person get by. They involve distracting oneself by keeping busy doing things, focusing attention away from the self and onto others, and self-soothing by doing good things for oneself that will provide comfort. In addition, Linehan suggested that people can improve the moment by means of positive imagery, prayer, relaxation, or taking a vacation from responsibilities.

Helping people create a working distance from intense emotions is a helpful method for working with distressing emotion. Here, rather than simply coping with the emotion by regulating its intensity, the emphasis is on getting the appropriate distance from the emotion to facilitate access to it in a manner that will assist in its processing. The client should be neither too close nor too distant from the emotion, neither so overwhelmed by it that it is impossible to symbolize it in words and see it as an experience of a larger whole nor so distant from the emotion that it is a purely conceptual experience. Coaches can ask their clients to move closer to or further away from an experience and can spend time doing just this. Thus, a coach might say, "Breathe, and try to move a bit further away from the feeling so that you can get a sense of it as just a part of you" or "Let's put that feeling here, in this chair. Can you describe it?" To get closer to the feeling, a coach might say, "Try to go into the feeling a bit more. What's it like?" or "Speak from the feeling. Can you enter the feeling, become it, and describe what you are like, something like, 'I am my sadness and I am a pain in my chest; I hurt'"?

A method to promote self-soothing that I have found most helpful is to ask the person to engage in a particular type of soothing internal dialogue. This is best applied when a person is expressing a lot of self-condemnation or self-contempt and appears unable to access any self-soothing capacities. This is often the case in people who commit self-harm or use self-medication to regulate their emotions (Korman & Bolger, 1999). In this intervention the coach asks a client to imagine a child sitting in a chair in front of him or her, a child who has suffered what that person has suffered in life. To evoke the child's plight the coach then describes the most poignant details of the person's history and asks, "What would you say to that child? What do you feel toward the child?" This typically evokes a compassionate response toward the child and the child's circumstances and a recognition of what the child needed. For example, a coach might introduce this dialogue with a client who is curling her lip, saying, "I wish that whining part of me would just get over it. So, my mother ignored me and my father emotionally manipulated me. So what, I should just quit whimpering." The coach might say, "Imagine an 8-year-old sitting here. Her mother hardly looks at her, never mind talks to her. Her father emotionally draws on her for all the love he can't get from his wife and then rejects her when he doesn't need her. What do you imagine it's like for her?" The coach might also ask, "What would you say to her if she were your child?" The client might answer, "I know she would feel so alone without anyone. She deserves more," and then the coach might say, "Can you give her some of what she needs?" Once the client recognizes the child's need and responds in a soothing manner to the child, the coach then asks the client if she could respond to the child in her in that same way. In this intervention it seems important to start with a stranger or a child in general, not with the part of the self that needs soothing or with the person's own inner child. Even though people understand the implication of what they are being asked to do they seem to be better able to soothe a child in general. Once the softening has occurred in relation to a child in need, it is easier to transfer this feeling to the self. Over time, doing this in conjunction with the empathic soothing provided by the coach's affective attunement helps the person develop his or her self-soothing capacity.

In relationships, being unable to self-soothe in response to momentary ruptures in connections or minor conflict with others results in a lot of distressing feelings. For example, a husband can become very anxious when his wife is upset with him because he was late or did not wash the dishes, and he simply cannot tolerate the disapproval. Then, while his wife is still annoyed, he presses her for reassurance that she still loves him. Instead of reassurance, he gets more annoyance. This produces the pushing away he was so anxiously trying to avoid. Had this anxious husband been able to soothe his own anxiety, or had his emotional self-soothing been so automatic that anxiety was not felt, these small breaks in connections would be more easily tolerated. It is important for coaches to help people learn the skills of self-care to help them improve their relationships. I discuss this in more detail in chapter 11.

Coaches thus need to help relationship partners learn emotion regulation skills to deal with dysregulated states that emerge usually most intensely in intimate relationships. Although people really are adults and don't have a baby within, the metaphor of taking care of their "inner child" can help people access self-soothing responses. To help resolve conflict between couples, people need to learn to feel compassion for themselves and be able to comfort themselves when their partner is angry or unavailable. This is a complex internal skill that can be learned over time in conjunction with learning to breathe regularly when distressed. As discussed earlier, behaviors such a treating oneself to a favorite activity, listening to music, relaxing, taking a hot bath, going for a walk, or calling someone for contact and support are self-comforting behaviors that can also be helpful when one is feeling bad about relational ruptures.

FACILITATING THE TRANSFORMATION OF MALADAPTIVE EMOTIONS AND DESTRUCTIVE THOUGHTS

Once a therapist helps a client access and regulate his or her distress and identify a healthier internal voice it is much easier for the client to combat the dominant negative voice within. A coach's job is to help clients find their alternate healthy feelings and to use these to transform their unhealthy feelings. This can occur by explicitly challenging the beliefs, experientially integrating the opposing feelings, or both. Change comes by accessing previously unacknowledged healthy feelings and needs in the context of the affective attunement and confirmation of these inner resources by an empathic other. Sharing dreaded feelings with another breaks the isolation in which these feelings are usually felt. This helps alleviate the terrible pain and despair and strengthens the self. This helps the person gain access to a more resilient sense of self and to internal resources. Coaches then put these in contact with the maladaptive feelings and negative beliefs. This means that coaches need to help their clients set two states in opposition. A coach can, for example, say, "What do you say to that voice that says you are useless?," or a coach can ask the person to enact a dialogue between the healthy feelings and the maladaptive ones.

For example, a client in therapy was able to express for the first time her feeling of worthlessness about the failure of her marriage. Her marriage had ended in a rather sudden and unexpected divorce. She said, "I feel so worthless" and sobbed with the full realization of the feeling. She realized that this feeling came from her mother having made her feel "You don't deserve to be loved." The coach helped this client focus on her emotional reaction to this harsh criticism. The client became angry at having been so unfairly treated and sad at the loss of support she so had so badly needed. With the help of her coach's supportive confirmation of her newly emerging experience, she realized that her new, survival-based goal was to get the support she needed. She now contacted an inner wellspring of self-worth, and a new voice arose. The coach invited her to speak from this place to that negative voice. Looking at her imagined critic in an empty chair in front of her, she said, "I am worthwhile; I do deserve to be valued," and "I have love to give, and I deserve to be loved." At this point the critical voice softened into compassion for her (cf. Greenberg, Rice, et al., 1993).

If people have been severely rejected or abandoned and are able to acknowledge that they feel shattered, they can begin once again to take charge of their feelings. First, they need to soothe themselves. This is an important skill that people must be able to exercise if they are to be able to take care of themselves. Second, when people acknowledge their own pain rather than being a victim of it, they begin to change how they view themselves. This stance emphasizes their active "I" self—"I feel broken" —rather than their shattered "me" self—"It happened to me." Once they adopt this more agentic view they are more in charge of their reactions and are more able to commit to new goals. As I have discussed, coaches can help this process along by, at the right time, focusing clients on their capacities for self-soothing and their emerging needs and goals. By asking questions such as "What do you need?" or "What has been missing?" coaches help clients pay attention to their capacities for self-supportive actions. Their emerging goals generally are no longer ones of, for example, passively needing a rejecting person's approval or love to prevent them from feeling shattered; rather, once a person has accepted a loss, the goal becomes one of actively supporting oneself or mastering the situation, accompanied by a life-sustaining desire to be close to, to be loved by, or to feel safe with others.

In working to change emotion with emotion in relation to trauma, coaches need to (a) acknowledge and validate the client's initial experience of hopelessness; (b) activate the emotional memories and associated dysfunctional beliefs by arousing, for example, fear and shame in reaction to an imagined scene, in the safety of therapeutic situation; and (c) activate healthy emotional resources in the person, such as anger at violation and sadness at loss, or self-soothing, as alternate responses to replace or help transform the person's maladaptive responses. This allows for the formation of new, more complex responses through a synthesis of the adaptive and maladaptive emotional responses and by transforming negative beliefs with newly accessed needs. Thus, fear responses become fused with anger responses, and action tendencies to flee are replaced or transformed by the assertive action tendencies of anger. With the aid of high attentional allocation to the new, healthier response tendencies, and with the support of the emotion coach, a person will construct a new emotional response by integrating elements of the previously evoked responses. Now, for example, a physically abused client will feel anger and disgust in place of her original fear at her cruel father's violence. From this empowered state she combats her previous negative view of herself as worthless. In addition, she feels sadness at the loss of protection from her mother, and this transforms her shame at her humiliation, and her view that nothing can help, into a desire for comfort and a belief in her lovableness. This allows her to access her capacity to self-soothe and to more effectively regulate her painful states.

As these new experiences are repeatedly processed over time, new, emerging tendencies are translated into action, and the traumatic memory fades. Old emotion memories are often affectively deactivated, replaced by another memory, or both. Throughout this process the coach validates and empathizes with the client's feelings, provides acceptance and comfort, and establishes the idiosyncratic meaning of the experience. These coaching actions provide a model that is internalized as self-empathy and self-soothing to help calm feelings of alarm. Toward the end of this process coaches also need to facilitate the development of a new narrative that incorporates the new emotion as well as the changed beliefs. This new view helps the client engage in new action in the world.

STRATEGIES OF INTERVENTION FOR TRANSFORMING EMOTION

The strategies for this phase are summarized in the following list and then described briefly.

1. Regulate undesirable emotions with desirable ones.
2. Access maladaptive beliefs.
3. Access positive feelings to counteract negative feelings and beliefs.
4. Integrate opposing feelings.

Coaches must help people *regulate undesirable emotions* with more desirable, soothing ones. They also must help people *access maladaptive beliefs* and articulate them in words. Clients also need to be coached toward *accessing positive feelings*, especially in the hopes of counteracting undesirable emotions. Coaches must find the healthy, striving emotions and resources in people and use these to combat their negative beliefs. Finally, bridges between opposing feelings must be built *and the opposing feelings must be integrated*. Coaches should help clients connect feelings of helplessness to feelings of strength and feelings of isolation to states of loving connectedness. They must help people remember forgotten possibilities.

EXERCISE 1: IDENTIFYING TRIGGERS AND THEMES OF MALADAPTIVE EMOTIONS

Identify a feeling you often regret having. Do you sometimes get angry and then wish you hadn't? Do you feel sad, desperate, or humiliated and regret what you say or do? Fill out the following sheet and keep it as a logbook.

1. What emotion do you feel that you would prefer not to?
2. Did you recognize the emotion yourself, or did others tell you?
3. What happened before you felt this emotion? Describe it in as much detail as possible.
4. What are the characteristics of the situation that led to this feeling? If you were to tell the story of what happened, what would the theme be? Who were the main players? What were the situation, the plot, and the conclusion? Was the theme one of abandonment, domination, being slighted, being deprived, or being dependent? How would you describe the theme that seems to trigger this feeling for you?
5. What are the origins of this story and its themes in your life? From where are you transporting this? Of what does it remind you?
6. Label this trigger for yourself. "I have an emotional reaction that I regret when X happens." Fill in the X with one of the following feelings:

- I feel deprived.
- I am being teased.
- I am feeling looked over or left out.
- I feel criticized.
- I feel controlled.
- I feel unimportant.
- I feel competitive.
- I am alone.
- Other. _____

7. Be aware that this situation is a trigger for your anger, sadness, fear, shame, or some other emotion you regret having. Next time you experience this feeling, ask yourself, "Am I reacting to a trigger?"

EXERCISE 2: EXPERIENCING AN EMOTION THAT GENERALLY AFFECTS YOU AND THEN SHIFTING OUT OF IT

Give yourself at least 20 minutes to practice this exercise.

1. Select music that relaxes you. Make yourself comfortable, and begin to listen. It is better to choose music of a slow tempo to help give you time to get into your feelings.
2. Imagine the situation that affects you.
3. Permit yourself to feel the first emotional reaction that comes.
4. Say "This first reaction (or this first feeling) makes me feel. . . . ." Put the feeling into words.
5. If thoughts enter your mind, focus your consciousness on how they make you feel.
6. Breathe deeply into your stomach. Continue to go deeper, allowing one feeling to lead to another until you discover the information that feels important. You will be able to sense when you have reached a core experience and received a valuable message. You will be glad you received it because it feels deep and real. This form of knowing provides a sense of satisfaction of knowing, regardless of whether the message is agreeable or disagreeable.
7. Shift your focus back to your external world. Redirect your attention and thoughts to your ongoing activities.

To go deeper into states of your feeling, you have to be willing to refuse the interference that comes from your thinking- and action-oriented brain. If you want to stay in a feeling long enough to receive the information it brings you, you need to free yourself of any need to come to conclusions or to decide on actions on the basis of feelings.

EXERCISE 3: DEALING WITH A DIFFICULT EMOTION

Sometimes, rather than simply experiencing a feeling, it is useful to get some objective distance from the feeling. This is particularly true for overwhelming, unhealthy feelings. You can do this in the following exercise by paying attention to process rather than to content. Then you can try and access another balancing emotion.

1. Imagine a situation or personal interaction that produces this difficult emotion. This might be a conversation with a parent or partner that leaves you feeling difficult emotions of rage, worthlessness, or undesirability.
2. As the emotion emerges, shift your attention to the process of sensing. Describe the sensations. Describe their quality, intensity, and location and any changes in these. Breathe.
3. Pay attention to accompanying thoughts. Describe the mental process in which you are engaging, whether it be thinking, remembering, or criticizing. Breathe.
4. Focus on another softer, good feeling, such as love, joy, or compassion. Imagine a situation or personal interaction in which you feel this. Feel it now. Allow the feeling to fill you.
5. Talk to the old, difficult feeling from your space in your new, healthier feeling. What can you say to the bad feeling that will help transform it to a better feeling? Say this.

EXERCISE 4: HEALING MALADAPTIVE ANGER ABOUT A PAST EVENT

In this exercise you will have an imaginary dialogue with a significant person from your past in order to work through your unresolved emotions. The goal is to affirm yourself and either hold the other person accountable, understand and possibly forgive, or move on.

1. Give yourself time, and make yourself comfortable. Although the situation you wish to heal may have occurred when you were very young, now you are an adult. You have a different body and mind and a great deal more knowledge. Visualize yourself now as a fully empowered adult, even though you are about to discuss a situation that occurred long ago.

2. Visualize the face of the other person, and imagine yourself face to face with him or her. Observe what you feel now as you make contact.
3. Begin to tell this person what you resent. Be specific.
4. Imagine the other person responding to your resentment.
5. Become yourself again, and identify what else you felt. Now let yourself go back to an earlier scene. Become yourself as a child in the scene and talk to the other person. Be sure to express both primary sadness about what you missed as well as your primary anger at what you felt was unjust. Express any core feeling you felt.
6. Tell the other person what you needed or how you wanted him or her to act differently.
7. Imagine the other person responding to you. When you pretend to be this other person, rather than defending or continuing the negative or hurtful stance, listen to what he or she is saying, and explain what it was like inside for you. What were the struggles, difficulties, or reasons that led you to be hurtful or negative?
8. Continue until you arrive at a resolution. Either hold the other person accountable for his or her actions, let go, or forgive him or her. Let each of you gain something from the other. When you succeed, you will feel more self-affirming and will understand and hold the other person accountable for what he or she did to you.
9. Go back and visualize the recent situation that caused your anger as an adult. Imagine yourself responding on the basis of the new dialogue you have just experienced.

EXERCISE 5: DEALING WITH CURRENT MALADAPTIVE ANGER

The purpose of this exercise is to help you link a current feeling to a past one, and to find self-caring and self-support.

1. Imagine the person with whom you are angry and the situation in which the angering incident occurred.
2. Make a shift from "you are the cause of my anger" to identifying what in you is leading to your anger. Identify what part of this situation is triggering something in you or your emotional history. See if it reminds you of previous situations in which you felt hurt because you could not get what you wanted.
3. Ask "when" and not "why." For example, instead of asking

"Why am I mad?" ask "When did this happen before in my life? This reminds me of . . ." Review your past. Stop at any situation that seems appropriate; often the earliest scenes with your parents are the most poignant. Because of your need for their love, early memories of not getting what you want often contain the most hurt or anger. Whatever situation you select, make sure it is similar to the situation in the present that makes you mad.

4. Visualize and feel the earlier situation again. See it, enter it, and be affected by it. Find a way of empathizing with yourself. Imagine yourself as a child sitting in front of you. How can you care for this hurting child? Remember that this child will continue to hurt until you feel empathy for yourself.

5. While you are feeling your pain in the situation, look for what you really needed or wanted at the time.

6. Will you give it to yourself now? Are you capable of giving it to yourself now, or do you want to continue insisting that the other person give it to you? You can either continue being angry at the other person for not giving it to you, or you can decide to give it to yourself. Either you end the vengeance by giving to yourself what the other was not able to or did not give you, or you continue feeling resentment and anger.

7. If you are willing to give yourself whatever the other person did not give to you, or did not do for you, ask yourself when, where, and how will I give myself that, or do that for myself, in the next weeks and months? Plan carefully, and honor any promises you make.

8. Visualize giving yourself what you need.

9. The more you realize that it was your anger with the other person that led you to discover something that was missing in your life, the better you will feel about him or her.

EXERCISE 6: IMAGERY RESTRUCTURING

This exercise applies best to areas of childhood maltreatment and abuse. The trauma should not be too severe, and it can be a more general sense of feeling neglected, invalidated, or criticized.

1. Re-enter the scene.
   Close your eyes and remember a childhood experience of yourself in a situation that was traumatic. If no situation is clear, then remember a core feeling associated with the pain-

ful experience. Imagine a concrete memory. Describe what happened. What do you see, smell, and hear in the situation? What is going through your mind?

2. View the scene as an adult now.
   What do you see, feel, and think? Do you see the look on the child's face? What do you want to do? Do it. How can you intervene? Try intervening in your imagination.

3. What does the child need?
   Become the child. What, as the child, do you feel and think? What do you need from the adult? Ask for what you need or wish for. What does the adult do? Is it sufficient? What else do you need? Ask for it. Is there someone else you would like to have come in to help? Receive the care and protection offered.

4. Review.
   Check how you feel now. What does all this mean to you in regard to you? What does it mean about what you needed? Come back to the present, to yourself as an adult now. How do you feel? Say goodbye to the child for now.

EXERCISE 7: GETTING TO NEEDS AND WANTS

The key to empowerment is to get to the need or want that is embedded in the feeling and to feel entitled to it. You must be able to say "I need love, comfort, space, rest," or whatever it is that will make you feel whole again. Getting to "I can" is very important to overcome the helpless feeling that robs you of your effectiveness.

1. Identify what you need or want that you think you cannot have now. Answer these statements:
   - What I lost, or my goal that was blocked, was _____, and what I wanted was _____.
   - What I can't get now is _____.
   - What I can get now or do is _____.
2. Feel the struggle between the "I can't" and the "I can."
3. Feel what you want or need.
4. Stay in your feeling of wanting until you receive new insights or thoughts that can help you achieve what you want. Wait until solutions appear. Your mind will try to come up with solutions if you know your goals and have a definition of the problem.
5. Feel the wanting until it moves you to action.
6. What action did you take? What happened?

EXERCISE 8: THE WHOLE PROCESS OF EMOTION COACHING

When your client is feeling upset about something, suggest the following to him or her:

1. Listen to your body.
   Pay attention to the basic sensations in the trunk of your body, stomach, chest, arms, and throat, and pay attention to your face. Ask yourself, "What is it like inside? What am I feeling in my body?"
2. Let yourself feel the emotion.
   Welcome the feeling. Do not negatively evaluate the feeling. Accept it.
3. Name the feeling.
   Put words to your feeling. Find words that help you articulate what it is like inside. Let the words come from the feeling as much as possible.
4. Identify your most basic feeling.
   Ask yourself
   - Is this what I truly feel at rock bottom?
   - Is this my most core feeling?
   To test this, ask
   - Do I feel something else that comes even before this?
   - Do I feel something in addition to what I am most aware of feeling?
   - Am I trying to accomplish something with this feeling?

If the client responds "yes" to any of the last three questions, the feeling is probably not a core feeling. Then ask the client to listen again to his or her body and go through Steps 1 and 2 once more. Otherwise, continue on.

5. Establish whether your feeling is adaptive or maladaptive.
   Ask yourself
   - Is this feeling helpful? Will it enhance my self or my bonds with others? or
   - Is this feeling a response to other past experiences rather than mainly a response to what's happening now?
   - Is there a pattern of recurrent bad feeling here?
   - Is this a familiar, stuck feeling?

If the client's answers to these questions are "yes," then it is probably an unhealthy feeling, and therapist and client should proceed to Step 6. If the client's answers to the above questions suggest that this is a fresh, new, healthy feeling in response to the present situation, then proceed to Step 7.

6. Identify the negative voice and destructive thoughts.
   - First, fully acknowledge the unhealthy emotion. Feel it and name it: "I feel shattered," "I feel enraged," or "I feel humiliated." Accept the feeling. Welcome it. Let it come in.
   - If the feeling is intense and scary, soothe yourself and say "It's OK. I know you feel so ashamed, so angry. It's all right. I'll take care of you. You're OK."
   - As you pay attention to the sensations, put the thoughts associated with the bad feeling into words. Get at your core beliefs, such as "I feel unworthy or worthless"; "I feel I can't survive on my own. I feel I will die without support"; or "I am useless, unlovable, and not good enough." These are the negative voices and dysfunctional beliefs that help maintain this unhealthy emotional state.
   - Put the hostile, negative thoughts against the self into "you" language. Say them to yourself: "You are worthless"; "You can't survive on your own." Elaborate these criticisms, and make them as specific as possible. These are the destructive voices that cause so much trouble.
7. Search for your healthy voice that is based on adaptive primary feelings and needs that might be there, in the background. Identify your healthy core feelings in response to the destructive criticisms. Figure out what the healthy feelings are telling you. The following are examples of healthy emotions.
   - Anger tells you that you are being violated.
   - Sadness tells you that you have lost something.
   - Fear tells you that you are in danger.
   - Shame tells you that you are overexposed.
   - Disgust tells you that what you are experiencing is bad for you.
   - Pain tells you that your sense of yourself is being shattered.

Accept the feeling and use it as a guide to the action for which it has organized you:

- anger to protect a boundary
- sadness to cry or withdraw
- fear to flee
- shame to hide
- disgust to expel
- pain to not repeat the painful event.

If your primary feeling is pain, then face it, live through it, and learn that you will survive it.

Identify your need or goal. Identify your most basic unmet needs or your primary concerns or goals. Articulate these. They will provide you with the will to survive and the capacity to grow. Note that this is not an intellectual process; it is a feeling process. You must feel your unhealthy emotion, and then you must sense a new, healthy feeling emerge. Then you experience a heartfelt need. Identify these needs: the unmet need in the unhealthy feeling and the healthy need in the new, adaptive feeling. Both needs can help you remobilize yourself to change.

To help with this, ask yourself the following questions:

- "What do I need?" Let an answer come from your emotional state.
- "When do I feel the opposite of my unhealthy feeling? When do I feel worthwhile, safe, competent, and more integrated?" Focus on that state of being. Feel the emotion of this alternate state. This, too, is you. Then ask again, "What do I need?"
- "What can I do to help get my need met?" or, simply, "What can I do to help myself?" See if you can give yourself what you need.
- "To whom else can I turn to get some of what I need?"

If you are suffering, respond to the need in your suffering. Imagine yourself as a child experiencing the unhealthy feeling. What can you give to or do for this child? To further help articulate what you want or need, and what you wish to do, ask yourself

- What is my goal here?
- What do I want changed or different?
- What do I want to do?

Here are some guidelines as to what your needs or goals might be:

- If you are angry, is it protection against an offense?
- If you are sad, is it contact and comfort?
- If you are afraid, is it safety and escape, or soothing?
- If you are ashamed, is it privacy or validation?
- If you are feeling disgust, is it to get rid of something bad?
- If you are feeling pain, do you need nurturing and healing?

Now ask

- How can I get my need met?
- What am I prepared to do to get it met?
- Are my feelings and needs prompting any action that conflicts with any of my values?

- What are the consequences, the costs, and benefits of this course of action?
- Will this action help me express my feeling now, or should I put it on hold?

Make sense of what the feelings and needs are telling you. Clarify this by asking yourself

- What about the situation makes me feel this way?
- What is the real issue?
- Who is responsible for what?

Help the client decide what to do, and help him or her identify blocks in the basic process. If a client gets stuck in the previous process, you might find that the client has hit one of the very basic problems, named next, that cause these blocks.

Identifying Blocks

Intense Self-Criticism and Self-Manipulation

Clients might get stuck in their "no goods" and "shoulds." Their internal critics can be very strong and might crush them by saying such things as "You are worthless." Then you facilitate letting this voice speak and help people attend to how it makes them feel. Next, get them to respond from the feeling side of their selves to their critics. Have them tell their critics how the critics make them feel. Help clients identify what they need from their critics. Instruct clients to tell their critics to back off or tell their critics that they need comfort rather than criticism. See if you can help clients contact what is driving their critical voices. Try to help clients voice any fear or concern that the critical voice may have and help them listen to this.

Self-Destructiveness and Extreme Self-Contempt

If only highly contemptuous, destructive self-criticisms are present, it is better not to activate or enact these. When people say "I am disgusting, defiled, soiled, worthless"; "I belong on a garbage heap, I don't deserve to breathe other people's air"; or "I just occupy a space in the world," then it is better to help them access compassion for their wounded selves and to practice self-compassion. Here the goal is to actually cultivate a mental attitude toward the self. There is a deficit of self-soothing, and this capacity needs to be inculcated and practiced. It is useful to first ask a person to access compassion and loving kindness toward another person, often a small child. Ask the person to imagine a small child experiencing the type of distress that the client is suffering. This helps evoke the compassion that eventually will be felt toward the self. This involves the deliberate development of a new skill, and much practice is needed.

Suppression and Avoidance of Emotional Experience and Expression

Clients might find it hard to contact any feeling, and thus coaches need to help them become more aware of and take charge of the processes that interrupt their experiencing of their emotions. Help them become aware of how they interrupt themselves. Turn this into an activity, if you can. Do it more actively to get control over this process. Suggest to clients that they squeeze their jaws tighter, or tell themselves to be strong and to not feel. Help them do whatever they do to block their feelings. Then pay attention to their feelings and needs and use these to challenge the interruptive process.

Unfinished Business With a Significant Other

At times an unresolved bad feeling toward another person will emerge that people cannot seem to get past. Coaches need to help people rework their feelings in a past relationship by identifying, experiencing, and expressing these in a safe environment. The goal is to mobilize unmet needs. Help clients give a voice to the unexpressed resentment, anger, sadness, or fear. If a person feels the block of resignation, help him or her give this resignation a voice. Help the client say "I feel resigned. What's the use?" Listen for the sigh, the breath, and for any sign of life under the resignation. Help clients contact their core feelings. If they are stuck in anger, help them express sadness. If they are stuck in sadness, help them express anger. Then help them contact the need in the new feeling.

Painful and Traumatic Memories

If a particularly painful experience keeps intruding, coaches need to help people emotionally reprocess the experience in small steps and help them face the experience until they have assimilated and reorganized it, until it no longer intrudes. The best way to do this is to have them repeatedly tell the story of what happened at an emotional level, or write it in a journal. Ask them to talk, write, or imagine the scene until it loses some of its potency. Instruct clients to breathe and relax while doing this.

Fragility and Vulnerability of the Whole Self

People might feel very shaky and insecure; if they do, they need connection with, and support and validation from, another person to provide safety. They need to disclose their vulnerable feelings to a person and receive empathic confirmation from him or her. Therapy is often the best way to get this kind of sustained supportive environment.

8. Transform the unhealthy feelings and beliefs. Clients can also complete the following part of this exercise:
   - Soothe your painful feelings. Imagine your feelings are those of a small child. What would you say to comfort the child? Say this to yourself. Adopt a stance of compassion and empathy toward yourself. Enter a state of loving kindness. Give yourself warmth and patience.
   - Dispute your negative beliefs with the help of your healthy feelings and needs. If your belief is that you are not good enough, dispute that with your need for support. Say "I need support, not criticism." If your belief is that you cannot survive alone, ask yourself for comfort.
   - Overcome your negative state with the healthy, core emotion and self-compassion that you have found. Let these serve as a basis of strength, possibility, and value. Search for your inner calm under your wretched feeling. Let it soothe you.
   - Let your healthier, more positive side contact your less healthy side. Let the two combine into a healthier way of being. Integrate your shame and pride into a sense of worth, your fear and courage into strength, your anxiety and your desire for connection into sensitivity.

EXERCISE 9: EMOTION RESTRUCTURING TRAINING

Use the emotion restructuring sheet that follows to help people work through some of their unhealthy emotions. The steps are provided in narrative form and in a table (the emotion restructuring sheet) in a slightly truncated version for ease of application. The sheet will give therapists structure regarding what to ask people to do to achieve change. For it to work, people will have to experience all the feelings, not just conceptualize them. They will have to experience the new feelings and needs, and their new voices will have to actually emerge experientially. This is a difficult process, and it will take time to experience a real change in an unhealthy feeling. Answers to the questions can be written below each step or in each column in the table.

Step 1

What is your primary unhealthy feeling in your body? Allow it to come up, and welcome it.

- How intense is it now? (1–10)
- Do you need to regulate or create distance from the feeling? If so, how? Do it.
- Try to soothe and comfort yourself.

What are you feeling in your body?

_____

_____

Step 2

What are the destructive voices, the negative thoughts, or beliefs in your head that accompany the feeling?

- Identify the feeling tone of these voices (usually contempt or hostility).
  Where do these voices come from?
- Continue to soothe yourself.
  What are your negative thoughts? List them here.

_____

_____

Step 3

What else are you feeling in addition to the predominant bad feeling? What other feelings can you access? Identify an alternate emotion that can be used as a resource. Imagine another, helpful feeling. How can you evoke this feeling? Imagine a situation in which you experienced this feeling. Try entering this situation or feeling emotionally. What else are you feeling?

_____

_____

Step 4

What is the basic need, goal, or concern embedded in your newly identified, healthier emotion?
My need is

_____

_____

Step 5

Bring your healthy feelings and needs into contact with your unhealthy state. Let them transform it.

- Combat your destructive thoughts with your new feelings and needs.
- How can you integrate your strengths and resources to change your unhealthy feelings?
- How can you continue to soothe yourself?
- What changes?

_____

_____

Emotion Restructuring Training Sheet

Step 1	Step 2	Step 3	Step 4	Step 5
What is the primary maladaptive feeling in your body? Welcome it. ■ How intense is it? (1–10) ■ Do you need to regulate or create distance? If so, how?	What are the destructive voices, thoughts, and beliefs in your head? ■ What is the feeling tone of the voices (usually contempt or hostility)? ■ Where does it come from?	What else are you feeling? Identify a healthy, emotional response. Give it a voice. ■ Imagine a helpful feeling or situation in which you feel that emotion. ■ Enter this feeling or situation.	What is your basic need, goal, or concern in your primary adaptive emotion? What do you need from yourself? From others?	Bring your adaptive feelings and needs into contact with your maladaptive state. ■ Combat your destructive thoughts with your feelings and needs. ■ Integrate your strengths and resources.

IV

APPLYING THE SKILLS OF
EMOTIONAL INTELLIGENCE

9

LESSONS ABOUT ANGER AND SADNESS FROM PSYCHOTHERAPY

In this chapter I offer some examples of actual treatments using emotion coaching. In studies of videotapes of more than 100 therapy sessions from individual and couples treatments, I have found that of all the emotions people work on in therapy, anger, sadness, fear, and shame are by far the most frequent sources of problems. Of course, other, more complex feelings, such as jealousy, envy, guilt, inferiority, and boredom, arise, but not as frequently. These other feelings often involve a blend of the previous four feelings, as does emotional pain, which appears to be very important in resolving many problems in living. Psychotherapy also attempts to remedy the lack of the more pleasant emotions of joy, excitement, interest, and love. In this chapter I focus on working with anger and sadness in therapy, because these are the most prevalent primary adaptive emotions that arise in emotion coaching.

ANGER

All anger is not the same. Some anger masks another feeling, and some anger is directed at someone or something else even though it is felt at the present time. Some anger is downright manipulative or destructive. Even if a person senses that his or her current angry reaction at someone for being late (for example) is a core, healthy anger at feeling wronged and the person decides that expressing it is wise, the person still needs to figure out, keeping Aristotle's edict in mind, the purpose of the anger and when, how, with what intensity, and possibly even with whom to express the anger. Getting one of these wrong can cause a lot of problems. It may also often be a wise option to decide not to express even core anger, especially immediately. However, a chronic inability to deal constructively with anger can become a major problem leading to feelings of ineffectiveness, hopelessness, and meaninglessness. These inabilities include not recognizing that one is angry; recognizing but not being able to ever express anger (this occurs for a variety of fears); expressing anger, but doing so inappropriately, with too much intensity, starting off fine but getting carried away into destructive blaming or attacking; or being chronically angry and overreactive.

Anger is something people feel for a reason. People need to listen to their anger and respect it rather than trying to avoid what it is telling them. Their anger is a message that their boundaries are being invaded, they are being hurt, their rights are being violated, their wants or needs are not being adequately met, or that progress toward a goal is being frustrated. Anger may signal that the person is doing or giving more than he or she wants to. Anger helps people say "Enough! I won't take it anymore!" Anger helps set boundaries and limits and motivates people to say "No."

There is of course another side to this coin. As much as feeling anger is a signal of a problem, venting anger will not provide a solution. Expressing anger, especially intense anger, can be destructive and can hurt others and produce misunderstanding. Expressing anger often leads to escalating cycles of attack and counterattack, or to defense, and prevents listening and collaboration. Awareness of anger and expression of anger are thus two totally different tasks and require different skills. Awareness involves paying attention to how one's body feels and the ability to describe in words what one is feeling rather than acting it out. The goal of this is to be informed. On the other hand, expressing anger generally has a goal of informing others and influencing them in some way, and this requires great interpersonal skills to do effectively. Even if a person is skilled in communicating anger, one can never predict the other person's reaction. The skill thus also involves knowing what to do after one has expressed anger or experiences a sense of being wronged. Emotional intelligence involves being able to handle other people's reactions to one's expression of emotion. People should not express anger unless they are able to deal with what comes after the expression. It is usually a complex interaction. Rather than reacting impulsively, or controlling and suppressing anger, people generally do best when they steer a middle course. This involves integrating the wisdom of bodily feelings with social and cultural know-how on dealing with emotion. This is often as complex, or even more so, as solving any math problem. It just requires a different kind of intelligence: emotional intelligence.

Another major anger problem that often arises in psychotherapy involves unresolved anger from the past. This is often unfinished business with a significant other in a person's life. This type of anger causes a large amount of psychological distress. All people probably remember incidents that still make them angry. There also is a sharp difference between events that merely annoy or irritate and those that produce tremendous anger. Serious experiences of anger affect people quite differently than the ones that simply come and go. As time passes, annoying incidents lose their capacity to arouse people's anger. Certain other experiences, however, do not fade. They often boil and burn inside. These are the ones that arise in therapy.

The episode or series of events that produced the anger may have occurred years—even decades—ago, but even though the experience is long past, anger remains. Anger that lingers is often directed at spouses who betrayed or abandoned one, divorced parents, a father who abandoned his family, or a neglectful mother. This anger persists into the present and prevents loving relationships from developing. Even though many of the situational details are forgotten, the emotions remain, and people feel them again and again as if the event were occurring right now. What makes this happen is that the major violation was so arousing and overwhelming that people were unable to cope with the intensity of the hurt and anger at the time. They were unable to make sense of it and assimilate it into their understanding of the world. Instead, it was stored in emotional memory as an intense feeling. Long after people have forgotten the details in their semantic memory system, the emotional memory can be evoked, and they can feel the anger in the same intense and unprocessed fashion that it was originally stored. They may have been too young, too scared, or just too overwhelmed to process and make sense of it at the time. Since then they may have covered up their anger or tried to distract themselves from feeling so powerless and frustrated, instead of resolving their angry feelings.

Unfortunately, this way of coping produces the equivalent of a deep wound that was not cleaned or exposed to the air to allow the natural healing process of scab formation and regeneration of tissue. Had the person allowed him- or herself to heal, the incident might have left only a slight scar. Failing to deal with an emotional wound leaves people with the equivalent of an infected emotional sore from which the pus of intense hurt and resentment occasionally oozes. For example, a woman might feel helplessly angry 12 years after her husband walked out on their marriage. "He just walked out, without a word" she says, as her anger smolders but still remains tightly controlled.

I now present some examples of people in psychotherapy resolving problems with anger.

UNRESOLVED ANGER IN THERAPY

A client in her late 40s had been divorced almost 20 years and had grown children. She sought therapy because she found herself pushing away potential relationships, although she wanted companionship and the intimacy of a relationship "before I get much older." She was fearful of allowing anyone to get close enough to hurt her and shatter her life, as had happened many years earlier when her husband walked out on her and their small children. She described herself as being in a state of shock at the time and struggling to keep her head above water. She had coped by controlling her emotions. She had not allowed herself to feel the anger and pain of the abandonment, because she feared falling apart. Being "strong" in this way was reinforced by well-meaning friends who cautioned, "Don't shed one tear over that bastard; he's not worth it." The woman had postponed dealing with her feelings for 20 years.

Although she had done well in her life since then, she had never completely dealt emotionally with the loss of her marriage. She had not grieved this loss; neither had she fully allowed herself to express her intense anger at her ex-husband for the pain and hardship he had caused. She felt anger not only because he had left her but also because of his self-centeredness and lack of caring throughout the marriage. Therapy provided a safe place for her to express these things and deal with her fears of getting involved again in an intimate relationship.

The first important step in therapy was for this client to acknowledge her long-suppressed experience of anger at her ex-husband. This was not the intellectual process of saying "I'm angry at him." This she knew and had probably said many times before. She needed to *feel* the anger in a full-bodied way, experiencing the burning anger in her stomach rising up in volcanic surges. Once she gave herself permission to feel, a floodgate of suppressed and overcontrolled feelings opened.

During the seventh session she began to talk about her husband walked out on her. She exclaimed in an astonished and angry tone, "And he just walked away. I hate him for that! I hate him for that!" I asked the client to imagine that her husband was in the room and to speak directly to him. She proceeded to say, "I hate what you did; I really hate you! I hate you; I really hate you." When asked how she felt, she replied "I feel better. I feel better that I hate him."

Feeling already empowered by her anger, she reflected on her marital experience, saying that she and the children "didn't deserve what he gave us . . . if I had been a bad mother and a bad wife I could understand, but I wasn't; I loved him." Imagining him in an empty chair that I had placed in front of her, she said, "I loved you, and you didn't deserve it—you didn't deserve for me to love you, and my love turned to hate, and I hate you now, I hate you! I hate you for all those years I've wasted, trying to make something that wasn't there." After absorbing what she had expressed, she began to elaborate her feelings. I responded to the sense of wasted years I was picking up from her and, validated by this, she said "Yes, it was a big loss, and the loss is what hurts me, the loss and the wasted years, and for somebody that wasn't worth it. He wasn't even worth it; how could anyone waste that much time on somebody who's not worth it?"

She then spontaneously began to feel her pain. She began to weep deeply for the devastation and intense vulnerability she felt at the time he walked out on her. I acknowledged and validated her pain and how vulnerable she felt and said that I knew that her pain "must feel almost unbearable." She felt validated in her experience of having been so terribly wronged. Now, feeling entitled to her pain and anger, she allowed herself for the first time since that awful night when he walked out to fully feel and express her feelings of being wronged. She sobbed,

> How can anybody hurt someone else so much? How can they, and then walk away without even feeling any emotion out of it? My conscience would tell me if I'm hurting somebody . . . it is unforgivable . . . and he is just nothing in my eyes, just nothing.

Looking at the empty chair and clenching her fists, she yelled "I hate you. How can anybody hate anybody so much; I didn't think I had that much hate in me." I encouraged her to hit a pillow, pretending it was her ex-husband, and to allow herself to feel the full fury of her rage and express it in the safe confines of the therapy room.

The woman expressed her anger and rage and experienced the full satisfaction that her anger desired. She imagined exposing him to all their friends and family for the selfish bastard he truly was. She expressed her contempt, humiliating him for all that he had done and not done for his children. She felt proud that she had the courage now, finally, to face her rage and direct it at him in this way.

After this experience the client said, "I felt the pain; the anger again, as if it were all happening again, only more intensely." She said that it was her vulnerability that she had feared experiencing again. It was this that had prevented her from opening up in new relationships and that she needed to feel some ability to regulate. She feared that she again might allow herself to become so dependent on someone else that she could again be so devastated. After she explored all these feelings, she articulated some of the unhealthy beliefs that were preventing her from achieving intimacy. She talked about her secondary anger at herself for having put up with so much from her ex-husband. Shame also emerged in her expression of grief. She said there must have been something wrong with her: "How could anyone put up with that and keep coming back for more?"

Having her intense anger, distress, and vulnerability validated; letting all those tears come; and acknowledging all those years of hurting led this client finally to reflect on how she must have been pretty desperate as a young woman and how much she wished now that she could have stood up for herself. She said "I guess it bothers me how I allowed it to happen —How *did* I allow it to happen? There must have been something wrong with me." Having articulated this unhealthy belief, she explored and confirmed her current strengths. She recognized that now she was no longer a young mother with little children, no longer so dependent and vulnerable. Empowered by the legitimacy of her anger, she was able to draw on her current resources to challenge and change the belief that she was helpless and the fear that she might repeat this desperation or lack of assertion in another relationship. At the end of treatment she felt stronger and had created a new view of herself and believed now that she could maintain her autonomy in a new relationship. Her decision to get involved with someone would be determined more by her willingness to make compromises than by her fear.

What can be learned from this therapeutic experience? First, overcontrolled anger can turn into highly problematic emotional memories. This client had difficulty in feeling the anger and hurt at the time of the event because she felt she would not be able to bear the pain, which led her to close off and cover up a part of herself. This coping style, supported by friends and family and social injunctions against showing weakness, had major negative repercussions in her life. At the time, her minister encouraged her to grieve, but she could not. In the long run this strategy of closing up did not prove best. Control sometimes seems to work, but only when the hurt and anger are more minor. Each time people control or cut off a significant experience of anger, they not only cut themselves off from important information from within, but they also cut themselves off from others. Each unexpressed feeling of anger that remains unresolved burns within a person as resentment and becomes a barrier to intimacy. These bricks of resentment, imperceptible at first, soon combine to form a nearly impenetrable wall of anger and distance. I often see couples between whom the wall of 20 years of unresolved resentment is difficult to dismantle— possible, but extremely difficult. If only such couples had started much earlier to deal with their feelings of being offended, accommodated less for the sake of peace, and asserted their boundaries and needs, these walls would not be quite so difficult to break down. Anger expression at violation is sometimes necessary to protect one's health and relationships, both present relationships and the possibility of future ones. This example does not mean that anger should always be expressed, or that this form of therapeutic expression is called for in everyday life. It does, however, point to the damage of unexpressed, overcontrolled anger. This is the kind of suppressed anger that can cause physical health problems, ranging from headaches to digestive problems, as well as causing emotional problems. Paradoxically, people often feel that getting angry in situations of hurt, betrayal, or abandonment is a sign of weakness. It is like admitting they were hurt and that whatever occurred really did violate them. To be able to get angry, people have to both feel strong enough to be weak and feel sufficient support from another person to feel angry.

The form of expression of anger in which this client engaged was not done for the purposes of getting rid of her anger, as many people mistakenly think is the aim of this type of expression. Her anger was not just sitting in some storage tank, waiting to be drained off. It would not have helped her much, once her anger was fully experienced and expressed, to go back and repeatedly express her anger to further drain it off. Many academics, correctly critical of a cathartic view of this type, do not think it is a good idea to express anger. However, they fail to see that the true therapeutic purpose of this form of expression is to validate the feeling and produce change in the meanings things have (Greenberg & Safran, 1987).

Allowing herself to experience this degree of anger was a way for this client to acknowledge the extent of the violation and to put in motion a lot of important other change processes that would have been difficult to promote without her first feeling entitled to and expressing her anger. This type of anger awareness and expression, rather than draining off anger, informs and mobilizes. It also helps uncover unhealthy beliefs that accompany the emotion and exposes them as untrue. Often these are the same beliefs that have kept the anger under wraps. Such beliefs could include "My anger will destroy others or my relationships with them," "I will not survive my own anger," or "I have no right to feel this anger." Expressing anger in a healthy way in therapy results in empowerment and is a path to the changing of destructive beliefs. It certainly takes time to feel empowered, and so revisiting the anger may be important, but not for the purpose of draining it off. Creating the new meanings that help resolve past angers takes continued work, but repeated expressions of rage will not help with this. Rather, it is the initial acknowledgment and expression of the anger, in the intensity that it initially was felt, that is highly strengthening. It helps give a person permission to feel what was previously not allowed and begins the process of assimilating the experience and making sense of it. This leads to understanding and changes in meaning; people come to see themselves and others in a new way.

It is important to see from this example that both core anger and sadness were present for this client. These two emotions are frequently associated with disappointments and injuries to self-esteem in adult attachment relationships and with unresolved disappointments with parents. One of the goals of therapy is to differentiate the anger and sadness in these situations and have the client fully experience, express, and work through each one. Often people are able to express sadness once their anger has been validated and expressed aloud. Tracking moment-by-moment experience is critical in working with anger and sadness, because clients working on these issues in therapy frequently shift quickly between these two emotions. It is important to recognize that both anger and sadness can be core emotions and that they need to be validated and deepened so clients can access healthy components of each. Thus, people need to be coached to allow themselves to feel fully their anger and sadness. They should not be too afraid of them. They need to listen to both of them and discern what each emotion is telling them. A helpful guideline to follow is that the experience that is most alive at any moment is the one on which a person should focus. However, people generally need to work harder on, and need more help with, accessing the emotion that is more difficult for them to acknowledge and express. Some people are more comfortable with sadness than with anger. I certainly am. Others are more comfortable with anger than with sadness. People need to value them both and learn what these emotions do for them and what happens to them if they try to cover the emotions. Accessing one's most deeply inhibited core emotional experience usually enhances growth and makes accessible experiences that are associated with new and healthy information.

DEALING WITH UNEXPRESSED SADNESS IN THERAPY

As with minor anger, minor sadness and disappointment flow through people and are soon forgotten. However, people are usually haunted by the intense sadness at a major loss that was blocked and not expressed. In the therapeutic episodes that follow, unacknowledged or suppressed core sadness and distress were the clients' most salient experiences. In these episodes the sadness was often accompanied by anger. Readers will see that it was an incredible relief for the clients to say what had been missed and to acknowledge what had been lost. This helped them accept the losses and move on to otherwise satisfy their unmet needs. Allowing themselves to experience their sadness also helped these clients articulate unhealthy beliefs, making these available for exploration and change in therapy.

Core sadness due to deprivation is frequently covered by anger. The importance of distinguishing between sadness and anger was vividly illustrated in therapy with a 7-year-old boy. This child had been abandoned by his mother and shuffled from foster home to foster home. He had been abandoned, rejected, betrayed, and deprived of love all his life and had told his therapist that "no one loves me." He had temper tantrums every time his foster parents said "no" to him in his current foster home. Part of his therapy involved emotion awareness training. In one of the activities, he was asked what a person is feeling when he or she says "I hate you" (something he said to his foster parents in his tantrums). This child responded that the person is feeling "sad." There is no doubt that this child is legitimately angry about being abandoned, but his core experience is one of sadness. If he grows up to be a man who has not been able to acknowledge his core hurt and sadness and has no skills for accurately describing and communicating his emotional experience, his needs for love and connection will never be met. His anger will push others away rather than pull them in for the nurturance he desires.

A 37-year-old divorced woman came to therapy experiencing chronic feelings of insecurity and loneliness. Beginning in approximately the 10th session, she began to talk about her childhood experience of abandonment. She focused on her anger at her father for having abandoned her when she was a child. Her mother had died when she was 7, and her father had placed her and her younger brother in a foster home because he could not cope. She remained in the foster home for several years until the father remarried and reclaimed them. When he and his new wife had children of their own, the client continued to feel neglected and unimportant, like the "stepchild." As an adult she had come to have a decent relationship with her father and believed that he loved her but, despite "understanding" his limitations as a parent, harbored deep resentments toward him. She felt like he had cheated her and should never have abandoned her no matter how rough things were. She believed he had never been there for her even after the foster care and that he should have been a better father.

At the time of therapy he was a sick and frail old man, and she feared his death and being abandoned by him for the second time. These painful feelings evoked episodic memories of herself as a little child holding onto her little brother's hand as though it were a lifeline. She remembered sitting with her brother on the steps of their house, waiting to be taken to a foster home, feeling utterly alone and forgotten. She wanted to resolve these feelings of abandonment with her father and did not want this "unfinished business" haunting her after he died. At the same time, she believed he was too old and feeble to be confronted directly.

I began the next session by acknowledging and validating the client's feelings of abandonment and her anger at her father by saying "How lonely and frightening that must have been—like being thrown to the lions" and saying that she must have felt "so angry at him, like 'how could he have done that to us!'" Together, the client and I collaborated to focus on her painful memories of abandonment in this session. Her emotion-filled memories of being abandoned by her father were evoked in the session in the context of the ongoing empathic relationship.

I then helped the client pay attention to and explore her bad feelings, her feelings of pain and fear at being suddenly left all alone in the world with no one to care for her. She explored many aspects of her terrible experience of abandonment and her feeling of great responsibility that it was up to her to take care of her brother and herself. As she talked about the abandonment, she began to access her grief and express her core anger at her father for not being there for her. It was an anger she had felt at the time, and often thereafter, but had been unable to express. It was important at this point to help her to not cancel out her anger again, as she had done in the past. She had done this in various ways: by being too understanding of her father's position, by frequently dismissing her own needs and pain, and by paying attention to his needs. I helped her become aware of the ways in which she interrupted her anger, and I encouraged her to acknowledge her emerging anger rather than interrupt its expression. This involved, among other things, helping her become aware of, and reinspecting, her belief that her anger would result in the loss of her father's love and would damage him. I encouraged her to direct her anger at the strong adult man he used to be, not at the sick and feeble man he currently was. The client then experienced and expressed her anger at him for his choices and for the pain it caused her. She imagined she was the 7-year-old child who had lost her mother. She said that she needed comfort and protection from him and that he had not been there for her. In addition, she said how angry she was that he also had been blind to her pain as an adult in subsequent years.

Once the client was able to fully express her anger and receive empathic validation of her experience, she grieved more fully the loss of her mother and of her father's support. A transformation occurs when one is able to grieve one's losses. Grieving often involves expressing angry protest at a loss before one can access tears of sadness.

The client was able to change her unhealthy emotions of feeling worthless by acknowledging her simultaneous feelings of sadness and super-responsibility and feeling unentitled to her anger. The change occurred by her acknowledgment of her core healthy emotions and by accepting that her needs for support and comfort were legitimate. She realized that she could, and should, expect support from others in her life. She came to feel more entitled to her sadness and her anger and to having her needs met.

In this process of reworking her feelings she also changed her views about her father's neglect. She came to believe that her father was not as abandoning as she had believed but rather that he was somewhat unable to take care of her and would have responded to her if he had been aware and known how. She also felt that if he knew how she felt he currently would want to help her and make amends. She was able to let go of her anger toward him, grieve fully for her losses, and forgive him. She created a new account of her past. She felt a lot stronger, because in this new account she affirmed herself as being worthy of his love. She was subsequently able to feel the uncomplicated pain and sadness of loss when he died a few months later.

In this session I was guided by what was emotionally alive and poignant for the client. Focusing on what was alive evoked her childhood memories of abandonment, which I helped her begin to change in the supportive atmosphere of therapy and by helping her access her anger and sadness, her need for support, and a sense of entitlement to these emotions. This provided her with a new experience of herself and helped her reform her view of herself and transform some of her life story.

From this therapy example one learns first about the many ways people have of interrupting their anger. People need to be helped to identify their own ways of interrupting their anger and sadness and to bring these interruption processes into awareness and under control. They need to learn whether they deflect their experience of anger, whether they pay attention to others' needs rather than their own, and whether they believe that their anger is dangerous. It is important to be able to regulate anger and sadness, not only so that one does not express them at certain inappropriate times, but also so that one can express them at other times. Otherwise people become prisoners of their own automatic ways of interrupting their feelings.

Another important point in this therapy example is that the experience of feelings does not stop with expression. It is very important to get to the needs and concerns associated with the feelings. Thus, this client's experience and expression of anger helped her acknowledge her need for support, to claim this as her right, and to have this right affirmed by her therapist. As I have pointed out, emotion coaches must help people get to the need, goal, or concern that their emotion is telling them is relevant to their well-being in the situation. Once people acknowledge the importance of their concerns, they reorganize themselves in light of them.

LESSONS

The therapy examples described in this chapter demonstrate the following lessons:

- Unexpressed emotion and its overcontrol can cause problems.
- Feelings of blame, complaint, and hurt need to be differentiated into core anger and sadness.
- Appropriate expression of emotions about past violations promotes changes in their meaning.
- Emotional expression in therapy can lead to changes in one's view of others, letting go, or forgiveness.
- People need to become aware of the many ways they interrupt their expression and experience of feelings.
- Expressing emotion helps one access one's unhealthy beliefs about oneself and the world and about the dangers of emotional expression.
- Awareness of the needs, goals, and concerns that are embedded in the emotions are important in helping reorganization.
- Anger legitimizes that one feels wronged.
- Sadness and grieving help one let go and move on.

10

TRANSFORMING FEAR AND SHAME IN PSYCHOTHERAPY

The following clinical example illustrates a variety of the aspects of emotion coaching discussed so far: promoting emotion awareness, regulating emotion, and changing emotion with emotion. It also illustrates how the therapist empathizes, validates, and promotes exploration and the restructuring of emotional experience. This case example demonstrates how to work with fear and shame and how to change these with anger and sadness. In this treatment the client's maladaptive fear and her shame related to her childhood maltreatment were accessed in therapy and restructured by accessing her anger at violation and acknowledging her sadness at loss and her pain at having being trapped in an abusive family.

The client was a woman in her early 50s who sought therapy because of chronic loneliness and feelings of alienation. She had been married and divorced several times. She presented herself as highly attractive and well-dressed, with a dramatic interpersonal style. She seemed independent and aloof. She reported an inability to connect with others and had difficulty in forming relationships, apart from those with her four children from different marriages. At intake, she described her primary experience as one of excruciating loneliness and at times described herself as "climbing the walls" because she felt so cut off. As a child she felt like she had been separated from the world and had often felt like she was "living in a glass bubble," feeling untouched by life, with only brief moments of feeling like she was "participating." She had been physically and emotionally abused as a child. Her experience had been constantly invalidated. She had been continually told that she was "crazy" and "stupid" and that she was "exaggerating" when she was upset. All of this childhood maltreatment resulted in predominant feelings of fear, anxiety, and shame while growing up. She feared her parents, who had completely dominated her life, and she was often confused about her own perceptions and emotional experience. She had learned to be afraid of close interpersonal contact and feared her own experience of weakness and neediness. She learned to cope by withdrawing into self-sufficiency and by avoiding painful memories, emotions, and vulnerability. This left her alienated and alone as well as disoriented and out of touch with her feelings and needs. She stated that fear and anxiety—particularly an ongoing fear of her parents—had dominated her life. A major goal of therapy for her was to be free of the influence of these maladaptive emotions. Additional stated goals of therapy were a desire to connect with others and to learn to know and trust what she was experiencing.

Part of this client's treatment focused on helping her deal with her pain and sadness related to the childhood abuse and lack of love. She worked on resolving her unmet dependency needs as a child plus her chronic difficulty in forming lasting attachments in her adult life. Many sessions focused on exploring her internalized messages of worthlessness and her fears about being weak and needy. She succeeded in getting past her maladaptive fears to contact how deeply she had been hurt, and she began to heal these wounds. In the beginning she found it difficult to acknowledge that she had been hurt. She said she would never let her parents know she needed anything from them or that they had hurt her and said that it was difficult to be open and weak. I helped her acknowledge her vulnerability through repeated validation, directing attention to her internal experience of pain and sadness and symbolizing that experience in awareness.

An important focus of the treatment was the provision of interpersonal safety and a positive emotional experience with the therapist. This positive relational experience helped the client disconfirm her dysfunctional beliefs about close relationships. Another important change process involved the allowing and accepting of her previously painful emotional experience and memories regarding her unmet attachment needs. By means of this process, adaptive information from her primary emotions and needs was integrated into her current constructions of reality. The emotion coaching also aimed at accessing, often through memory evocation, core maladaptive fear and shame structures related to childhood maltreatment so that those originally self-protective emotional responses—the associated beliefs and avoidant behaviors, which now were no longer adaptive to current contexts—were transformed. I now describe how this occurred.

DEALING WITH THE CLIENT'S FEAR OF HER PARENTS

This therapy focused on overcoming the client's core maladaptive fear by accessing her sadness at loss and anger at violation and mobilizing her current abilities to protect herself. I spent the first three sessions establishing an empathic bond and then focused on her primary fear of her abusive parents. This fear had been originally adaptive in that it had helped somewhat in keeping her out of harm's way. It was now maladaptive in that it continued to dominate her current relationship with her parents and with others. I aimed my interventions at accessing this fear structure by talking about her childhood and experiencing and reprocessing her fear to help strengthen her sense of self. Approximately midway in this 20-session treatment I also addressed her fear of her dependence, weakness, and vulnerability. She had learned, through parental invalidation and ridicule, to distrust her internal experience and in particular to avoid painful experiences associated with unmet attachment needs. In therapy, these painful experiences needed to be acknowledged and accepted as part of her core self-structure.

Thus, a major focus of therapy was the client's ongoing fear of her parents, particularly of her father. She described a recent incident in which she had returned to her country of origin and visited her parents and found that she was still frightened as an adult. Her father now used a walking stick, and she had felt terrified that he would hit her with the stick. I validated how deeply ingrained her fear was and that it was an automatic response, and I acknowledged her struggle to be free of it. We collaboratively agreed to focus on overcoming her fear and on self-empowerment as goals of therapy.

The evocation of the emotional memories that were critical in the development of this client's anxious–avoidant self-organization was important in intervention. One of her earliest memories was of her father forcing her to watch him drown a litter of puppies. This was to "teach her a lesson about life," and the client believed that he enjoyed it. The client accessed a core self-organization, which included her "suppressed scream of horror" from this experience, while reliving this scene in therapy. I guided her attention toward the expression of disgust in her mouth while she was feeling afraid. Doing so mobilized this subdominant adaptive emotion to be a resource to help her begin to build a stronger sense of self. I helped her evoke and explore other memories of her father's violence and threatening sexuality. Imaging herself back in her family home brought the traumatic scenes alive for her, thus accessing her core emotion schemes and some of her coping responses, like that of "slinking away like a dog." The client re-experienced how she had learned to keep quiet and disappear. She articulated her sense that there was no escape or sense of protection and how fear had overwhelmed and overpowered all her other experiences.

She talked about beatings; of being left alone with no support, with no one to turn to, with no protection or safety; and of being "unable to speak" about her plight. The client recalled that, as a child, she would frequently dream about being left alone, abandoned and utterly unable to protect herself. My empathic responses, such as "So life was just full of fear, just trying not to be seen so you wouldn't provoke an attack" or "You never knew when it would come, you were just so afraid and alone in your fear," highlighted primary fear as a core part of her construction of her self and the world.

Like many abused clients, this woman expressed a desire to distance herself from her parents, to sever ties to gain control of her life. She simultaneously wanted to have the courage to face them unafraid, that is, to overcome her fear. I responded to this desire with "So, the best thing would be that they not have so much power over you." The client responded that, although her parents had real power when she was a child, now that she was an adult their power was in her mind. I responded by asking, "Something up here (point to head) keeps you tied, victimized?" This led to a focus on how her internal processes gave the power to her parents and resulted in her current experience of fear and disempowerment. This was a first step in feeling some control.

The client also felt that she should directly confront her parents. It was her desire to do this, rather than an actual behavioral confrontation, that I acknowledged and supported at this point. Although clients are not explicitly discouraged from such confrontations, they are more likely to be successful in doing this after they have explored and clarified their issues and developed a stronger sense of self. The desire to confront the parents is a healthy, adaptive response, and I supported it by encouraging the client to "speak your truth" in the session. She found it helpful to write a letter to her parents, but she did not send it. In the fifth session I helped the client confront her father in her imagination. Imagining her father sitting in front of her evoked disgust and fear. As when she was a child, her fear initially overpowered all other emotions and made engaging in an enacted dialogue with him very difficult. I helped her stay with the process and gain control, maintaining a safe distance by putting her imagined father across the room and directing only crucial, self-empowering statements (anger) at him. Expression and exploration of her vulnerability (fear and sadness) took place, not in response to the imagined father but in the affirming and safe dialogue with me.

These imaginary confrontations with her father evoked the client's fear and her painful memories of childhood beatings, of being told she was bad, and of being aware of nothing but her desperate need to escape. I responded supportively to her overwhelming fear and powerlessness at the time and asked how she felt, now, as she thought about herself as a little kid going through those experiences and what she had needed. This directed attention to her internal experience and helped her access her primary anger at being treated so cruelly. Access to her primary adaptive emotion mobilized her self-protective responses, and she began to stand up for herself, saying such things to him as "I don't really think I was bad; you are bad." I was attuned to and supported the emergence of such self-empowering challenges to her old views. I encouraged her to direct these statements to her imagined father in the empty chair: "Let's say that to him." Interventions to intensify anger expression and experience ("Say it again"), attend to internal experience ("Tune inside and see how it feels to say that"), and access the need for safety and protection ("What did you need?") helped restructure her fear scheme. Anger replaced her fear, and I supported her newfound sense of power, heightening her awareness of her strengths. This motivated further assertion and self-validation.

DEALING WITH SHAME

The client's frequent expressions of shame and embarrassment in therapy were often mixed with fear. Her parents had disciplined her with harsh criticism and ridicule, as well as physical abuse, and she stated that her greatest pain was that "they never believed in me." She was called stupid, crazy, a whore, and a slut, and she grew up utterly paralyzed in interpersonal relationships. She had internalized these beliefs about herself as inferior or weird and that she would amount to nothing. In therapy, there were indicators that shame was a core part of her sense of self. For example, she cringed at the thought of being the center of attention or having the spotlight on her. These were excruciatingly embarrassing experiences. At times, her shame interfered with her ability to attend to her internal experience. She experienced a kind of performance anxiety in which she feared being scrutinized and judged. Attending to and acknowledging her feelings of shame, plus the provision of safety and empathic affirmation in therapy, especially when she felt vulnerable (e.g., when she felt anxiety about exposing her experience for fear of being judged as ridiculous or a phony), helped her attend to and express sensitive material.

There were other times when shame mixed with fear in therapy. For example, in one session when the client's feeling of shame was evoked, she felt small and insignificant in front of her imagined parents. At first she was completely unable to imagine facing them or looking them in the eye, and she shrank away from being the object of their scorn. The shame associated with her father was mixed with fear and disgust at recalling his sexual innuendoes. One of her objectives in cutting off ties with her parents, physically distancing herself, was to free herself of their influence, to see "what I could be, or accomplish," if she were free of the constant name calling, ridicule, and negative expectations.

In such an invalidating early environment the client learned to be ashamed of, and to distrust, her feelings. She had internalized parental injunctions against "sniveling," being weak, and seeking attention, which made it difficult to admit to neediness or pain or to expose herself, cry, or ask for help. She viewed her feelings as "stupid" or "foolish." All this was evoked in therapy. It was embarrassing for her to imagine herself showing any signs of affection or emotional tenderness toward her mother. The thought of doing so literally made her shudder—"Yuck," a response of disgust or distaste often closely related to shame. She found experiences of emotional weakness, admitting to pain in therapy, embarrassing: "It is embarrassing to be so hurting." Having evoked the shame, I helped her explore and overcome it: "It's as if you have learned that there is something distasteful or shameful about your own experience, who you are." She found it humiliating to recall incidents of abuse, images of herself cowering like a dog, feeling like "garbage," and to experience how truly victimized she had been, realizing she had been used. She felt shame and humiliation at having been damaged so. Again, empathic affirmation provided safety so she could access and allow this painful experience in order to access the maladaptive sense of herself, formed at the time of these experiences, which generalized to lack of confidence and social avoidance.

Evocation of the memory of her mother's rejection when the client was first pregnant evoked painful memories and a longing for her mother's love and support. It was not only painful but also embarrassing to admit that she still needed her mother. She was unwilling to even use the word *need*. This unwillingness came in part from distrusting that her mother would respond and in part from the pain of rejection as well as from the shame of feeling like an abandoned child. I responded to how hard it was to admit to be needy with statements such as "You're kind of reduced to feeling like a needy little waif, so desperate for affection and love," and "It's hard to feel so needy as a grown woman; somehow you feel you should be more put together." *Damaged* or *broken* were terms used to further evoke and explore the pain of rejection. This helped the client access and allow herself to experience her neediness and to articulate how deprived and unloved she felt. She symbolized clearly that her core emotion scheme was one of feeling fundamentally flawed, defective, unlovable, that there must be something wrong with her. Seeing that this was her view of herself and understanding how this affected her gave her a new vantage point. She realized that she was both fearful and ashamed of the intensity of her desire to be close to others, that her intense neediness felt somehow inappropriate, unacceptable, immature, and desperate and that it needed to be controlled or hidden. I reflected that, having experienced such deprivation, of course she felt like a starved child. Accessing this emotion scheme of shame made it accessible to new information and restructuring. Alternate feelings of anger at violations and other internal resources, such as her capacity for self-empathy and self-soothing, were accessed to help overcome the shame.

In terms of overcoming shame of internal experience, the client distinguished between "admitting" that she had been hurt in a kind of objective, matter-of-fact way and "admitting" the pain into herself. The word *admit* suggests shame, as in admitting to some wrongdoing, flaw, or mistake. In one session, the client talked about seeing children's phone-in lines for abuse on television and how hard, humiliating, it was to see herself as one of them. I responded "Yes, so abused and unloved," and tears welled up in her eyes as well as anger at the unfairness of the children's situations. I used her ability to identify with other helpless children to help her acknowledge her anger about her own maltreatment and to restore her past. I validated that experiencing these painful feelings was understandably very difficult for her, remarked on her courage in having done it even a little in therapy, and expressed appreciation for both her weakness and her strength. I again used her anger to help her challenge her maladaptive beliefs about her worthlessness and restructure her core emotion schemes. Therapist validation and safety were also important in helping this client overcome her core sense of shame and years of parental invalidation. The therapy experience also left her less isolated. At the end of therapy she reported feeling less small and that her parents were "down to life size" and more human. This indicated that she was becoming self-validating and felt more empowered. She had overcome her sense of inferiority and fear and had begun constructing a new view of herself and her parents as well as a new life story in which she was now more of a heroic figure rather than a hopeless victim.

ACCESSING HEALTHY ANGER, SADNESS, AND PAIN

Evoking memories of parental criticism, ridicule, and beatings also helped this client access her primary sadness and the pain of her unmet childhood needs. I was attuned to the emergence of these, and I affirmed her needs for security and empathized with her terrible sense of loneliness. To strengthen her sense of control over her emotional experience, an appropriate distance from the intensity of experience was established. Whenever she felt overwhelmed or too tense I would tell her to breathe, reestablish contact with the present, feel her feet on the ground, and see me. When she was calmer I would invite her to return to the pain and face it. Helping her symbolize and explore the emotional experience associated with her father rather than simply being overwhelmed by it also helped make order of her inner chaos. In one session, the client first said she was in touch with her sense of dread as a child coming home, then, and how much she hated him, "wishing him dead many times, wishing on him all the punishment he gave me." I reflected her desire to destroy him and asked her to check inside as she said these things. She reported feeling uptight and tense, holding back. She needed help in overcoming her fear of her anger. She articulated that there were grave consequences for wishing one's father dead and that as a child this thought had increased her anxiety. This exploration slowly enabled her to overcome her fear of confronting him, in her imagination, and of expressing her anger directly to his image in the session. She accessed the adaptive action tendency associated with her anger and disgust and was able to tell him to get away and that she thought he was "gross." Again, this strengthened her sense of self and helped restructure her weak and bad sense of self and her fear-based schemes.

Early in treatment the client had been surprised by my use of the word *pain* to symbolize her experience; she had never thought of it that way. At first she found this difficult to admit and to experience how truly victimized she had been. Her confident and dramatic style distanced her from others; she needed to contact and communicate her neediness for companionship to overcome her fear of doing so. Heightening her awareness of her internal experience was a means of achieving these objectives.

There were also frequent moments of feeling embarrassed about being needy and hurt—"I don't want to be teary"; "It's embarrassing to be hurt." One form of expression of sadness occurred when her eyes welled up in tears in response to my empathic, caring responses. Attuned to her process, I reflected that "something touched you just now," and the client responded, in a little-girl tone of voice while sitting on her hands, that she could not "tolerate kindness from others." Subsequent interventions helped her attend to and symbolize that experience: "intolerable . . . like it hurts," "like it touches a sore spot inside," "kindness is somehow painful . . . you end up feeling like a desperately needy little girl." This last response illustrates how focusing on her expression of her little-girl, powerless tone of voice and sitting on her hands, suppressing her expression, led to increased awareness and experience. When I asked about memories of kindness as a child, there were none, only earlier deprivation and lack of love and invalidation. I again directed her attention to her unmet primary need, how she must have longed for some kindness as a child and how painful it was not to get it, and how kindness touched a deep longing and emptiness inside.

This triggered episodic memories of events with her mother. The client was particularly distressed by what she perceived as her mother's lack of love and indifference to her suffering as a child (e.g., her mother had watched while father beat her, asked her to leave home when she became pregnant as a teenager, and constantly invalidated her experience). Memories of beatings and of her mother's rejection evoked her confusion and fear at the time, and she experienced how these feelings dominated her perceptions; overshadowed everything; and caused her to withdraw into herself, unable to communicate. She realized how she came to believe that her own feelings and perceptions were not to be trusted and that there must be something wrong with her. This left her unable to communicate, isolated, cut off, and painfully alone. Underneath this fear and confusion were deep pain and sadness.

I helped the client acknowledge and symbolize her sadness at the loss of what might have been a friendship and mutually supportive relationship with her mother and how, in her adult life, she longed for this and yet knew it was impossible. It was a big loss for her that she and her mother were not friends. Also, she acknowledged how painful it was that it had taken her so long to actually be in charge of her life. She said it was as if she had been living in a kind of fog, automatically, and had wasted years. These realizations also helped motivate her not to waste any more of her life and to heal. She could express these vulnerable feelings to me but still could not imagine expressing them to her parents. She felt she could not trust them to hear her pain, could not let down her guard, and had not forgiven them. She felt a lot of blame toward them and at first could not experience any sadness that was free of blame.

The client had been dominated in her childhood by fear and had not had an opportunity to let down her guard, to grieve, or weep for herself. Also, she had been stopped by internalized messages such as "You're exaggerating," "You're making it up," and derision and mocking from her mother that she had internalized. At moments of vulnerability I empathically responded to her sadness at being so uncared for. She reflected into her tears how much she had needed a mother and how feeling this need was normal and acceptable. I helped her become aware of her reluctance to express her sadness and longing and her refusal to acknowledge that she had needed her mother. I did this by empathically understanding how painful it was for her to know that her mother would not respond to her need and by symbolizing how she had almost vowed never to need again, because it hurt so much. In this empathic environment the client attended to her internal experience of suppressing her pain and needs, of fighting against them and trying to make them go away. Therapy was a process of validating her experience, and this led to her accessing and accepting her hurt.

Accessing and accepting her hurt helped mobilize her deep longing for connection with others and helped her articulate how her fear and confusion had interfered with her awareness and ability to express this. This accessing of her sadness and of the action tendency to connect motivated her to persist in therapy; to face her painful memories; and to seek out, with my help, an ongoing social skills peer group. She was determined to change her life. Throughout, I validated her strengths at surviving despite her suffering and supported her capacity for self-care. I helped her draw on her experience as a parent to help her identify her own unmet childhood needs and their validity. She needed a lot of guidance and support, and I balanced support with more active exploration. The therapeutic relationship was an important source of new interpersonal learning—learning that the client could trust and be understood and comforted.

The following transcript from a session illustrates moment-by-moment emotion coaching to help deal with the client's difficulty in acknowledging her pain.

Client: I used to think if I even thought about my pain I would die about it.

Therapist: Can you say more about that? (encourage elaboration)

Client: I remember one time thinking that if I ever talked about, if I ever tried to do anything about the sadness I feel, I would die from it.

Therapist: Just so unbearable. (empathic understanding)

Client: I mean I know I wouldn't, but that's how it feels.

Therapist: So afraid, like you would be completely overwhelmed by your sadness. (empathic attunement and focus on a leading edge)

Client: Yes, overwhelmed, absolutely oozing it, I thought it would just wipe me out somehow. The thought of me weeping and wailing and howling and bawling and stuff like that . . . was so embarrassing.

Therapist: Something about weeping and wailing. To really weep about this would be very, very hard, embarrassing. (promote exploration)

Client: Yes, embarrassing to lose, such loss of control.

Therapist: So total a loss of control.

Client: And the ability to protect myself.

Therapist: Yes, so it is very important to feel like you can protect yourself, to feel your feelings and also have some control. One way you can do that is by dipping in a little at a time. (coaching on dealing with pain)

———————

Therapist: So you felt like she didn't really care about you.

Client: I was too busy at the time to pay much attention, but I would have liked it, some humane treatment.

Therapist: What were some of the things you would have liked, it seems important to put those things in words, what you missed. (coaching to symbolize)

Client: I don't know what I missed, anything would have done (weeps); anything at all would have done.

Therapist: Yes, stay with that, I really needed her to care.

Client: That was the second time that happened, first time was when I was pregnant and I wasn't married and I didn't know what to do.

Therapist: You needed her then, too.

Client: When I phoned and told her she said I wasn't to dare to come into the country.

Therapist: You must have felt so rejected, what would you have liked her to do, as your mother?

Client: She could have at least not stood in my way, some kind of human care and attention. This sounds so—I don't know (sits up in her seat and frowns evaluatively).

Therapist: What happens as you say that, something stopped you. (focus on interruptions)

Client: I'm thinking to myself, it sounds so juvenile, and so self-pitying and stuff like that, it sounds like I'm whining.

I continued to coach the client, saying such things as

- "In an ideal world, and if you could say what was in your heart to your mother, what would you say?" (accessing feeling or need)
- "What's happening? You feel . . . How could I be so hurt still?" (inquiring into experience and conjecturing)
- "So sort of like you desperately needed her, and the fact that she wasn't there has just cut you to the quick. (Client sniffles.) It's unbearable, almost. You desperately needed a mother." (reflecting feeling and need)
- "Sounds like you needed that more than anything." (reflection)
- "It makes sense what you're saying. It makes perfect, perfect sense." (validating)

OVERCOMING INTERRUPTIONS

I also was attuned to signs of anxiety and deflections in the session —laughing, rapid talk, diversions—and after an alliance and safety had been established I began to address the client's experience of interpersonal anxiety and interruption of emotion in the therapy session. I directed her attention to her current internal experience, and the client described herself as "a rabbit in a field, kind of twitching all over." I responded "kind of all jumpy inside" and encouraged her to stay with her experience if she could: "There's something threatening in here, too." This invited the client to attend to, explore, and speak from her current experiential state of nervousness. The client observed that when she was nervous in the sessions she talked a lot and wondered whether she was avoiding something. I asked what she thought she was avoiding. The client responded that she did not feel unsafe in the session but rather that she felt weepy. She recalled her difficulty writing the word *pain* in her journal and believed that her nervousness was about the difficulty of facing the emotional pain associated with her parents. She said she was always afraid of doing that, afraid that somehow she would be left unprotected. As well, she expressed fear that I would find her expressions stupid or think that she was a fraud. Thus, the intervention of focusing on what she might be avoiding, when she had identified that she might be avoiding something, helped her articulate her anxiety about her emotional experience. She began to explore how she avoided experiencing the pain of unmet needs and began to deal directly with her shame and anxiety about her internal experience.

This client's pain of unmet needs for love and support were consistently accessed as part of her memories but also generally were quickly interrupted. She would deflect, squeeze her jaw, or become frozen. Intervention consisted first of validating how painful her memories were and how difficult it was to feel needy and fear that she might be rejected or belittled and then of exploring and articulating her self-interruptive processes. At first, the client found it foreign to attach words such as *pain* and *abuse* to her own experience, distanced herself from the experience by minimizing it, and interrupted emerging experience with internalized messages that she was stupid or exaggerating. I commented that she often seemed to not take her pain seriously and raised her awareness of the ridiculing voice in her head that prevented her experience. Eventually the client was able to express her childhood unmet needs to me. She was never willing to express to her imagined parents that she "needed" anything from them. She explained how she always got nothing back from them, and I validated her by saying, "Why express yourself if you have no faith the other will hear or respond; why risk opening up?" She was, however, able to say to me what she had needed and missed and to express anger to her imagined parents. I supported the emergence of this healthy, self-validating stance.

Toward the end of therapy the client acknowledged that she was worthy and had deserved more than she got from her parents. She began to create a new identity narrative, one in which she was worthy and had unfairly suffered abuse at the hands of cruel parents. She also began to feel that it would be possible to need love and that she was now open to learn to love. At the end of therapy, she decided to cut off contact with her parents for the present time. This was something she had always wanted to do but had been unable to. I supported her in this decision and helped her accept that the decision was part of a process and did not have to be permanent if she changed her mind. In response to my statement "There's something important about it" the client said "Yes, it's a way of exercising control over my life."

11

COACHING FOR EMOTIONAL
WISDOM IN COUPLES

Bob and Marie are a young married couple. When they see each other at the end of the day they feel good. When Marie laughs at Bob's jokes, a pleasant feeling courses through his body, and if she doesn't laugh he is a bit deflated and feels like sinking, just a little, into the ground. When they cuddle they both feel warm and safe, like babies in their mothers' arms. When Bob and Marie are angry, they both feel threatened and feel all kinds of unpleasant sensations in their bodies.

People's relationships with each other are a wellspring of emotional experience. When two people connect it is like the meeting of two chemicals: All kinds of reactions occur. Unbeknownst to one another, intimate partners produce little squirts of neurotransmitters in each other that send messages pouring through each other's body. Affection is associated with pleasure, and the look or touch of a loved one launches endorphins on a complex journey through one's body. This is an especially pleasurable journey because endorphins are natural opiates that kill pain and produce pleasure. Other chemicals activated by different cues course through partners' bodies to make them feel and act differently. A relationship is a marriage of chemicals and receptor sites. It is a highly physiological process. One's partner affects one's heart rate, breathing, perspiration, and physical well-being. Affect at its base is neurochemical and physiological in nature. Conscious feelings and thoughts come later. The affective dance is continually in progress both in and out of our awareness.

Emotions are fundamentally relational. They link people to each other. Once they are in awareness, emotions give people information about the states of their intimate bonds, telling them if their bonds are in good condition, if they have been disrupted, or if they need maintenance. People are calm and feel good when all is going well between them and their intimate partners. They are disturbed and upset when all is not well. Emotions are of great importance in the everyday life of relationships. Emotion coaches can help people improve their relationships by guiding them to become aware of their attachment- and intimacy-related feelings and needs and to communicate these in nondemanding ways (Greenberg & Johnson, 1988).

INTIMACY AND ATTACHMENT EMOTIONS ARE THE BASIS OF RELATIONSHIPS

People have been primed by evolution to feel pleasant feelings when they are close to caretakers and unpleasant feelings when they are unwillingly separated from them. People basically feel joy when they are with loved ones and fear and anxiety when the bond is ruptured. Human beings need others to feel secure and happy. Healthy adult attachment and intimacy involve emotional availability and responsiveness, security and warmth. The need for other people becomes unhealthy only when a person cannot tolerate separation and flies into a rage or becomes depressed at loss, separation, or distance.

Couples generally know that their emotions govern their relationships. They know their emotions affect what they do with, and to, one another. However, even though couples know intuitively how important their emotions are, generally they do not know much about how to deal with their emotional experiences in their relationships. They simply have not been taught how to deal with their emotions. All they have ever been taught is that their negative, angry, or painful emotions are troublesome and ought to be avoided at all costs and that loving feelings are generally good. They have also learned from life experience that they sometimes can express their feelings and be responded to but that generally their feelings are ignored, discounted, or even ridiculed by others. People therefore often conclude that their feelings are best held in, controlled, or ignored until they disappear or change with time.

> Bob and Marie have had their first child. Bob feels abandoned and lonely now that Marie is so busy trying to fulfill her new roles as a mother and income earner. He is having difficulty accepting that he is feeling unloved and, rather than discussing his feeling of being ne-

glected, he begins to become critical of the way Marie does things, and he becomes more bossy. The criticisms and struggles begin.

It is often difficult for couples like Bob and Marie to cope with their more negative feelings, because they do not know how to handle their emotions well. They don't know what to do when they feel lonely, angry, and hurt. They don't know what to do when they feel inadequate or when they feel unloved and unlovable. They don't know what they can hope for from their partners or whether what they are feeling is mature or if it is childish and unacceptable. Coaches need to help couples learn that intimacy involves sharing hurt feelings, that problematic and conflicting emotions are usual in loving relationships, and that hating the one you love is inevitable at times. Couples also need to learn that as well as their attractions to their partners there may be repulsions and that resentments as well as appreciations are normal. Coaches need to help couples deal with the many and varied emotions that emerge in their relationships. They need to help people learn which feelings are problematic and need further work and which are healthy and should be expressed. I now apply some of what I have discussed thus far about emotion to coaching couples in the application of their emotion in intelligence.

EMOTIONS TELL PEOPLE WHEN SOMETHING IS WRONG

Emotions identify problems for people to solve. Thus, when Bob begins to feel angry that Marie is not available, or Marie feels frightened that Bob will be angry or disapproving, their feelings are automatic alarms saying "This is important; something is wrong here. My need for attention or support is not being met." Couples need to learn that this form of emotional feedback occurs all the time, telling them about how they are conducting themselves and how their relationship is going. Coaches need to help them pay attention to this feedback. If a person feels afraid, sad, or angry at her spouse, she is receiving information that something is wrong. If she doesn't pay attention to what she feels and what she needs, the relationship with her spouse will deteriorate. Emotions tell people that what is happening is relevant to their well-being and that a need of theirs is not being met. Then they have to start acting to do something about it.

Resolving difficult situations becomes easier if couples learn to deal effectively with their emotions, as demonstrated in the following vignette.

Bob and Marie become aware that something is going wrong, because they have learned to pay attention to their emotions. They can recognize what they feel. Bob is angry about feeling ignored and left out. Marie is afraid of his disapproval and overwhelmed. They now are in a position to use their awareness of their feelings to begin a nonblaming dialogue about what they feel and what they need from each other. Rather than accusing, judging, or trying to change each other, they are able to speak with minimum blame, listen nondefensively, and respond with acceptance and caring in the best way they can. Being human, they are not necessarily perfect, but at rock bottom their intentions to resolve rather than to blame, to discuss rather than to defeat, and to argue to a draw rather than to win, are apparent to each other. This helps them listen and respond to each other.

EMOTIONS COMMUNICATE

In the last few days Marie has been very busy at work as well as with the housework. She is tired and irritable but does not have the time or energy to talk about it. In fact, Marie has paid almost no attention to Bob for awhile. What she needs is for Bob to be sensitive to what she is feeling. Bob is aware that something is going on. He notices that Marie's voice is at times edgy and that she sometimes doesn't look at him directly when she speaks to him, as if she's distracted. These emotional signals tell him that she is stressed and does not want any demands from him. Reading these emotional signals can save them a lot of difficulty in their relationship.

Emotions play an important role in communication. They are the primary communicative signals in intimate relationships and in fact are primary signals from infancy onward. In infancy, emotions send messages that regulate caretakers' behavior. Yells bring caretakers running, coos make them overjoyed. Emotions continue into adulthood to be a primary form of communication, regulating others' responses. Emotions signal to others, especially to intimate partners, how well the partner is meeting one's relational needs and expectations. They also signal to one partner the states and intentions of the other partner. Couples therefore need to read each other's emotional signals carefully.

There has been a lot of confusion in the literature about how emotions are best expressed in couples (Greenberg & Johnson, 1988; Johnson & Greenberg, 1994). Some writers have argued that people always should express their feelings, whereas others caution that feelings are disruptive and should not be expressed. Some professionals promote radical responsibility, in which each person needs to own that he or she is the author of his or her own feelings and no statements such as "You made me feel . . ." are tolerated. It is the person's own responsibility. Others promote great empathy for and acceptance of the other and have been criticized as recommending that people treat their partners like babies. What is really needed in dealing with emotions in couple communication is an integration of both head and heart, of acceptance and responsibility.

Emotionally guided, reasoned expression and action seem best. Partners do not need to blurt out their anger at all times; rather, they need to use it to inform themselves that they feel violated, and then they need to use reason to analyze the situation. On the basis of the integration of reason and emotion, they express their concern in a reasoned manner, such as saying, "I don't like being criticized." This can occur only if people are aware of their emotions and feelings. Partners need to have some knowledge about how their own emotions work, what impact their expressions have on their partners, and what they can do with their maladaptive feelings. They need to take responsibility for how they handle their own feelings, and they need to practice acceptance of their partners' feelings.

> Marie, for example, knows that she sometimes feels overwhelmed because of her work situation. She is aware that she also feels that Bob is angry and unsupportive at these times. This has happened before, and Marie has learned something about her reactions. She used to feel a lot and say nothing. This led to a chain of internal dialogue that made her feel more and more depressed and angry; then she would eventually explode. After she saw that this didn't work, she learned it was better to express her feelings much sooner and that she needed to express only particular kinds of feelings, not everything. She learned that what helped resolve things was first speaking about her own experience and not about Bob's behaviors or motivations. Second, she needed to speak about her most core and deep feelings, usually feeling hurt or lonely, instead of relying on her more defensive feelings, usually anger. Third, she learned that to resolve the issue she needed to hear what Bob was feeling. Fourth, while listening to him, she needed to not forget about her own feelings and her desire to have them heard. She and Bob both learned that to resolve differences they both needed to speak and listen in a very intimate kind of manner to who they each were and to what their needs were. They needed to value their differences.

EMOTIONAL EXPRESSION AND THE CREATION OF INTIMACY

Creating and maintaining a satisfying, intimate relationship is a key life task. Intimacy involves people bringing their inner worlds of feelings, needs, desires, fears, perceptions, and fantasies into contact with the outer worlds of other experiencing people, their partners, and having their inner worlds accepted and confirmed by these intimate others. Intimacy results when people tell their partners their main feelings and concerns and experience that these are understood. This needs to be a reciprocal process. Everyone wants a partner who listens, understands, accepts, sympathizes, confides, forgives, and admits his or her part. Emotion coaches need to help couples become aware of and express their first, primary feelings to each other rather than their secondary, defensive or self-protective reactions. It is the disclosing of heartfelt experience between partners that breathes new life into relationships, especially when the relationship has grown cold and stale. Helping people express attachment-related feelings of fear and anxiety—even shame, sadness, and anger—brings or keeps them close.

Intimacy often involves expressing hurt feelings, because hurt often signals that which people most urgently need but for which they feel too ashamed to ask. People often cannot ask, because previously they have not had enough support to help them feel that their need is legitimate. People also might not trust that they can survive not being responded to or, because of past hurts, they might have vowed that they will not allow themselves ever to need again or be hurt again. Often then it is people's relationships with their own feelings, rather than with their partners, that prevent them from being intimate with others. Because a husband thinks his wife will reject him if he tells her what he is really feeling, he closes up. He tells himself to be strong. He often despises his neediness. He doesn't even give his wife the opportunity to respond. Many times in situations such as this the imagined rejection is more fantasy than reality. People really do not know how other people will respond to their feelings, but they are afraid to risk finding out. To be intimate, people have to be able to express whatever is going on within themselves and have trust in themselves that they can cope if another person does not respond as they hope.

> After a particularly difficult interchange, Marie accuses Bob of being controlling, of never saying what he wants but always expecting her to guess. She tells him this is a role she now refuses to play. Bob admits that he has this irrational need to be in control and, as he says this, he looks appealingly at her with a childlike look. This is a critical moment. Marie can either miss this moment because she is so involved in her own process, her resentment and hurt, or she can see the softening in Bob's face, the appeal, and the steel rod inside her can melt. She can feel tender and can return his look with one of concern. Supported by her look, Bob can begin to open up. He can say how often he watches her reactions, searching for signs of rejection, and of how much he wants to reach her but how afraid he is of being rebuffed. So he ends up trying to control things. He acknowledges that he doesn't reveal himself because he is afraid of being hurt. This softening of Bob can help Marie feel more open to talk about how she has given up trying to respond to him for fear that she will be criticized for getting it wrong. She has chosen instead to turn away and stay out of his way. She may now be able to talk about her sensitivity to criticism and to ask for his recognition and respect as a precondition of her support of him. The two may now look at each other. Something in the air is alive; something new has happened. Life has been breathed

back into the relationship. Much more work is still needed, but a new possibility has emerged: the intimacy of sharing vulnerabilities.

FEAR OF INTIMACY

Once hurt, many people vow never again to let themselves be vulnerable or need others. They move into a self-protective stance that is driven by a fear of intimacy. People fear emotional intimacy mainly because they fear being hurt again. They fear rejection, and they fear abandonment. The latter fear is built in biologically to infants to protect them from dangerous separations, and adults still carry the same programming. To ward off all these fears, people often avoid becoming dependent on anyone; they fear closeness. Shame also prevents intimacy. When people feel unlovable, they are afraid of getting close to others and of ruining things, so they protect themselves by staying distant. They fear that if they show themselves they will be found to be defective or deficient. The two maladaptive emotions of fear and shame interfere with people getting the love they need.

Accompanying the maladaptive feelings that prevent intimacy are the negative voices that can influence one's view of other people, especially people of the opposite gender. For example, running through women's heads often are statements they learned from their parents, culture, and experience, voices that say "You can't trust men; they don't have feelings, they are too dominant, you have to build a man's ego" and at the same time "If you don't have a man, you are a failure." Running through men's heads are voices that say "Women are too emotional, too demanding, and too controlling" and at the same time "If you don't make your woman happy, you are a failure." This creates great conflict in people who want but fear intimacy. Closeness can occur only when people overcome their fear and shame and change the negative beliefs that appear to protect them but in reality prevent them from achieving intimacy.

HOW PROBLEMS START IN COUPLES

The main problems experienced by couples emerge from conflicts related to needs for connectedness or intimacy and needs for separateness or autonomy and the struggle to change one's partner to meet these needs. Unresolved struggles of this nature lead to the development of certain escalating interactional cycles. Coaches need to work to identify these cycles and to access the underlying attachment-related emotions and needs to help change these cycles.

The Problem of Trying to Change One's Partner

Problems often initially arise in relationships because people don't say what they feel or need or, when they do try to explain to their partners what they need, their partners do not understand. This is a communication problem. However, often, over time, people might succeed in communicating their needs to their partners, but still there is a problem. Now it is no longer lack of communication or misunderstandings that leads to problems. As relationships develop, spouses often understand only too well what their partners need, but they are simply unable or unwilling to give their partners the response for which they are looking. Because partners differ, because each is a unique person who has his or her own needs, they are unable to always respond to each other in the right way at the right time. Often, one partner just doesn't feel the way the other wants him or her to feel. Partners do not always feel giving or concerned just when one needs this; neither do they do what one wants in just the right way. Then people often begin to feel that their partner is cold or uncaring. This is when the conflict starts. People begin to try to change their partners, and they begin to blame or to withdraw in service of these efforts. One of them may end up screaming "Give me, give me. You're so closed, you are afraid of intimacy," while the other may be screaming "Leave me alone—you're so demanding (or needy)." This is when the real problems begin. Cycles like this often emerge because of people's inability to express their most intimate feelings. How can couples resolve these conflicts? They need to be able to step out of the vicious cycle of attack and defend, or pursue and withdraw, and truly accept themselves and their partners. Partners need to change their interactions by expressing their primary attachment-related feeling and their needs for closeness and comfort. To do this, they often need to change themselves rather than their partners. Emotion coaches need to be alert to a number of problems that interfere with couples' open disclosure.

The Emergence of Destructive Cycles

Destructive cycles result from unexpressed primary emotions and needs. They are maintained by the expression of secondary emotions, such as blame and resentment, that mask primary feelings, or by instrumental emotional responses, such as hurt—pouting or crying when one is angry, as a means of getting what one wants from the other person. The cycles form around partner's most sensitive concerns, in regard to what each one feels most vulnerable about and needs most. One partner might want more closeness, be more anxious about connection, and need more reassurance; the other partner might be more inclined to feel inadequate, be overly concerned about being competent, need more compliments, or need space and be sensitive to intrusion. One partner might function more rapidly, be more decisive and more active, and become impatient if restrained. Partners' rhythms might be different: One might be quicker, while the other one is slower; one might need more rest and relaxation than the other. One might be bold, the other fearful. Two partners are never exactly the same. People sometimes do play different roles in different relationships: leader in one, follower in another, seeking out the other in one, and distancing in another. However, in their primary relationships people eventually become sensitive about the issue that evokes their deepest anxieties and unmet needs. Partners' buttons usually don't get pushed by the same concern, or at least not to the same degree. One might be concerned with closeness, the other with control. This leads to mismatched needs and conflict. Different types of cycles emerge between couples.

The Pursue–Distance Cycle

People are never perfectly matched with their partners in terms of needs. One usually wants a bit more closeness, more contact, more talk, more touch, or more time. The most common cycle that emerges is thus a pursue–distance cycle in which one partner is essentially pursuing the other partner for greater closeness or intimacy. Often the amount of blaming and complaining this partner may have resorted to, in order to get the closeness, doesn't make this need easily apparent. Even though the other partner may want to be connected, he or she feels overwhelmed. His or her autonomy and identity become threatened, and this might lead him or her to feel inadequate to the demands the pursuing partner is making.

The Dominant–Submissive Cycle

Given that identity is another major issue, power is another key concern. Who calls the shots more often and defines things more often might be an imperceptible issue at first but later can become a big issue. One of the partners is quicker to state needs, pick the movie, or choose the restaurant. The other goes along at first, maybe even enjoys not having to think about what he or she wants. Eventually this can become a second type of cycle—a dominant–submissive cycle—that can cause a lot of problems. One person takes over and overfunctions, and the other one gives up and underfunctions.

In a dominant–submissive cycle often one partner has to be right and get his or her own way. The dominant partner may feel that it is a matter of survival to prove that he or she is right. If challenged or even questioned, the dominant one becomes highly protective of his or her position. The other partner, after years of following, has forgotten how to choose, to make decisions, and is scared to make mistakes or speak up and produce conflict.

Problems start when one's feelings are not heard and relational needs are not met. Often, however, this occurs because people feel that their own feelings and needs are not acceptable, and therefore they don't say what they feel and need. When one partner is insecure or lonely and does not feel entitled to what he or she feels and needs, then these feelings are not expressed. People hope their partners will sense their feelings and needs, and when they don't partners end up feeling isolated. Then unexpressed sadness or loneliness and feelings of being unloved or neglected turn into anger, and people begin to criticize or blame. In the face of the criticism and contempt that one partner expresses, the other partner feels afraid or inadequate and withdraws or defends. Now the couple is locked into a cycle that takes on a life of its own. One blames, and the other withdraws. The more the withdrawer withdraws, the more the pursuing person blames, and the more the blamer blames, the more the withdrawer withdraws.

In general, the person who is doing the blaming feels lonely or un-heard, and the one who withdraws feels fearful or inadequate. The blamer generally feels even more abandoned in response to the partner's with-drawal. In reality the withdrawer is just trying protect him- or herself, and the blamer interprets this withdrawal as rejection. What the complaining or criticizing partner is really trying to do is get his or her needs met, but all that the receiver of blame feels is criticized. Withdrawers feel inadequate and then protect themselves. Often it is their initial feeling of inadequacy or anxiety that made them less available and helped evoke their partners' feelings of abandonment. So the cycle develops. In one type of cycle the pursuer pursues for emotional closeness but does so by blaming and criti-cizing, and the withdrawer withdraws for emotional protection. In another type of cycle the dominant person dominates, overfunctions, makes all the decisions, and then feels burdened. The partner who feels more insecure, unsure, or submissive underfunctions and doesn't do much, but then ends up feeling invisible, like he or she doesn't exist in the relationship.

> Bob feels lonely and unloved. He started to feel lonely because Marie is paying too much attention to her career, and although he first tries to express his feelings, he then feels that maybe he is too dependent, so instead he stifles his feelings. Over time, however, he finds himself feeling angry, and he begins to criticize Marie. Eventually, after many months of his criticisms, Marie begins to distance herself from Bob. She would come home; be criticized by Bob; and feel inadequate, like she was being told that she was not a good enough person. Rather than understanding that he is feeling hurt and lonely, which is very difficult to do when one's partner is blaming you, she keeps trying to defend herself, and eventually they lock into the cycle of attack and defend. She then just begins to withdraw and feel that talking or re-lating aren't worthwhile and that the safest thing is to stay out of Bob's

way when he is angry. Distance and alienation set in. Often the couple is unaware of the dynamics of the cycle and their feelings. They just become aware of the distance and alienation. They start saying "We're drifting; your interests are different; we've grown apart." In actuality they have closed off.

Once the blame–withdraw cycle gets going it really takes over. The crucial emotional issues remain unresolved. Intimacy is impossible, because both partners feel they have to protect themselves from further disappointment. This prevents them from risking revealing their innermost emerging feelings to their partners.

The Shame–Rage Cycle

A particularly important and difficult emotion sequence in couples is a shame–rage sequence when one person feels primarily humiliated and then gets angry. This can be very intense and eventually can lead to violence in couples. Here the person's rage is generally a response to his or her inability to deal with the more core feelings of shame and powerlessness.

If a partner feels rage, he or she needs to learn how to calm the rage and to get what is at the bottom of it. Usually it is a feeling of shame of powerlessness; of vulnerability and helplessness; or of feeling sad, lonely, and abandoned. If one often gets very angry, one needs to not only control one's anger but also to learn to experience and express the more vulnerable feelings that lie beneath the anger. Expressing underlying fear, shame, or hurt will have a very different impact on one's partner than will expressing destructive rage. Being aware of and getting in touch with core feelings as they arise, then, is a key way to prevent the development of destructive rage. People thus need to know, for example, that when they are defensively angry they need to express the fear that comes before the anger. Coaches need to help people develop the ability to soothe themselves and to soothe their partners. This is one of the best antidotes to negative escalation: the ability to soothe vulnerability in oneself and the other person.

The Disillusionment Phase

Eventually couples fight about how they fight, and this becomes the new argument. One of them says, "You are so blaming," or "You are so cold and unresponsive." The couple by now has entered the "change your partner" stage of the relationship. This stage often takes a number of years to develop. Partner renovation efforts, however, often do not go the way they hope. Deterioration rather than home improvement results. This is the disillusioning period. At first the couple may spend their efforts trying to communicate in the belief that once each partner knows what he or she needs and wants, then they both will get it. Then it begins to dawn on a person that his or her partner well knows what the person wants, that he or she has been a successful communicator; the partner just won't give the person what he or she wants. It is difficult for people to appreciate their partner's reasons, that they are each different from the other and that each have their own needs and struggles that prevent them from being a reliable supplier of what the other wants. At this stage the couple begins to doubt their love for one another and they start attributing reasons to explain why their partners are not giving them what is desired. Usually, as the partners feel more and more deprived, they don't say that their partners are tired or stressed. They stop attributing what's going wrong to the situation and go straight for the jugular: their partners' personalities. A person might say that his or her partner is too demanding, selfish, insecure, cold, afraid of intimacy, unable to express anger, and so on. Now the person needs to either change the partner's personality or leave the relationship. Both are unhappy options. It is better to find another path.

Both partners are usually quite hurt at this point and of course have been hurting all along the way. How could their hurt have been expressed more constructively? Is it possible for people to express their hurt without anger? Some authors have said that hurt is just unexpressed resentment. Can people feel hurt by their partners without being angry at them? The problem is that anger often pushes partners away; hurt and sadness, however, ask for comfort. When partners sense the other person's anger they will not be able to offer soothing comfort, because they are busily preparing a defense against the possible attack signaled by this anger. The hurt or angry partners, meanwhile, are waiting expectantly to have their hurt soothed, and they perceive their partners' nonresponsiveness as insult added to injury. In response to the insult of nonresponsiveness they now get really mad. How do couples get off this merry-go-round or, better yet, not get on it? Exercise 1, at the end of this chapter, helps couples identify and change their cycles. They do this by expressing their softer underlying feelings.

Difficult Emotional States

If partners do not pay attention to each others' core unmet needs, they will get entrenched in their cycle and begin a special kind of dance, a dance of couple insanity. In these dances both may shift into what later will often be seen as "crazy" states. They will later say that what was felt and what was said in these states was untrue—it was "not really them." These "not me" states seem to have a mind of their own. They are maladaptive emotional states. In such states, people might begin to yell at each other rather than speak to each other, or they might cut each other off and not listen. They probably have repeated these fights before and have resolved them or understood and forgiven each other many times, but it happens all over again. They can even see it coming, but once they enter these unhealthy emotional states of threat, violation, or humiliation, which often are based on past wounds, they are transformed into their other selves. In the man a sense of longing might become physical, and he may yearn for something from his partner, from deep within his body, or the woman might feel a desperate need to protect herself from destruction. She fears becoming overwhelmed by her partner; she sees her partner as intrusively powerful, and she closes up, becoming rigid, feeling icy, and walling out any contact. These extreme states generally reflect maladaptive emotion states. They often are not people's initial, primary responses to their partners. Instead, they result from both unhealthy internal and interactional sequences. An example of the unhealthy states entered during an emotional thunderstorm of this type is given next.

> In a particular cycle a wife, in response to her husband's demands, begins to feel overwhelmed by his reactions to her. She hears his voice, sees that familiar angry expression on his face. She doesn't know exactly what happened, but she just feels this is dangerous. Something in her begins to close up. She becomes cold and feels tremendously attacked and powerless. He just seems to keep coming at her with angry words, questions, and accusations. She doesn't listen; she just wants him to stop and go away. He keeps demanding, intruding into her, and she just wants him to leave her alone. She needs to escape, get away. She can't think. She explodes and says something awful to get him to stop. At this moment she hates him. Then she withdraws just to try to get away, to make it all stop.

> A husband wants to be close to his wife, but she is distant. He reacted to something she had said and felt hurt and ignored. He had hoped to be close and make love. He feels hurt and angry and sees her as cold and rejecting. He tries to tell her what he is feeling and gets angry because she won't listen. He explains what she is doing that is so damaging to him, and he interrogates her about why she does this. He feels he desperately needs her softness and begins to feel intensely powerless and then angry. He loses all contact with her and just senses the wall she has put up. He becomes enraged at the wall, and all he can think of is destroying it because it is preventing him from getting what he so desperately needs. He sees his wife as cruelly withholding herself, and he wishes to destroy the barrier. He hardly recognizes her explosion because he is so intent on removing the barrier. He feels distant and cold.

DEALING WITH HURT AND ANGER: TWO MAJOR ELEMENTS IN THE WALL OF ISOLATION

Once cycles have been identified and brought into awareness, emotion coaches need to help couples deal with the feelings that are keeping them apart and help them deal with their crazy states. Without doubt, one of the most important ways couples get into difficulties is related to the inability to deal with their own and their partner's anger. Although, as I have discussed, anger in response to violation is a healthy feeling that needs to be expressed, anger is often a secondary response to a more primary feeling of hurt or a fear of feeling unloved or unsupported. Many of the "harder" emotions partners express, such as anger, resentment, and contempt, might often be aggressive attempts to protect themselves from their partners or to protect themselves against their more painful, "softer" emotions of sadness, fear, and shame (Greenberg & Mateu Marques, 1998).

Hurt and anger are normal parts of relationships. How does an emotion coach help people deal with these two unwelcome feelings so that they don't become bricks in a wall of alienation and isolation? How does a coach help them handle these feelings without turning them into the single most poisonous element of relationships: blame and the contempt into which it eventually develops?

The problem with hurt and anger is that they are so difficult to express without shaming or belittling the other person or becoming demanding and controlling, yet if partners do not express these emotions they start building a wall. It is important to recognize that sadness is generally at the base of hurt, and hurt clearly is often at the base of anger. One of the difficulties is separating anger from sadness. As I have discussed in regard to unresolved emotional memories, the two often are fused into a hurt, angry ball that is expressed mostly as complaint, feelings of victimization, and blame. To be able to successfully express these emotions, partners first have to be able to be clearly angry and cleanly sad, with each emotion uncontaminated by the other.

Each partner's anger needs be expressed clearly, without blame and, if possible, with a show of good intention. One of the skills I have personally tried, with some success, is to say "I don't want to feel angry, but I do feel angry at ——." This communicates a desire for harmony and can be reassuring to one's partner. People have to learn to own their anger. The tone must not convey contempt or scowling, sneering hostility. Anger that wants to destroy will not work. Anger that asserts and informs one's partner of a boundary, or of a boundary violation, although not always easy to receive, is what is needed. "I'm angry; you have not done what I asked. It makes me feel like I'm not important to you." It is partners' nonverbal communication and their attitudes that truly count: If they are contemptuous, their anger will be destructive; if they are respectful, it will not.

Anger in the form of unexpressed resentment and subsequent withdrawal or closing off is the poison of relationships. Closing off is often the withdrawer's attempted solution to resolving conflict. It does not work. Contact works. Expression of hidden resentment is helpful, first because it brings the withdrawer out of hiding, and second, much to the withdrawer's surprise, because the pursuer finds the anger much easier to deal with than distance. It feels more like emotional contact than stony silence or cold distance. Contact is what the pursuer wants, and so expression of anger by a withdrawer can enhance the intimate bond.

The problem with anger, however, is that it can escalate, or the interactions around it can escalate. Once partners get angry, unless they are met with an understanding response quite soon in the sequence, they will tend to get carried away. There is almost a pleasure or joy in some people's expressions of anger. Once started, it is hard to stop. All emotions are a combination of letting go and restraint. I once witnessed an older person, who was losing some of his capacities to regulate different aspects of his functioning, begin to get angry at a slight provocation. He started off appropriately requesting termination of the provocation but then couldn't stop his rapidly escalating irritation, which exploded into full-blown rage. Being able to regulate expression and not let it run away is important.

More problematic in couples is the runaway escalation. One partner gets angry, even in an acceptable way, and the other partner, sensing a boundary violation, responds with equal anger. Now two fighters are poised in a ring. The general sequence proceeds thus: As soon as one partner ups the anger level, so does the other, and soon they are delivering blows below the belt. The spouse's character, mother, and the kitchen sink all get thrown into the ring. These are usually painful and destructive fights. Sometimes the fight is a precursor to the sweetness of making up, often with making love. A kind of intensity, passion, and closeness can come in healing wounds created by a fight, but fighting in order to make up eventually backfires. The fighting becomes so destructive that there is no making up. Often one partner prefers to fight. For this partner the intense contact of anger feels better than the tense, cold distance. The problem is the other partner is probably different and finds the fights too frightening or hurtful. Fights themselves are not the problem; it is the inability to resolve the fight that causes distance and eventual dissolution of the intimate bond. The worst-case scenarios are when there is a very rapid escalation, when contempt and defiance are expressed—for example, when a wife says to her husband, "Clean the dishes," and he says "Yeah, make me." These are signs of future divorce (Gottman, Katz, & Hooven, 1997).

The solution to hurt and anger involves separating the sadness and anger so each comes out in a pure form. Anger should be an assertion of clear boundaries, and sadness should be a call for comfort, unaccompanied by demand. Anger needs to be an expression of personal boundaries, firm but in no way attacking. Hurt needs to be seen not as an inevitable response to a damaging act but truly as people's unique response based on who they really are and their own sense of loss. Rather than the hurt being seen as caused by the other person, hurt is seen as a function of one's own emotional makeup. If, on the other hand, people see their partner as having intentionally been hurtful or damaging, then anger is the appropriate response.

SOOTHING ONESELF

To help people deal with the "crazy states" they enter in a fight, emotion coaches need to help them learn to soothe themselves. Some people may feel unable to self-soothe, because they lack the internal emotional structures or processes to relax and to calm or nurture themselves. They might not have received enough of this as children and might not have built an internal, nurturing parent representation on which to draw. When relationships are momentarily disrupted, such people feel desperate and have difficulty holding onto the sense of security generated by the lived history of the relationship. Then it is difficult for them to buffer even minor disruptions, and they are unable to project a vision of a secure future to the relationship. They thus experience tremendous threat, or a sense of violation, as though the distance or slight rupture means the relationship is over. This may sound foreign or overly extreme, but it occurs to all of us at some moments no matter how secure we feel.

Think about a difficult fight you have had with an intimate partner. At least one of you probably entered a state of anxious attachment; that is probably why the situation escalated into a fight. One of you lost perspective, and it suddenly felt like unless you resolve this and get close right now, your relationship, or you, won't survive. Your partner probably felt an identity threat, that unless he or she was heard right then, you would forever misunderstand, and he or she would be invalidated. Neither of you necessarily think this realistically, but an anxious part of each of you is acting this way in a do-or-die effort to protect something. Unfortunately, your attempted solutions of protecting by trying to point out, convince, or blame usually become the problem. What is needed is to be able to calm yourself with images of past security and caring and the knowledge that bad moments in the past have again turned to good. You need to work with your anxiety to soothe it by reassuring yourself that "this too will pass," as it has always passed before. Coaches thus need to help their clients self-soothe at times when their partners are not able to be responsive. The skills discussed in chapter 8 in regard to dealing with maladaptive emotion and emotion regulation are relevant here.

WHAT DO COACHES NEED TO DO FOR COUPLES WHO ARE IN TROUBLE?

Research on how couples change in therapy has indicated that the single most effective way of resolving couples conflict, of moderate and milder forms, is to expose the partners' vulnerable feelings and their attachment and intimacy needs (Greenberg & Johnson, 1988; Johnson & Greenberg, 1985). Intimacy can be created by sharing feelings without complaining. Sharing hurt feelings can be the antidote to acrimonious relating. I am not suggesting this method when violence is present or when rage is too strong. However, partners engaged in moderate conflict who revealed and expressed their previously unexpressed emotions of sadness at loss, fear at threat, and anger at offense had a magical effect on each other. When partners actually saw each other's tears, and heard their fear or anger, they snapped out of their trancelike state of repeating their position over and over again or defending it. Instead, they became more alive, compassionate, softer, and more interested and concerned. Couples can be coached quite quickly to realize that because emotions form the basis of relating, expressing genuine feelings has incredible power to change interactions. Authentic vulnerability disarms and evokes compassion, whereas nonmanipulative anger sets a limit and evokes respect and attention.

Many educators and therapists have talked about teaching the skills of good communication, such as making "I" statements, being nonblaming, listening, and so on. All are correct. All these skills will help people break the cycle that maintains the conflict. The issue, however, is how people get organized to adopt these more conciliatory stances. They do this by means of their emotions. People's compassion, caring, love, and interest organize them to attend and listen. Their unexpressed fear and anger organize them to be defensive and far less conciliatory.

Coaching Partners to Express Core Feelings of Hurt

How do emotion coaches help people to feel healing concern and caring? How do they help people get concern and caring from their partners? The answers are a little unexpected. I don't know how to easily help people to feel loving, compassionate, and understanding but, as indicated earlier, I have discovered something about how to help one partner get the other partner to experience these feelings toward him or her. By sharing attachment- and intimacy-related feelings and needs, partners generally soften their stance toward each other (Greenberg, Ford, Alden, & Johnson, 1993; Greenberg, James, & Conway, 1988; Johnson & Greenberg, 1985). When people genuinely express their needs for closeness or identity in a nonblaming manner, their partners listen and relax. Once both partners are feeling heard and seen, they are much more likely be able to participate in a more conciliatory engagement, and then both will start to access more loving feelings.

The best a coach can do is help partners present their feelings and needs as honestly and openly as possible, in such a way that their partners are most likely to hear and see them. This does not mean that partners plead or become self-effacingly pleasing to try and win favor; rather, with the coach's support and validation of their primary experience, they become strong enough to risk revealing attachment needs and, if these needs are not responded to, are able to tolerate delays of gratification. The ability to tolerate nonresponsiveness involves having the capacity to remember that the partner was available in the past and will again be available in the future. This faith in their partners' availability allows people temporarily how to move away from their at-present-nonresponsive partners and be able to turn to themselves graciously, even though they have not been satisfied. If people are later able to turn back to their partners without resentment but with humor, the ability to laugh at themselves, and a philosophical acceptance of the inevitability of conflict, this will help foster reconnection. Reconciliation is itself an art that requires the emotional intelligence of sensitivity to and empathy for one's own and one's partner's states and the skills of good timing.

> In the last few months Bob's business has not been going well, and Marie's comments that her brother has bought a beautiful car make Bob feel inadequate. When Marie talks about her brother's car Bob feels that she is complaining because they don't have enough money, and he feels a sense of shame, one that is difficult for him to accept. Then the rage emerges, and he begins to yell. Bob is simply unable to acknowledge and express his feelings of devaluation or shame. He needs to struggle to be more aware of, and express his core feelings. The defensive and manipulative feelings of anger and rage are not helpful. If expressed, they create distance and destroy connections. A coach would need to help Bob approach his feelings of shame and inadequacy and to help him disclose to Marie how he feels when she makes these types of comments.

People have to learn to express their hurt, without blaming and without demanding to be comforted. They need to be coached to express hurt that allows their partners to feel free of attack and free to respond in accord with the dictates of their own feelings. Coaches can achieve this by helping people recognize that they are hurt because of their own vulnerability, their own need, and that the other person had been under no obligation to not have not done what he or she did or to not have said what he or she said that was hurtful.

Say, for example, a husband did not listen while his wife was telling him about something important to her, or at a moment of intimacy for the husband, his wife changed the topic or showed a lack of interest in sex. These are all situations in which people could feel hurt or angry. For example, a partner felt hurt by a sexual rebuff, and this was part of a pattern in the couple. The husband was generally more interested in sex but generally waited for his wife to make the advances. Both had discussed this and agreed that it was a good system to avoid him feeling rebuffed. Still, sometimes he made advances, and each time his wife, even though she was willing to go along, was not eager, and he felt the excitement and mutuality disappear and then felt hurt or angry. In this situation he is stuck. If he proceeds in silence he will begin to split into two parts: One part will hide, and the other will engage with his wife. This is not a fulfilling solution. If he expresses hurt or anger he may cause an even greater rupture, a tear in the couple's connection. This will not happen if he expresses his anger in a nonblaming manner and from his heart. If he says "I'm finding this difficult because I'm feeling my hurt feeling again, like you don't love me or don't want to be close, and I'm struggling to stay in contact with you," his wife is free to respond as she sees fit. This is the key. If the wife in any way feels coerced, then the husband might get a complaint response, and he will later end up as the recipient of more resentment from his wife than it was worth. Exercise 2 at the end of this chapter provides couples with a guide to fighting constructively.

Owning Feelings

People often go through life without really telling their partners what is in their hearts and on their minds. It seems so hard to speak from one's inner feelings. People are so afraid: afraid of appearing foolish, of being rejected, or of not getting the response they desire. In marital therapy one of the almost universal myths that unfortunately has to be shattered, or at least put to rest, is the "fishbowl" fantasy: believing that one's spouse should be able to see into the other and see all the feelings and thoughts swimming around inside. People operate under the damaging assumption that their partners should know what they feel and need without them having to ask for it. They also might believe that if they have to ask, what is given is not of the same value as that which is given spontaneously. There is some truth to the notion that a spontaneous gesture gives one proof of one's partner's intentions—more specifically, of a partner's love. Constantly requiring proof of love, however, is no way to run a long-term relationship. Being able to express what one feels, and ask for what one wants and needs, is the best way of ensuring satisfaction and a more smoothly running relationship. When what is asked for is given with good grace, this is sufficient proof of caring.

When partners are in trouble as a couple, when they are locked into anger, disappointment, and distance, they need to be helped to focus on what they are most truly feeling and try to express these feelings in a nonblaming fashion. Generally they will be feeling sad or afraid at the loss of connection. Partners have to be able to listen to these feelings in a nondefensive fashion in themselves or in their partners. Not blaming and not defending are at the core of re-establishing intimacy. This means that each partner has to be able to self-focus, to talk about "I" rather than about "you." Helping each partner to focus on the self and say what it's like inside helps to undo the blaming.

Talking in this way, owning hurt by saying "I'm feeling my hurt" rather than "You hurt me, you so and so," is clearly feeling talk, and people have to be coached to be able to do this and to be comfortable with it. Consider a 220-lb football player, or a tough young woman who wants to be independent, or a high-powered executive who is used to giving orders. If they cannot accept feeling weak, hurt, and needy without getting mad, and they cannot communicate this in their own way, then they are going to be doomed to difficult, less satisfying intimate relationships. Everyone is needy at times, like a baby, and everyone sometimes needs to be taken care of. There is nothing wrong with this. Adult attachment needs involve needing caring as much those of a child do. This is not infantile; being able to express one's needs is a highly adult capability. It is mature as long as people can integrate their heads with their hearts and tolerate frustrations if their partners cannot respond to their dependence needs. Partners also need to learn how to alternate caretaking and being taken care of. Being vulnerable and in need, when the other is available to truly soothe and tend to one's needs in a caring, contacting way, is wonderfully nourishing and replenishing. It becomes a problem only when both partners need to be taken care of at the same time. Just as it is very difficult having two needy babies in the house at the same time, it is difficult to deal with two adults who have dependence needs. When both are feeling depleted and in need of caring, one has to grow up rather quickly; otherwise, both end up yelling in a demanding fashion. The roles of caretaker and dependent must be flexible, with partners able to alternate roles.

An additional important element in resolving conflict is that each person be clear on the need or goal that is motivating his or her interactions. When a partner's current highest level goal is getting along, and this person has a real desire to preserve and enhance the relationship, his or her responses will be as constructive as possible. Many couples dance the endless control waltz of "I'm right; you're wrong." To make relationships work, partners have to decide that it is more important in life to be happy than to be right. Then they will begin to see that disagreement is a matter of being different rather than being right or wrong.

Coaching Appreciation of Partners

Another important element of getting along is feeling and expressing appreciation of the other. People need to be able to express both their positive and negative feelings to their partners. Although it makes sense that people need to express more positives than negatives, people in relationships soon forget this golden rule (Gottman, 1997). Some couples get into trouble because the positives are so taken for granted that they end up expressing only the negatives. On the other hand, some couples feel they are not allowed to express the negatives and avoid them altogether. Neither of these strategies is constructive. Coaches need to help people express appreciation for each other and engage in giving behaviors that make each person feel cared for. A little bit of positive goes a long way in helping people maintain good attachments.

EXERCISE 1: IDENTIFYING AND CHANGING CYCLES

1. Identify your role.
   Select which role you occupy and which your partner occupies.
   - Intimacy-related roles
Pursue	Distance
Cling	Push away
Demand/nag	Withdraw
Attack	Defend
Intrude	Wall off
   - Identity-related roles
Dominate	Submit
Right	Wrong
Lead	Follow
Overfunction	Underfunction
Helpful	Helpless
   - Identify what secondary, "harder" emotions go with these roles.
2. Identify the core "softer," attachment-related feeling that underlies your position.
   - If you are feeling the need to pursue your partner, search for underlying feelings of vulnerability, loneliness, and sadness.
   - If you are feeling withdrawn because of fear, search for underlying feelings of a need for connection, inadequacy, or unexpressed resentment.
   - If you are feeling dominant, search for underlying feelings of anxiety or insecurity that are possibly guiding your need to control.
   - If you are feeling submissive, search for underlying feelings of fear of anger and unsureness.
3. Identify and express attachment needs for closeness, connectedness, and identity.
   - Say "I feel sad, lonely, or afraid."

- Say "I need recognition of my needs, boundaries, and preferences."
- Don't complain; rather, express your core feelings and needs.

4. Listen to and accept your partner's feelings and needs.
   - Try to understand your partner's experience. Put yourself in your partner's shoes. See things from his or her perspective.
   - Communicate your understanding and appreciation of your partner's perspective.

EXERCISE 2: FIGHTING TO A DRAW

Once you figure out what destructive cycles you and your partner get into, try to determine the core feelings that you and your partner are feeling. Your goal is to reveal your attachment-related feelings and needs to your partner. Once you are able to understand your partner's core feelings, you will be able to respond differently, and this will change how you relate to each other. This new understanding needs to be maintained and supported.

1. Identify that this is a fight.
   - Often, neither of you thinks you are fighting.
2. Identify your core feeling.
   - What is the "softer" feeling under your "harder" feeling?
   - Are you feeling lonely, abandoned, or anxious?
   - Are you feeling unsure, inadequate, or afraid?
3. Clarify your core attachment-related concerns and goals.
   - Do you want closeness?
   - Do you want to set a boundary?
   Your goals and intentions will be strong determinants of your actions.
   - If your primary concern is harmony and preserving the relationship, then anger escalations such as attacking or insulting will be avoided.
   - If your primary concern is to repair self-esteem, then anger-escalating behaviors are more likely. Try instead to identify your shame and what has made you feel damaged.
4. Express your core emotion and concern directly.
   - Either say "I feel hurt or wounded" or "I feel angry," signaling that you are concerned with your identity.
   - Say "I want to preserve harmony," signaling a collaborative, conciliatory stance.

- Identify whether this feeling is related to your sensitivity, your well-known vulnerability to feeling abandoned, criticized, unwanted, or unappreciated.
- Own the feeling as yours rather than blaming the other person.
- Express how you feel: "I feel scared to lose you," "I feel like I'm failing you," "I'm afraid of your anger," "I'm angry at your clinging to me," or "I need more space."

5. Identify your basic need. What do you really need or want now?
- Communicate this in a nonblaming and nondemanding manner.
- Do not try to force your views on your partner, however justified you feel. Your partner feels equally right. Trying to prove that your partner is wrong is futile. Fight to draw or to both win.

6. Identify the walls that are preventing you from expressing your need.
- Notice what is preventing you from listening to your partner's noncoercive, attachment need.

7. If your partner is unable to respond, practice self-soothing.
- Remember that now is not all there is. Yesterday and tomorrow exist, and your partner is able to respond differently at different times.

EXERCISE 3: HANDLING DIFFICULT EMOTIONAL STATES

Once a person has learned to recognize the difficult emotion states one enters into in relationships the following things are helpful:

1. You need to become comfortable with your vulnerable states and bring them into your relationship with your partner. Tell your partner how you feel.
2. Avoid triggering difficult states in each other.
3. Help your partner shift out of aggressive and protective states.
4. Take breaks to calm or shift states.
5. Give your partner time and space to work out his or her difficult states.

12

EMOTIONS IN PARENTING

Avi is a child who likes only chocolate ice cream and can't stand vanilla. He is 3 years old and is attending a friend's birthday party for the first time. The party is ending, and it's been an exciting time, but everyone is tired and getting cranky. Out comes the ice cream! It is vanilla. Disappointed, Avi begins to look very unhappy. He goes to his father and says "I want chocolate ice cream." Dad says "Sorry, Avi; they don't have anything but vanilla."

"I want chocolate," Avi begins to whine. The other parents look at Dad. He becomes tense. How should he handle this? Dad knew he couldn't get Avi a substitute, but he realizes that his son is upset, and he can provide understanding and comfort.

"You wish you had chocolate ice cream." Avi looks up and nods.

"And you are angry because we can't get you what you want."

"Yeah."

"You wish you could have it right now, and it seems unfair that the other kids have ice cream and you don't."

"Yeah," Avi says more assertively but no longer whining.

"I'm sorry we can't get you your favorite ice cream, and I know that it's really frustrating."

"Yeah," Avi says, looking a lot less upset.

"I am really sorry."

Avi looks relieved and when his father suggests "We can get some chocolate ice cream when we get home." He looks quite pleased and

279

runs off to play. Many years later Dad learns that some people who have sensitive tastes find vanilla aversive.

This type of empathic understanding of a child's feelings is central to emotion coaching in parenting. The father's actions were so much more effective than coaxing Avi to have what he doesn't want or telling him that he is ungrateful, that he should be more flexible and eat what he is given. If parents were able to enter their children's shoes and see the world through their eyes, chances are that children would feel a lot let isolated and lonely. Ignoring children's feelings does not make the feelings go away; rather, bad feelings tend to shift when children can talk about them, put them into words, and feel understood and soothed by parents' comfort and concern. The children then see their parents as allies in their struggle to make sense of things in their inner and outer worlds, and they then turn more often to their parents for support.

As easy as it is to understand what empathy is, it is extremely difficult to practice with one's own children. I speak from experience. Parents have to be able to slow themselves down and be able to rid themselves of the many anxieties that might stop them from feeling empathic. Anxieties such as wanting to protect one's child from the rejections he or she suffers, worries that their children won't turn out "right," expectations of how one wants one's children to be, and self-conscious concerns about others watching and wanting to do parenting right are all part of being a parent. If one's daughter comes home and says her friends rejected her, it is important to stop and respond to her hurt rather than rushing in to solve it, give advice, or try to get her to be less sensitive. This style of relating is part of emotion coaching.

Emotion coaching of parents involves helping parents become emotion coaches with their children. This involves guiding parents toward awareness and management of their own emotions as well as teaching them how to deal with their children's emotions. At times, work with parents involves coaching the parents alone on how to help their children focus on and manage their emotions. At other times, work with parents together with their children is indicated. In the latter case parents are coached on how to respond to their children's emotions as they emerge in actual interactions. For example, parents who are having problems with their children can be coached in how to hold their infants, how to be vocally responsive, and how to be more attentive and reciprocating in their gazes.

EMOTION COACHING IN PARENTING

John Gottman, a psychologist who has studied parenting emotion philosophies, found that children of parents with an *emotion coaching* philosophy functioned much better in a number of domains than did children of parents with an *emotion dismissing* philosophy (Gottman, 1997). In Gottman's (1997) study parents' attitudes toward emotions and their interactions with their 5-year-old children were measured at Time 1. Three years later, at Time 2, the children, who were now 8 years old, were again studied on a number of indexes. These included teacher-rated peer relations, academic achievement, parent reports of the children's need for emotion regulation, and the children's physical health. The children with emotion coaching parents at Time 1 had better academic performance at Time 2. Controlling for IQ, their math and reading scores were higher. They were also getting along better with their peers, they had stronger social skills, and their mothers reported that they had fewer negative emotions and more positive emotions. These children had lower levels of stress in their lives, as measured by stress-related hormones in their urine, lower resting heart rates, and quicker recovery from stress. They also were reported to have had fewer infections and colds. The general conclusions of this study were that parents whose children were doing best on the above indexes at Time 2 showed specific characteristics at Time 1.

The parents of the successful children showed higher levels of emotion awareness of their own and their children's emotions. They had an emotion coaching philosophy that offered acceptance of and assistance in dealing with anger and sadness. Also, rather than being either derogatory (intrusive, critical, mocking) or simply warm (positive but not emotion focused) in their behavior, they were not only warm but also more focused on emotion and able to provide direction when needed and praise when the children's behavior was goal appropriate. This provision of structure and praise was provided in a relaxed manner, for example, stating simply the goals and procedures of a game to be played and not overwhelming the children with too much information. These parents waited for their children to act, not pushing them, and then commented primarily when the child did something right. Parents who were low on this dimension gave little structure and too much information to children, which either excited or confused them. They commented on mistakes and were usually critical.

Emotion coaching helped these children regulate their emotions and develop the ability to soothe themselves. Emotion-focused mentoring of children's feelings had a soothing effect on children, and this led to change in their parasympathetic nervous system responses, affecting such things as heart rate and attentional abilities. Of great interest is that children who at age 5 received emotion coaching—the ability to talk about emotions while having them—were not overly emotional with their peers at age 8. In fact, just the opposite was observed. Being appropriately cool was the norm, and children with good emotion coaching seemed to be most competent with their peers because they had developed the skills to handle situations appropriately. They probably were more aware of their emotions, could regulate their upset feelings more easily both physiologically and behaviorally, and could better attend to salient aspects of the situation. They probably had also learned how to learn in emotion-evoking situations.

Parental characteristics that had such a powerful effect on their children that defined emotion coaching were

1. Awareness of even low-intensity emotions in themselves and their children.
2. Viewing their children's negative emotions as opportunities for intimacy or teaching.
3. Empathizing with and validating their children's emotions.
4. Assisting their children in verbally labeling their emotions.
5. Problem solving with their children, setting behavioral limits, discussing goals, and offering strategies for dealing with negative-emotion-generating situations. (Gottman, 1997)

These parents clearly possess all the elements of emotional intelligence, emotion awareness, empathy, and the ability to think about and regulate emotions. Notice that parenting with emotional intelligence involves more than either warmth or limit setting, alone or in combination. It involves an emotion coaching style of attending and managing: being aware of, and being able to deal with, emotion. Parents need to feel comfortable with their own emotions. They do not need always to express them, but they must not ignore them. A crucial element of emotion coaching is being able to talk to children while they are experiencing their feelings and helping them put these feelings into words. This helps the children make sense of their feelings and the situations that evoke them. As with adults, putting emotions into words for children is a way of integrating reason and emotion and creating new links between different parts of the brain. This helps integrate feelings into a meaningful story that explains things. In addition, helping children make transitions from one emotional state to another is an important aspect of coaching. Here bridges between different states are built, and flexibility in moving between states is encouraged. A crying child first is soothed and then is offered a new, exciting stimulus, such as a funny face and sound or an experience, like being swiftly raised in the air with a sound of a new wheel. This helps the child transition into a new emotional state. Repeated experiences of this type help the child develop his or her own ability to soothe and shift states.

An emotion-dismissing parental attitude, in contrast, viewed children's sadness and anger as potentially harmful to the child. These parents believed they needed to change these emotionally disruptive experiences, as quickly as possible, and that the child needed to realize that these negative emotions were not important and would soon disappear if the child just rode them out. It is not that these parents were necessarily insensitive to emotion, but their approach to sadness, for example, was to ignore or deny it as much as possible and to mollify anger or punish it. They said such things as "Seeing my child sad makes me uncomfortable" or "Sadness needs to be controlled" (Gottman, 1997). These are not the parents to whom emotion is a welcome addition to life. Rather, they believe it is "not OK" to have feelings, that feelings need to be minimized and avoided, and that negative feelings are dangerous and even from the Devil. Some parents minimize sadness in themselves—"What's the good of being sad?"—and in their children—"What does a child have to be sad about?"

Parents have a tremendous opportunity to influence their children's emotional intelligence. Babies learn from their parents' responses to their emotions that emotions have a sense of direction and that needs can be satisfied. They learn that it is possible to go from one feeling to another rather than become overwhelmed by their emotions. In particular, they learn that it is possible to go from distress, anger, and fear to feelings of calmness, satisfaction, and joy. They begin thereby to build the bridges that will be so important in life to help them transition from disturbance to calm. Babies with unresponsive parents learn that when they are in distress and cry out they experience only more distress. They have never had a guide who conducts them from one place to another, who guides them from distress to comfort, so they don't learn how to soothe themselves. Instead, a bad feeling is a black hole that swallows them up.

Coaches need to recommend to parents that they should begin very early to teach emotional intelligence skills to their children and continue this teaching all the way through childhood. The skills in which parents need to be coached include opening channels of emotional communication with their children right from infancy, so that they help their children develop an early "emotional vocabulary" on which to build. Parents need to learn to encourage their children to talk about how they feel about the events in their lives and to listen to how their children feel without passing judgment. Parents need to recognize the less intense emotions in their children, not only the intense ones. If a child seems hesitant or nervous about the choir audition tomorrow, it is better to talk to him or her about it today than for the child to freeze tomorrow. Providing activities and playthings that help children explore and express their feelings also is very helpful in developing an emotional vocabulary. To develop their children's emotional intelligence, parents should choose toys and games that help kids recognize their feelings, identify their feelings, communicate their feelings, and hear what other people are saying about their feelings.

PARENTS AND THEIR INFANTS

Emotions are central to how parents and children relate. Through emotional expression parents and children come to learn about each other's desires, intentions, and points of view. Children's emotions signal what is working or not working for them in their relationships long before they can talk. Being aware of children's emotions from birth onward is thus one of the most central tasks of parenting. Infants are very labile and easily aroused. Unable to control their own responses, they are prone to sudden frustration, boredom, and fatigue. They depend on adults to read their emotion signals.

At first, attending to children's emotions comes naturally to many parents. At birth and in the first years parents listen and watch attentively to every nuance of expression, trying to understand this wondrous little being and all of the desires of his or her majesty. The child cries, and they run to comfort him or her. The child smiles, and they are overjoyed. Parents generally are incredibly attuned to their infants, far more so than any other species. Human infants are born far more helpless than other mammals: They need caretakers. Children are totally dependent on parents for their survival. Parents are so attuned that not only are they fascinated and attentive by every coo and gurgle but they even go in the quiet of night and check to see if their children are breathing. At the other end of the parenting spectrum are those parents who not only are not attuned to their infants but also bewildered by the little bundles of emotions. They cannot fathom why infants don't come with operating manuals. These parents need more explicit training in recognizing emotions, in understanding what they mean and what to do. In such cases parent–infant coaching is highly indicated (Stern, 1995). Van den Boom (1994) found that a 3-month coaching intervention for irritable 6-month-olds and their mothers designed to enhance maternal sensitive responsiveness improved the quality of mother–infant interaction, infant exploration, and infant attachment. At the end of the 3 months of training mothers were more responsive, stimulating, visually attentive, and controlling of their infants' behavior. Infants had higher scores on sociability, self-soothing capacity, and exploration, and they cried less. At 12 months the infants who had received the intervention were more securely attached than those who had not received the intervention.

Human infants, as well as being far more dependent than other species, have also far higher neural plasticity. Because they are so ready to learn, what happens to them early on, especially in their emotional experience, shapes them in profound ways. Family life provides infants with their first emotional lessons. It is in this intimate school that children will learn who they are on the basis of how they are treated. They will learn how others will react to their feelings, and from this they will begin to form attitudes about their own feelings and will learn how to handle them. It is not that infants come into the world as blank slates to be written on by experience. They have their own temperaments, capacities, and emotional tendencies. Infants definitely are active agents who promote their own development, but they need a lot of assistance from caretakers to help them find their feet. Once they do, they are truly up and running, all over the place.

Amazing as it is, the brains of these dependent little beings contain the seeds of many of their future capacities for mastery of their worlds. These seeds are just waiting for an opportunity to develop. Infants are born with lots of emotional capacities that provide all they need to survive in a close bond with a caretaker, the closest emotional bond they will ever experience. Of special significance are the capacities for connection pro-vided by an innate emotion system. How these emotions are responded to lays a foundation for further emotional development.

A nursing baby whose needs are responded to with loving attention and cradling affection absorbs his or her mother's loving gaze and receptive arms along with the milk and drifts contentedly back to sleep. This child learns that people can be trusted to notice one's needs and can be relied on to help and that his or her own efforts at need satisfaction will meet with success. A child who encounters the tense arms of an irritable, over-whelmed mother, who looks vacantly ahead, waiting for the feeding to be over, learns another lesson. Tensing in response to the mother's tension, this child learns that no one really cares, that people can't be counted on, and that his or her efforts to get needs met will not prove satisfying (Stern, 1985). Depressed mothers have been found to spend less time looking at, touching, and talking to their infants; show little or negative affect; and often fail to respond to infants' signals. Their infants in turn show abnor-mal activity levels and less positive affect. It appears that because of their frequent exposure to their mothers' maladaptive responses, these infants themselves develop a dysfunctional style of interacting (Field, 1995). A parenting style that is responsive and sensitive to children's signals results in infants high in social and cognitive competence.

Legerstee and Varghese (2001) studied the role of mothers' affect mirroring or empathic responsiveness on the development of 2- to 3-month-old infants. Mothers were classified as *high affect mirroring* if they exhibited the following behaviors: were more attentive, maintaining, join-ing, or following their infant's focus of attention by, for example, com-menting "Are you looking at your socks? Those are pretty socks, aren't they?"; were warm and sensitive in their response to their infant's affective cues, including promptness and appropriateness of reactions, acceptance of the infant's interest, amount of physical affection, positive affect, and tone of voice; and were socially responsive, imitating the infant's smiles and vocalizations and modulating negative affect. Notice the similarity between these dimensions and those of empathic following recommended for em-pathic emotion coaching. Infants with mothers who responded in these ways were found to be more responsive, reflecting back the mothers' affect and smiling, cooing, and gazing at their mothers more than at mothers who were characterized as *low affect mirroring*. These infants showed more social behaviors, more often shared affective states with their mothers, and discriminated between live interactions with their mothers and film replays of their mothers. They interacted more with their real mothers than with a film of them, whereas infants with low affect mirroring mothers did not.

Infants enter the world with a highly interpersonally responsive emotion system that is raring to go. They respond positively to facial configurations soon after birth. Masks shaped like a face soon evoke a smile. Young children respond with fear to looming shadows and even avert their gaze from fast-approaching objects. The latter response was shown in an experiment by simulating a fast-approaching missile with an expanding dot on a TV screen (Sroufe, 1996). The dot grew rapidly to fill a screen on which the infant's gaze had been fixed. The babies automatically turned their heads and eyes away to protect their faces from the apparently fast-approaching missile.

Infants also begin to learn very early in their development. By the time they have reached the ripe old age of about 4 days, they can discriminate and show preference for a breast pad saturated with their own mother's milk over one saturated with a stranger's milk. Soon they distinguish between animate and inanimate objects, showing greater interest in and preference for living over nonliving objects. Novel stimulation, even novel sequences of the same flashing lights, attracts their attention more than the same old thing over and over. The first weeks and months are very busy, not only for caretakers but also for infants as their brains grow and develop, and more differentiated, neuronal connections, lay down a set of pathways of great consequence. The roads less traveled will wither and simply fade away, while those most practiced will become well-constructed highways to the future.

Learning helps the brain grow. Children who regularly practice violin or piano early on, say between ages 4 and 10, show many more developed neuronal connections in the music-related areas of their brains. This includes much more highly differentiated areas related to finger and eye–finger coordination. Maestros' brains therefore are being developed by early practice, in a way and at a rate that never occur again. Future musical geniuses are being formed by childhood practice that occurs soon after leaving the cradle. So too are areas of the youthful brains of soccer and baseball players being developed on childhood playgrounds. As they kick and hit balls, or anything that resembles them, the brain grows new connecting links that govern motor coordination.

Children are therefore active, forming beings from Day 1. How parents respond to their primary communications—emotions—is of great significance to children's well-being. Awareness of children's emotions is virtually a natural ability, especially if one has experienced good parenting as a child him- or herself or has had other good relationships. Children also appear to be highly talented emotional beings. However, this talent tragically often erodes as they develop. As infants grow to maturity, and develop language, parents often attend less and less to their feelings, and in the busyness and stresses of life, parents often expect their children to speak up for themselves. By the time kids are teenagers they don't want parents to know what they are feeling, and parents have often lost interest. It is in the small, everyday emotional exchanges, as well as in the big ones, that templates are laid down. Parents too often send messages such as "I'm busy with something important—don't bother me." Why is it that parents stop attending to their children's feelings as they grow?

One important reason is the parents' own philosophy of emotion management (Gottman, 1997). To the degree that parents feel that their own and others' emotions need to be suppressed, controlled, and avoided, they stop attending to their children's emotions. Parents believe that their children need to learn the lessons of emotional control and the merits of no longer being babies. Adulthood, in this view, involves reining in one's emotions, at worst through physical punishment and at best by promoting rational control over one's emotions. The view of the benefits of emotional control is rewarded by its apparent validity. Parents generally don't want their children to be crybabies or wimps. Popularity does not go with emotional lability in childhood or adulthood. Being strong is a much-admired and -desired quality. Strength and emotional intelligence, however, in the long run come, as I have argued, from the integration of reason and emotion rather than from control over emotion.

It is parents' own feelings and thoughts about their emotions that are the major influence on how they handle their children's feelings. Parents raise children in their own images. Gender-stereotyped ways of dealing with emotion, for example, have been shown to be influenced by parents' ways of telling stories to their children (Chance & Fiese, 1999). Mothers tend to tell stories with themes of disappointment and sadness. Fathers overall are less likely to use any emotion themes in their stories. Mothers are more likely to tell stories of sadness to their daughters than to their sons and have also been shown to demonstrate greater expressivity toward daughters than toward sons, which may explain girls' greater sociability and stronger tendency to smile in social interchanges (Magai & McFadden, 1995). The way parents tell stories to their children and express emotions to their children appears to be an important avenue of imparting gender-related information about emotion and its expression. Mothers have also been found to influence the expressions of their infants over time. Magai and McFadden (1995) summarized their longitudinal study of expressive development of infants and mothers over a 5-year period. They found that mothers engaged in behaviors that could be understood as an attempt to moderate the emotional expressions of their infants. Mothers restricted their modeling to the more socially positive signals of interest and joy, and over the years they increased their matching responses to these emotions in their infants and decreased their matching responses to infants' expressions of pain. Infants who received higher rates of maternal modeling of joy and interest showed higher gains in these emotions between 2½ to 7½ months of age.

Parents thus must learn to see their children's emotions as intimate opportunities for connecting with their children, as opportunities for getting close to and validating their children's experiences. This is the first step in helping children learn about intelligent management of emotions. Parents should not invalidate and dismiss their children's emotions; ignore them; or treat them as undesirable intrusions or disruptions to be eliminated, controlled, or got rid of.

I now look at coaching parents in how to deal with the emotions in their children that later trouble adults so much.

DEALING WITH CHILDREN'S SADNESS

The cry to be loved breaks all people's hearts. Babies' needs for love and tender care move virtually all people to provide these things. Infants who do not receive love and tender care fail to thrive and become sad and depressed. Loneliness and powerlessness are the instigators of sadness, for old and young people and, when prolonged, produce depression. Loss of friends, esteem, disappointment; failure to attain a goal; and loss of first and later loves all produce sadness in children. Not feeling loved, and insufficient autonomy or a sense of helplessness, brings on adolescent despair.

How can parents mentor their children about the sadness of life, without the experience of which no one can mature? Parents shape their children's emotions by how they respond to these emotions, by the language they use to describe the emotions, by the specific emotions they themselves display, and by responding to some emotions rather than to others. Feeling talk is very important in children's development. In one study (Sroufe, 1996), the more mothers talked to their 3-year-olds about their feeling states, the more skilled the children were when they were 6 years old at making judgments about the emotions displayed by unfamiliar adults. Witness the following feeling talk interaction between a mother and her 2-year-old son, Dennis.

Dennis: Eat my Cheerios. Eat my Cheerios. (crying)

Mother: Crying? We're having a real struggle, aren't we, Dennis? One more mouthful now. And oh, my, what do you do, you spit it out.

Dennis: Crying! (pretends to cry)

Mother: Dennis is crying. Doesn't want Cheerios. Mommy wanted
           him to have one more. Dennis is sad. Crying.

Dennis: Dennis sad. Crying.

Here mother and child are beginning to develop a shared experience in which they are learning to better understand each other. No one truly knows why Dennis was originally crying, but his mother is trying to understand, and Dennis is learning what his mother thinks about why he is crying. Together they are constructing a shared view of what is occurring. The mother is a mentor, a type of emotion coach, who here is simply helping Dennis put words to feelings and connect them to the situation. Later, as Dennis develops, his mother will do more coaching, helping him with appropriate forms of expression and action. By age 3, when children see another child crying or hurt, they respond with concern and might run to get the child's mother. Even earlier than this they understand causes of feelings and common antecedents of sadness, saying such things as "Mommy sad; what Daddy do?" or "I cry. Lady pick me up and hold me." Parents need to be coached to engage in feeling talk.

STEPS IN DEALING WITH SADNESS

Parents can deal successfully with their children's sadness by following these proposed steps. These steps can be taught in a psychoeducational group and can be given to parents as a guide.

1. Be aware of even low-intensity sadness in yourself and your child. You need to pay attention to nonverbal signs or mild verbal ones of disappointment, loneliness and powerlessness, or giving up, not only to crying and more noisy forms of distress.

2. View your child's sadness as an opportunity for intimacy or teaching. Intimacy often involves sharing hurt feelings. There can be nothing as precious as sharing your child's hurt feeling; this is a real opportunity to be close. Being able to help alleviate sadness as a bonus will bring relief and will send you soaring to heights of satisfaction and gratitude. Don't be scared of your child's sadness; you will then only teach your child a fear of sadness. Don't avoid sadness; if you do, your child will learn to do this, too. However, as children get older and reach adolescence they begin to separate from parents and form their own identities. Being autonomous becomes the important goal. Now you have to change your style to suit your child's mood. Your adolescent's sadness now can be discussed or shared only by invitation. Don't miss the op-

portunity. If your child shows you that he or she is sad, this is a sufficient invitation. You can say you would be sad if that had happened to you. Your mentoring should continue as your child grows, but when your child is older, don't say your child is sad until he or she does. Approaching too close to a feeling that has to do with weakness, such as sadness, when the adolescent is struggling with issues of competence and strength and is not yet ready to deal with these feelings, is potentially disastrous. Approach will result in your adolescent shrinking away and may hurt his or her pride rather than promote the openness you seek.

3. Validate your child's sadness. This is crucial. It is painful enough to be sad; to have this invalidated with "Don't be a crybaby" or "There is nothing to be sad about" is shame producing. Validation involves saying something like "It is sad or disappointing when X doesn't work out." Find some ways of truly understanding the validity of your child's sadness.

4. Assist your child in verbally labeling his or her emotions. As in the earlier example of Dennis and his mother's feeling talk, starting from an early age, talking about feelings is an important way of helping your child develop awareness about his or her own emotions as well as empathy with others' feelings. Both are crucial aspects of emotional intelligence. It is important to notice sadness and disappointment early, put them into words, and open them up. This prevents the sadness from escalating into withdrawal. It is important, however, with children to distinguish early on among primary, secondary, and instrumental sadness. Most children learn pretty quickly that sadness sometimes gets them their way. Thus they try using it to achieve their aims. To validate sadness that is expressed deliberately on a child's face, so that he or she can get his or her way, is to validate the wrong thing. Rather than responding to an instrumental expression of sadness with "Mikey is sad," it would be best to say "Mikey wants a candy," and some coaching might be helpful; for example: "You don't have to be sad to get a candy."

5. Finally, problem solve with your child. Set behavioral limits where necessary, and discuss needs and goals involved in the sadness and strategies for dealing with sadness-generating situations. After the sadness has been validated, proposing solutions in a nonimposing fashion can be helpful. When Amanda is sad that the blocks she was so carefully erecting into her own leaning tower collapsed, she cries. Mommy says, "It's so disappointing when the blocks fall that you just want

to cry. Mommy's sad too when it doesn't work." (Amanda is still crying.) "You don't want the blocks to fall down. When we're sad when the blocks fall down we cry a little, and then we wipe our tears. There we are." (Amanda stops crying and starts looking around at the blocks.) "Now, let's see where those silly blocks are that fell down. Let's see if this time we can put the big one on the bottom." Rather than ignoring Amanda's sadness and starting to build blocks straight away, the mother recognizes her crying as an opportunity for closeness and teaching, and she coaches Amanda on dealing with sadness. Note the conducting from one state to another that is occurring.

DEALING WITH CHILDREN'S ANGER

Toddlers are among the angriest people in the world. They are small and helpless—their skills for mastering the world are just beginning to develop. Much that they do, they do poorly. This produces loads of frustration. If adults become exasperated with them it only increases their sense of hopeless failure. Children's anger is explosive—a brief burst of it and they return to normalcy with bewildering speed. Children between the ages of 1 and 2 years can be pretty ferocious together in a playpen. They might bite, scratch, hit, pull hair, and steal each other's toys.

Even at these young ages children express different kinds of anger: helpless anger, just standing and screaming when a toy is stuck behind the couch; more goal-directed anger, by pulling angrily on the toy to free it; and retaliatory anger at the child who stole the toy. As children grow, so does their retaliatory anger. Most parents are shocked to see their child destroy a toy in a fit of anger. A severe lecture or punishment often follows this unacceptable behavior. The child's hostility must be subdued. What happens instead is it becomes hidden. It is remarkable that, in a culture in which people stress the importance of learning how to spell, starting with the ABCs and building up to an adult vocabulary, that people don't see how important it is to learn one's emotional lessons step by step until one is emotionally eloquent. Learning math requires first differentiating between 1 and 2, then learning to count to 10, and so on. Learning emotion regulation similarly is a complex learning process; one cannot learn it all at once. In learning to regulate emotional expression, a global emotional response such as anger needs to become differentiated by experience into a variety of subtle and appropriate responses. First one needs to be aware of one's anger; then name it; and then, in small steps, learn what to do to achieve its aim. Only then will children be able to differentiate their anger so as to satisfy Aristotle's requirement of being angry with the right person, to the right degree, at the right time, for the right purpose, and in the right way. Anger and aggression in adolescents have become a problem in North America that has no easy solution. Prevention is what I propose here. Emotion coaching from early on will provide the connection and the integration of emotion tolerance and regulation skills that will help prevent adolescent explosions. Parents need to connect with their children to address the emptiness, pain, isolation, and lack of hope felt by so many of them.

Angry children who receive no emotional guidance, no coaching or mentoring, become angry adults. Unless parents can sit patiently with their children's anger, assimilate it, tolerate it, empathize with it, and validate it, and then, at a pace appropriate to the child, begin to put words to it and guide it in constructive ways, it has no opportunity to develop and grow. Only with this kind of attention will anger grow into more differentiated, socially appropriate forms of expression. Children's retaliatory anger peaks in their early school years and then diminishes until it almost disappears in most teenagers. Teens tend to sulk and be oppositional, and they get angry with those who impose on them. They get especially angry with siblings and when they feel too confined, are lied to, or are shamed.

Many parents deal with their children's anger by driving it underground rather than helping their children make sense of their anger and use it in problem solving. Children come into the world with different temperaments and differ in their degrees of irritability and anger. Crabby babies can become happy adults, but infants who begin life with bad moods will not be as easily soothed and may grow into angry children, especially if they happen to have parents who are too harshly controlling or anxiously unsure. The following guidelines can be given to parents to help them deal with their children's anger.

STEPS IN DEALING WITH ANGER

1. Be aware of anger in yourself and in your child. You need to pay attention not only to your child's tantrums but also to his or her irritability and resentment.
2. View your child's anger as an opportunity for getting closer to what is happening in him or her and for teaching. Recognize this anger episode as one in which you can help your child learn something about how best to deal with this anger. Don't drive the anger underground—it is not a toxic product to be buried. Also, don't allow yourself to be dominated by a tantrum and give in to get rid of it. View it as an opportunity for your child to learn and you to teach, not a disaster.
3. Validate your child's anger. To validate anger rather than see-

ing it as a volcanic eruption to be capped you are going to need to be comfortable with your own anger and its expression. Remember, anger is saying, "I'm offended." Find out about the offense your child has experienced and discern your child's reasons for being angry. Seeing how your child's experience makes sense is one of the most important parts of validation. Convey this understanding even if you feel it important to set a limit, for example, "I know you are angry (or upset) that your brother took the toy. I know you want it, but I want you to let him have it now. It is his turn." It is also helpful to empathize with your child's anger against you. Saying "I can understand how you would be angry at me for limiting your TV" is helpful. This maintains a connection and validates the child's anger.

4. Assist your child in verbally labeling his or her anger. This is generally done first by offering words, but as the child grows and is able to name feelings, first ask, "Are you angry?" and later ask, "What are you feeling?"

5. Problem solve with your child, set behavioral limits when necessary, and discuss goals and strategies for dealing with anger-generating situations.

DEALING WITH CHILDREN'S FEARS

The fear of separation is many children's most basic fear and becomes anxiety over a lack of safety. Most babies show a fear of heights, of falling, and of sudden noise. Many fears grow with imagination. At about age 8 months the fear of separation begins. This is the time at which babies' cognitive capacities have developed sufficiently that they can recognize familiar people and objects. Separation from familiar caretakers produces imagined consequences too frightening to anticipate, and the appearance of strangers presents them with a sight too terrifying to behold.

Many fears are learned. Children often fear what their parents fear, or they learn the lesson of fearfulness and begin to fear other things. Studies have shown (Magai & McFadden, 1995) a correlation between the number of fears held by children and their mothers. When parents themselves are anxious with other people, children will interpret this as a fear of strangers. If adults are highly anxious about their children's health or injury, the children will conjure up dire consequences. Fear of the dark, fear of water, and fear of cows or dogs are other common childhood fears. On the other hand, often fears come of their own accord and tend to disappear as the child grows.

Severe or harsh punishment produces fear, as does a parent's explosive temper. Children who have come from homes in which there has been violence or intense marital or familial dispute tend to walk through life on eggshells. This is a survival skill learned in the family so as not to precipitate the inexplicable wrath that could descend at any moment. The direct result of frightening or unpleasant family situations is an increased load of anxiety on the children. Domination, lack of respect, constant criticism, expectations that are too high, and having to take sides in parental disputes all produce a weaker sense of self and anxiety. Growing up in an environment of suppressed hostility between parents is highly confusing and anxiety provoking for many children, who sense the danger but cannot quite identify its source. They just feel anxious.

Overprotective parenting also will create fearfulness in children that they are not well equipped to survive on their own and that they require protection. Children raised in a warm environment in which their fears are noticed, in which they are helped and encouraged to put their feelings into words, and in which actions are taken to deal with their fears will have lower levels of fear. No one can be inoculated against all fear, but children who are raised in a secure emotion coaching environment are less likely to suffer from deep anxieties later in life.

Fears of inadequacy, which none of us overcomes entirely, begin in childhood as children become more autonomous and have to face the world alone. This fear is most acute in teenagers, who have a stronger need than most to belong or fit in. They fear being criticized, mocked, or made fun of. They form ideal images that they often find hard to live up to. Overconfidence, with no doubts, does not make for ideal adaptation; a certain amount of unsureness is healthy. The following guidelines for dealing with fear can be given to parents.

STEPS IN DEALING WITH FEAR

A child comes running in the night, afraid of the dark in his room. The noises outside scare him, and he imagines all kinds of monsters out there, in his closet, or under his bed. Provided these are not chronic and too overwhelming, in which case underlying problems might be signaled, how do parents handle the child's fear? The following steps will help.

1. Be aware of even low-intensity fears in yourself and your children. The issue here is being realistic. If you are overattentive to fears—your own or your children's—you will produce overanxiety, but if you ignore your children's fears they will not go away. Statements such as "Be a big boy or girl" in response to fear will only produce shame about the fear. Notice whether your child is afraid when you put him or her to

bed or whether he or she asks urgently for water or too hurriedly comes out of the room with some excuse.

2. View your child's fear as an opportunity for intimacy or teaching. Rather than simply mollifying your child or minimizing his or her fear with "There is nothing to worry about," take it seriously. Recognize that something more is needed. Attempt to give what is needed and not more.

3. Validate your child's fear. For some reason, perhaps because adults are so afraid of their own fear, adults tend to humiliate children for being afraid. Even with the best of intentions, either thinking the child is cute or remembering their own fears, adults often are amused by children's fears, laugh about them, and say things like "Don't be silly." This is very humiliating. Children's fears and anxieties are valid, not silly. Once the child has been validated at least he or she now no longer feels alone in a fear that no one understands. Possibly a child's fear is the emotion with which adults most need to empathize, because being connected to a secure adult helps calm a child's fears. Nothing is worse than being ridiculed for one's fears. I still remember picnicking with my extended family on a family holiday and being afraid of cows that were approaching our picnic site. I struggled, trying not to show my fear. No one else seemed afraid, and I wanted to be a big boy, but my fear overcame me. Although my mother usually was protective, she was influenced by the context of relatives, particularly by one who took the "don't pamper him; he has to grow up" and mocking "don't be a sissy" approach, and so I was left to suffer on my own. I felt so alone in my obviously irrational fear. Even the other children weren't afraid, and my mother was providing no protection. I ran back to the car and in humiliation ate my hot dog in the safety of the back seat. I still remember the awful feeling in my stomach and the suppressed tears of shame and anger at my relative. This did not help me deal with my fear. I got over my fear on other occasions, when my mother, unembarrassed and unconstrained by a family chorus, helped me approach cows, reassured me of their harmlessness in spite of their size, and showed me how to feed them grass and even touch them. The ability to do these things was exhilarating, and I felt proud of myself, as I felt my mother was.

4. Assist your child in verbally labeling his or her fear. The answer lies in naming the fear, either with questions such as "What are you afraid of?" or, if you and your child don't know, taking the opportunity to explore this together. Make

helpful comments or conjectures, such as "I understand you are afraid of the cows" or "Are you afraid of the dark and the sounds outside?"

5. Problem solve with your child; set behavioral limits; and discuss needs, goals, and strategies for dealing with fear-generating situations. When a child is afraid of the dark, sleeping in the parents' room is not a good solution even though that's what the child wants and would solve the immediate problem. A clear "No, that is not a good idea; Mommy and Daddy need to sleep in their beds and you in yours" sets the limit. Solutions might involve nightlights, a certain amount of checking under the bed, and investigating the sources of noise to reassure the child that there realistically is no danger. Soothing is also important to help the child relax. Facing fears in small steps is the right approach, but this must always be done in a validating, understanding context.

DEALING WITH CHILDREN'S SHAME

Shame is among the most excruciating of childhood experiences. Children need to be proud of their small selves in order to feel big. To be belittled when one is so small is too diminishing. Children need to be the apples of their parents' eyes. Their excitement needs to be seen and validated, otherwise they shrink, red-faced into the floor. To them this is a fate worse than death and is avoided at all costs, especially as the child grows into adolescence. Embarrassment develops with age. By the time the child recognizes him- or herself as a separate person and can evaluate the self from the perspective of another person, the capacity for embarrassment has begun. If a parent ignores a child's pride the child will feel shame. Support and validation are the antidotes to shame. If a parent shames a child, the parent must correct this immediately by reaffirming the child's importance to the parent. Prototypic of more intense shame experiences for a child is loss of bladder or bowel control and soiling oneself in public. This is the worst sort of humiliation. Reassuring the child that he or she is not defective for having made a mistake, or for his or her inability to control this time, puts the accident in a temporary context and removes it as a basic flaw of the self.

STEPS IN DEALING WITH SHAME

1. Become aware of even low-intensity shame or embarrassment in yourself and your children. Name it. Validate the child,

and help him or her recognize that mistakes are acceptable and do not diminish the child's self in the eyes of you or others.

2. View your child's shame as an opportunity for intimacy or teaching. Teach him or her that all people mistakes and that this does not make your child an unacceptable person.

3. Validate your child's shame. Acknowledge and normalize the child's experience: "It feels awful to think that others will tease you," "You are not the only one whom this has happened to," and "I remember when . . ." all help.

4. Assist your child in verbally labeling his or her shame. Give a name to this feeling of wanting to shrink into nothing and hide from the eyes—and, in the case of loss of bowel control, the noses—of others.

5. Problem solve with your child. Set behavioral limits and discuss goals and strategies for dealing with shame-generating situations. Discuss with your child how such a situation could have been prevented. Teach the child that telling the parent who is giving one a ride home that one needs to go to a toilet is better than trying to hold it in until one gets home. Tell the child that you understand that it might be difficult to ask but that this is the best way.

DEALING WITH ONE'S OWN EMOTIONS AS A PARENT

If anyone had told me the depth of emotion, especially difficult emotions, I would experience in parenting, I would have thought the person greatly prone to exaggeration. Sure, I expected to feel love, joy, happiness, excitement, worry, and frustration, but I did not expect to be pushed to the farthest limits of my experience. In addition to the feelings I expected, I have felt extreme helplessness, rage, pride, fear, anxiety, and worry beyond anything I had ever felt before. I have also felt sadness, a deeper and more poignant sadness than I could have imagined: sadness at my children's hurts that I could not heal; at their disappointments and failures that I could not prevent; and at their leaving, which I could not stop, nor wished to. I needed every ounce of emotional intelligence I had to negotiate the most challenging of life's tasks: parenting.

One of the most remarkable parts of this emotional journey was the extent to which I had to confront my own feelings and grow emotionally. My children were a mirror for my own emotions, and keeping clear what they truly felt and not confusing it with what I felt was highly challenging. Parenting made me realize many things about myself. Sometimes—often, I hope—I was able to see and hear them and understand what they felt, but at other times my own feelings would become so strong that they obscured the separation between us. If they were sad, I would be sad. I would overidentify with their sadness and become overtaken with my own sadness. On other occasions I would imagine they were hurting when they were not and feel my own hurt through them. This is not some strange insanity. All parents do it. The conspiracy of silence that surrounds the emotional experience of child rearing needs to be broken. The issue is not whether all parents to some degree project their feelings onto their children and become so enmeshed that they lose their boundaries. In these states a child's hurt is the parent's hurt, the child's loss is the parent's loss, the child's victory is the parent's victory. Instead, the issue is whether parents can distinguish fantasy from reality. Can parents recognize and find out what they are feeling rather than believing what they imagine, that their feelings are really their children's? Even when parents' feelings and their children's are the same, it is very different to hear and respond to a child as a parent versus overidentifying and being overwhelmed by one's own unresolved feelings triggered by one's children's feelings or circumstances.

In addition to adults confusing their feelings with those of their children, an area of definite difficulty is that of parents overreacting to their children: feeling threatened by their anger, defensive at their criticisms, hurt by their separations, needing their attention, and feeling rejected by their disinterest can evoke parents' own maladaptive responses. These will impair parents' ability to be a mentor or emotion coach. Parents who often feel anger, sadness, or fear in their parenting experience these emotions too intensely, have difficulty calming down, and are out of control. Coaches need to work with these parents to help them deal with these maladaptive states. Angry feelings are usually the most difficult ones with which parents must deal. They need to acknowledge their anger but learn to regulate it so that they don't lash out and then feel guilty afterward, although if they do so, an apology is always welcomed by children, who need the love of their parents and can be very forgiving. It is important for parents to be able to express anger when they are mad at their children, but it is doing this constructively with which they may need help. This means communicating anger with "I" statements and not condemning or criticizing the child, for example, saying "I am mad," not "You are bad." Parents need to be able to talk sensibly about their anger, to disclose it as information to be dealt with rather than to attack. Throughout their expressions of anger they need to continue to communicate their caring and respect for their children and communicate that what their children do matters to them. Sometimes it would be a lot better if parents saw their children as they see other adults—as sensitive, feeling beings—and applied the same rules of interaction to them. For some reason parents tend to lose sight of the fact that their children have feelings, and even though they have the best intentions toward their children they try to teach them or control them and just end up nagging and arguing. It is so easy as a parent to forget that children are real people, too. This is in part because children don't yet speak in a way parents can understand, so the parents lose sight of their children's inner worlds. Parents need to remember that their children do feel, all the time.

Children are simultaneously the most forgiving and the most condemning of their parents. An infant bears no grudge at a parent's neglect, and children tolerate parents' moments of anger and impatience the way few others would. But if there is no lasting love, and especially if no understanding is developed, this precious bond becomes contaminated with anger, hurt, and recrimination. As much as children grow to seeming independence they, as do parents, always remain interdependent beings. People always need, and benefit from, human connections of some kind. Family ties are the strongest of all emotional bonds. Parents need, therefore, to pay special attention to their children and learn to be good emotion coaches.

EPILOGUE

People are emotional for a reason. Emotions are a part of human intelligence. The split between emotional and rational, and inside and outside, needs to be healed in a new cultural evolutionary step, in which the integration of heads and hearts is facilitated in schools and institutions and most importantly, in the home, the place where the major emotional lessons are learned. People thus need to learn to attend to their emotions. Emotions are one of people's most precious resources. People go to such great lengths to protect them; therefore, they must be very precious.

Psychological life begins for all of us with affect. All human beings experience the world through feeling and are motivated by the desire for certain feelings. As we develop, our emotions remain under the control of one part of the brain, and speaking about our emotions falls under the jurisdiction of another part. As adults we are left in a process of constantly having to make sense of our emotions. Because people are most aware of the verbal, more rational part of their brains they often assume that all parts of their minds should be amenable to reason and argument. This is not so. Much of our brains do not respond to rational commands. We cannot direct our emotional lives by reason. Moods and emotions are parts of the human condition; they cannot be avoided. Moods and emotions do change, provided we work with them in a harmonious fashion and have emotional wisdom.

The following list summarizes all that I have said in this book about developing emotional wisdom. People need to develop

- greater awareness of their emotions,
- greater empathy to their own and others' feelings,
- greater capacities to make sense of their emotions by symbolizing them in awareness and reflecting on them,
- improved emotion regulation and self-soothing skills, and
- the ability to link emotional states to each other and integrate them to change emotion with emotion.

People benefit from awareness of their own emotions and the ability to recognize emotions in others. Being aware of what they are feeling helps people orient themselves in their worlds and helps them function in an integrated manner within themselves. If people are not aware of what they feel, they become split. Feeling sad or threatened will move their body sense in one direction while their minds race off in another. Without awareness of their emotions people become torn and end up feeling inexplicably ragged. Being aware of feelings while they are happening is the sine qua non of a healthy orientation toward life. When people ignore, suppress, or become frightened of their emotions they become divided selves.

Just prior to writing this book I experienced once again, as if for the first time, the importance of the emotion processes I have written about: the process of both having emotions and regulating them. I found myself dramatically thrown into the process of interrupting my own tears. This took place at the unveiling of my mother's tombstone. I had traveled 20,000 miles for this event, to South Africa and, standing there by the graveside, I at first automatically controlled my tears. I felt them welling up in me. Against my better judgment, I tightened my throat and fixed my concentration in an attempt to deliberately control them. I struggled with crying in this public way, a struggle made especially difficult for me because I was responsible for reading a prayer and therefore was a center of attention. It was only at the end, when I received the consolation of my niece and felt her arms around me after the ceremony, that I was able to sob those tears, which I had come all that way to cry. This was good for me, as it is for all of us. The postponed emotion, suppressed for one reason or another, expresses itself when one senses it is safe to feel the emotion. This reminded me how important others can be in providing us with the safety to experience what we feel. As I write this now, the tears well up, and they are good. They tell me that I am still grieving, that I am alive, that I care and feel tender. They wash over me like a soothing balm, poignant and comforting. I am reminded of a quote from Rilke (1934), who said of sadness that these are the moments when something new has entered into us, something unknown: our feelings grow mute in shy perplexity, everything in us withdraws, a stillness comes, and the new, which no one knows, stands in the midst of it and is silent. (p. 17)

Sadness of this type gives meaning to life and leaves us in some unique way feeling both invigorated and tired, maybe from the intensity of it all. Feeling no doubt takes energy and uses our resources. After experiencing emotions we need time to recover and replenish. I notice that I feel the energy drain of my emotion more now, as I age.

Having believed deeply, in my early adulthood, in the importance of trying to live a rational life and rise above both the sentimentality and the horrors of life, I tried to develop a philosophical approach. This resulted in my adoption of a dispassionate stance espousing views such as that pain, suffering, and loss are inevitable, so there is no purpose in being distressed about them. Control, or immunity from pain, was really my aim. With the wisdom of life experience I came to see the error of this view. With the wisdom of age I came to see that quality of life is improved by giving up the attempt to try to control my reactions and to recognize my process nature. I came to understand that my emotional process needed to be allowed rather than controlled, and so I grew to accept the emotional side of my nature and to respect the mind in my heart. Rather than rejecting the importance of rationality, I gave it a different role: that of making sense of my feelings and helping me reflect on them in order to make meaning. The construction of personal narratives is crucial to one's sense of identity. We order our reality by forming stories that tell who we are. No story is significant without emotion, and no emotion exists without a story to provide its context. We thus integrate head and heart in authoring who we are.

Validating the existence of people's emotionality through coaching is crucial to helping them toward a more satisfying life. People need to dwell in their emotional moments as well as in the emotional moments of others and to be able to validate these emotions. People need to be coached on how to not run from difficult feelings, be distracted from them, or try to talk themselves out of them. Unfortunately, feelings do not respond well to reason. Certain effects of emotion are impenetrable to reason. Telling oneself it is not rational to be so anxious or depressed is not very effective. In therapy people cannot easily be cured by reason alone. Connections from the emotional centers of the brain to the rational ones are much stronger than those in the reverse direction (Le Doux, 1996). Thus, people are moved far more by their emotions than they are able to move their emotions by rational control. This is a fact of cerebral architecture. Thus, it is easier to change emotion with emotion. Mood over mood is more effective than mind over mood. People need to live in harmony with the emotions that move them rather than live by a code of rational control and self-manipulation. In the long run, even the sensible "shoulds" of life, such as "I should exercise or eat healthier food," have to be emotionally important, and not be the product of willpower alone to be successful.

Although the ability to defer action is quintessentially human, to be cut off from one's spontaneity is dangerously alienating. Being purely rational denies one's access to a sophisticated source of emotional knowing that adaptively informs action and aids problem solving and decision making (Damasio, 1994). Overcontrol of emotion often leads to its opposite —the possibility of breakdown in rational control. Emotional control most often fails when stress becomes too great. In addition, the inner life of emotional experience that is not exposed to the light of human confirmation does not grow and differentiate into socially appropriate forms. Left on their own in murky darkness, emotions can become painfully tortured and twisted. This occurs when, for example, bottled up, unresolved anger turns to thoughts of revenge. Emotional coaching can help to bring feelings into the light of day, where they can be developed into socially appropriate expressions.

As I have argued throughout this book, emotion coaches can help people achieve this goal by seeing clients as trainees whom they help arrive at their emotions. This can be done by helping them identify what they are feeling in the moment in their bodies. By helping them pay attention to their internal sense of complexity, so filled with meaning, they make sense of their feelings and emotions. Emotion coaches also help people by coaching them to use their healthy emotions as a guide to adaptive action and problem solving. Finally, coaches also need to help people recognize and interrupt nonproductive patterns of emotional responding and to leave behind emotions that are not productive.

ADDITIONAL RESOURCES

For additional information on Emotion-Focused Therapy, refer to the following sources:

Web Site

www.emotionfocusedtherapy.org

Films and Videos

American Psychological Association (Producer). (n.d.). *Process experiential psychotherapy* (APA Psychotherapy Videotape Series I: Systems of Psychotherapy). (Available from the American Psychological Association, 750 First Street, NE, Washington, DC 20002-4242; www.apa.org/videos/)

Psychological & Educational Films (Producer). (n.d.). *Integrative psychotherapy* (Part 5: A demonstration with Dr. Leslie Greenberg). (Available from Psychological & Educational Films, 3334 East Coast Highway, #252, Corona Del Mar, CA 92625; www.psychedfilms.com)

REFERENCES

Adams, K. E., & Greenberg, L. S. (1996, June). *Therapists' influence on depressed clients' therapeutic experiencing and outcome.* Paper presented at the 43rd annual convention of the Society for Psychotherapy Research, St. Amelia Island, FL.

Allen, R. (Ed.). (1990). *The concise Oxford dictionary.* Oxford, England: Clarendon Press.

Angus, L., Lewin, J., & Hardtke, K. (2001, May). *Narrative processing modes and therapeutic change in brief experiential therapy for depression: An empirical analysis.* Paper presented at the conference of the Joint UK–Europe Society for Psychotherapy Research, University of Leiden, Leiden, The Netherlands.

Aristotle (1941). Rhetoric. In R. McKeon (Ed.), *The basic works of Aristotle.* New York: Random House.

Atkinson, B. (1999). The emotional imperative. *Family Therapy Networker, 23*(4), 22–33

Bargh, J. A., & Chartrand, T. L. (1999). The unbearable automaticity of being. *American Psychologist, 54,* 462–479.

Beck, A. (1976). *Cognitive therapies and the emotional disorders.* New York: International Universities Press.

Berkowitz, L. (2000). *Causes and consequences of feelings.* Cambridge, England: Cambridge University Press.

Beutler, L. E., Clarkin, J. F., & Bongar, B. (2000). *Guidelines for the systematic treatment of the depressed patient.* Oxford, England: Oxford University Press.

Bohart, A. (1977). Role playing and interpersonal conflict reduction. *Journal of Counseling Psychology, 24,* 15–24.

Bohart, A., Elliott, R., Greenberg, L. S., & Watson, J. (in press). Empathy redux. In J. Norcross (Ed.), *Psychotherapy relationships that work.* Washington, DC: American Psychological Association.

Bohart, A., & Greenberg, L. (Eds.). (1997). *Empathy reconsidered: New directions in psychotherapy.* Washington, DC: American Psychological Association.

Bolger, E. (1999). Grounded theory analysis of emotional pain. *Psychotherapy Research, 99,* 342–362.

Bonanno, G., & Keltner, D. (1997). Facial expressions of emotion and the course of bereavement. *Journal of Abnormal Psychology, 106,* 126–137.

Borkovec, T. (1994). The nature, functions, and origins of worry. In G. Davey & F. Tallis (Eds.), *Worrying: Perspectives on theory, assessment, and treatment* (pp. 131–162). New York: Wiley.

Bowlby, J. (1969). *Attachment.* New York: Basic Books.

Buber, M. (1958). *I and thou* (2nd ed.). New York: Scribner's.

Bushman, B. J., Baumeister, R. F., & Stack, A. D. (1999). Catharsis, aggression, and persuasive influence: Self-fulfilling or self-defeating prophecies? *Journal of Personality and Social Psychology, 76,* 367–376.

Chance, C., & Fiese, B. H. (1999). Gender-stereotyped lessons about emotions in family narratives. *Narrative Inquiry, 9,* 243–256.

Clarke, D. (1996). Panic disorder: From theory to therapy. In P. M. Salkovskis (Ed.), *Frontiers of cognitive therapy* (pp. 318–344). New York: Guilford Press.

Cummings, J. (1997). The role of emotional experience in the psychotherapeutic process: A qualitative research study. *Dissertation Abstracts International, 56*(1-B).

Cushman, P. (1995). *Constructing the self, constructing America.* Reading, MA: Addison-Wesley.

Dahl, H. (1991). The key to understanding change: Emotions as appetitive wishes and beliefs about their fulfillment. In J. Safran & L. Greenberg (Eds.), *Emotion, psychotherapy, and change* (pp. 130–165). New York: Guilford Press.

Damasio, A. (1994). *Descartes' error: Emotion, reason, and the human brain.* New York: Putnam's.

Damasio, A. (1999). *The feeling of what happens.* New York: Harcourt, Brace.

Darwin, C. (1872). *The expression of emotions in man and animals.* New York: Philosophical Library.

Davidson, R. (2000). Affective style, mood, and anxiety disorders: An affective neuroscience approach. In R. Davidson (Ed.), *Anxiety, depression, and emotion* (pp. 88–102). Oxford: Oxford University Press.

Diamond, G., & Liddle, H. A. (1996). Resolving a therapeutic impasse between parents and adolescents in multidimensional family therapy. *Journal of Consulting and Clinical Psychology, 64*(3), 481–488.

Ekman, P., & Davidson, R. (1994). *The nature of emotion: Fundamental questions.* New York: Oxford University Press.

Ekman, P., & Friesen, W. (1975). *Unmasking the face.* Englewood Cliffs, NJ: Prentice Hall.

Ellsworth, P. C. (1994). William James and emotion: Is a century of fame worth a century of misunderstanding? *Psychological Review, 101,* 222–229.

Epstein, S. (1994). Integration of the cognitive and psychodynamic unconscious. *American Psychologist, 49,* 709–724.

Field, T. (1995). Psychologically depressed parents. In M. Bornstein (Ed.), *Handbook of parenting* (Vol. 4, pp. 85–99). Hillsdale, NJ: Erlbaum.

Flack, W., Laird, J. D., & Cavallaro, J. (1999). Emotional expression and feeling in schizophrenia: Effects of specific expressive behaviors on emotional experiences. *Journal of Clinical Psychology, 55,* 1–20.

Foa, E. B., & Kozak, M. J. (1986). Emotional processing of fear: Exposure to corrective information. *Psychological Bulletin, 99,* 20–35.

Forgas, J. (2000). *Feeling and thinking.* Cambridge, England: Cambridge University Press.

Fosha, D. (2000). *The transforming power of affect.* New York: Basic Books.

Fredrickson, B. L. (1998). What good are positive emotions? *Review of General Psychology, 2,* 300–319.

Fredrickson, B. (2001). The role of positive emotions in positive psychology: The broaden-and-build theory of positive emotions. *American Psychologist, 56*(3), 218–226.

Freud, S. (1961). The ego and the id. In J. Strachey (Ed. & Trans.), *The standard edition of the complete psychological works of Sigmund Freud* (Vol. 19, pp. 1–66). London: Hogarth Press. (Original work published 1923)

Freud, S., & Breuer, J. (1949). On the psychical mechanism of hysterical phenomena: A preliminary communication. In J. Strachey (Ed.), *Standard edition* (Vol. 2, pp. 1–13). London: Hogarth Press. (Original work published 1893)

Frijda, N. H. (1986). *The emotions.* Cambridge, England: Cambridge University Press.

Gamble, M. (2001). *The role of emotion in therapeutic change.* Unpublished honor's thesis, York University, Toronto, Ontario, Canada.

Gendlin, E. T. (1962). *Experiencing and the creation of meaning.* New York: Free Press.

Gendlin, E. T. (1996). *Focusing-oriented psychotherapy: A manual of the experiential method.* New York: Guilford Press.

Gergen, K. (1985). The social constructionist movement in modern psychology. American Psychologist, 40, 266–275.

Gilbert, P. (1992). *Depression: The evolution of powerlessness.* Hove, England: Erlbaum.

Gottman, J. (1997). *The heart of parenting: How to raise an emotionally intelligent child.* New York: Simon & Schuster.

Gottman, J. M., Katz, L. F., & Hooven, C. (1997). Parental meta-emotion philosophy and the emotional life of families: Theoretical models and preliminary data. *Journal of Family Psychology, 10,* 243–291.

Greenberg, L. S. (2000). My change process: From certainty through chaos to complexity. In M. Goldfried (Ed.), *How therapists change: Personal and professional reflections* (pp. 247–270). Washington, DC: American Psychological Association.

Greenberg, L. S., & Bolger, E. (2001). An emotion focused approach to the over-regulation of emotion and emotional pain. *In-Session, 57,* 197–212.

Greenberg, L. S., & Elliott, R. (1997). Varieties of empathic responding. In A. Bohart & L. Greenberg (Eds.), *Empathy reconsidered: New directions in psychotherapy* (pp. 167–186). Washington, DC: American Psychological Association.

Greenberg, L. S., Elliott, R., & Lietaer, G. (1994). Research on humanistic and experiential psychotherapies. In A. E. Bergin & S. L. Garfield (Eds.), *Handbook of psychotherapy and behavior change* (4th ed., pp. 509–539). New York: Wiley.

Greenberg, L. S., Ford, C., Alden, L., & Johnson, S. (1993). In-session change processes in emotionally focused therapy for couples. *Journal of Consulting and Clinical Psychology, 61,* 68–84.

Greenberg, L. S., & Geller, S. (2001). Congruence and therapeutic presence. In

G. Wyatt (Ed.), *Roger's therapeutic conditions: Vol. 1. Congruence* (pp. 131–149). Ross-on-Wye, Herefordshire, UK: PCCS Books.

Greenberg, L. S., James, P., & Conway, R. (1988). Perceived change process in emotionally focused couples therapy. *Journal of Family Psychology, 2,* 1–12.

Greenberg, L. S., & Johnson, S. M. (1988). *Emotionally focused therapy for couples.* New York: Guilford Press.

Greenberg, L. S., Korman, L. M., & Paivio, S. C. (2001). Emotion in humanistic therapy. In D. J. Cain & J. Seeman (Eds.), *Humanistic psychotherapies: Handbook of research and practice* (pp. 499–530). Washington, DC: American Psychological Association.

Greenberg, L., & Mateu Marques, C. (1998). Emotions in couples systems. *Journal of Systemic Therapies, 17,* 93–107.

Greenberg, L. S., & Paivio, S. C. (1997). *Working with the emotions in psychotherapy.* New York: Guilford Press.

Greenberg, L. S., & Pascual-Leone, J. (1995). A dialectical constructivist approach to experiential change. In R. A. Neimeyer & M. J. Mahoney (Eds.), *Constructivism in psychotherapy* (pp. 169–191). Washington, DC: American Psychological Association.

Greenberg, L. S., & Pascual-Leone, J. (1997). Emotion in the creation of personal meaning. In M. Power & C. Brewin (Eds.), *The transformation of meaning in psychological therapies* (pp. 157–174). Chichester, England: Wiley.

Greenberg, L. S., & Pascual-Leone, J. (2001). A dialectical constructivist view of the creation of personal meaning. *Journal of Constructivist Psychology, 14*(3), 165–186.

Greenberg, L. S., & Rhodes, R. (1991). Emotional change processes. In R. Curtis & G. Stricker (Eds.), *How do people change* (pp. 39–58). New York: Plenum.

Greenberg, L. S., Rice, L. N., & Elliott, R. (1993). *Facilitating emotional change: The moment-by-moment process.* New York: Guilford Press.

Greenberg, L. S., & Rosenberg, R. (2000, June). *Varieties of emotional experience.* Paper presented at the International Conference of Client Centered and Experiential Psychotherapy, Indian Hills, IL.

Greenberg, L. S., & Safran, J. D. (1987). *Emotion in psychotherapy: Affect, cognition, and the process of change.* New York: Guilford Press.

Greenberg, L. S., & van Balen, R. (1998). Theory of experience centered therapy. In L. Greenberg, J. Watson, & G. Lietaer (Eds.), *Handbook of experiential psychotherapy: Foundations and differential treatment* (pp. 28–57). New York: Guilford Press.

Greenberg, L. S., & Watson, J. (1998). Experiential therapy of depression: Differential effects of client-centered relationship conditions and active experiential interventions. *Psychotherapy Research, 8,* 210–224.

Griffiths, P. (1997). *What emotions really are.* Chicago. University of Chicago Press.

Gross, J. J. (1999). Emotion and emotion regulation. In L. A. Pervin & O. P. John (Eds.), *Handbook of personality theory and research* (pp. 525–552). New York: Guilford Press.

Guidano, V. F. (1991). *The self in process.* New York: Guilford Press.

Guidano, V. F. (1995). Self-observation in constructivist therapy. In R. A. Neimeyer & M. J. Mahoney (Eds.), *Constructivism in psychotherapy* (pp. 155–168). Washington, DC: American Psychological Association.

Hendricks, M. N. (2001). Focusing-oriented/experiential psychotherapy. In D. J. Cain & J. Seeman (Eds.), *Humanistic psychotherapies: Handbook of research and practice* (pp. 221–252). Washington, DC: American Psychological Association.

Henry, W., Schacht, T., & Strupp, H. (1990). Patient and therapist introject, interpersonal process, and differential psychotherapy outcome. *Journal of Consulting and Clinical Psychology, 58,* 768–774.

Hume, D. (1739). *Treatise on human nature.* London: John Noon.

Isen, A. (1999). Positive affect. In T. Dagleish & M. Power (Eds.), *Handbook of cognition and emotion* (pp. 520–542). London: Wiley.

Iwakabe, S., Rogan, K., & Stalikas, A. (2000). The relationship between client emotional expressions, therapist interventions, and the working alliance: An exploration of eight emotional expression events. *Journal of Psychotherapy Integration, 10*(4), 375–402.

Izard, C. E. (1991). *The psychology of emotions.* New York: Plenum.

James, W. (1950). *The principles of psychology.* New York: Dover. (Original work published 1890)

Johnson, S., & Greenberg, L. S. (1985). Differential effects of experiential and problem solving interventions in resolving marital conflict. *Journal of Consulting and Clinical Psychology, 53,* 175–184.

Johnson, S., & Greenberg, L. S. (1994). *The heart of the matter.* New York: Guilford Press.

Kabat-Zinn, J. (1993). *Full catastrophe living.* New York: Delta.

Kant, I. (1953). *Critique of pure reason* (N. K. Smith, Trans.). London: MacMillan.

Kennedy-Moore, E., & Watson, J. C. (1999). *Expressing emotion: Myths, realities, and therapeutic strategies.* New York: Guilford Press.

Klein, M. H., Mathieu-Coughlan, P., & Kiesler, D. J. (1986). The Experiencing Scales. In L. Greenberg & W. Pinsof (Eds.), *The psychotherapeutic process* (pp. 21–71). New York: Guilford Press.

Korman, L., & Bolger, E. (1999, June). *A task analysis of a self-soothing event.* Paper presented at the annual meeting of the International Society for Psychotherapy Research, Braga, Portugal.

Kottler, J. (1996). *The language of tears.* San Francisco: Jossey-Bass.

Lane, R., & Nadel, L. (2000). *Cognitive neuroscience of emotion.* New York: Oxford University Press.

Lasch, C. (1979). *The culture of narcissm: American life in an age of diminishing expectations.* New York: Warner Books.

Lasch, C. (1984). *The minimal self: Psychic survival in troubled times.* New York: Norton.

LeDoux, J. E. (1993). Emotional networks in the brain. In M. Lewis & J. M. Haviland (Eds.), *Handbook of emotions* (pp. 109–118). New York: Guilford Press.

LeDoux, J. E. (1996). *The emotional brain: The mysterious underpinnings of emotional life.* New York: Simon & Schuster.

Legerstee, M., & Varghese, J. (2001). The role of maternal mirroring on social expectancies in 3-month-old infants. *Child Development, 72,* 1301–1313.

Leventhal, H. (1984). A perceptual motor theory of emotion. In L. Berkowitz (Ed.), *Advances in experimental social psychology* (pp. 117–182). New York: Academic Press.

Levine, S. (1989). *A gradual awakening.* New York: Anchor Books.

Lewis, M., & DeHaviland, J. (2000). *Handbook of emotions.* New York: Guilford Press.

Lietaer, G. (1993). Authenticity, congruence and transparency. In D. Brazier (Ed.), *Beyond Carl Rogers* (pp. 17–46). London: Constable.

Linehan, M. M. (1993). *Cognitive–behavioral treatment of borderline personality disorder.* New York: Guilford Press.

Luborsky, L., & Crits-Christoph, P. (1990). *Understanding transference: The core conflictual relationship theme method.* New York: Basic Books.

Magai, C., & McFadden, S. (1995). *The role of emotions in social and personality development.* New York: Plenum.

Mahoney, M. (1991). *Human change processes.* New York. Basic Books.

Mayer, J. D., & Hanson, E. (1995). Mood-congruent judgment over time. *Personality and Social Psychology Bulletin, 21,* 237–244.

Mayer, J. D., & Salovey, P. (1997). What is emotional intelligence? In P. Salovey & D. Sluyter (Eds.), *Emotional development and emotional intelligence* (pp. 3–31). New York: Basic Books.

Mergenthaler, E. (1996). Emotion-abstraction patterns in verbatim protocols: A new way of describing psychotherapeutic processes. *Journal of Consulting and Clinical Psychology, 64,* 1306–1315.

Mineka, S., & Thomas, C. (1999). Mechanisms of change in exposure therapy for anxiety disorders. In T. Dagleish & M. Power, *Handbook of cognition and emotion* (pp. 747–764). New York: John Wiley & Sons.

Myers, D. (1996). *Social psychology.* New York. McGraw-Hill.

Neimeyer, R. A., & Mahoney, M. J. (1995). *Constructivism in psychotherapy.* Washington, DC: American Psychological Association.

Oatley, K. (1992). *Best laid schemes: The psychology of emotions.* New York: Cambridge University Press.

Orlinsky, D. E., & Howard, K. I. (1986). The relation of process to outcome in psychotherapy. In S. L. Garfield & A. E. Bergin (Eds.), *Handbook of psychotherapy and behavior change: An empirical analysis* (2nd ed., pp. 311–381). New York: Wiley.

Paivio, S., & Greenberg, L. S. (2001). Introduction to special issue on treating emotion regulation problems in psychotherapy. *In-Session, 57*, 153–156.

Palfia, T. P., & Salovey, P. (1993). The influence of depressed and elated mood on deductive and inductive reasoning. *Imagination, Cognition, and Personality, 13*, 57–71.

Pascual-Leone, J. (1991). Emotions, development and psychotherapy: A dialectical–constructivist perspective. In J. Safran & L. Greenberg (Eds.), *Emotion, psychotherapy and change* (pp. 302–335). New York: Guilford Press.

Pennebaker, J. W. (1990). *Opening up: The healing power of confiding in others*. New York: Morrow.

Pennebaker, J. W. (1994). Emotion, disclosure, & health: An overview. In J. W. Pennebaker (Ed.), *Emotion, disclosure, and health* (pp. 3–10). Washington, DC: American Psychological Association.

Pennebaker, J. W., & Traue, H. C. (1993). Inhibition and psychosomatic processes. In J. W. Pennebaker & H. C. Traue (Eds.), *Emotion, inhibition and health* (pp. 146–163). Gottingen, Germany: Hogrefe & Huber.

Perls, F. (1969). *Gestalt therapy verbatim*. Lafayette, CA: Real People Press.

Perls, F., Hefferline, R. F., & Goodman, P. (1951). *Gestalt therapy*. New York: Dell.

Pierce, R. A., Nichols, M. P., & DuBrin, J. R. (1983). *Emotional expression in psychotherapy*. New York: Gardner.

Pizer, S. (2000). The capacity to tolerate paradox: Bridging multiplicity within the self. In J. C. Muran (Ed.), *Self-relations in the psychotherapy process* (pp. 111–131). Washington, DC: American Psychological Association.

Polanyi, M. (1966). *The tacit dimension*. Garden City, NY: Doubleday.

Polster, I., & Polster, M. (1973). *Gestalt therapy integrated*. San Francisco: Jossey-Bass.

Plutchik, R. (2000). *Emotions in the practice of psychotherapy: Clinical implications of affect theories*. Washington, DC: American Psychological Association.

Rennie, D. (2001). *Reflexivity in person centered counselling*. Manuscript submitted for publication.

Rilke, R. M. (1934). *Letters to a young poet* (M. D. Harter, Trans.). New York: Norton.

Rogers, C. R. (1959). A theory of therapy, personality and interpersonal relationships, as developed in the client-centered framework. In S. Koch (Ed.), *Psychology: A study of a science* (Vol. 3, pp. 184–256). New York: McGraw-Hill.

Sachse, R. (1993). The effect of intervention phrasing on therapist–client communication. *Psychotherapy Research, 3*(4), 260–277.

Sachse, R. (1998). Goal-oriented client-centered therapy of psychosomatic disorders. In L. S. Greenberg, J. C. Watson, & G. Lietaer (Eds.), *Handbook of experiential psychotherapy* (pp. 295–327). New York: Guilford Press.

Safran, J., & Muran, C. (2000). *Negotiating the therapeutic alliance*. New York: Guilford Press.

Salovey, P., & Mayer, J. D. (1990). Emotional intelligence. *Imagination, Cognition, and Personality, 9,* 185–211.

Salovey, P., & Sluyter, D. J. (1997). *Emotional development and emotional intelligence.* New York: Basic Books.

Scherer, K. R. (1984a). Emotion as a multicomponent process: A model and some cross cultural data. In P. Shaver (Ed.), *Review of personality and social psychology* (Vol. 5, pp. 37–63). Beverly Hills, CA: Sage.

Scherer, K. R. (1984b). On the nature and function of emotion: A component process approach. In K. R. Scherer & P. Ekman (Eds.), *Approaches to emotion* (pp. 293–317). Hillsdale, NJ: Erlbaum.

Shaver, P., Schwartz, J., Kirson, D., & O'Connor, C. (1987). Emotion knowledge: Further exploration of a prototype approach. *Journal of Personality and Social Psychology, 52,* 1061–1086.

Sicoli, L., & Greenberg, L. S. (2000, June). *A task analysis of hopelessness events in therapy.* Paper presented at the International Society for Psychotherapy Research, Indian Hills, IL.

Singer, J., & Salovey, P. (1993). *The remembered self.* New York: Free Press.

Spinoza, B. (1967). *Ethics (Part IV).* New York: Hafner.

Sroufe, L. A. (1996). *Emotional development: The organization of emotional life in the early years.* New York: Cambridge University Press.

Stanton, A., Danoff-Burg, S., Twillman, R., Cameron, C., Bishop, M., & Collins, S. (2000). Emotionally expressive coping predicts psychological and physical adjustment to breast cancer. *Journal of Consulting and Clinical Psychology, 68* (5), 875–882.

Stein, R. (1991). *Psychoanalytic theories of affect.* New York: Praeger.

Stern, D. (1985). *The interpersonal world of the infant.* New York: Basic Books.

Stern, D. (1995). *The motherhood constellation.* New York: Basic Books.

Stuart, J. (2000, June). *Client perceptions of experiencing emotion in counseling.* Poster presented at the International Meeting of the Society for Psychotherapy Research, Indian Hills, IL.

Taylor, C. (1989). *Sources of the self. The making of modern identity.* Cambridge, England: Cambridge University Press.

Thelen, E., & Smith, L. B. (1994). *A dynamic systems approach to the development of cognition and action.* Cambridge, MA: MIT Press.

Titchener, E. B. (1909). *Experimental psychology of the thought-processes.* New York: MacMillan.

Tomkins, S. (1963). *Affect, imagery and consciousness: The negative affects* (Vol. 1). New York: Springer.

Tomkins, S. (1983). Affect theory. In P. Ekman (Ed.), *Emotion in the human face* (pp. 137–154). New York: Cambridge University Press.

Truase, C., & Carkhuff, R. (1967). *Toward effective counselling and psychotherapy.* Chicago: Aldine.

Tugade, M., & Frederickson, B. (2000, August). *Resilient individuals use positive emotions to bounce back from negative emotional arousal*. Paper presented at the annual conference of the International Society for Research in Emotion, Quebec City, Quebec, Canada.

Van den Boom, D. (1994). The influence of temperament and mothering on attachment and exploration: An experimental manipulation of sensitive responsiveness among lower-class mothers with irritable infants. *Child Development, 65*, 1457–1477.

Van der Kolk, B. A. (1993). The body keeps the score: Memory and the evolving psychobiology of posttraumatic stress. *Harvard Review of Psychiatry, 1*, 253–265.

Vygotsky, L. (1986). *Thought and language*. Cambridge, MA: MIT Press.

Wachtel, P. (1997). *Therapeutic communication*. New York: Basic Books.

Warwar, N., & Greenberg, L. (2000, June). *Emotional processing and therapeutic change*. Paper presented at the annual meeting of the International Society for Psychotherapy Research, Indian Hills, IL.

Watson, J., & Greenberg, L. (1996). Emotion and cognition in experiential therapy: A dialectical–constructivist position. In H. Rosen & K. Kuelwein (Eds.), *Constructing realities: Meaning-making perspectives for psychotherapists* (pp. 221–249). San Francisco: Jossey-Bass.

Weston, J., & Greenberg, L. (2000, June). *Interrupting emotion in psychotherapy*. Paper presented at the International Meeting of the Society for Psychotherapy Research, Indian Hills, IL.

Whelton, W., & Greenberg, L. (2000). The self as a singular multiplicity: A process experiential perspective. In C. J. Muran (Ed.), *Self-relations in the psychotherapy process* (pp. 87–106). Washington, DC: American Psychological Association.

Whelton, W., & Greenberg, L. (2001). *Emotion in self-criticism*. Manuscript submitted for publication.

White, R. (1959). Motivation reconsidered: The concept of competence. *Psychological Review, 66*, 297–333.

Wiser, S., & Arnow, B. (2001). Emotional experiencing: To facilitate or regulate. *Journal of Clinical Psychology, 57*(2), 157–168.

Weiser Cornell, A. (1996). *The power of focusing*. Oakland, CA: New Harbinger.

Wundt, W. (1912). *An introduction to psychology*. London: George Allen.

Young, J. (1990). *Cognitive therapy for personality disorders: A schema-focused approach*. Sarasota, FL: Professional Resources Exchange.

Zajonc, R. B. (1980). Feeling and thinking: Preferences need no inferences. *American Psychologist, 35*, 151–175.

Zimbardo, P., Ebbesen, E., & Malasch, C. (1997). *Influencing attitudes and changing behavior*. Reading, MA: Addison-Wesley.

AUTHOR INDEX

Adams, K. E., 57
Alden, L., 9, 271
Allen, R., 55
Angus, L., 58
Aristotle, 6, 40, 141, 230, 291
Arnow, B., 42
Atkinson, B., 61

Bargh, J. A., 28
Baumeister, R. F., 8, 41
Beck, A., 9, 28
Berkowitz, L., 63
Beutler, L. E., 7
Bohart, A., 6, 76
Bolger, E., 60, 137, *146*, 147, 208
Bonanno, G., 95
Bongar, B., 7
Borkovec, T., 16
Bowlby, J., 203
Breuer, J., 9, 10
Buber, M., 182, 204
Bushman, B. J., 8, 41

Carkhuff, R., 77
Cavallaro, J., 31, 63, 197
Chance, C., 287
Chartrand, T. L., 28
Clarke, D., 7
Clarkin, J. F., 7
Conway, R., 271
Crits-Christoph, P., 15, 185
Cummings, J., 67, 68, 72
Cushman, P., 15

Dahl, H., 51
Damasio, A., 3, 4, 12, 18, 19, 304
Darwin, C., 5, 62
Davidson, R., 3, 63, 96, 197
DeHaviland, J., 3
DuBrin, J. R., 8

Ebbesen, E., 64
Ekman, P., 3, 5, 19, 32, 197

Elliott, R., 76, 77, 83, 184
Ellsworth, P. C., 27

Field, T., 285
Fiese, B. H., 287
Flack, W., 31, 63, 197
Foa, E. B., 60
Ford, C., 9, 271
Forgas, J., 27
Fosha, D., 3, 74, 76
Fredrickson, B. L., 64
Freud, S., 9, 10
Friesen, R., 32
Friesen, W., 5, 19
Frijda, N. H., 3, 5, 11, 27, 33

Gamble, M., 72
Geller, S., 73, 100
Gendlin, E. T., 119, 202
Gendlin, M., 117
Gergen, K., 17
Gilbert, P., 203
Goodman, P., 9, 60
Gottman, J., 55, 59, 269, 274, *281*, 282,
    283, 287
Greenberg, L. S., 3, 7, 8, 9, 10, 19, 25,
    26, 27, 28, 41, 55, 57, 60, 61,
    64, 65, 66, 72, 73, 76, 77, 78,
    79, 83, 93, 94, 100, 118, 126,
    137, 146, 149, 180, 183, 184,
    186, 210, 235, 256, 258, 268,
    271
Griffiths, P., 19, 32
Gross, J. J., 33
Guidano, V. F., 25, 27, 62

Hanson, E., 64
Hardtke, K., 58
Hefferline, R. F., 9, 60
Hendricks, M. N., 8
Henry, W., 75
Hooven, C., 269
Howard, K. I., 8

317

Isen, A., 64, 96
Izard, C. E., 11

James, P., 271
James, W., 26, 196
Johnson, S. M., 9, 256, 258, 271

Kabat-Zinn, J., 15, 206
Kant, I., *141*
Katz, L. F., 269
Keltner, D., 95
Kennedy-Moore, E., 8, 41
Kiesler, D. J., 57
Kirson, D., 32, 89
Klein, M. H., 57
Korman, L. M., 7, 55, 208
Kottler, J., 14
Kozak, M. J., 60

Laird, J. D., 31, 63, 197
Lane, R., 3
Lasch, C., 15
LeDoux, J. E., 3, 27, 303
Legerstee, M., 285
Leventhal, H., 10
Levine, S., 206
Lewin, J., 58
Lewis, M., 3
Lietaer, G., 77, 100
Linehan, M. M., 43, 61, 83, 182, 207
Luborsky, L., 15, 185

Magai, C., 287, 293
Mahoney, M. J., 9, 17, 27
Malasch, C., 64
Mateu Margues, C., 268
Mathieu-Coughlan, P., 57
Mayer, J. D., 5, 10, 12, 58, 64
McFadden, S., 287, 293
Mergenthaler, E., 8
Mineka, S., 7
Muran, C., 75
Myers, D., 64

Nadel, L., 3
Neimeyer, R. A., 9, 17
Nichols, M. P., 8

Oatley, K., 10, 12, 19, 26
O'Connor, C., 32, 89
Orlinsky, D. E., 8

Paivio, S. C., 7, 19, 26, 41, 55, 60, 93,
    137
Palfia, T. P., 65
Pascual-Leone, J., 25, 28, 61, 66, 118
Pennebaker, J. W., 6, 8, 31, 61, 90
Perls, F., 9, 15, 60
Pierce, R. A., 8
Pizer, S., 80
Plutchik, R., 189
Polanyi, M., 91
Polster, L., 15
Polster, M., 15

Rennie, D., 25
Rhodes, R., 73
Rice, L. N., 76, 83, 184, 210
Rilke, R. M., *302–303*
Rogan, K., 7
Rogers, C. R., 9, 60, 100
Rosenberg, R., 78

Sachse, R., 58, 77
Safran, J. D., 10, 60, 75, 235
Salovey, P., 5, 10, 12, 15, 55, 58, 65
Schacht, T., 75
Scherer, K. R., 18, 27, 140
Schwartz, J., 32, 89
Shaver, P., 32, 89
Sicoli, L., 186
Singer, J., 15
Sluyter, D. J., 55
Smith, L. B., 27
Spinoza, B., 62, 171
Sroufe, L. A., 286, 288
Stack, A. D., 8, 41
Stalikas, A., 7
Stanton, A., 6
Stern, D., 17, 78, 79, 284, 285
Strupp, H., 75
Stuart, J., 71

Taylor, C., 5, 25
Thelen, E., 27

Thomas, C., 7
Titchener, E. B., 26
Tomkins, S., 11
Traue, H. C., 8
Truase, C., 77
Tugade, M., 64

van Balen, R., 27, 79
Van den Boom, D., 284
Van der Kolk, B. A., 3, 61, 90
Varghese, J., 285
Vygotsky, L., 82

Wachtel, P., 190
Warwar, N., 8, 66, 137

Watson, J., 8, 25, 41, 61, 65, 72, 76
Weston, J., 126
Whelton, W., 61, 64, 94, 118, 149,
    183
White, R., 203
Wiser, S., 42
Weiser Cornell, A., 117, 119
Wundt, W., 26

Young, J., 184

Zajonc, R. B., 5
Zimbardo, P., 64

SUBJECT INDEX

Abandonment
    fear of, 261
    unexpressed sadness and anger in,
        236–237
Acceptance
    of emotion, 174
    of experience
        in change, 72
    facilitation of, 87–88
    of pain, 146–147, 219
    of partners' feelings, 258, 259
Accessing emotions
    adaptive, 95–98, 124–125, 194–196,
        242–243
    in hopelessness, 188–190
    interventions in, 188–189
    maladaptive, 177–183, 211, 242–243
    strategies in, 189–190, 208
Accessing positive feeling, 210
Adaptation
    in coaching, 82
Adaptive emotions. *See also under* Pri-
        mary emotion(s)
    accessing
        as alternative to destructive beliefs/
            views, 94–95
        attention shift in, 194
        enactments in, 196–197
        expression by therapist in, 199
        facilitation of, 95–98
        identification of needs and goals in,
            194–195
        imagery in, 195–196
        memories in, 197–199
        to transform maladaptive primary
            emotions, 66
    in creation of adaptive structures, 66–
        67
    example of, 20–21
    experiencing of
        exercise for, 129, 131–133
    functions of, 21–23
    in organization of adaptive action, 66
    primary, 44, 114, 138–148
Adaptive feelings
    action following, 219

examples of, 219
Adolescents
    anger in, 292
    fear of inadequacy in, 294
    feelings of, 287
    sadness in, 289–290
Affect mirroring
    maternal, 285–286
Aggression
    in adolescents, 292
Allowing of emotion, 127–128
Amygdala
    in arousal, 61
Anger, 229–232. *See also* Rage
    acceptance of
        in child, 281
    adaptive, 140–142
        activation of, 141–142
    in adolescent, 292
    Aristotle on, 6, 40, 141, 230, 291
    awareness of, 230
    in children
        awareness of, 292
        parental handling of, 282–283
        problem solving for, 293
        types of, 291
        validation of, 292–293
        verbal labeling of, 293
    in couples relationships, 268–269
    as defense, 157
    destructive, 152
    evaluation of, 140–142
    expression of, 166, 230–231
        appropriate, 152–153
        in couples relationships, 268–269
        for negotiation, 166–167
        as validation, 235
    as expression of boundaries, 269
    from fear to contentment and, 65
    function of, 39, 145
    and gentleness, 142–143
    healthy, 97, 98
    healthy primary
        function of, 140
        sources of, 141
        vs. aggression, 140

Anger (*continued*)
 historical view of, 141
 instrumental, 161–162
 interruption of, 239
 lessons about, 239
 maladaptive, about past event
  healing through imaginary dialogue,
   214–215
 maladaptive, current
  link with past, 215–216
 maladaptive primary, 151–153
  evaluation of, 150–153
  replacement of, 63
  sources of, 152
 outbursts of, 142–143
 overcontrolled
  consequences of, 234
 of parent, 292, 298
 power in, 167
 regulation of, 157, 291
 in sadness, 236–238
 sadness in, 235–236
 secondary, 156–158
  in couples relationships, 267–268
  working with, 125
 secondary sadness in, 155
 sensations and thought in, 26
 separation from sadness, 268, 269
 suppression of, 141, 142, 231
 of therapist toward client, 75
 in three-step sequence, 124–125
 in toddlers, 291
 as trap, 153
 in two-step sequence, 124
 types of, 229–230
 as unexpressed resentment, 268–269
 unresolved (*See also* Unresolved anger)
  description of, 231
 varieties of, 39–40
 at violation, 142
Anger—sadness—shame—anger cycle,
 125
Anxiety
 about another feeling, 159
 adaptive, 143–144
 anticipatory, 16
 maladaptive core, 93
 maladaptive primary, 143–144
  evaluation of, 154
  source of, 154
 as secondary emotion, 158–159

 as secondary feeling, 48
 self-soothing for, 270
Aristotle
 on anger, 6, 40, 141, 230, 291
Arousal
 for change, 62–63
 in change, 67
 contraindications to, 43
 regulation of, 61
 relationship to outcome, 65, 66
Art
 in changing emotion, 200
Articulation
 of emotion, 117–119
 of maladaptive emotion, 219
 of need, 220
Assessment
 context and, past and present, 52–53
 effect of emotion in, 53
 emotional style of client in, 53
 empathy in, 53
 knowledge and function of adaptive
  emotion in, 52
 principles for, 52
 process diagnosis in, 51–52
Assimilation
 in change, 67
Assimilation analysis
 of adaptive emotion replacing maladaptive, 66
Attachment
 anxious
  in fight, 270
 in couples relationships, 256–257
 emotions in, 256–257
 need for, 203
Attachment needs
 in couples conflict
  revelation of, 271, 272
 in couples relationships, 275–276
  expression of core emotions in, 275–
   276
  identification of, 275
Attention
 to emotion
  facilitative environment and, 118
 entry to emotion, 27
 shifting to adaptive state, 194
Authenticity
 self-awareness in, 100
 transparency in, 100

Automatic emotions
  regulation of
    through positive alternatives, 96–97
Autonomy
  in couples relationship, 263
Avoidance
  awareness of, 127
  as block to change, 222
  of disturbing emotions, 205–206
  focusing on
    in abuse case, 252
  overcoming, 72
  of pain
    effect of, 147
Awareness
  bodily, 87
  in change, 67
  of child's emotions, 281, 284, 286–287
  of emotions, 32, 128–129
  as experience, 60
  facilitation of, 73
  focusing on vaguely felt emotion in,
    119–121
  of interruption, 126–127
  of needs, 171–172
  nonverbal, 86–87
  in overcoming avoidance, 60–61
  of parental emotions, 281
  of present, 30
  promotion of, 86–87
  reflective state of, 30
  steps in, 85–86
  symbolization in, 61
  training sheet for, 164

Basic emotions, 50
  words for, 89
Belief(s). *See also* Destructive beliefs
  unhealthy
    transformation of, 223
  in unresolved anger, 234, 235
Blamer
  in blame withdraw cycle, 264–265
Blame—withdraw cycle
  in couples relationship
    submission and dominance in, 264–
    265
Blocking
  anger in, 157
Blocks
  identification of, 221–223

Bodily sensation
  differentiation from emotion, 134
  in focusing, 119–120
  focusing on, 133–135
Body
  in expression of emotion, 63–64
Boredom
  of coach, 75
Brain
  emotion and, 3–4
  of infant, 285
Bridging
  between experience and action, 175
  of opposing states
    facilitation by coach, 80–81

Caring needs
  in attachment, 274
Change
  coaching steps in, 67
  of emotion, 35–36
  emotion in, 7–8
  emotion work in, 68–72
  expression in
    physical, 63–64
  general principles of, 60–72
    awareness, 60–61
    of emotion with emotion, 62–67
    regulation, 61–62
  of partner *vs.* self, 262
  through emerging goals and opportuni-
    ties, 98–99
Childhood abuse and neglect
  restructuring through imagery, 216–217
Childhood abuse victim, 241–253
  accessing core maladaptive fear and
    shame in, 242–243
  dealing with
    accessing primary sadness in, 247
  fear and shame in, 241–253
  fear in, 243–245, 249
    distancing from, 244, 247–248
    imaginary confrontation with father
      in, 244–245
    reexperiencing of, 243–244
    restructuring in, 245
  pain in, 247, 250–251
  rejection in, 246, 247, 248–249
  sadness in, 249
  self-validation and
    in therapy, 252–253

Childhood abuse victim (*continued*)
  shame in, 245–247
Children
  emotions of
    as opportunity for parental connec-
      tion, 288
    feeling talk with, 288–289
    as mirror of parents' emotions, 297–
      298
Clear emotion
  description and expression of, 117
Client
  as explorer, 80
Coach
  authentic presence of, 73–74
  definitions of, 55
  emotions of, 74–75
  empathic attunement of, 78–79, 81
  as facilitator, 55, 82
  feelings of, 74–75
  as follower and leader, 81
  function of, 304
  as guide, 80
  guide for
    from client reports, 71–72
  internal experience of
    relationship to doing no harm, 100
  process suggestions of, 81
  self-awareness of, 99–103
  as trainer, 55
  training of, 99
Coaching. *See also* Emotion counseling
  of children
    parental characteristics in, 282, 283
  co-exploration partnership in, 56
  concept of, 56
  in couples conflict
    appreciation of partners in, 274–
      275
    for expression of core feelings of
      hurt, 271–273
    ownership of feelings in, 273–274
  emotional intelligence in, 58–59
  experiential learning in, 56
  parenting in, 59
  phases in
    arriving, 85–92
    leaving, 92–99
  processing in, 58
  reflection in, 57–58
  steps in
    acceptance, 87–88

accessing adaptive emotions and
  needs, 95–98
awareness, 86–87
evaluation of primary feeling, 92–93
identification of beliefs/views in maladaptive primary emotion, 94–95
identification of primary emotions,
  90–91
transformation of maladaptive emotions, 98–99
verbalization, 88–90
summary of work in, 82
teachable moment in, 82–83
training as treatment in, 56
Coaching process, 59–60, 105
  with client feeling upset, 218–219
  evaluation in, 18
  identification of blocks in, 221–222
  identification of need or goal in, 220–
    221
  in practice vignette, 103–105
  transformation of unhealthy feelings
    and beliefs in, 223
Coaching relationship, 72–76
  authentic presence of coach in, 73–75
  facilitation of affective competencies
    in, 73
  feedback in, 73
  negative feelings in, 75
  process directives in, 79–81
Cognition
  reason and, 14
Communication
  by coach, 101–102
  emotions in, 258–259
Communication skills
  for conflict resolution, 271
Compassion
  generation of, through imagery, 196
Complex emotions
  description of, 50
Congruence
  communication in, 100
  internal awareness component of, 100
  self-awareness and transparency in, 100
Connections
  in emotion work, 68
Construal
  destructive, 183–186 (*See also* Destruc-
    tive beliefs)
  destructive beliefs in, 94–95

Containment
  of disjunctive states, 80
Context
  in coaching, 85
  expression in, 176
Control
  of emotion, 302
  instrumental anger in, 162
  parental teaching of, 287–288
  primary emotions and, 88
  of primary feelings, 46
Conversation
  in coaching, 79–80
Core emotions. *See also* Instrumental
      emotion(s); Secondary emo-
      tion(s)
  adaptive, 138–148
  maladaptive, 148–155
Core feeling
  evaluation of, 109
Counseling experience
  clients' perceptions of, 67–68
  distressing emotions in, 67, 68
  therapeutic issues in, 67–68
Couples conflict
  coaching in, 270–271
  intimacy *vs.* autonomy in, 261
  resolution of
    communications skills in, 271
    exposure of needs in, 271
Couples relationships, 255–277
  alternation of caretaker and dependent
      roles in, 274
  anger in, 268–269
  crazy states in, 266–267, 268, 270
  destructive cycles in, 262–266
  emotional feedback in, 257–258
  fights in, 266, 276–277
  hurt in, 267–270
  intimacy and attachment emotions in,
      256–257
  needs in, 261
  problems in, 262–267
Crazy states
  in couples relationships
    behavior in, 266–267
    dealing with, 268, 270
Crying
  instrumental use of, 161
  in sadness, 139, 156
Curiosity need, 203

Deprivation
  sadness and anger in, 236–237
Desensitization
  of states and feelings, 190
Despair
  in maladaptive primary sadness, 148,
      149
Destructive beliefs
  alternatives to, 94
  identification of, 183–186
    content in, 185–186
    imaginary dialogue in, 184
  schemes in
    bad other, 185
    bad self, 184
    weak self, 184–185
  transformation of, 223
  verbalization of, 183, 184
Destructive cycles
  in couples relationships, 262–266
  identifying and changing, 275–276
Destructive thoughts
  transformation of, 209–211
Dialogue
  imaginary
    in identification of destructive be-
        liefs, 184
    in identification of hopelessness,
        186–187
    in maladaptive anger, 214–215
    in resolution of maladaptive anger,
        214–215
    in unresolved anger, 233
  with imaginary child
    in self-soothing, 208–209
Difficult emotional states
  recognizing and dealing with, 190–191
Difficult emotions
  dealing with, 214
  handling of, 277
Disclosure
  by coach
    of feelings, 75, 101–102
    interpersonal stance in, 102
    of thought, 102
Disillusionment
  in couples relationship, 265–266
Disordered emotion, 48
Distancing
  in abuse case, 252
  from abusive parents
    client desire for, 244

Distancing (*continued*)
  for accessing emotion, 208
  from emotion, 214
  from feelings
    from childhood abuse, 247
  from painful emotions, 206
  in regulation of emotion, 99, 206
  self as observer in, 206–207
Distress
  in emotion work, 71
  response to
    healthy emotions in, 97–98
  self-soothing in, 209
Distress tolerance
  differentiation from regulation skills,
    207
Dominance
  in blame—withdraw cycle, 264
Dominant—submissive cycle
  in couples relationship, 263

Embarrassment
  in children, 296
  development of
    age and, 296
  with feelings
    by childhood abuse victim, 246, 247
  with needs and feelings
    from childhood abuse, 248
Emotion—action responses, 27
Emotional intelligence, 10–13
  abilities in, 58
  in children
    parental influence on, 283
  in coaching, 58–59
  complex emotions in, 50
  definition of, 58
  in instrumental emotions, 50
  primary emotions in, 44
  teaching of, 283
Emotional states
  difficult, 190–191
  shifting out of, 200–201
Emotional wisdom
  development of, 302
Emotion counseling. *See also* Coaching
  steps in
    access adaptive emotions and needs,
      95–98
    evaluation of primary feeling, 92–94
    facilitation of acceptance, 87–88

identification of beliefs/views in maladaptive emotion, 94–95
identification of primary emotions,
  90–92
promotion of awareness, 86–87
promotion of verbalization/expres-
  sion, 88–90
transformation of maladaptive emotions and destructive beliefs, 98–
  99
Emotion log, 128–129, 130
Emotion(s). *See also* Adaptive emotions;
    Maladaptive emotions; Primary
    emotion(s)
  acceptance of *vs.* reactions to, 174–
    175
  assessment of, 51–53
  awareness and knowledge of, 128–129
  basic, 50
  categories of, 138
  changing with emotion, 62–67
  children's
    parental gender-stereotyping and,
      287
  clear, 117
  common language of, 18–19
  as communication, 258
  complex, 50
  conduct of life and, 13–14
  creation of, 117–118
  as data of existence, 12
  difficult, 214, 277
  evaluation of, 110–113
    criteria for, 173
  experience of, 41–43
    distinctions in, 41–42
    identification of, 164
  expression of, 8, 14–15, 41–43, 175–
    177
  facilitation of, 42
  form and function of, 39–40
  guidance of, 35
  instrumental, 49–50, 161–163
  interruption of, 125–128
  in learning, 23–25
  "me" and "it," 51
  measurement of, 5
  overcontrol of, 304
  parental
    dealing with, 297–299
  physical basis of, 255
  as pointers in relationships, 11–12

primary, 44–45, 138–155
regulation of, 42, 205–209
in response to external cues, 35, 112
in response to internal processes, 35, 112
secondary, 45–49, 155–161
self-soothing and, 208–209
as signal, 10–11, 13
situation effect on, 41
studies of
  historical perspective, 4–10
and thought, 25–31
vague, 116–117
virtual, 16
vivid, 116
Emotion schemes, 10, 19, 184–185
Emotion sequences, 28
  in primary adaptive emotions, 123–125
    three-step, 124–125
    two-step, 124
Emotion system, 10
Emotion work
  connections in, 68
  experiential learning in, 70
  guide for coaches, 71–72
  intense emotion in, 69
  missing, 70
  negative emotions in, 68, 69, 70
  pain in, 69–70
Empathic attunement
  of coach, 75–76
  strengthening of self in, 78–79
Empathy
  of coach, 59
  in coaching relationship, 76–79
  functions of, 76
  maternal
    infant development and, 285–286
  of parent for child, 280
  as process, 78
Empowerment
  through getting to needs and wants, 217–218
Enactment
  in accessing alternative adaptive emotion, 196–197
Environment
  in coaching, 85
    facilitative, 99
Evaluation
  of emotion, 110–113
  of primary feeling

acceptance for, 93
  as adaptive or maladaptive, 92
  collaboration in, 92–93
Expectations
  catastrophic
    anxiety in, 159
Experience
  construction of, 27
    language in, 118–119
  depth of
    therapeutic outcome and, 7–9
  in evaluation of emotion, 111
  of feelings, 174
  of pain, 146
  suppression and avoidance of, 222
  technique for, 213
Experiential learning
  in emotion work, 70
Exploration
  of concrete situations, 190
  in evaluation of emotion, 110, 111
  of healing grief, 165–166
  of idiosyncratic meanings, 190
  joint
    in coaching, 84
  of maladaptive emotions, 179–180
  of past experiences, 190
Exposure therapy, 7
Expression
  in changing emotion
    methods for, 199–200
  by coach
    characteristics of, 101–102
    on client's behalf, 199–200
    comprehensive, 101
    disciplined, 101
    facilitative, 100
  in couples relationships, 258
  in creation of intimacy, 259–261
  of emotion
    physical, 197
    by therapist, 199–200
  of emotions, 175–177
  in induction of emotion, 63–64
  integration of reason and emotion in, 258–259
  of negative emotions, 69
  physical
    in change, 63–64
  of range of emotions, 190
  regulation of, 88

Expression (*continued*)
  suppression of, 222
  verbal, 88–90
vs. experience, 176

Facilitation
  of access to adaptive emotions/needs
    by focusing on needs, goals, con-
      cerns, 96
    shifting focus of attention to back-
      ground feelings and, 95–96
  contraindications to, 43
  criteria for, 42
Fear
  of abusive parents
    dealing with, 243–254
  adaptive, 143–144
    in childhood abuse, 243
  adaptive primary
    evaluation of, 143–144
    for survival, 143
  in blame—withdraw cycle
    in couples relationship, 264
  in children
    awareness of, 294–295
    from familial discord and violence,
      293–294
    as learned emotion, 293–294
    as opportunity for intimacy, 295
    from overprotective parenting, 294
    problem solving for, 296
    of separation, 293
    validation of, 295
    verbal labeling of, 295–296
  disorganizing, 154
  function of, 145
  of inadequacy in adolescents, 294
  instrumental, 162
  of intimacy, 261
  maladaptive primary, 143–144
    evaluation of, 153–154
    replacement of, 63
  ongoing after childhood abuse
    distancing from, 244
    reexperiencing of, 243–244
    restructuring of, 245
  of owning feelings, 273
  replacement of, 65
  as secondary emotion, 158–159
  self-invalidation of
    in abuse case, 249

Fear of separation
  in children, 293
Feedback
  for recognition
    of instrumental feelings, 115–116
  in relationships, 257–258
Feelings
  about feelings, 46
  of coach, 74–75
  consciousness and, 12–13
  creating aspect in, 117–118
  differentiation of, 110–111
  disclosure of
    by coach, 102–103
  expression in couples relationship
    open and honest, 271–272
  as information *vs.* conclusions, 173–
    174
  meaning of, 118
  message in, 133
  owning of
    in relationships, 273–274
  primary
    evaluation of, 92
    recognition of, 111
  as process, 176
  reflection on, 13
  relationship with *vs.* relationship with
    partner, 260
  shift in
    through focusing, 120–121
  unhealthy
    transformation of, 223
Feeling state
  entering into, 132–133
Fighting
  in couples relationships, 266
    handling of, 276–277
  expression of core emotions in, 276
  identification of, 276
  self-soothing in, 277
Focusing
  on bodily felt sense, 133–134
  on bodily sensation, 119–121
  description of, 119–120
  in experiential search for feeling, 117
  on missing components, 189
  verbalization in, 134
Future
  emotion in relation to, 16–17

Gentleness
    anger and, 142
Goals
    in accessing adaptive emotions, 194–
        195
    clarification of and change, 96
    focusing on, 203
    identification of, 220
Grief
    anger in, 238
    complicated, 151
    healing, exploration of, 165–166
Guidano, V. F., 62
Gut response. *See* Primary adaptive emo-
        tions

Healing moments
    in authentic presence, 74
Hopelessness
    accessing primary feeling in, 187–188
    adaptive, 196
    facing, 147–148
    identification of
        imaginary dialogue in, 186–187
    overcoming, 186–188
    secondary, 196
        to core experiences, 186
    self as agent of, 187
    statements of, 186
    underlying feelings in
        adaptive, 188
        maladaptive, 188
Humor
    in changing emotion with emotion,
        199–200
Hurt feeling
    in anger, 156–157
    in couples relationships, 267–270
        anger and sadness in, 268–269
        constructive expression of, 266
        expression of, 271–273
        owning of, 274
        sharing for conflict resolution,
            271
        solution to, 269–270
    expression of
        in intimacy, 260

Identification
    of directional tendency, 190
    of emotion type, 43

of healthy feelings and needs, 97
    of primary emotion
        coach in, 111–112
    of primary experience, 90–91
    of trigger, 189
Identity
    in couples relationship, 263
    roles related to
        in couples relationship, 275
Imagery
    in empathy, 78
    positive
        in generation of alternate feelings,
            195–196
    in restructuring childhood abuse, 216–
        217
Imagination
    about future, 16–17
    in regulation, 62
Infants
    learning by, 284–286
    parents and, 283–288
Information
    emotions as, 87
    feelings as, 173–174
    from "it" emotions, 51
    processing of, 36
Instrumental emotions
    emotional intelligence in, 50
    expression of
        conscious and automatic, 49
    intentions in, 49–50
Instrumental feelings
    identification of, 115
    integral to personal style, 115
    recognition of, 115
        feedback for, 115–116
Integration
    in change, 67
    of emotion and thought, 26
    of past, present, future, 17–18
    of reason and emotion, 5–6, 10, 14–15
        coaching for, 109
        in expression, 258–259
    reflection in, 37
Intention
    as bridge between experience and ac-
        tion, 175
Interest
    need for, 203
Interruption of emotion, 125–131
    awareness of, 126, 129, 131

Interruption of emotion (*continued*)
    motivation for, 126
    overcoming, 251–253
    processes in, 126–127
Intimacy
    in couples relationships, 256–257, 275
        in conflict with autonomy, 261
    emotions in, 256–257
    fear of, 261
    in pursue—distance cycle, 263
    roles in, 275
    shame and, 261
It emotions
    in response to external cues, 51

Kant, I
    anger and, 141
Kindness
    sadness reactions to, 151
Knowledge
    biological, 17–18
    language-based, 17

Language
    coach's use of, 118–119
    in construction of experience, 118–119
    to elicit emotion, 190
    evocative, 190
    in reflection back to client, 57–58
Learning
    emotional, 23–25
    of emotional experience, 14
    experiential, 56, 70
    infant
        brain growth and, 286
        of emotions, 284–285
    of maladaptive emotion, 44, 45
    traumatic, 45
Limit setting
    for anger, 293
    for fear, 296
    for shame, 297
Loneliness
    of blamer, 264–265
Loss
    dealing with, 164–165
    pain in, 145
    unresolved, 151
Loss of control
    shame and, 144, 145

Maladaptive emotion(s), 31–33
    accessing, 177–183
    articulation of, 219
    basic, 45
    characteristics of, 177–178
    client as author *vs.* as victim of, 180
    complex, 45
    destructive beliefs or views in, 94–95
    destructive effect of, 179
    evaluation of
        criteria for, 173
    examples of, 178
    experiencing of, 182–183
    exploration of, 180
    identification of
        dreams in, 178–179
    identification of negative voice and de-
        structive thoughts in, 219
    interventions in
        levels of, 188–189
        strategies in, 189–190
    learning of, 32, 44, 45
    primary, 44–45, 114–115, 148–155
    replacement with adaptive emotion, 63
    sources of, 44
    transformation of, 209–211
        dialogue between healthy and mal-
            adaptive feelings in, 210
        facilitation of, 209–211
        healthy feelings in, 98
        possibilities for, 181–182
        strategies for, 211–212
    triggers and themes of
        identification of, 189, 212–213
    validation of, 179, 181
Maladaptive feeling(s)
    core
        in childhood abuse, 93
        control through experience and
            naming of, 97
        fear—anxiety and, 93
        rage, 93–94
        shame and, 93
Manipulative feelings. *See* Instrumental
    emotions
Meaning
    construction of, 35, 37
Meditation
    in regulation of emotion, 206
Me emotions
    internal sources of, 51

Memory
    in accessing alternative emotion, 197–
        199
    in clarification of need/goal, 96
    of feelings
        actual *vs.* meaning of, 112–113
    in generation of emotion, 15–16
    painful and traumatic
        as block to change, 222
Message
    in feeling, 133
Metaphors
    in expression of emotion, 89
Mirroring. *See also* Reflection
    maternal
        infant development and, 285–286
    of parent's emotions, 297–298
Monitoring
    of feeling and emotion, 91
Mood
    thinking and, 64–65
Mother
    affect mirroring by
        infant development and, 285–286
Motivation
    of interactions
        in couples relationships, 274
    for interruption of emotion, 126
Music
    in changing emotion, 200
Mutuality
    in coaching relationship, 74

Naming
    of emotions, 117–118
    in regulation, 89–90
Need(s)
    in accessing adaptive emotions, 194–
        195
    action on, 220–221
    articulation of, 220
    attachment, 203, 271, 272, 275–276
    awareness of, 171–172, 203–205
    caring, 274
    clarification of and change, 96
    classification of, 203
    in couples relationships, 261
        destructive cycles and, 262–266
        identification of, 275–276
    curiosity, 203
    evaluation of, 204–205

focusing on, 202–203
function of, 204
identification of
    in fight, 277
    guidelines for, 220
    mismatched in couples, 262–263
of partner
    problems with, 262
in primary feelings, 188
sadness-associated, 249
in transformation of emotion, 220–221
Negative beliefs
    transformation of, 223
Negative emotions
    discovery of, 68
    expression of, 69–70
    normalization of, 69
Negative feelings
    client, 75
    disclosure to client, 75
Negative voice
    in couples relationships, 261
    in expression of destructive beliefs, 94
Novel moments
    from therapeutic presence, 74

Ownership
    of feelings, 273
Owning
    reowning and, 72

Pain
    acceptance of, 219
        in change, 146–147
    acknowledgment of
        in abuse case, 250–251
    adaptive, 145–148
    avoidance of, 147
    from childhood abuse, 242, 243
        acknowledgment and acceptance of,
            250–251
    definition of, 145
    example of
        in unresolved anger, 233
    experience of, 146, 219
        in emotion work, 69–70
    facing, 168
    of rejection
        in childhood abuse victim, 246, 247

Pain (*continued*)
  as symbol of childhood abuse, 248
  transformation through, 146
  of unmet needs, 247
Panic, 154
Parenting
  anger and, 291–292
    steps in, 292–293
  coaching in, 59, 280–283
  with emotional intelligence, 282
  fear and, 293–294
    steps in, 294–296
  infants' emotions and, 283–288
  parental emotions in
    dealing with, 297–298
  responsive style of
    role in infant development, 285–286
  sadness and, 288–289
    steps in, 289–291
  shame and, 296–297
Parents
  coaching of, 280
  as emotion coaches, 280
  emotion coaching by, 59
  maladaptive anger in, 298
  overreaction to child's emotions, 298
  philosophy of emotion management,
    280, 281, 287
Power
  in couples relationships, 263
Powerlessness
  in anger, 156–157
  crying and, 161
  rage and
    secondary, 265
Presence in the moment, 100
Present
  embodied, 18
  emotional response to, 15
Primary emotion(s)
  adaptive, 44, 114, 138–148
    differentiation from secondary emo-
      tions, 47–48
    emotion sequences in, 123–125
    evaluation criteria for, 172–173
    as information, 173–175
  automatic evaluation of external and
    internal experience, 91–92
  in couples relationships, 262
  identification of, 110–113
  maladaptive, 44–45, 114–115, 148–
    155

Problems
  in couples relationships
    destructive cycles, 262–265
    difficult emotional states, 266–267
    disillusionment, 265–266
    needs and, 261
    trying to change partner, 262
  in emotion work, 71
  identification of
    emotions in, 257
Process diagnosis
  in assessment, 51–52
Process directions
  in coaching, 79–81
Processing
  coach as guide to, 60
  shift to internal experience, 58
Pursue—distance cycle
  in couples relationship, 263

Rage. *See also* Anger
  in childhood abuse, 93–94
  secondary to shame, 157–158
  secondary to shame and powerlessness
    in couples relationship, 265
Reason
  in emotional life, 301
  emotion and, 303
  integration with emotion, 5–6, 10,
    14–15
    coaching for, 109
    in expression, 258–259
Reconciliation
  in couples conflict
    requirements for, 272
Reflection. *See also* Mirroring
  in coaching, 57–58
  on emotion, 25–26
    information in, 29–31
  on feelings, 30, 37
Regulation, 33–37
  attention shift in, from content to pro-
    cess, 207
  avoidance in, 205–206
  behavioral techniques in, 207
  in change, 67
  criteria for, 42
  distancing in, 206–207
  distress tolerance in, 207
  facilitation of, 73
  levels of, 34–35

meditation in, 206
in partner relationships, 209
self-soothing in, 208–209
skills for, 61–62, 206
strategies in, 34–35
from victim to agent in, 207
Rejection
fear of, 260, 261
feelings of
in blame—withdraw cycle, 264
imagined
in couples relationship, 260
maternal
of child, 248–249
Relationships. *See also* Couples relationships
dealing with emotions in, 257–258
emotions as monitors of, 11–12
neurochemistry of, 255
Resilience
positive emotions and, 64
Response(s)
empathetic, 76–78
exploratory, 77
interchangeable with client, 77
understanding, 77
Responsibility
for feelings, 258, 259
Restructuring training, 223
steps in, 226
Role play
in change, 64

Sadness, 40
acceptance of
in child, 281
adaptive, 138–140
adaptive primary *vs.* maladaptive primary
evaluation of, 150
in adolescents, 289–290
in anger, 235–236
anger in, 140
in divorce case, 236–237
in couples relationship, 264
awareness of
in self and child, 289
in child
awareness of, 289
as opportunity for intimacy teaching, 289

parental handling of, 282–283
problem solving and, 290–291
validation of, 290
verbal labeling of, 290
crying in, 139, 156
experiencing of
exercise for, 129, 131–133
healthy, 97, 98
healthy primary
description of, 139
evaluation of, 138–140
function of, 128
instrumental, 161
lessons about, 239
at loss, 140
in abuse case, 249
maladaptive primary, 148–151
effect of, 149
obscuring anger, 124, 125
parental mentoring and, 288–289
primary
dealing with, 164–165
Rilke on, *302–303*
as secondary feeling, 48
secondary to anger, 155–156
sensation and thought in, 26
separation of anger from, 268, 269
sources of, 288
as state of mind, 149–150
unexpressed
dealing with, 236–239
Secondary emotions, 45–49, 155–161
about primary emotions, 46
from control of primary, 46
in couples relationships, 262
definition of, 45
as symptoms of core feelings, 46
from thought, 46–47
Secondary feelings
differentiation from primary maladaptive primary emotions, 113–114
identification of, 113–115
in reaction to primary experiences, 114
Self
as observer, 206–207
vulnerability and fragility of
as block to change, 222
Self-awareness
of coach, 59, 99–103
in congruence, 100–101

Self-contempt
    as block to change, 221–222
    in destructive beliefs, 183–184
Self-criticism
    as block to change, 221
    as secondary anger, 158
    shame from, 159–160
Self-destructiveness
    as block to change, 221–222
Self-esteem
    shame and, 145, 155
Self-manipulation
    as block to change, 221
Self-soothing, 208–209
    development of
        in children, 281
    in fight, 277
    imaginary dialogue in, 208–209
    in partnership conflict, 209
    in regulation, 61–62
    in relationships, 270
Self-talk
    negative, 112–113
    in production of secondary emotions, 112
    in secondary reactions, 114
Self-worth
    sense of
        shame and, 144
Sensations
    attention to, 87
Sense of self
    empathy and, 78–79
    maladaptive, 246–247
    maladaptive feelings and, 177
    as partial vs. as possible self, 180–181
Sense of worthlessness
    shame and, 155
Shame
    adaptive primary, 144–145
        evaluation for, 144–145
    alternatives to
        anger and sadness, 97
    from childhood abuse
        restructuring of, 246–247
    in children, 296
        awareness of in self and child, 296–297
        as opportunity for intimacy, 297
        problem solving and, 297
        validation of, 297

    in couples relationship
        rage secondary to, 265
    at diminishment, 145
    instrumental, 162–163
    of internal feelings
        by childhood abuse victim, 246, 247
    intimacy and, 261
    maladaptive
        anger in transformation of, 247
        core, 93
        primary, evaluation of, 154–155
    mixed with fear
        ongoing after childhood abuse, 245, 246
    rage secondary to, 157–158
    secondary, 159–160
        dealing with, 160–161
    sources of, 144
Shame—rage cycle
    in couples relationship, 265
Shifting out of emotional states, 200–201
    technique for, 213
Slowing down
    in entering feeling, 132–133
Social relations
    shame and, 145
Stuck in sadness, 151
Submission
    in blame—withdraw cycle, 264
Suffering
    response to need in, 220
Suppression
    of anger, 231, 232, 234
    of emotional experience and expression
        as block to change, 222
    temporary, 176
Symbolization
    of emotion, 61
    of experience, 132
    of feelings, 30, 37, 60

Talking about emotion
    to access new emotion, 199
Teachable moment
    in coaching, 82–83
Themes
    of maladaptive emotions
        identification of, 212–213

Therapist
  response of
    experiential focus of, 57
    as processing proposal, 58
Therapy
  emotion in
    problematic aspects of, 71
Thoughts
  awareness of, 87
Threat
  physical
    fear and, 144
  sensed
    anxiety and, 144
Three-step sequence
  accessing adaptive emotion in, 124–125
  accessing of maladaptive emotion in, 124
  acknowledgment of secondary emotion in, 124
  unproductive, 125
Time
  emotion and, 15–18
    future, 17
    past, 16–17
    present, 15
    in reflective processing of emotional experience, 30–31
Tolerance
  facilitation of, 73
Toleration
  of disjunctive states, 80
Transformation
  of emotion, 35–36
  intervention strategies for, 211–226
  steps in, 86
  of vague feelings
    focusing in, 121, 201–203
  of victim to agent, 210–211
Transparency
  in congruence, 100, 101
  facilitative, 100–103, 102
Trauma
  transformation of response to, 211
Traumatic experience
  control of
    through verbalization, 90
Traumatic learning, 45
Triggers
  of maladaptive emotions
    identification of, 189, 212–213

Trust
  of emotions, 71
  of self
    in emotional expression, 260–261

Unfinished business
  with significant other
    as block to change, 222
Unresolved anger
  against other, 232–233
  secondary
    imaginary dialogue in, 233
    loss in, 233
    pain in, 233
  against self, 233
    therapeutic experience in divorce scenario, 232–234
  suppression in, 232, 234
Upset feeling
  coaching and, 218–219
  dealing with, 217
  as signal, 48–49

Vague emotion
  experiential search for, 116–117
  focusing on, 119–121
  meaning in, 120
Vague feelings
  attention to, 122
  empathic focusing in, 122–123
  experiencing of, 122
  focusing on
    bodily felt shift in, 201–203
  transformation of, 121, 123, 201–203
  verbalization of, 123
Validation
  of client feeling/experience, 81–82
  by coach, 59–60
  of emotional experience, 117
  of emotionality, 303
  of maladaptive emotions, 179, 181
Verbalization
  coaching for, 88–90
    in children, 282
  of destructive beliefs, 183, 184
  of emotion, 88–90, 117–119, 189–190
  promotion of, 88–90
Victim
  transformation into agent, 210–211

Violence
  witness/victim of
    anger in, 152
Vivid emotion
  description of, 116
Vulnerability
  in conflict resolution, 271

Wall of isolation
  in couples relationships, 267–270

Zone of proximal development
  emotion coaching and, 82–83

ABOUT THE AUTHOR

Leslie S. Greenberg, PhD, is a professor of psychology at York University in Toronto, where he is director of the Psychotherapy Research Clinic. A primary developer of Emotion-Focused Therapy for individuals and couples, he is the leading authority on working with emotions in psychotherapy. His integrative work has been embraced by practitioners from diverse theoretical backgrounds, including cognitive–behavioral, psychodynamic, interpersonal, and solution-focused. He is coauthor of several major texts in the field, including *Emotion in Psychotherapy: Affect, Cognition, and the Process of Change* (with Jeremy Safran); *Emotionally Focused Therapy for Couples* (with Susan Johnson); *Facilitating Emotional Change: The Moment-by-Moment Process* (with Laura Rice and Robert Elliott); and *Working With Emotion in Psychotherapy* (with Sandra Paivio). Dr. Greenberg is a founding member of the Society for Psychotherapy Integration, a founder of the Society for Constructivism in Psychotherapy, and a past president of the Society for Psychotherapy Research. He has published extensively on research on the process of change.